AMERICAN BABY GUIDE TO PARENTING

AMERICAN BABY GUIDE TO PARENTING

Consultant Editor

DAVID A. LINK, M.D.

GALLERY BOOKS
An Imprint of W. H. Smith Publishers Inc.
112 Madison Avenue
New York City 10016

CONTENTS

The Authors

Miss Mary Anderson
Consultant Obstetrician
at the Lewisham Hospital, London

Dr Kate Costeloe
Consultant Paediatrician
and Senior Lecturer in Child Health, Department of
Neonatal Medicine, Homerton Hospital, London

Caroline Flint
Senior Midwife
and Member of the Royal College of Midwives

Dr Catherine James
formerly Consultant Obstetrician and Gynaecologist,
St Thomas' Hospital, London

Dr Sue Jenkins
Senior Clinical Medical Officer
in Paddington District Health Authority

Dr Josephine Likierman
General Practitioner

Mrs Margaret Polden
Senior Obstetric Physiotherapist,
Hammersmith Hospital, London

Dr Leon Polnay
Consultant Paediatrician,
Nottingham Community Health Service and
University Hospital, Nottingham

Dr Diane Smyth
Consultant Paediatrician in the Child Development Unit,
Paddington Green Children's Hospital, London

Dr John Stroobant
Consultant Paediatrician
at Whipps Cross Hospital, London

Illustrations by Elaine Anderson and Kathy Wyatt
Special photography by Ron Sutherland

The publishers would like to thank the following for their
kind permission to use photographs in the book: Ace
Photo Agency/Michael Bluestone 17; Ace Photo Agency/
Anthony Price 227; Ace Photo Agency/Gabe Palmer half
title page; Bubbles Photo Library/Loisjoy Thurstun 33;
Bubbles Photo Library/Julie Fisher 51, 104, 289; Sally
and Richard Greenhill 59, 189, 237; Susan Griggs Agency
Limited 249; Jerrican/Clement title page; Camilla Jessel
106, 128, 133, 199, 231; Steve Lyne 117, 124-125; Tony
Stone Photo Library 9, 103, 110, 225; Jennie
Woodcock 137; Tim Woodcock 163.

First published in 1988 by
the Hamlyn Publishing Group Limited
a division of the Octopus Publishing Group
Michelin House, 81 Fulham Road
London SW3 6RB

This edition published in 1989 by
Gallery Books
An imprint of W.H. Smith Publishers Inc.
112 Madison Avenue
New York, New York 10016

© the Hamlyn Publishing Group Limited, 1988, 1989
ISBN 0 8317 0293 1

Produced by Mandarin Offset in Hong Kong

PREFACE

Babies do not arrive with an owner's manual. Just when your exhilaration, curiosity and anxiety peak with the birth of your baby, you begin to discover how little you know about taking care of them. *American Baby Guide to Parenting* aims to provide basic knowledge for child rearing and hopes to reduce parental anxiety as well. Every pediatrician quickly learns that most of parents' worries stem from a lack of familiarity regarding what is normal in various stages of child development, beginning in the womb and running right through adolescence. While this book does not try to present a coherent theory of child development, it does strive to provide the essential factual knowledge pertaining to pregnancy, labor, delivery, and early childhood so that new parents can understand what is happening. Throughout, we have relied upon the dual strengths all parents have – common sense and a curiosity to learn. For those who require more information than we can provide in our topical chapters, there is an extensive list, at the end of the book, of reference books, agencies, and foundations which deal with some of the specialized problems of parenting and children.

This book embraces no single philosophy of child-rearing. As we come to the end of the 1980s, developments in both fields discussed in this book – obstetrics and pediatrics – point to a more flexible and less rigid understanding of how to manage and "what to do". Increasingly, we recognize the power of inborn temperament. You will find that your children are not simply the result of the environment and what you put into them; rather, they come into this world endowed with a whole set of personality traits and individual qualities that vary tremendously from one child to the next in the family. Furthermore, over the decades, we have learned that there are many perfectly sensible approaches to solving some of the problems in childhood, and we need to take an adaptable stance toward all the key processes of fertility, pregnancy, delivery and child rearing. In fact, I would suggest that you beware of anyone preaching a strict orthodoxy about "proper parenting". That is why we have endeavored throughout this book to take a very practical and down to earth approach to the problems we review.

The development of any child still contains many mysteries, even to the so-called specialists. It is a beautiful, exciting, and sometimes perplexing process that permits a fertilized egg to grow up into your child with all his or her precious and unique gifts. Along the road of parenting there will be problems to solve, decisions to make, and, sometimes, very difficult times to get through. I hope this guidebook comes in handy along the way.

I also feel it is important that you realize how much the medical experts who have written this book struggle with bringing up their own children. As a pediatrician, married to a psychiatrist, I have to assure you that I get confused and derailed with my own children just as you will. That is part of the challenge and part of the fun. I also need to confess that the longer I practice pediatrics, the less authoritative I become. Experience has a way of humbling any expert who takes care of children on a professional basis. Do not be alarmed – the chapters in this book are not full of fuzzy ideas or confused thinking. Rather, we have all striven to put our experience and expertise together in order to write a practical handbook which represents our best assessment of current scientific thinking and our best recommendations for how to manage. We sincerely hope you find the *American Baby Guide to Parenting* useful. Just recall that our principal aim is to bolster your self-confidence and make our information fit in with your own common sense.

David A. Link, M.D.
Cambridge, Massachusetts

INTRODUCTION

The birth of a baby is not only exciting and wonderful; it also causes many anxieties for the parents. We believe that parents – both mothers *and* fathers – should be given as much information as possible about pregnancy and child development, so that they can fully understand what may happen – that is the reason for this book.

Books on pregnancy and child care at one time only stressed the normal. This was a little naïve because it ignored genuine problems which do arise; it was also a symptom of the wish to cloud medicine from the public. For example, it was common to leave out any mention of serious illness in the first few days after birth. In fact, about ten per cent of newborn babies need what is called 'special care.' This means that they have to be admitted to a special unit for observation and treatment. Some of them need intensive care using modern life-saving equipment, such as ventilators to keep them breathing. In this book we have not shied away from describing the illnesses that affect some babies and what you might expect if your baby is among the one in ten to be admitted to the special care unit. Hopefully you will have the chance to visit the unit in your own hospital fairly early in pregnancy, so that you are familiar with the surroundings if your baby is unlucky enough to go there.

One of the major advances in the last decade has been the discovery of the importance of the relationship between parents and their newborn baby – one could probably say *rediscovery*, since many of the concepts are really a reiteration of the virtue of being kind and caring. We must not get too carried away, however, in our enthusiasm for the rediscovery. For example, skin-to-skin contact between the mother and her baby is clearly a very good thing if it is possible immediately after birth; it seems to promote a special feeling between the two of them and is also good for breast feeding. If it is not possible, however, it would be sad for a mother to feel that irreparable damage has been done. After all, babies can be adopted very satisfactorily, so it is clearly not essential for normal human life. Unfortunately, it sometimes cannot happen because the baby is not well. For instance, urgent treatment may be needed to make sure that breathing has started, or the baby may have been born very prematurely allowing you only time to give a quick cuddle before the baby is taken to the special care unit. We have tried to explain all such issues much more than in the past.

Each one of us knows that a hospital can be an unnerving and even frightening place. Feelings are very important in medicine, so caring for the emotions is as necessary as caring for the body. We have not set out to be frightening, but have planned the book to be realistic. We hope we have succeeded in finding a middle way between the extremes of giving no explanation except a rose-tinted view of natural childbirth and a fearsome account implying that all childbirth is abnormal.

Every year brings new advances and problems. We were anxious that the book should be really up to date, because modern obstetrics and pediatrics produce many questions which need to be answered. Ultrasound and fetal monitoring were unknown a couple of decades ago, and such modern technology is bound to raise questions about safety and whether they interfere with the normal course of a pregnancy. It will be important for new methods to be carefully evaluated, not only to be certain that they work and are safe, but also that they do not have hidden side-effects such as producing unnecessary distress for parents.

The book is not only about pregnancy. The first few months and years of a child's life are tremendous fun, but also a period of worry. The main thing that parents need is common sense. The approach *you* feel you should adopt in looking after your baby will almost certainly be the best; other members of the family can be helpful with advice and support, but don't let them take over. The first baby is always more of a worry because you don't known what to expect, so we have tried to set a framework of what is normal. The information in the book comes from the experience of many people, both professionals and parents, and we hope it is presented in such a way that you have plenty of objective advice to lean on. It cannot be stressed too much that each baby is an individual and that you, as parents, are the right people to judge what is best for your baby.

Like so many authors, we have struggled with the question of whether to use 'he' or 'she' for the baby. All of us have an aversion to 'it' or 'he/she.' We have decided to let the author of each chapter choose which pronoun they prefer, and believe that this has produced a comfortable mix.

BEGINNINGS

The physiology of reproduction and how to prepare yourself for pregnancy

Having a baby is always a major event, whether it is the first, or third, or even the sixth child in a family. From early pregnancy on, this new person places physical and emotional demands on his or her parents which, as any grandparent knows, continue well into adulthood. Yet parenthood is uniquely rewarding, bringing with it the uncomplicated and unquestioning love of the young child.

For many parents, however, taking on the responsibility of parenthood means careful planning and difficult decision-making. Many babies are still unexpected, though none the less loved, but for other couples, deciding to have a baby means facing up to serious discussions about timing, career prospects, financial considerations, housing, the effect on their relationship, and simple apprehension about the loss of personal freedom. After all, the first baby increases the family unit by 50 per cent.

Becoming a parent changes your life permanently, so preparing yourselves for it both emotionally and practically does pay dividends. No one can really describe how any individual person is going to feel when he or she becomes a parent – it is a new experience every time. However, before you start, there are pointers which can help you make decisions about your well-being, your chances of conceiving and your ability to bring a healthy child into the world.

THE REPRODUCTIVE PROCESS

The potential for reproduction is something which is determined in its broadest terms from the time of a person's own conception – for it is at this moment that the genetic sex is decided and a chain of events is set in motion which will eventually lead to development into men and women of the human species. The many changes and adaptations which are involved in the production of such fundamentally different beings are so subtle and complex as to seem miraculous indeed, but the ways in which these two such apparently disparate bodies are so perfectly designed to generate new life is perhaps the most fascinating of all. To set the scene for successful pregnancy everyone has to undergo a long period of development and maturation until the body's anatomy and physiology, whether it be male or female, is in full working order for this complicated function.

BASIC ANATOMY

In men the external organs of reproduction are the penis and testes (testicles). The testes are contained in a bag of skin called the scrotum, lying outside the body cavity in the genital region. Although two testes are the norm, reproduction is still possible when only one is present. The testes produce the spermatozoa (sperm) which are required to fertilize the female ovum (egg) – the first step in the formation of a new life – and they also produce the male hormone testosterone. Testosterone is responsible for male development at puberty and the maintenance of sexual function thereafter.

The testes have a rich nerve and blood supply and are very sensitive to painful stimuli, as is well known. It may seem rather illogical that these delicate structures which are so vital for reproduction should have evolved to occupy such a vulnerable position, when the ovary, the equivalent structure in the female, is well protected within the bony pelvis. As with many things in nature, there is, however, a sensible explanation – the sperm could not survive if exposed to the heat within the body cavity, and require a lower environmental temperature for optimum development. Abnormalities in the scrotum can raise the temperature, reducing sperm production and causing male infertility.

Lying alongside the testis, is the epididymis, which is the main storehouse of the sperms and in which they become more motile (active) and mature. Arising from the epididymis is the vas deferens (sperm tube) by which sperms are transported to the seminal vesicles, structures which lie just behind the bladder and prostate gland. (It is this sperm tube which is divided for male sterilization in

Being a parent can be uniquely rewarding, but careful preparation is always invaluable.

the operation of vasectomy, when further pregnancies are not desired.) The seminal vesicles are also involved in the short term storage of sperm but their main function is to provide the sticky fluid which forms much of the volume of the ejaculated semen.

The penis is a flaccid cylindrical structure which is capable, under appropriate stimulation, of becoming hard and erect, because of its ability to be engorged with blood. At the moment of orgasm seminal fluid is ejaculated from the penis via the urethra, the hollow tube which runs along its length from the bladder and to which the seminal vesicles are connected, thus allowing the deposition of sperm into the female vagina. Both processes are fundamentally controlled by complex nerve pathways under the influence of some of the highest centers in the brain, and as such are very much affected by psychological and emotional factors.

Sperm are being constantly formed in the male from puberty onwards until their production declines in old age. Each mature sperm is about $1/100$ of an inch long and consists of a head, neck, body and tail. The tail gives motion to the sperm and allows it to make swimming movements from the vagina up into the uterus and Fallopian tube. In any one ejaculate there will be about 200 million sperm contained in about half a teaspoonful of fluid.

In women the organs of reproduction are all contained within the bony pelvis and consist of the vagina, the uterus and cervix, the Fallopian tubes and ovaries. Surrounding the entrance to the vagina there are external folds of skin known as the labia (lips) and just inside the vagina are the openings of tiny glands which produce the mucus secretions required for lubrication during intercourse. The vagina itself is an elastic muscular canal about 3-4in long into the top portion of which protrudes the cervix (neck of the womb).

The cervix is an integral part of the uterus (womb) and together they are usually directed forwards at almost a right angle to the length of the vagina, to take up what is called a position of anteversion. The cervix plays a special part in the process of conception by producing mucus which, at the time of ovulation (egg production), is particularly favorable to the passage of sperm.

The uterus is capable of enormous expansion – in its prepregnant state it is similar in size to an egg, but by the end of pregnancy it occupies the whole of the abdomen and its weight has increased more than tenfold. Attached to the upper part of the uterus are the Fallopian tubes – these are delicate hollow structures whose frond-like ends (fimbriae) are closely applied to the ovaries. Fertilization of the ovum (egg) by the sperm takes place in the Fallopian tube and its gentle squeezing movements transport the newly formed embryo into the uterine cavity where it will implant and grow.

The ovaries are the female equivalent of the testes – they lie in close relation to the outer ends of the Fallopian tubes and produce the mature ova (eggs) which are essential to reproduction. In a newborn baby girl the ovaries contain thousands of ova, but these remain undeveloped until the time of puberty.

THE MENSTRUAL CYCLE

As a result of complex hormonal mechanisms at puberty, the ovaries begin to function in a monthly cycle, ripening and releasing one ovum each time. This menstrual cycle, as it is called, is regulated by interdependent hormones produced not only by the ovaries but also by the pituitary gland and the hypothalamus in the brain. At the start of a cycle one or other ovary will start to develop a follicle which contains the ovum designated to mature that month. This stimulates the production of the hormone estrogen from the ovary, which in turn influences the follicle to rupture (ovulation) and releases the ovum, which passes into the Fallopian tube. In a normal 28 day cycle this would take place on the fourteenth day from the beginning of menstruation.

The ruptured follicle now becomes known as the corpus luteum; as well as estrogen, it produces another hormone called progesterone. This hormone helps to prepare the lining of the womb (endometrium) for an ensuing pregnancy. If fertilization of the egg does not take place, then the corpus luteum disintegrates after approximately fourteen days and the endometrium is shed with the four to five days of bleeding we recognize as menstruation (monthly or menstrual period).

This regular process of monthly preparation for pregnancy goes on for many years, but is not always totally efficient. Sometimes ovulation does not take place regularly, and this is particularly likely in the early years just after periods start, in middle age (the late thirties and early forties) as the menopause approaches, immediately after a pregnancy, and after stopping the oral contraceptive pill. Without ovulation pregnancy cannot occur and this is one of the many reasons for infertility.

CONCEPTION

During the act of sexual intercourse, sperm contained in the seminal fluid are deposited in the upper part of the vagina, by the mechanisms already described. There could be as many as 400 million in any one ejaculate and they immediately start on their journey, using their tail structures to swim up

THE WOMAN'S REPRODUCTIVE ORGANS

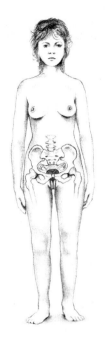

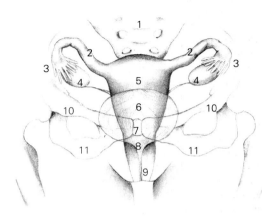

1 Sacrum

2 Fallopian tubes

3 Fimbriae

4 Ovaries

5 Uterus

6 Bladder (in front of uterus)

7 Symphysis pubis

8 Cervix

9 Vagina

10 Pelvic girdle

11 Ischial tuberosities

THE MAN'S REPRODUCTIVE ORGANS

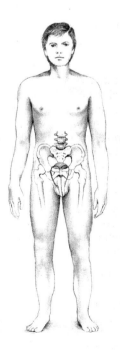

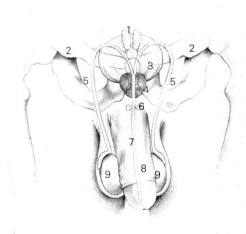

1 Seminal vesicles

2 Pelvic girdle

3 Bladder

4 Prostate gland (below bladder)

5 Vas deferens

6 Cowper's gland

7 Urethra

8 Penis (containing erectile tissue)

9 Testes

through the cervix towards the Fallopian tubes, which they reach in about 30 minutes. Many sperms are lost on the way and only a few thousand actually reach their destination. Only one sperm will succeed in fertilizing the ovum which has been released from the ovary and once this has happened the activity of all the other sperm is inhibited.

The survival times of ova and spermatozoa are very short; for a pregnancy to result, intercourse has to be carefully timed to the monthly cycle. The ovum survives for only about 24 hours after it has been released so, ideally, sperm should be already present in the Fallopian tube to fertilize it. A sperm can survive a little longer than the ovum, up to 48 hours, so if pregnancy is planned, your best chance of success is to have intercourse around the time of ovulation – the day before being the very best of all.

You can calculate when you ovulate from observation of your monthly cycle. Ovulation takes place about fourteen days before your next period would start; if you have fairly regular cycles you can work out your most fertile time of the month from the calendar. You can also examine the nature of the mucus produced by your cervix. The change that takes place in this around the time of ovulation has already been mentioned and it is quite easy to notice in your normal vaginal secretions – the mucus becomes clear and rather 'tacky'. If your periods tend to be irregular it is more difficult to predict when an egg will be released and you may have to use the temperature method to check when ovulation has occurred. Because of effects of the hormone progesterone, body temperature rises by about 2°F after ovulation and this change can be seen if you take your temperature each day. Using this method can be quite difficult and it is not necessary unless you are having fertility problems.

PRE-PREGNANCY PREPARATION

The early months of pregnancy are a time of great importance in a baby's development – it is during this time that the organs are formed and that very rapid growth is taking place. However, for many couples, the possibility of pregnancy may be unsuspected until this formative time is well under way. We know there are harmful influences which can affect a baby at this time and that these risks can be reduced if they have been considered before the baby is conceived. For this reason many prospective parents like to prepare ahead for pregnancy – a little like getting fit for a race or planning your holiday. Of course many pregnancies are not premeditated and are no less successful because of that, but a little forward thinking will make you feel even more confident.

When discussing pre-pregnancy counseling it is logical to think in terms of advice that is generally useful to all, and then to consider couples who may have specific problems or needs. Often the first decision that has to be made is when to stop using contraception. If you are using a barrier method or intrauterine device, then once its use has been discontinued you can try to conceive straight away. If you are using the contraceptive pill, however, it is best to stop this two or three months before you plan a pregnancy and use an alternative method such as the diaphragm or condom. This gap allows restoration of your natural menstrual cycle and the resumption of ovulation already referred to. It also makes it easier to calculate the baby's due date when you become pregnant (see below).

If you are planning your pregnancy in order to have your baby at a particular time of year, perhaps to fit with work schedules or older children's school holidays, it is perhaps appropriate here to explain how doctors and midwives talk about the duration of a pregnancy. They nearly always refer to the length of a pregnancy in weeks, it being more accurate than to talk of months (see p. 14). (To illustrate this point – a pregnancy lasts on average 40 weeks, a length usually equated with nine months in popular parlance. However, many people would calculate one month to equal four weeks, because this is the cycle associated with 'monthly periods', which would then make the average pregnancy ten months long – so you can see how confusion may arise!)

For medical purposes, duration of pregnancy is always calculated from the first day of the last menstrual period and not from the time of conception, so what is referred to as 'four weeks pregnant' is about the time when the majority of women would be missing their first period, rather than being four weeks from the time they have conceived. Unfortunately, the last menstrual period is only an accurate guide to the duration of pregnancy provided the cycle is regular each month, with ovulation occurring on day fourteen. If periods are erratic then the length of pregnancy may have to be calculated by ultrasound. In this book, any discussion about lengths of pregnancy follows the medical convention of weeks from the last period, with the assumption of conception two weeks later.

You may also want to take into account financial and career considerations in deciding the age at which your pregnancy is planned. With modern obstetric care, even the older mother can expect a relatively trouble-free time if she is generally fit and healthy, but the most favorable decade for having your family from the point of view of medical risk is between 20 and 30 years.

PRE-PREGNANCY AVERAGE WEIGHT FOR WOMEN

Height without shoes (ft, in)	Women Weight without clothes (lb)		Height without shoes (m)	Women Weight without clothes (kg)	
	Acceptable average	Acceptable weight range		Acceptable average	Acceptable weight range
4 10	102	92–119	1.45	46.0	42–53
4 11	104	94–122	1.48	46.5	42–54
5 0	107	96–125	1.50	47.0	43–55
5 1	110	99–128	1.52	48.5	44–57
5 2	113	102–131	1.54	49.5	44–58
5 3	116	105–134	1.56	50.4	45–58
5 4	120	108–138	1.58	51.3	46–59
5 5	123	111–142	1.60	52.6	48–61
5 6	128	114–146	1.62	54.0	49–62
5 7	132	118–150	1.64	55.4	50–64
5 8	136	122–154	1.66	56.8	51–65
5 9	140	126–158	1.68	58.1	52–66
5 10	144	130–163	1.70	60.0	53–67
5 11	148	134–168	1.72	61.3	55–69
6 0	152	138–173	1.74	62.6	56–70
			1.76	64.0	58–72
			1.78	65.3	59–74

HEALTH, WEIGHT AND DIET

Before you try to become pregnant, there are a number of things you should check, such as your immunity to rubella (German measles). Rubella is a viral illness which is mild in adults but can severely damage a fetus, particularly in the first semester of pregnancy, causing serious disabilities such as heart problems, deafness and blindness.

Since 1967, children in the United States receive rubella immunization at age fifteen months. More recently, rubella vaccine is combined with mumps and measles as the MMR shot. Most school systems require this shot for kindergarten entry so it is very likely you are immune. Furthermore, many states mandate testing for rubella immunity before obtaining a marriage license. But, if there is a question, your immunity can be checked by a blood test. If it is found that you are not immune you can be immunized by your doctor. Pregnancy should be

avoided for three months afterward. You can then be confident that you are no longer at risk, as immunity usually lasts for life, except in rare circumstances where the injection does not 'take'. If you were told you have already had the infection, it is best to check for certain via the blood test.

Another test some obstetricians perform is a toxoplasmosis titer. By checking early in pregnancy, and again toward the end, your doctor can be certain that you have not had this illness. Like rubella, it can cause defects in a fetus. Practice varies on this test, and you may wish to discuss the matter with your obstetrician.

As a potential mother, you should give some thought to your weight and diet. Of the many factors which may influence the course and outcome of pregnancy, nutritional status around the time of conception is one of the most important. Check your weight against the chart given above. If you find that you are very much over or under the weight range recommended then it would be sensible to correct this before pregnancy, as either state increases the likelihood of pregnancy complications. In particular pregnancy is no time for dieting.

As well as starting your pregnancy at the optimum weight it is important to eat a healthy and balanced diet to provide all the vitamins and nutrients essential for the baby's growth. There has been much debate about the advisability of taking vitamin and mineral supplements in the pre-pregnancy period and as yet their value for general use remains unproven, although they are almost certainly not harmful. More to the point are the general principles of healthy diet – choosing unrefined foods and fresh foods, and selecting a wide range from the four main groups: meat and fish, bread and cereals, milk and dairy products, and fruit and vegetables.

AVOIDING SMOKING

There are of course some habits, dietary and otherwise, which are best avoided when planning a pregnancy, the most important of which are smoking and alcohol consumption. We all know of people who have smoked heavily and consumed large quantities of alcohol all through pregnancies and had perfectly healthy, well grown babies but the medical evidence is overwhelming that indulging in these habits puts the baby at more risk. It is best if possible to give up smoking altogether, but the information about alcohol is not quite so clear. Obviously if you can avoid drinking then you are taking no risk but the occasional glass of beer or wine is probably not harmful. This advice applies to *both partners* trying for a successful pregnancy since excessive alcohol and tobacco consumption can affect male fertility by depressing sperm production and motility, as well as damaging the fertilized ovum.

Do try to avoid taking any pills, medicines or other drugs around the time of conception; even common remedies and pills should be checked with your doctor. If you are receiving regular medication it is sensible to discuss your plans for pregnancy with your doctor in case a change is needed. Seeing your doctor is also a good opportunity to have your blood pressure checked and to have a pelvic examination and cervical smear test if these have not been done recently at your family planning clinic. At this time you can also find out about prenatal supervision and delivery, and discover whether your obstetrician practices in a group. For some specific medical conditions such as diabetes, kidney disease, heart disease and high blood pressure prepregnancy advice and preparation is very important.

SPECIALIZED ADVICE

For some couples, rather more specialized advice may be required. One of the commoner situations in which this may arise is in counseling the older woman about the risks of having a baby with a chromosomal congenital abnormality – the one most often encountered being Down syndrome (once known as mongolism). The chances of having an affected baby increase with maternal age as shown in the graph on page 27. Although you will be counseled again in pregnancy it is easier to have thought through your response to the question of prenatal diagnosis, should you be in the at risk age group, particularly now that chorionic villus sampling can be used for diagnosis as early as eight to ten weeks from the last period (see p. 28). Other situations where prepregnancy information may be needed is for those couples who are at risk of carrying a hemoglobinopathy (see p. 26) who can be checked by means of a simple blood test, those who have had problems in previous pregnancies, and those where there is a family history of inherited disease for whom it is possible to arrange genetic counseling. If you think that you may need advice of this kind then your doctor should be consulted.

GENETIC COUNSELING

Many parents who have a relative with a handicapped child, or who have one themselves (see p. 280), worry about the same problem occurring with future children. If this is your situation, then the advice and reassurance of a genetic counselor could help to sort out your anxieties.

Genes are carried on chromosomes and are the fundamental basis of all inherited characteristics. At conception each person inherits thousands of genes from their parents. Sometimes one or two of these are harmful and can cause disease or handicap. The possibility of this happening is greater if the parents are related before marriage, such as cousins, for it is more likely they will carry the same genes because they inherited them from a common ancestor.

Genetic counseling can help parents in different ways. Not all parents want all that the service can offer. That does not matter. The doctor or clinical geneticist who gives the advice must first make an accurate diagnosis of affected family members and this may involve them being examined, some investigations and acquisition of relevant reports.

The correct diagnosis then allows the geneticist to calculate the risks of recurrence in subsequent children, or of recurrence in other family members. He or she can give advice about the cause and course of the disease, the risk to future children and ways to prevent it happening again. Help and support can also be provided in making difficult decisions once the facts are established.

PROBLEMS WITH FERTILITY

It is by no means usual for a couple to achieve a pregnancy the first time they try, even when intercourse has been perfectly timed, and it may take several months before success is accomplished. Most doctors would not regard a couple as subfertile until they have been trying for a pregnancy for at least a year. Sadly, however, infertility can occur and is known to affect about one in ten couples in the Western world. Failure to conceive can be due to one or more reasons affecting the man, the woman or both.

MALE INFERTILITY

The only true test of a man's fertility is his ability to father a child. Short of this, some indication of male fertility or infertility is given by the sperm count, which reports on the number of sperm present, their shape and motility. Fertile men usually produce between 50 million and 150 million sperm per milliliter of ejaculated fluid. Men with sperm counts under ten million per milliliter are usually infertile. But the quality of the sperm matters as much as the number produced. Men are occasionally fertile despite low sperm counts and, conversely, men with high counts may not always be fertile.

Some men produce no sperm at all – this may follow infections such as some venereal diseases and mumps, sterilization by vasectomy, radiation therapy for cancers in the genital region or such men may have a rare disorder of their chromosomes (genetic make-up). Sperm counts may also be greatly reduced in men who smoke tobacco or marijuana, and also those who drink alcohol heavily.

The treatment of male infertility is largely angled at removing the cause – stopping excessive smoking and drinking, reversing a vasectomy, tying off abnormal scrotal veins and so on. Sometimes powerful hormone injections may improve sperm production, with steroid drugs to decrease the effects of an antibody interference.

Sometimes normal sperm may be rendered inactive when they arrive at the cervix, because the mucus through which they must pass there is thick, acid and therefore hostile. This may be counteracted by treating any infection present which might cause this, and by giving the woman estrogen tablets to make the mucus flow clear and plentiful at the time of ovulation.

FEMALE INFERTILITY

One of the most common causes of female infertility is ovulation failure. Ovulation can be achieved by giving the woman pills which help the pituitary gland stimulate egg ripening or by powerful injections of hormones which stimulate the ovaries directly. In this case there is an increased likelihood of multiple births. By and large, however, the treatment for ovulation problems using closely monitored modern medical techniques is successful. Multiple births are usually limited to twins.

Another frequent cause of female infertility is blockage of the Fallopian tubes, which prevents fertilization of the ovum. Tube damage may follow severe pelvic infections or the formation of adhesions (bands of scar tissue) after surgical operations. Fallopian tubes may also be artificially blocked for sterilization.

The unblocking of Fallopian tubes is relatively straightforward, thanks to up-to-date microsurgical techniques. The blocked portions are removed and the ends joined up again. However, if the lining of the remaining pieces of Fallopian tube has been damaged by previous infection, then the fertilized ovum will not be sustained and nourished in the tube as usual and a pregnancy will not develop, despite the tubes being open again.

A neat way of by-passing the tubes is by in vitro fertilization (IVF) – the test tube baby approach. In this technique eggs are removed from the woman's stimulated ovaries and mixed with her partner's sperm in a dish, under specially controlled conditions. The fertilized eggs are then placed inside her uterus some hours later. Their development is then monitored – usually only one embryo survives to grow into a healthy baby, and the pregnancy proceeds in the normal way. It should be stressed, however, that IVF requires considerable motivation on the part of both prospective parents and that the number of women suited to this treatment is very small.

Recent technical improvements in IVF make it easier than previously. Eggs can now be harvested using a vaginal probe ultrasound with attached needle guide egg harvester and the process can be carried out in the x-ray department rather than in an operating room.

INVESTIGATING INFERTILITY

If you are worried about your fertility, talk it over with your obstetrician who can give you general advice, explain what special tests may be necessary and refer you to a specialist. There are also self-help groups who can support you with counseling.

PRENATAL CARE

**The pattern of pregnancy care and its importance
for the health and well-being of you and your baby**

Pregnancy is not an illness. The majority of mothers-to-be are healthy women who go through the normal process of bearing a child without any problems beyond the minor discomforts associated with the development of the fetus in the uterus. Occasional problems can occur, however, which may threaten the health of the baby or the mother, or both. And some women with existing conditions, such as diabetes or some form of physical disability, need extra help during pregnancy. For these reasons, regular prenatal check-ups are important – to reassure you that all is well and to act quickly when it is not.

THE LENGTH OF PREGNANCY

You usually have your first full prenatal check-up between the tenth and twelfth weeks of pregnancy, during what is sometimes known as the first trimester. 'Trimester' is a term used by doctors to mean a three month period: for convenience pregnancy is divided into three trimesters (weeks 1 to 12, 13 to 28 and 29 to 40). These divisions are not particularly significant.

People have traditionally thought of pregnancy as being nine months long, but doctors and midwives prefer to use a more accurate method to establish the estimated date of confinement (EDC). The average pregnancy lasts 38 weeks from conception, which for most women will take place in the middle of their menstrual cycle (see p. 10). However, since this assumes that all women have a regular 28 day cycle, which is by no means the case, your EDC is usually calculated from the first day of your last menstrual period. A simple way to calculate your EDC is to add 40 weeks from the date of the start of your last period, or alternatively to add seven days to the first day of your last period and then add nine months to that. For example, if your last period started on 14 June, add seven days (21 June), then add nine months (21 March) which becomes your estimated date of confinement. Bear in mind that these dates are only estimates: a normal pregnancy can be anything from 38 to 42 weeks long.

If for some reason you don't know or can't remember the date of your last period, or if your cycle is very irregular, during your first prenatal check-up the doctor or midwife will try to establish the size and therefore the age of the fetus by measuring the size of your uterus during an internal examination (see p. 23), or you will be given an ultrasound scan (see p. 25).

CONFIRMING THE PREGNANCY

The first sign of pregnancy for most women is a missed menstrual period (known as amenorrhea) which is a sign that the developing embryo has embedded in the endometrium (see p. 39). However, if your periods are irregular you may notice other signs first (see p. 43). In fact, if you have partially suppressed periods for a month or two, you may not even know that you are pregnant for a while.

Your breasts may enlarge and become quite tender. You also notice that the nipples and areola (the area round the nipples) become darker, and the areola will develop small protuberances, called Montgomery's tubercles, glands which help to keep the nipples supple. Some women experience nausea (morning sickness) right from the start, though this usually develops over the first six weeks or so, subsiding at about twelve to fourteen weeks (see p. 44). You may also notice a need to urinate more often, and you might also become aware of increasing tiredness.

You can confirm the pregnancy before you see your doctor by having a urine test. Family planning clinics and health centers may offer pregnancy testing, and home pregnancy testing kits, using a urine specimen, are available from drug stores.

VISITING YOUR DOCTOR

When you think you may be pregnant, visit your family doctor or obstetrician as soon as possible. Unless you have a particular condition which requires urgent decision-making, or you or your doctor think your pregnancy may already be fairly advanced, your doctor is unlikely to do more at this stage than to congratulate you, check that you are

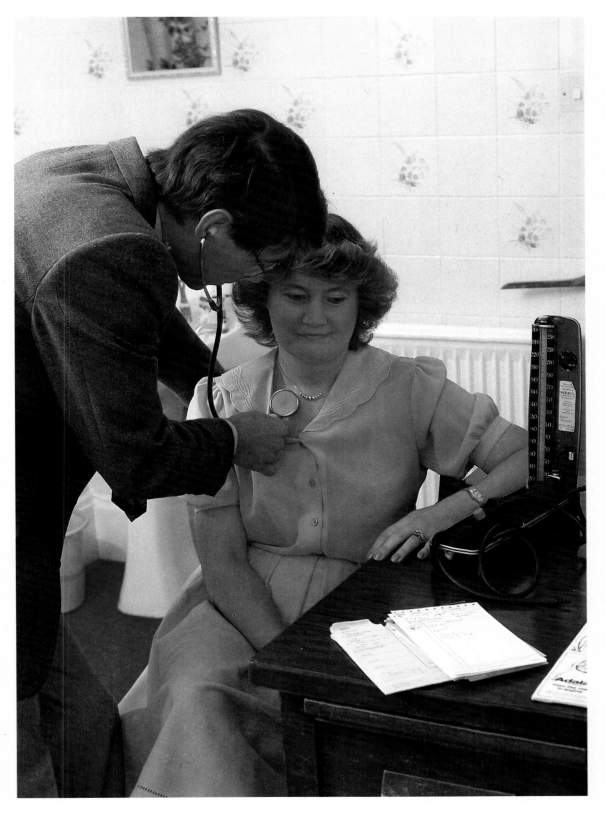

generally well and make arrangements for prenatal care, depending on where you want to have your baby.

It is worth thinking about birth options before you have this discussion with your doctor. If you are not sure, talk about it with your doctor and defer the decision for a few days, after which you can make the necessary arrangements through your doctor at another consultation. The information given in the next few pages about pregnancy care and the pros and cons of hospital or home births may help you make up your mind.

PREGNANCY CARE

Pregnancy care varies in different parts of the country; in some areas you will have a wide range of choices, in others very few. Three different care givers can provide prenatal care – your family doctor, a midwife, or a specialist doctor called an obstetrician.

Family practice doctors, or general practitioners, carry out their prenatal checkups in the office. They perform this component of medical care as part of overall family medicine. Obstetricians are sometimes hospital-based; most have their own offices away from the hospital and provide care only in the area of obstetrics and gynecology. Midwives are often affiliated with obstetrical departments in local hospitals and may work independently, or collaborate with an obstetrician depending on state laws. Midwives are expert in normal childbirth, and if all goes well with your pregnancy and birth it will be a midwife who delivers your baby and who will give you much of your pregnancy and postpartum care. Generally, if complications arise during the pregnancy or during delivery, midwives will refer you to a hospital delivery setting, and, typically, will involve the expertise of an obstetrician. There are different combinations of prenatal care. Depending upon where the birth will take place, you may be followed in a hospital office or clinic, a doctor's office, a free-standing health center, or even at home by an independent midwife.

WHERE TO HAVE THE BABY

You can either have your baby at home or in hospital. Most women have their babies in hospital and there is some controversy about the relative merits of a home or hospital delivery. Increasing evidence shows that if you are healthy and want to have your baby at home, there is no reason why you shouldn't. The difficulty nowadays is to find a doctor and community or independent midwife in your area who are willing to offer this service, as

To use the chart to calculate your estimated date of confinement (EDC), first find the date of your last period in the upper rows of figures. The date below it is your EDC.

JANUARY	1	2	3	4	5	6	7	8	9	10	11	12	13	14	15	16	17	18	19	20	21	22	23	24	25	26	27	28	29	30	31	**JANUARY**
OCTOBER	8	9	10	11	12	13	14	15	16	17	18	19	20	21	22	23	24	25	26	27	28	29	30	31	1	2	3	4	5	6	7	**NOVEMBER**
FEBRUARY	1	2	3	4	5	6	7	8	9	10	11	12	13	14	15	16	17	18	19	20	21	22	23	24	25	26	27	28				**FEBRUARY**
NOVEMBER	8	9	10	11	12	13	14	15	16	17	18	19	20	21	22	23	24	25	26	27	28	29	30	1	2	3	4	5				**DECEMBER**
MARCH	1	2	3	4	5	6	7	8	9	10	11	12	13	14	15	16	17	18	19	20	21	22	23	24	25	26	27	28	29	30	31	**MARCH**
DECEMBER	6	7	8	9	10	11	12	13	14	15	16	17	18	19	20	21	22	23	24	25	26	27	28	29	30	31	1	2	3	4	5	**JANUARY**
APRIL	1	2	3	4	5	6	7	8	9	10	11	12	13	14	15	16	17	18	19	20	21	22	23	24	25	26	27	28	29	30		**APRIL**
JANUARY	6	7	8	9	10	11	12	13	14	15	16	17	18	19	20	21	22	23	24	25	26	27	28	29	30	31	1	2	3	4		**FEBRUARY**
MAY	1	2	3	4	5	6	7	8	9	10	11	12	13	14	15	16	17	18	19	20	21	22	23	24	25	26	27	28	29	30	31	**MAY**
FEBRUARY	5	6	7	8	9	10	11	12	13	14	15	16	17	18	19	20	21	22	23	24	25	26	27	28	1	2	3	4	5	6	7	**MARCH**
JUNE	1	2	3	4	5	6	7	8	9	10	11	12	13	14	15	16	17	18	19	20	21	22	23	24	25	26	27	28	29	30		**JUNE**
MARCH	8	9	10	11	12	13	14	15	16	17	18	19	20	21	22	23	24	25	26	27	28	29	30	31	1	2	3	4	5	6		**APRIL**
JULY	1	2	3	4	5	6	7	8	9	10	11	12	13	14	15	16	17	18	19	20	21	22	23	24	25	26	27	28	29	30	31	**JULY**
APRIL	7	8	9	10	11	12	13	14	15	16	17	18	19	20	21	22	23	24	25	26	27	28	29	30	1	2	3	4	5	6	7	**MAY**
AUGUST	1	2	3	4	5	6	7	8	9	10	11	12	13	14	15	16	17	18	19	20	21	22	23	24	25	26	27	28	29	30	31	**AUGUST**
MAY	8	9	10	11	12	13	14	15	16	17	18	19	20	21	22	23	24	25	26	27	28	29	30	31	1	2	3	4	5	6	7	**JUNE**
SEPTEMBER	1	2	3	4	5	6	7	8	9	10	11	12	13	14	15	16	17	18	19	20	21	22	23	24	25	26	27	28	29	30		**SEPTEMBER**
JUNE	8	9	10	11	12	13	14	15	16	17	18	19	20	21	22	23	24	25	26	27	28	29	30	1	2	3	4	5	6	7		**JULY**
OCTOBER	1	2	3	4	5	6	7	8	9	10	11	12	13	14	15	16	17	18	19	20	21	22	23	24	25	26	27	28	29	30	31	**OCTOBER**
JULY	8	9	10	11	12	13	14	15	16	17	18	19	20	21	22	23	24	25	26	27	28	29	30	31	1	2	3	4	5	6	7	**AUGUST**
NOVEMBER	1	2	3	4	5	6	7	8	9	10	11	12	13	14	15	16	17	18	19	20	21	22	23	24	25	26	27	28	29	30		**NOVEMBER**
AUGUST	8	9	10	11	12	13	14	15	16	17	18	19	20	21	22	23	24	25	26	27	28	29	30	31	1	2	3	4	5	6		**SEPTEMBER**
DECEMBER	1	2	3	4	5	6	7	8	9	10	11	12	13	14	15	16	17	18	19	20	21	22	23	24	25	26	27	28	29	30	31	**DECEMBER**
SEPTEMBER	7	8	9	10	11	12	13	14	15	16	17	18	19	20	21	22	23	24	25	26	27	28	29	30	1	2	3	4	5	6	7	**OCTOBER**

health authorities tend to concentrate resources for pregnancy and childbirth on hospital care, and many doctors are not convinced of the safety of home deliveries. At the same time, many hospital maternity units are trying to relax their atmosphere to make it as comfortable for mothers as possible.

HOME DELIVERIES

If you decide to have your baby at home, you will need to find a midwife who can look after you. Many hospitals advertise home delivery programs and midwife programs; further information is available through the department of obstetrics or the community health department of the hospital. Your family practitioner or internist can also help you with this referral. Many obstetricians also co-practice with midwives engaged in home delivery. Your local Medical Society can often provide a list with such particulars on it. Likewise, friends and neighbors are a helpful resource regarding what practices are locally available.

Many general hospitals run prenatal classes and the leaders of these typically can help you with a referral to any style of practice and delivery arrangement you prefer.

HOSPITAL DELIVERIES

Having a hospital delivery does not necessarily · mean having a long stay in the postpartum ward nowadays. There is a tendency for mothers to leave hospital earlier, both because of pressure on beds and because it is not medically necessary for them to stay longer. Some women go into hospital when labor starts and stay there for a few days after the baby is born; others, especially if they have a child or children already, only stay for 24-48 hours and then go home to be looked after by their family and friends.

THE BIRTHING ROOM

Many hospitals now have delivery room suites called 'birthing rooms'. The idea behind this is simple. The hospital tries to provide a room which looks like a normal home bedroom, but is especially equipped for a delivery. In some instances, the space is both well designed and decorated so that it closely resembles a 'normal' bedroom. However, concealed behind drapes or other decorative features are the various pieces of equipment which might be necessary should an emergency arise during labor or delivery. In other hospital units, the attempt to mimic a home birth setting is less successful. However, even the small amenities of a

birthing room may make you feel more comfortable and less at the mercy of high technology medicine. Moreover, since these suites are located nearby the hospital delivery rooms, you have access to all the modern kind of treatment techniques which could, conceivably, help minimize any risk to mother or baby. For many couples, this kind of compromise is very attractive. A little research on your part will turn up the locations of these units near you. Hospitals generally welcome you to visit the unit so that you can have some idea of the ambience.

PROS AND CONS

The main risks of a home delivery are usually defined as excessive bleeding of the mother or problems with the baby's breathing at birth, which are difficult to deal with safely outside hospital. However, midwives usually carry drugs to help the uterus contract in case of bleeding and also carry the equipment to administer intravenous fluids to increase blood volume. Midwives also carry resuscitation equipment for the baby if there is any difficulty with breathing, but they cannot provide care comparable to a hospital if an emergency arises.

If any emergency crops up during a home delivery the mother can be transferred to hospital by ambulance. About one in ten of women having a first baby at home end up having a hospital delivery instead, but fewer women having their second or third babies at home end up in hospital.

Women having babies at home feel that they are taking responsibility for their birth and for their babies right from the start. For many women, a home delivery is relaxing and intimate: only your immediate family and a midwife or doctor that you know will be present and you do not have to interrupt the progress of your labor with a journey to the hospital.

THE RISKS OF HOME BIRTHS

Most doctors advise against home deliveries for a first baby. There are also valid arguments against having a baby at home if you have any medical problems such as kidney disease, very high blood pressure, a heart condition or diabetes. Women who have had a cesarean section in the past have a 1 in 100 chance that the scar on their uterus could give way during a subsequent labor, so many doctors and midwives feel that the risk is too great and are very reluctant to agree to a home delivery for a woman who has had a previous cesarean section. In addition, women who are 5ft 2in or less in height have a greater chance of needing a cesarean section, so you will probably be safer if you arrange for a hospital delivery. You would be safer with a hospital delivery if you are having twins, and if your baby is breech you will be advised to go into hospital, even if you had arranged a home birth originally.

It is always a good idea to ask your mother how she gave birth to you and your brothers and sisters. If she gave birth normally, your pelvis is probably like hers and you will be able to give birth normally too. If she needed a cesarean delivery it may mean that her pelvis was narrow at some points and you may have inherited that. If she had a forceps delivery it may have been for the same reason.

In many areas it is very difficult to organize a home delivery, and a hospital delivery is inevitable. Many women prefer this anyway; they like the security of knowing that if anything goes wrong at the last minute there will be up-to-date equipment and specialist staff available immediately to deal with the emergency. Some women, especially first time mothers, prefer to have a few days in the postpartum ward to get used to their babies and to have the option to call on a nurse day or night to advise them. It is also an opportunity to meet other mothers, some of whom may be more experienced. And although it may be a wrench to leave older children at home, some second or third time mothers like the fact that even 36 hours in hospital gives them the opportunity to be alone with the new baby without the extra pressures of family life.

THE RISKS OF HOSPITAL BIRTHS

The risks to women of having a baby in hospital are not often discussed because most women have their babies there, but they do exist. They are usually seen as being two-fold – the risk of infection due to the large number of people using the hospital, and the risk from interference in a normal physiological experience which may have an adverse effect on labor. For instance, in hospital you are more likely to be electronically monitored (see p. 81). Although monitoring may be necessary it sometimes is not, and, unless there is a 'remote control' facility, it does mean that the mother cannot move around as she would normally do in labor. As a result the pain she feels may be more intense because she is unable to do anything physical to relieve it. This in turn may lead to the use of more painkillers which may affect not only the way the baby is delivered but also the baby's condition.

In addition to these possible inconveniences during labor, a few hospitals still remove babies from their mothers to a nursery, especially at night. This may not worry some mothers who would be

glad to hand over responsibility to the staff in the hospital, especially if they are very tired after a difficult labor. But it is not particularly pleasant for a mother who feels well and wants to keep her baby with her all the time to be denied that choice.

A hospital is a large institution catering for a wide section of the population, and like all large institutions it cannot always fit in with every individual's needs even though everyone working there does their best, whereas if you are at home you are probably the center of attention. If you are fortunate and have the choice of several different types of service for your prenatal care and birth, weigh up all the pros and cons according to your own feelings and expectations. These expectations may not always be possible to fulfill – every labor is different and things can change at the very last minute, but at least you will feel that you have made the initial decisions.

THE FIRST PRENATAL CHECK-UP

You have decided whether to have your baby at the hospital or at home, and know whether you will be using a midwife, family practitioner, or obstetrician. Telephone for an appointment when both of you can meet the doctor or midwife together and review your earlier decisions. If your medical history includes problems or complications, it is best to obtain a referral letter from your regular doctor stating a summary of these issues. Depending on the appointments system, you could be there for up to three hours on the first visit. Go prepared with a drink, and a book or something else to while away the time in case you have a long wait. You will need to bring medical insurance information as well, and you may wish to prepare a list of questions or problems to review with your provider.

While practice details may vary somewhat, the description which follows is both standard and typical. When you arrive at the clinic, you will probably be weighed and your height measured. You will be weighed at every subsequent prenatal visit. Weight gain is one indication of the progress of pregnancy – excessive gain can cause problems but it is also important that you put on enough weight according to your height and build (see page 46).

THE URINE TEST

You will be asked to bring a clean sample of urine to every prenatal visit, and will probably be given a special container. At the office you may be asked to provide a 'mid-stream specimen of urine' for testing. This is a specimen uncontaminated by mucus or discharge, and you will be given a special sterile

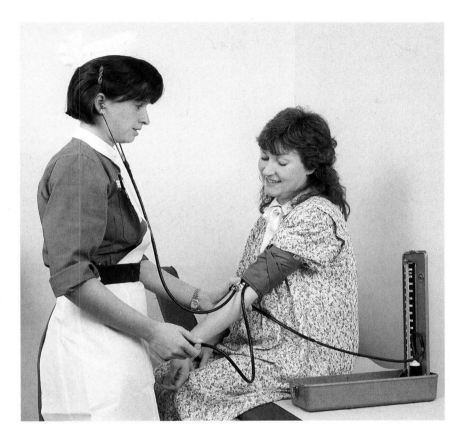

Blood pressure is a useful indicator of the health of your pregnancy and will be measured by the midwife or doctor at every prenatal check-up.

cleansing pack with instructions for use. Sterile water and cotton wool swabs are provided to clean your genital area; you then pass a small amount of urine into the lavatory, stopping the flow in 'midstream', catching the next part of the stream in the jar provided. You take this to the assistant for testing. Some women find they can stop and start the flow of urine with ease because of the strength of their pelvic floor muscles (see p. 32), while others find it more difficult. It is worth persevering since you may be asked for another sample if the first is contaminated. Your urine sample will be checked immediately for the presence of protein and sugar, and also be cultured for infection.

These tests give important signals about your health and the progress of your pregnancy, which is why you are asked to bring a sample every time. Protein in urine may indicate kidney infection, or, later in pregnancy, may be a symptom of pre-eclampsia (see p. 70), especially if associated with high blood pressure. Sugar in urine is a possible sign of diabetes, but many non-diabetic women have sugar in their urine during pregnancy due to hormonal changes. This will be double-checked with your blood test (see p.22). Your urine will also be checked for the presence of ketones (also known

as acetones) which appear when the body is short of glucose. This could be due to dietary deficiency, excessive nausea or dehydration, and you will receive treatment for it.

BLOOD PRESSURE

At this first and every subsequent prenatal visit your blood pressure and pulse will be measured, using a special instrument called a sphygmomanometer.

Blood pressure is an important gauge of the health of your pregnancy. It is measured in terms of the pressure at the peak of a heartbeat (systolic pressure) and when the heart relaxes between beats (diastolic pressure). Normal blood pressure can range from 90/60 to 130/85, and the systolic pressure can vary widely according to how active you are being at the time. The diastolic level should, however, remain about the same. Blood pressure should drop as your pregnancy advances because of the action of the hormone progesterone. If the diastolic level rises more than a certain amount, it may be a symptom of pre-eclampsia. Although you may feel perfectly well, you will probably be advised to have bed rest (see p. 70) to prevent the condition from developing to a severe stage.

BLOOD TESTS

At some point during your first visit you will be asked to give a blood sample. This may be taken by a doctor or midwife, or you will have to go to a special department to have the sample taken by a specialist technician. This first sample is very important as it gives a lot of important information about your health and the health of your baby. It will be used to establish your blood group (A, B, O or AB). The hemoglobin level (Hb) of your blood will also be checked to see if you are anemic, and you may be given iron and folic acid pills to prevent anemia (see p. 52).

Your blood will also be tested for the rhesus factor (Rh). If like most of the population your blood contains this, you are 'rhesus positive', and have no further problems. If however you are 'rhesus negative' (no rhesus factor), there may be future difficulties if your baby has rhesus positive blood. Rh positive and Rh negative blood are incompatible, and if during pregnancy or birth some of the baby's blood crosses from the placenta into the mother's bloodstream the mother may develop antibodies which would destroy the rhesus factor in the blood of a subsequent baby. The baby could be born severely anemic, requiring an exchange blood transfusion (see p. 122).

Fortunately this situation is now very rare since the condition can be treated. If you are found to be Rh negative, you may be given a dose of rhesus antibody (immunoglobulin Anti-D) after the birth. In some circumstances you may be given this during pregnancy, for instance after an amniocentesis or an obstetric hemorrhage (see p. 62). Some units even give it routinely at 36 weeks to rhesus negative women.

Your blood will also be tested to see if you are immune to rubella (German measles), which can have a catastrophic effect on the baby if contracted during pregnancy (see p. 13). If you are not immune you will be offered immunization after the birth. (Never be inoculated during pregnancy. Rubella immunization involves a 'live' vaccine, so it could have the same effect on your unborn baby as the disease itself.) Some doctors also screen for toxoplasmosis, an uncommon disease which can cause birth defects.

Your blood will also be screened for sexually transmitted diseases, especially syphilis. Although very few women now have this disease, those who do may not know it and it can be transmitted to the fetus after about 20 weeks. If the disease is found before 20 weeks, it can be successfully treated. Blood is not automatically screened for AIDS at the moment, but if you think you may be at risk from this disease you can ask the doctor to arrange this for you (see also p. 29).

THE INTERVIEW

Apart from the physical examination by the doctor, which is usually the last item in the schedule, by far the longest time will be spent on your 'medical history'. This takes the form of an informal interview conducted in private. It consists of a long series of personal and medical details about yourself, your family and your partner which gives the medical staff information which may be helpful in the management of your pregnancy and birth, and possibly in the subsequent care of your baby. This information is confidential so don't be shy about giving complete details of your medical history, particularly any gynecological details such as a termination of pregnancy (abortion), pelvic infection or sexually transmitted disease.

The most important questions will concern the progress of your present pregnancy and that of any earlier pregnancies, even if they ended in miscarriage or abortion. You will be asked the date of your last period, its duration, what your periods are usually like, and whether you are suffering from headaches, nausea or other discomforts. The week of pregnancy at which any previous children were born, or when miscarriages took place, are also important, as are any abnormal deliveries.

The midwife or doctor will want to know social details of your life as well. You will be asked about your past health and that of your partner, and of your parents and grandparents. They will want to know if any handicapped babies have been born to either family (if you don't know it's worth enquiring of relatives before you go to hospital), and how your mother gave birth to you and your brothers and sisters. She will also want to know whether you were breast or bottle fed and whether you have decided which method of feeding you prefer for your own baby.

When recording your medical history and that of your partner the midwife will ask whether you suffer from any chronic condition, what infectious diseases you and your partner have had, and whether either of you has had heart disease, tuberculosis, mental illness or allergies, or whether there are any members of your families who suffer or suffered from these conditions. Don't worry if you don't know all the answers to these questions, but if you find out subsequently tell the provider at your next prenatal check-up.

Your provider will review with you whether you are eligible for the WIC program (Women, Infant, Children food supplement coupons), and help

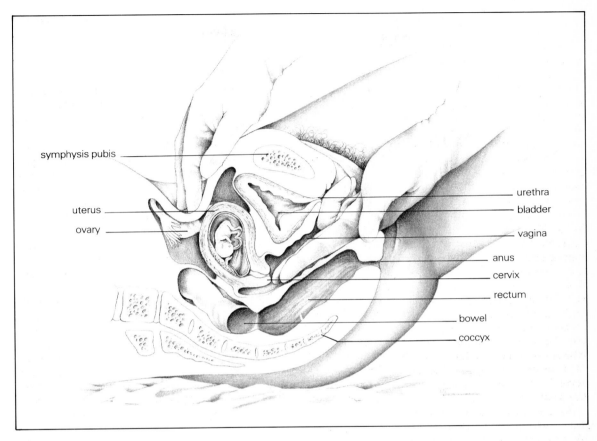

symphysis pubis

uterus

ovary

urethra

bladder

vagina

anus

cervix

rectum

bowel

coccyx

To check the size and position of the uterus, the doctor inserts two fingers into the vagina while pressing on the abdomen with the other hand.

arrange for social service consultation as well.

The provider may well ask you if there is anything special you were thinking about for labor – any special way you want to be looked after, or would prefer to be delivered if possible. If she doesn't talk about this, raise the topic yourself. You may well be shell-shocked by this 'interrogation' but this is a good time to ask questions if you have any, and your partner may like to as well if he is with you. If you haven't decided about how you want to conduct your labor yet, you can have this part filled in at a later visit, but it is best to discuss it as early in your pregnancy as possible so that it can be recorded in your chart, rather than leaving it to the last minute. Trying to make special requests on a busy labor ward can make communication difficult.

THE PHYSICAL EXAMINATION

At the first prenatal visit, the physical examination should be carried out by your provider.

There may well be another long wait before you see the doctor. If you especially want to see a woman doctor, you should always ask when you make the appointment.

The doctor will examine your breasts and nipples and give advice on their care if you intend to breastfeed. He or she will listen to your heart and lungs and ask you if you smoke. If you do you will be advised to give it up (see p. 46). While the examination will focus on your pregnancy, the doctor will also take time to check any other health problems you may have. For example, if you have diabetes he is likely to perform a careful heart examination, and will also examine your legs very carefully with respect to your blood circulation.

THE INTERNAL EXAMINATION

The most important part of this first examination is the palpation of your abdomen and the internal examination. You will be asked to lie on the couch and the doctor will press (palpate) your abdomen to feel whether the uterus has grown big enough to be felt above the symphisis pubis (see p. 41). This does not happen until about the twelfth week of pregnancy, so it is a useful guide to the exact stage of your pregnancy. The doctor will then give you an internal examination to assess the size of the uterus by pressing on your abdomen with one hand and feeling the position of the cervix with the other. This is particularly useful if you were not sure of the date of your last menstrual period, and you may find that you are further on with the pregnancy than you thought. If this is the case the doctor is likely to arrange for you to have an ultrasound scan as soon as possible to confirm his or her own findings.

You may also have a cervical smear taken if you have not had one done recently. The doctor will insert a speculum into your vagina and gently scrape a few cells from your cervix to be examined for abnormal cells by a specialist cytologist in the laboratory. You will probably get the result at your next appointment, but any treatment required will probably be left until after the birth.

If you already have a history of miscarriage the doctor may decide to avoid making an internal examination until later in your pregnancy, perhaps at about fifteen or sixteen weeks, after the vulnerable period for early miscarriage has passed. In this case he will almost certainly refer you for an early ultrasound scan as well.

FATHERS AT THE PRENATAL VISIT

Your partner will always be made welcome at your prenatal visits – it is useful for him to know how your pregnancy is progressing first hand. Fathers are invariably invited into the consulting room, and may have useful information to contribute to the medical history about their families' medical history and their own feelings concerning the forthcoming birth. Your partner will also be able to give an outsider's view of how you have been during your pregnancy – whether you have been more irritable or more emotional than usual. He will also be able to hear for himself advice about diet, giving up smoking and reducing alcohol – it could help you both to stop or cut down on these.

Your partner may also be better able to remember the questions you wanted to ask, and take in more of the information and advice given to you toward the end of your pregnancy when your concentration begins to waver. It is useful to have someone with you with whom to discuss the conversations afterwards. And a final important benefit for fathers at prenatal visits is the insight it will give them into the whole process of childbirth. Most hospitals welcome fathers into the labor ward nowadays, and most women want to have their partners with them during labor and birth. However there are still some men who are reluctant or diffident about being

there. Attending prenatal check-ups with their partners can help to demystify childbirth for them and prepare them just as it does mothers, especially if these visits are combined with preparation classes (see p. 30).

OTHER ADVICE

Before you leave the office you may well be invited to talk to one or two other health workers who are there to help you. Many hospitals invite couples to an introductory talk on parenting in which midwives and physiotherapists give advice on how to stay healthy and fit during pregnancy. They will also tell you how to join regular classes on parenting and preparation for childbirth (see p. 30).

There is usually a hospital dietician attached to the prenatal clinic who will advise you about healthy eating during pregnancy (see p. 46). If you are a vegan (a vegetarian who eats no animal produce at all) she will make sure that a midwife supplies you with extra Vitamin B12 supplements, since this vitamin is essential for the healthy growth of your baby and is only present in animal products. In some hospitals Asian women are advised to take extra Vitamin D. Vitamin D is usually produced through the action of the sun shining on skin; because many Asian women wear clothes which cover them almost completely they may not make enough Vitamin D for their needs. This is not a problem for Afro-Caribbean women.

If the midwife has reason to believe from your interview with her that you need special financial or welfare assistance, she may suggest you talk to the hospital social worker. This is particularly helpful if you are a single parent or if either you or your partner is unemployed or has housing problems. It is a good idea to set the wheels in motion early in pregnancy in order to make your life easier once the baby is born. The social worker can help you assess your rights to the various benefits both before and after the birth.

SPECIAL PRENATAL TESTS

Most women require no more than the routine prenatal checks described above throughout their pregnancies. If however the midwife or doctor has any reason to be concerned about the health of yourself or the fetus, or if you are among a small minority of women who might be at risk of passing on certain inherited diseases or abnormalities to your baby (see p. 14), then it is likely that you will be offered one of a number of special screening tests which are designed to diagnose such problems as early as possible.

ULTRASOUND

The use of ultrasound scanners in obstetric care is one of the most beneficial technical advances of the past twenty years. Almost all maternity units have this facility, and some of the machines in use are extremely sophisticated. Ultrasound was developed during the First World War as a means of detecting submarines under water; it works by bouncing very high frequency sound (sonar) waves off solid objects which show up as a picture on a visual display unit. It is mainly used to check fetal age and health, since accurate measurements can be taken of the diameter of the head, the length of the spine or thigh bone, all of which can be used to compute fetal age. Position and presentation of the fetus can be ascertained, multiple pregnancies can be diagnosed with certainty at a very early stage, and a skilled operator can often distinguish the sex of the fetus (although they won't usually tell you!).

In addition more sophisticated machines can check the position and health of the placenta and the cervix, enabling early diagnosis of such conditions as placenta previa or cervical incompetence (see pp. 60 and 63). Ultrasound can also be used to detect fetal abnormalities such as spina bifida, and uterine abnormalities such as fibroids. It can also be used to diagnose whether a miscarriage is likely to be inevitable as early as six or seven weeks of pregnancy, and is also used for amniocentesis and chorionic villus sampling (see p. 28).

The ultrasound machine is completely harmless to the mother – indeed it avoids the need for an internal examination in many cases so can be seen as positively beneficial. It is also extremely interesting for both parents to see the baby on the screen, literally bringing the pregnancy to life. This can be particularly meaningful for fathers who sometimes feel excluded from the excitement of the pregnancy because they have no direct physical involvement. Some hospitals will provide you with a photograph of the image as a keepsake.

There is no evidence that the use of ultrasound in pregnancy harms the fetus, although this has not yet been proven with certainty by long term research. Many hospital consultants confine routine scanning to a single appointment at about sixteen or seventeen weeks, others prefer to have a second scan done routinely later in pregnancy at perhaps 30 or 32 weeks. Occasionally you may be scanned more frequently if your doctor wants to check something specific, particularly if you experience any bleeding or if the doctor or midwife wants to check that the baby is growing properly (see p. 72).

In early pregnancy you will probably be asked to come to an ultrasound appointment with a full bladder. This can cause some discomfort if you are kept waiting, but it does help to give the radiographer a better view of your uterus on the screen. To be scanned, you lie on a couch in a darkened room. Your abdomen is smeared with warm oil or a special gel which allows the transducer (the scanning probe) to pass across your abdomen with ease and to give a clear image with less interference to

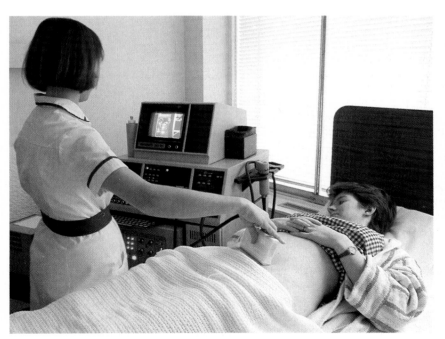

Most pregnant women are now given a routine ultrasound scan at sixteen to seventeen weeks to check the size, gestational age and health of the fetus and placenta. Ultrasound is also used to help diagnostic techniques, such as amniocentesis and chorionic villus sampling, and to look for problems such as placenta previa or perhaps the presence of more than one baby.

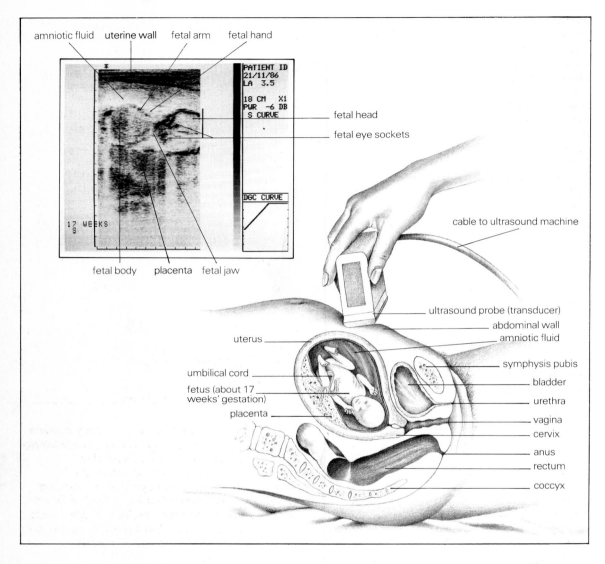

amniotic fluid · uterine wall · fetal arm · fetal hand

PATIENT ID
21/11/86
LA 3.5

18 CM   X1
PWR -6 DB
S CURVE

fetal head

fetal eye sockets

DGC CURVE

17 WEEKS

fetal body · placenta · fetal jaw

cable to ultrasound machine

ultrasound probe (transducer)

abdominal wall

amniotic fluid

uterus

symphysis pubis

umbilical cord

bladder

fetus (about 17 weeks' gestation)

urethra

placenta

vagina

cervix

anus

rectum

coccyx

Top: *The film positive taken from an ultrasound scan of a fetus of seventeen weeks' gestation.*
Above: *A cross-section of the mother's uterus, with a seventeen-week fetus. Ultrasound can now show congenital abnormalities of internal organs at this stage.*

the sound waves. The radiographer (sometimes called an ultrasonographer) moves the transducer from side to side to produce the image on the screen which can then be interpreted.

SPECIAL BLOOD TESTS

In addition to the routine blood tests requested from all mothers at prenatal checks, some women will be tested for a specific group of blood disorders which are passed on by inheritance – these disorders are known as 'hemoglobinopathies', and include sickle cell anemia and thalassemia. They are caused by an abnormality of hemoglobin, the substance that gives blood its red color and carries oxygen round the body in the red blood cells. The type of hemoglobin you make depends on the genetic material you inherit from your parents. Sometimes an unusual hemoglobin may be inherited from only one parent (a 'carrier state' or 'trait'), or, more rarely, from both, when it can cause a serious and disabling illness. People with the 'trait' are not ill but could pass on the full blown condition to their children if their partners were similarly affected.

For couples at such risk prenatal diagnosis is possible and counseling can be made available. Sickle cell disease is particularly common among people from West Africa or the Caribbean, while people of Mediterranean origin are more likely to have types of thalassemia. Other groups such as Arabs and those from the Indian sub-continent have a lesser but significant incidence. If you come from any of these parts of the world, or if you are descended from someone who did, it is important that you have the simple blood screening test performed. If you are not offered it at the prenatal clinic please ask your midwife or doctor. It can even be done before pregnancy if you so wish.

Another blood test may be offered to certain women at about fifteen weeks of pregnancy which measures alpha feto protein (AFP) levels. Alpha feto protein is a substance in the blood of babies in the uterus which can spill over into the mother's bloodstream. If the level of AFP is very high, it can indicate that the baby has spina bifida (a defect in which the skin of the back does not close properly, leaving the spinal column exposed), so if found an ultrasound or amniocentesis may be suggested as confirmation. The AFP test is not 100 per cent accurate – high levels may not mean abnormality at all (they are one sign of a multiple birth, for instance) and as many as one in five women may be found to have high AFP levels but their babies are perfectly all right. Conversely a negative AFP test is not unfortunately a guarantee that no abnormality is present.

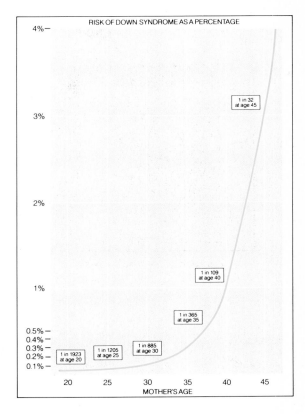

This graph shows how the risk of having a Down syndrome baby rises steeply in women over the age of 35. Most maternity units will now offer amniocentesis to detect this condition to all pregnant women over the age of 35. However it should be remembered that 50 per cent of Down babies are born to women under that age, simply because proportionately more women have babies then than between the ages of 35 and 45.

AMNIOCENTESIS

Amniocentesis is the name given to the procedure by which a sample of amniotic fluid is drawn from the uterus by means of a hollow needle inserted through the abdominal wall. Before the needle is inserted, an ultrasound scan is made to find the position of the fetus and the placenta so that the needle can be inserted in a safe place. A local anesthetic is given in the abdominal wall so that you will feel no pain. It is advisable to rest for a day or so after an amniocentesis as the technique may irritate the uterus. If you feel any pain, experience any bleeding or leakage of fluid from the vagina after an amniocentesis, contact the hospital at once.

Amniocentesis is only used where it is considered important to check the chemical content of the fluid, or fetal cells floating in it for chromosomal abnormalities, especially those indicating Down syndrome (which used to be called mongolism). If any abnormality is found the mother may then be offered a termination of pregnancy. This is a difficult and distressing decision for any couple to have to face and you will be given sympathetic counseling to help you. If you would not want a termination of pregnancy under any circumstances, you do not

have to accept an amniocentesis if it is offered. On the other hand, if you do have an amniocentesis and the result shows an abnormality you may find that even so you cannot face a termination. In this case every effort will be made to help you prepare yourself for the future (see p. 280).

Statistically, the older the mother the greater is the risk of chromosomal abnormalities occurring, so most of the larger hospitals offer amniocentesis to all women over 37. These women have a higher risk of producing a Down syndrome baby, and by the age of 39 or over, the risk – about one per cent – is as great as the chance of miscarrying as a result of the amniocentesis itself. It is difficult to weigh up the risk of miscarriage against the risk of bearing an abnormal baby – information given on the graph above may help you.

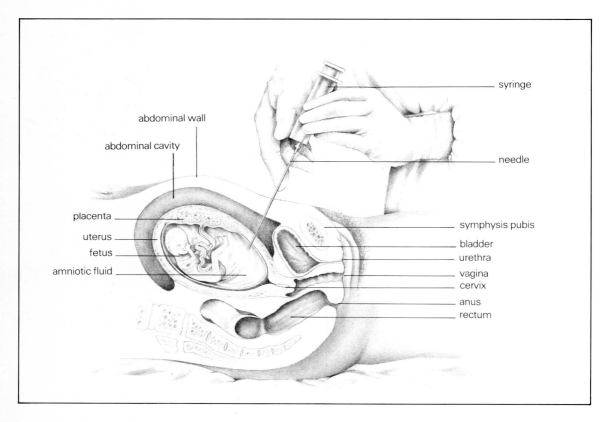

For amniocentesis, the skin of the abdomen is anesthetized and a fine needle is inserted with ultrasound guidance into the top of the uterus. Amniotic fluid is then drawn out with a syringe.

Remember also that no test has yet been developed which can discover all types of congenital abnormality; amniocentesis only helps rule out some of the most distressing. And statistics can always be looked at another way – even when a mother is as old as 49, the chance of her having a normal healthy baby is as high as 91 per cent.

The earliest the test can be done is about fifteen weeks. Waiting for the result can be an anxious time as it can take as long as four weeks for the results of the amniocentesis to come through from the laboratory, by which time you may well be able to feel your baby moving. As a result many women who have amniocentesis do not let themselves become involved in the pregnancy until they have the result – they detach themselves as much as possible from their growing baby and keep their feelings suppressed. This of course does not mean they are any less upset if they have to have their pregnancies terminated; it is always a terrible decision to make.

If you are unlucky enough to have an unfavorable result after an amniocentesis and you opt for a termination of pregnancy, you may find that your doctor recommends inducing a premature labor, rather than an operation. However, in the former case you will of course be given all the pain relief you want.

CHORIONIC VILLUS SAMPLING

Most ways of detecting inherited diseases or congenital abnormalities cannot be performed until well into the second trimester. However, chorionic villus sampling is a new technique, only available in a few centers, which enables the doctors to find out as early as nine to eleven weeks whether a baby is likely to be affected.

Chorionic villus sampling is used to examine fetal chromosomes and detect genetic disorders such as Down syndrome, Tay Sachs disease, thalassemia and cystic fibrosis. The early stage at which it can be performed means that if anything abnormal is found the parents can have the option of an early termination of pregnancy, if they so wish. However, the technique has not yet been perfected and there is a fairly high risk of miscarriage attached to it, although this is now well under ten per cent, and for this reason, it is only offered to women whose babies are most at risk from these serious congen-

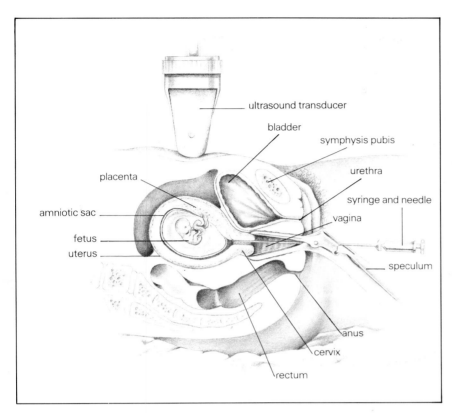

ultrasound transducer

bladder

symphysis pubis

placenta

urethra

syringe and needle

amniotic sac

vagina

fetus

uterus

speculum

anus

cervix

rectum

Chorionic villus sampling is usually achieved by inserting a fine needle through the vagina and cervix with ultrasound guidance which removes a tiny sample of the villi near the internal os (neck of the uterus).

ital problems. On the other hand, since many miscarriages happen spontaneously at this stage of pregnancy, often because the fetus is abnormal, it is difficult for doctors always to be sure that a miscarriage associated with chorionic villus sampling would not have happened anyway.

Chorionic villus sampling is performed with the help of ultrasound. Using a fine tube inserted either through the abdominal wall or through the cervix, the doctor guides it towards the chorionic villi, tiny root-like projections which eventually bed into the uterine wall to become the placenta (see p. 39). A few of these tiny projections are drawn out by a syringe and sent to the laboratory for testing. Although they are not part of the fetus, they have the same genetic make-up. It usually takes between seven and ten days to obtain the result – occasionally as much as two weeks – but even so, the waiting time is much less than that required for the result of an amniocentesis.

AIDS IN PREGNANCY

You will no doubt have heard a lot about this condition recently and may be anxious about its relevance to you and your baby. AIDS is a disease caused by a virus named the human immune

deficiency virus (HIV) for which at present there is no cure. Acquisition of this virus means that the body's defense mechanism against disease becomes impaired and in many sufferers this leads to death from overwhelming infections. Not all people infected with the AIDS virus, however, have symptoms – some just carry it in their blood, but they could infect others under appropriate circumstances.

The disease is spread in three ways: by transmission in the blood, by sexual contact with an infected person, and from an infected mother to her baby. Although the disease was first reported in homosexual communities it is now clear that it can equally be spread by heterosexual partnerships.

AIDS is especially serious if associated with pregnancy because not only is there a strong possibility that the mother's disease may worsen, but there is a 50 per cent chance that the baby will acquire the infection in the womb and a very high chance that the child will die as a result. Because these risks are so great, women who are known to be infected are strongly advised to avoid pregnancy and should they become pregnant termination of pregnancy is recommended.

In the light of this it is now the policy of many obstetric units to offer prenatal screening for AIDS to certain mothers who are recognized to be in 'high

<table>
<tr><td colspan="1">

WOMEN AT RISK FROM AIDS

☐ Women with symptoms of the disease

☐ Intravenous drug abusers

☐ Women with bisexual partners

☐ Women who have become pregnant by artificial insemination by a donor unscreened for AIDS

☐ Women from central and east African countries, Haiti, or women whose partners are from these areas, where AIDS is very common in the whole population

☐ Partners of hemophiliacs unscreened for AIDS

☐ Prostitutes

</td></tr>
</table>

well. You will notice that the fetal heartbeat is about twice as fast as yours – between 120 and 160 beats a minute.

The provider will want to know when you first feel fetal movements (usually around the twentieth week for a first baby, but earlier for mothers who have had several children). Towards the end of pregnancy the presentation and position of the fetus will be checked, and any complications will be dealt with immediately they crop up.

If you have any worries between your prenatal appointments don't be afraid to call your provider for advice, or go and see your own doctor at an ordinary appointment. If you have any queries about the minor discomforts of pregnancy (see pp. 44 and 50) it is a good idea to write them down so that you remember to mention them at your next appointment.

risk' groups. The test is simple, involving only the taking of a blood sample, and the table summarizes those at risk. This 'at risk' group of the population is very small, so for most pregnant women AIDS will not be an issue they have to face. However, if you are at all anxious that you may be a carrier of infection for whatever reason then talk it over with your midwife and doctor who can easily arrange the screening test for you, if necessary.

You may be particularly worried about blood transfusions as it is recognized that this has been a way of transmitting the virus in the past, although very rarely. Nowadays, you can be reassured that all the blood collected for transfusion in the USA is screened, so if you have the misfortune to require a blood transfusion in your pregnancy you will not acquire AIDS.

FURTHER PRENATAL VISITS

Most women in the USA have about fourteen prenatal appointments. Up to 28 weeks of pregnancy your prenatal checks will be at four-weekly intervals, unless there is some special reason to make them more frequent. From 28 to 36 weeks the appointments will be every two weeks, and from 36 weeks to birth the midwife or doctor will want to see you every week.

At each visit you will be asked to give a sample of urine, you will be weighed and your blood pressure taken. The size of the fetus will be measured by palpation, and the fetal heart rate monitored either through a small ear trumpet or with a portable ultrasound which amplifies the sound of the baby's heartbeat. If your partner comes with you to later prenatal appointments, he may be able to listen to the baby's heartbeat through the stethoscope as

PREPARATION CLASSES

As you approach the end of your pregnancy it is worth thinking about labor and how you want to deal with it so that you can discuss it with the midwife at the prenatal clinic, if you haven't already done so. Do you want your partner with you or some other person, like your mother, sister or a close friend? Decisions about positions for labor and delivery cannot always be made in advance, and many a firm resolve falters once labor starts. However you can discuss the options with your midwife and your partner beforehand, so that you can let the hospital know that you are thinking about adopting a squatting position for delivery, or using a birthing chair, or having an epidural anesthetic to help you in labor.

All these topics are covered in the preparation classes that are provided by most hospitals, or sometimes in health clinics. Some classes take place in the home of trained instructors. Hospital or clinic classes are usually run by midwives with the help of obstetric physiotherapists who are skilled in dealing with the physical aspects of pregnancy, birth and the postpartum period.

Wherever the classes are held, and whatever they are called, they have the same aims and function. Do not underestimate their usefulness. These classes give you an opportunity to get to know other people in your area who are expecting babies at the same sort of time as you are. This is more important than might appear at first – there is nothing more isolating, especially for first-time parents, than suddenly finding yourselves at home with a baby when you don't know other people close by with whom you can share experiences. Preparation classes teach you about what happens in labor, about pain

Prenatal classes welcome both mothers and fathers to prepare for labor and birth and offer an opportunity for questions and advice.

relief, about feeding, changing, bathing and other aspects of parenting. Classes are usually held informally, so they give an opportunity to ask questions and air your views. Fathers are welcome to all sessons; if classes are held in the day time, there is often a special evening 'fathers' session' at some point during the course to which you should try to take your partner.

In nearly all classes you will learn some type of relaxation. This is very important not just for your labor but for your life in the future. Babies can cause a great deal of stress and tension as well as joy, and learning to relax will help you cope with the stress more easily.

PRENATAL EXERCISES

Preparation classes which involve obstetric physiotherapists may include some basic prenatal exercises to keep mothers more comfortable during pregnancy and to prepare them for labor. Even if you don't normally take any special form of exercise, it pays to be aware of the changes in your body which affect your muscles, ligaments, joints and posture. As your pregnancy progresses, and your growing uterus and baby rise out of your pelvis, your

abdominal muscles stretch and may separate (see p. 134). You may find yourself leaning back to compensate, which can affect your back. Even if you have never suffered from back pain before, the action of progesterone makes your joints more vulnerable during pregnancy (see p. 53). Your pelvic floor hammock, too, is taking the additional strain of up to 14 pounds of extra weight by the end of your pregnancy, and with the increased pressure on your bladder this could lead to stress incontinence (see p. 53) unless you pay attention to exercising these muscles. All these points, and more, are usually covered by the physiotherapists, but if you do not have the opportunity to join a class the following basic exercises will help.

FEET AND LEGS

To improve the circulation in your legs and help prevent swelling and varicose veins, pump your feet up and down vigorously 30 times several times a day. This can be done sitting on a chair with your legs stretched out on a foot-stool. If you don't have a foot-stool, do one leg at a time, but do not cross your legs. If your ankles swell, do the exercises lying down with your legs raised on a stool so that they are higher than your head. In addition, you can circle your ankles ten times in each direction – this has a nice mobilizing feeling as well as being good for your circulation.

PELVIC TILTING

Pelvic tilting is a simple movement which, once you have learned it, can be done as you go about your daily routine, whether sitting, standing, kneeling or lying down. It helps to strengthen the abdominal muscles, helps correct your posture and gives relief to the backache that often accompanies postural problems during pregnancy. More specific advice on coping with sacro-iliac back pain (a particular problem of pregnancy) is given on page 55.

To practice pelvic tilting, start off by sitting on the edge of a chair with your knees apart and your hands resting on them. Rock backwards on your 'sitting' bones (the ischial tuberosities, as they are called, which are part of the pelvic girdle), drawing your abdominal muscles firmly in and rounding your back. Then gently rock the other way, releasing your abdominal muscles and curving your back the other way. This can be done slowly, holding the abdomen well pulled in while you count up to twelve, or as a small, faster movement to loosen a stiff back after you have been sitting still for a while.

Pelvic tilting on all fours is probably the best position for strengthening the abdominal muscles and relieving a tired back. Do the movement slowly and carefully, holding the abdominal muscles in for a count of twelve and then gently releasing them while allowing your back to hollow out as much as is comfortable.

The pelvic tilt done while standing corrects the posture as well as being good for the abdominal muscles and back. Stand with feet slightly apart and lift your ribs away from where your waist used to be. (Make sure your shoulders are relaxed and that you are not holding your breath.) Tilt the pelvis backward and forward, drawing your abdominal muscles in and your buttocks under, before relaxing to allow your back to arch slightly behind your waist. Make sure you finish the exercise with your baby pulled well into your pelvis, otherwise you may stretch your abdominal muscles unnecessarily and pull your spine forward.

THE PELVIC FLOOR

Although the pelvic floor is pierced by three openings, two of which we can normally control separately, in fact the muscles work as one unit when being exercised. Pelvic floor tightening can be done in any position – but perhaps it's easier to begin while sitting down, knees and feet apart, and with body leaning forward and your elbows resting on your knees.

Pull tight on the ring of muscle round the opening of your back passage (anus) at the same time as you

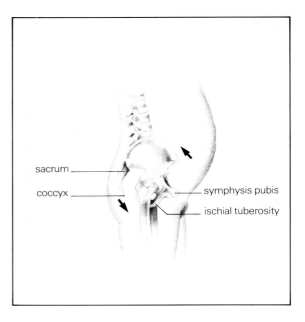

The pelvic tilt involves tipping the bones of the pelvis forward and up while drawing in the abdominal muscles at the same time. Although shown here in the standing position, it can also be done lying, sitting, kneeling, or on all fours.

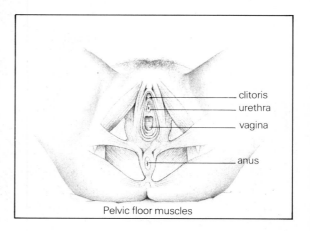

Pelvic floor muscles

The pelvic floor muscles act like a sort of hammock for the pelvic organs, forming a figure of eight around the front and back passages (the urethra and anus) and the vagina. Exercising them as described is extremely beneficial for all women, but especially during pregnancy and after delivery.

try to close the muscle supporting your urinary passage (urethra) and draw your vagina inward and up. Hold while you count to four – then relax. Some people find it helps to imagine that the pelvic floor is an elevator which should normally be standing on the ground floor; by tightening and drawing in and up, the elevator ascends to the first floor. (Pregnancy and birth take the elevator down to the basement!)

A useful test to see if you are exercising your pelvic floor correctly is to try to stop the flow of urine midstream – you will need to be able to do this every time the midwife wants a midstream sample of urine (see p. 20). Another test is to tighten and relax your pelvic floor during lovemaking, to see if your partner notices the difference.

This is the most important female exercise and should be done religiously by women, young and old, pregnant or not, many times every day. It can frequently be the answer to stress incontinence (see p. 55), slight prolapse and can help make sexual intercourse more satisfying for both partners. Being able to relax your pelvic floor can also make an internal examination more comfortable, and may relieve the 'dropping out' sensation which many women feel at the end of their pregnancy.

An awareness of tension or relaxation in the pelvic floor is also invaluable during the second stage of labor and while your baby is actually being born (see p. 88).

RELAXATION

Your body responds to stress (pain, fear or anger) by becoming tense. A typical 'tension posture' involves hunching your shoulders, clenching your fists and gritting your teeth. At the same time your heart beats more rapidly, your breath becomes faster and your body begins to burn up your store of energy as you try to 'run away' from whatever is upsetting you. A certain amount of stress and tension in everyday life is useful, and in fact helps people to perform better; but when the response to events gets out of hand problems begin to arise, giving a constant feeling of anxiety which can be exhausting. Relaxation can alter this state, giving you a feeling of ease and calmness.

Pregnancy carries its own stresses. Just being pregnant makes your body work overtime, and the fact that by the end of 40 weeks you are actually carrying an extra 22 to 25 pounds in weight increases your fatigue. Worrying about labor and after ('Will the baby be all right? Will *I* be all right?') can increase your stress response.

Prenatal classes are sometimes called 'Relaxation Classes' because it has been recognized for the

Relaxation during pregnancy should not be confined to your preparation classes. In the last weeks, try to find time to put what you have learned into practice, even if it is only for ten minutes a day.

past half century that relaxation can help a woman cope with the normal physiological stress of pregnancy, labor and new parenthood. There are many different techniques for teaching relaxation but the easiest and most logical was devised by a physiotherapist, Laura Mitchell, and is known as 'The Mitchell Method' of physiological relaxation. It is based on the body's response to stress and also on the fact that when one muscle group works, the group that performs the opposite movement has to rest; this is known as 'reciprocal relaxation' and is described in detail in Laura Mitchell's book *Simple Relaxation*.

To deal with the three most common bodily responses to stress (gritted teeth, hunched shoulders and clenched fists) the orders given to your body to change this and to achieve relaxation are:

Jaw: 'Drag your jaw downwards, stop doing it'; now register the comfortable new position in your mind (teeth slightly separated). You have eliminated tension in your jaw muscles.

Shoulders: 'Pull your shoulders toward your feet (making your neck longer), stop pulling' – now register their new position of ease and comfort – your shoulder girdle is no longer in its hunched up position.

Hands: The order is 'Long'; let your hands remain supported on your lap or tummy, then stretch out your fingers and thumbs, stop doing this, and register the new supported position of ease.

Although relaxation is usually taught in a comfortable lying down or sitting position it wouldn't be much use to you if you couldn't use the technique while you are standing or walking. Ideally you should practice relaxation in any and every position you can think of; once learned this art can be used every day of your life to help you cope with stress and your tension response; relaxation is not just for labor, it's for living.

Positions for relaxation and labor
By practicing some of these positions and experimenting with others during pregnancy you can familiarize yourself with different ways to help yourself cope with the pain of labor.

During the first stage many women find that sitting astride a chair with a fairly high back is comfortable (top), resting your head on your arms and with a pillow for support.

BREATHING WITH RELAXATION

The way you breathe can increase your tension response or help you remain calm and relaxed in moments of stress. We've all experienced 'panic breathing' – fast deep gasps, usually accompanied by a dry mouth and pounding heart. Try this little experiment: sitting comfortably, count how many times you breathe out in a minute; probably somewhere between twelve and 25 times. Now slow down your respiration rate by pausing briefly between finishing an outward breath and then letting as much air as you need gently in to your chest; once again count how many times you breathe out. This time it will probably be about half your previous score. This slower, calm, quiet

Another position that you will probably find more comfortable than lying on your side as the first stage progresses, is to kneel across a bean bag, allowing it to take the whole weight of your abdomen (above left).

Being supported by your partner (above) is helpful and reassuring. Lean against him with your arms round his neck. You can either stand or kneel on a chair or the end of the bed. Rock backward and forward gently during a contraction to help cope with the pain.

Practice squatting during pregnancy to stretch your ligaments and pelvic floor muscles (above), and perhaps to prepare yourself for a more upright position for the first stage. If you aren't used to squatting, start up against a wall with your heels on a book, and progress to unsupported squatting as shown.

During pregnancy, and in the early first stage of labor, it is restful to relax lying down with your head and shoulders supported by two pillows and your abdomen and upper leg supported by more pillows (main photograph).

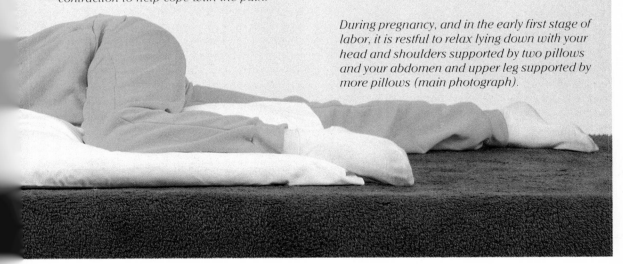

breathing will actually help you increase your sense of relaxation and control during times of stress; standing in the line in the Post Office when you're late, dealing with a saucepan that's boiling over on the stove, comforting a screaming baby when you've tried everything to soothe him, or coping with the contractions of the first stage of labor.

BREATHING IN LABOR

Some prenatal teachers compare labor contractions to waves on the sea as it gets rougher and rougher, or to mountains getting progressively higher (see p. 82). Your aim is to cope with one contraction at a time; begin each one with a breath out and a command to your whole body (but especially shoulders and jaw) to relax; then breathe comfortably and quietly as you ride your 'wave' or climb your 'mountain', then make your way down the other side. As you breathe out say to yourself 'relax' or 'let go' – each outward breath can increase your sense of relaxation and control and help unwind the tight internal coil of tension.

This slow breathing may be all you need for quite a while in labor, but as the first stage progresses you will probably find that your breathing needs to be slightly shallower and faster at the peak of a contraction. Relax your face and take very gentle sighing breaths through relaxed lips – imagine you're blowing dandelion seeds away one at a time. At the end of each and every contraction, take a deep relaxing breath in, and then out, to make sure there is plenty of oxygen circulating in your body for you and your baby, and also to return you to a relaxed state if you found the contraction a tension-making ordeal.

Until fairly recently all sorts of patterns of breathing were taught for use in labor. Some of these lead to 'over-breathing' (hyperventilation) in the mother and a subsequent decrease in the amount of oxygen reaching her baby. Nowadays we know that labor breathing should be very simple and as near normal breathing as possible. If you begin to feel dizzy and notice tingling or 'pins and needles' in your fingers, hands and face, it could mean that you are 'over-breathing' and have blown out too much carbon dioxide from your body. Immediately cup your hands together, put them over your nose and mouth, keep breathing, and you will be replacing the carbon dioxide.

Occasionally, at the end of the first stage of labor, you may get the urge to push before your midwife feels you are ready; to stop yourself, try saying 'I won't push' out loud. This will keep you breathing and will prevent you holding your breath and bearing down, which could lead to you 'pinching' your cervix between the back of your pubic bones and your baby's head if the cervix isn't yet fully dilated (see p. 88).

Pushing in the second stage of labor may take a while to get right: some people like to hold their breath as they push down; others find it easier to push with a steady breath out. When you are in labor, the best advice is to listen to your midwife or labor coach. She will tell you exactly how to breathe for pushing, and will also tell you when she wants you to stop pushing and pant instead.

PRACTICING POSITIONS FOR LABOR

Many prenatal classes will include some ideas for exercises, relaxation positions and movements to help you cope with labor contractions, which you should use together with breathing and relaxation. If you can get used in pregnancy to positions you may not normally rest in, you will find it easier to use them during labor. It is particularly useful if your partner learns these routines too since he will be able to remind you of the different techniques during labor.

When the uterus works in labor, as well as drawing the cervix over your baby's head, it tries to tip forward as it contracts. For this reason early first stage contractions can be coped with best by using forward leaning positions. Many couples find it mutually comforting if the woman puts her arms round her partner's neck and leans against him, both rocking together. Many women find it comfortable to sit astride a chair or to lean on a chair seat resting the head on a cushion. Kneeling on all fours often eases backache labor, while gentle or firm massage on the back, abdomen and thighs is very helpful when contractions reach their height.

You may already have discussed positions for delivery with your midwife during prenatal check-ups, and in many classes this subject will also be discussed. Many birth experts now favor an upright position for delivery, either as supported squatting, kneeling, or using a birthing chair or special bed. The most common position is sitting propped upright, with knees apart and your hands hooked behind your thighs for support.

Even if you do not want to adopt a squatting position for delivery, it is worth practicing simple squatting on flat feet since it helps to stretch your pelvic ligaments and the pelvic floor muscles, making them more supple for birth. Squatting can be uncomfortable at first if you aren't used to it, so start by practicing against a wall with your heels on a book, or wear shoes with low heels. You can gradually progress to unsupported squatting as you become looser.

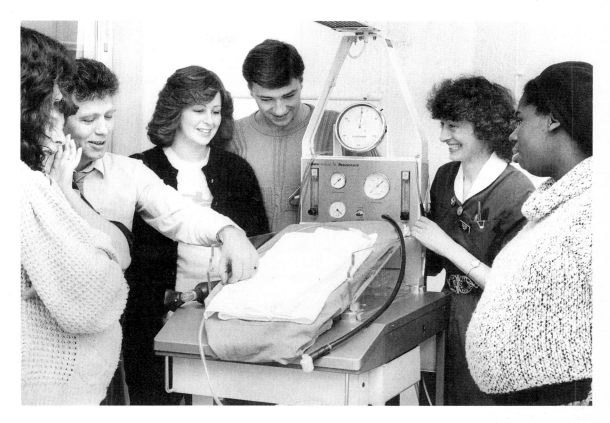

If you have the opportunity, visit the labor ward during your pregnancy so that you can familiarize yourself with the layout and the equipment, such as the baby resuscitation cart.

VISITING THE LABOR WARD

During most hospital classes there is an opportunity to visit the labor ward where you will have your baby. If you miss this it is worth telephoning to ask if you can come round at another time. If your partner or someone else is going to be with you during labor, it would be helpful if he or she could come with you. The nurse will probably give you a time when she expects to be less busy than usual – on the weekend or in the evening, or when a lot of staff are scheduled to be on duty.

WHAT TO LOOK FOR

Many women find it really comforting to lie in the bath while in labor, so find out where the bath is. Others find it helpful to walk around during labor, so have a look and see if this is going to be possible. Many women like to give birth in a position such as standing, squatting, or on a bean bag or birthing chair – ask to see if either of the latter would be available and if they have mattresses to make the floor more comfortable. If this kind of equipment isn't available at your hospital it might be worth bringing your own. Discuss it with the doctor at your next prenatal check. It is very sad nowadays if a hospital cannot cater for a woman's needs in this fairly simple way, but most will respond readily.

In the labor ward, discuss pain relief; ask to see the baby resuscitator – this is used quite routinely in many births but might upset you at the time if you don't know what it is for (see p. 102). Get to know the layout of the labor ward and the individual rooms – remember that one of them will become your room when you are in labor for maybe as long as 24 hours. Think about what you might like to bring to make it more comfortable – after all it is going to be one of the most important rooms you have ever spent any time in.

Standing here in the labor ward and sensing for the first time the concrete reality of childbirth, you can begin to form a list of how to cope with the hospital experience. Like any other major event in life, there are many details to think of and advanced planning makes it all so much easier. The more you can shape the experience of your childbirth to your own preferences, the more likely it is that you will find the experience as satisfying and pleasant as possible.

CHAPTER THREE

EARLY PREGNANCY

**Your baby's development in the first twenty weeks
of pregnancy and how it affects your body**

The potential for new life begins when the male sperm fertilizes the female ovum (see p. 12). It is at this point that the sex and physical characteristics of your new baby are determined, such as the color of the hair and eyes and the bodily physique when he or she grows to adulthood. All such information is carried in the chromosomes which are made up, in turn, of many thousands of genes which are inherited from our parents, grandparents and so on. Each person's unique chromosome and genetic pattern is repeated in every cell in the body, but when life begins it is just as one cell, created from the fusion of the mother's ovum with the father's sperm.

CHROMOSOMES AND GENES

The fertilized egg contains 46 chromosomes – 23 inherited from the mother and 23 from the father. Two of them are the sex chromosomes, of which one is inherited from each parent. The sex chromosome in the ovum is always the same and is known as the X chromosome. In the sperm the sex chromosome can either be X or Y. If the ovum is fertilized by an X-carrying sperm then a baby with XX sex chromosomes will develop; this is the pattern for a girl. If the ovum is fertilized by a Y-carrying sperm then a baby with XY sex chromosomes will result – the pattern for a boy. The

Fetal development in the first twenty weeks
In the first few weeks the embryo is so small that it is shown here several times life-size: at four to five weeks its crown-to-rump length is only about ³⁄₈ inches, while at eight to ten weeks it doubles in size to about ³⁄₄ inches. At twelve weeks the uterus can be felt just above the pubic bone. At sixteen weeks the fundus (top of the uterus) is about half way to the navel, and by twenty weeks a woman is noticeably pregnant, with the fundus at the level of the navel.

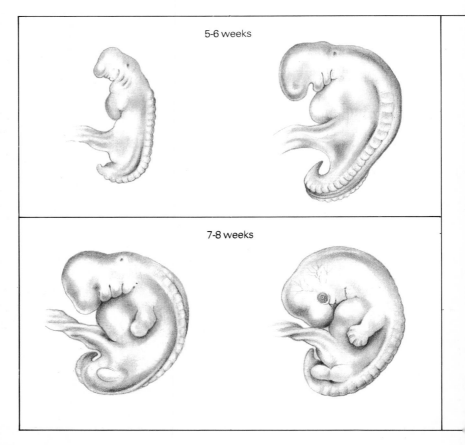

5-6 weeks

7-8 weeks

remaining 44 chromosomes, which are unrelated to the determination of sex, carry the genetic material which decides the outward appearance, the way the body works, and to a certain extent the intelligence and personality.

Since the composition of the genetic material in each sperm and ovum is slightly different, the new life created by their fusion will be unique. You can observe this in your own family. Because you inherit similar genes from your parents and grandparents, there may be quite strong resemblances between you, but no two individuals look exactly the same unless they are identical twins.

TWINS

Identical twins develop when a single sperm has fertilized a single ovum but very early on it has split into two, allowing the development of two babies instead of one, both of whom have exactly the same genetic make up. Non-identical twins develop when two ova have been released at the same time instead of the usual one, and both have been fertilized by two different sperm. The twin babies in this situation are no more alike than sisters or brothers within the same family; they just happen to develop at the same time and be born on the same day. Identical twins are always the same sex; non-identical twins may or may not be.

DEVELOPMENT OF THE EMBRYO

Once fertilization (the joining of the egg and sperm) has occurred, growth of what is now called the embryo (a word derived from the Greek, meaning 'to grow') now starts to take place. The single cell formed by the union of the ovum and the sperm divides rapidly as it passes along the Fallopian tube, encouraged by the gentle squeezing movements of the tube known as peristalsis. It takes about four days for the embryo to reach the uterus, then it spends a further four days lying free in the cavity preparing its attachment (implantation) into the wall of the uterus which has been specially prepared to receive it by the hormones produced from the ovary, particularly progesterone.

Soon after implantation, the mass of cells now forming the embryo begin to separate into several distinct parts. The outer cells will burrow into the uterine wall, making connections there with blood

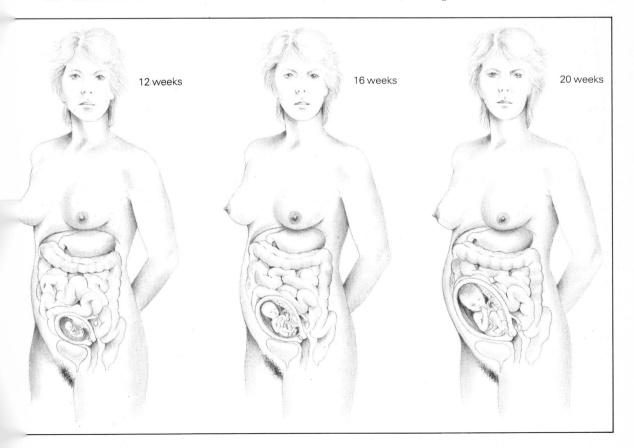

12 weeks   16 weeks   20 weeks

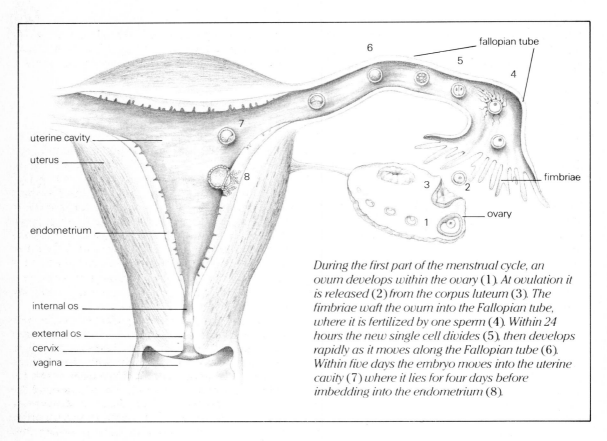

uterine cavity

uterus

endometrium

internal os

external os

cervix

vagina

6

5

4

fallopian tube

7

8

3

2

1

fimbriae

ovary

During the first part of the menstrual cycle, an ovum develops within the ovary (1). At ovulation it is released (2) from the corpus luteum (3). The fimbriae waft the ovum into the Fallopian tube, where it is fertilized by one sperm (4). Within 24 hours the new single cell divides (5), then develops rapidly as it moves along the Fallopian tube (6). Within five days the embryo moves into the uterine cavity (7) where it lies for four days before imbedding into the endometrium (8).

vessels from the mother's circulation. These cells will eventually form the placenta through which the baby will receive oxygen and nutrition while in the uterus. The inner group of cells form themselves into three layers, called the endoderm, mesoderm and ectoderm, from which the baby will develop. The endoderm will be responsible for the formation of the lungs, the stomach and the gut; the mesoderm for the skeleton and its muscles, the heart and circulation, the kidneys and the sexual organs; and the ectoderm for the brain and spinal cord, the face, the eyes, the ears and the skin. All this has happened within two to three weeks of an ovum being fertilized, just about the time when the first period will be missed.

FOUR TO FIVE WEEKS

By week four to five, recognizable structures within the embryo are beginning to form and the blood vessel connections to the placenta via the umbilical cord are becoming established. Once the sixth to eighth week has been reached the uterus has enlarged to the size of a tangerine and the embryo has become curled up and developed a large swelling at one end where the head and brain are

being formed. Little protuberances and indentations indicate the sites from which the limbs will grow and the eyes and ears will evolve. The primitive nervous system begins to develop, seen as a ridge of tissue down the length of the embryo, and the amniotic sac now contains a small amount of fluid. Also by this time the heart has formed sufficiently to start beating and can be detected by an ultrasound scan. The length of the embryo from the crown (top of the head) to the rump (bottom) is now about ⅜ inches.

EIGHT TO TEN WEEKS

Between the eighth and the tenth weeks, the uterus has enlarged to the size of an orange and the baby's face has become more recognizable – the eyes have formed and a mouth and jaw can be seen. The head remains disproportionately large for the size of the body, making up about 50 per cent of the baby's total size at this stage. Around this time it is conventional for this tiny embryonic human to start being called a fetus, a word derived from the Latin meaning 'offspring', which indicates that the developing baby now has recognizable human form. All the internal organs are well on the way to being completely formed and the size is rapidly increasing – by ten weeks, the crown–rump length is approximately ¾ inches, a 100 per cent increase in the space of two to three weeks.

TWELVE TO FOURTEEN WEEKS

By the twelfth to fourteenth weeks the baby has developed fully. All the muscles, bones, fingers and toes are in place – as are all the organs, including those of reproduction – and the fetus is even moving about the uterus, although these movements are too tiny to be felt by the mother. At this stage the baby's length has reached about 2¼ inches, it weighs about 1 ounce, and the size of the uterus has grown to that of a large grapefruit. It is around this time that the doctor or midwife will be able to feel the uterus when palpating the abdomen – prior to this it has been protected within the confines of the bony pelvis. The placenta is now recognizable as a separate organ.

FOURTEEN TO TWENTY WEEKS

Having completed basic development, from the fourteenth to the twentieth week, the baby now grows rapidly. As the weeks go by, the fetus's appearance becomes more and more like that of the newborn baby with which most of us are familiar. The relationship of the size of the body to the head becomes more proportionate and hair is beginning to appear. Concomitant with the growth of the baby, the uterus also continues to enlarge. By sixteen weeks the top of the womb (the fundus) has reached half way up to the navel (umbilicus) and by twenty weeks the fundus is level with it. At around eighteen to twenty weeks the baby's movements become sufficiently strong for them to be felt as a fluttering sensation. The exact time when movements are first felt does vary and may be a little later or earlier depending on whether this is your first or subsequent baby.

THE IMPORTANCE OF EARLY DEVELOPMENT

From this description of the early development of your baby, you will see that all the organs and vital structures are actually formed by the twelfth week of pregnancy. These first few weeks of life in the uterus are a time of very rapid growth when the baby is at particular risk of damage from harmful outside stimuli such as certain drugs and alcohol which can cross the placenta (see right). Yet you may not even know you are pregnant until several of these early weeks have passed. If you can plan ahead it is best to avoid any known situations which might possibly harm your newly formed baby (see p. 12), but if you have become pregnant accidentally do not worry too much; babies in the womb are remarkably resilient and can withstand many an unfavorable circumstance.

THE PLACENTA

During the second week after conception (about four weeks of pregnancy in medical terms), the embryo starts to imbed in the wall of the uterus. Part of the structure burrows into the soft spongy lining of the womb now called the decidua and forms an implantation cavity. The outer layer of cells of the embryo, called the trophoblast, puts out tiny blood vessels which form links with those of the mother which supply the uterine wall. These tiny, linking blood vessels form the beginnings of a network which will allow exchange of waste products and nutrients between the baby's and the mother's blood.

Numerous little finger-like projections called villi grow out from the trophoblast in which are contained the blood vessels from the fetus, and these villi form a close relationship with the mother's tissues in the uterine wall. Within a week or two the villi become confined to a circular area around the site of the umbilical cord and their base becomes a layer called the chorion. This circular area forms the placenta and the chorion covers the surface that faces the baby. It is the fact that the chorionic villi are formed from the developing embryo which forms the basis for the test of chorionic villus sampling (see p. 28) for the diagnosis of chromosomal or genetic abnormalities in the baby.

The placenta not only functions as the supplier of the baby's oxygen and nourishment and the eliminator of waste products, but it also has a vital role in the production of hormones essential for the maintenance of the pregnancy. These hormones are discussed in more detail later, but in early pregnancy the most important of these is human chorionic gonadotrophin – the hormone which is the basis of most pregnancy testing kits (see p. 16).

The placenta also provides an important barrier to the passage of harmful substances, but unfortunately it does not prevent some getting through, especially drugs such as alcohol and nicotine from smoking. A number of infectious organisms such as rubella (German measles) also pass across quite freely. Fortunately the mother's antibodies which protect her from infection also cross the placenta and so can provide the baby with some passive resistance, especially to some of the most dangerous infections for small babies, such as measles.

The placenta may develop at any site on the walls

of the uterine cavity. Its commonest location is on the posterior (back) wall, followed by the anterior (front) wall and the sides of the uterus. Rarely the placenta forms in the lower part of the uterus next to or covering the cervix. This can give rise to problems later in pregnancy (see p. 62).

THE AMNIOTIC FLUID

Very early in intrauterine life when the embryo is forming its inner and outer layers, a hollow cavity appears between them. This is the amniotic cavity and is lined by a thin membrane called the amnion. Clear fluid collects in this space and there is a net increase of about a teaspoonful per day until at full term (40 weeks) there is a volume of about 2 pints. The amnion takes the form of a fluid-filled sac which surrounds the developing fetus. The amniotic fluid originates from several sources. Some of it is made by the amnion itself and some seeps through from the mother's circulation, but quite a large proportion comes from the baby's urine. This is particularly the case in later pregnancy when the urine output may be as much as 1 pint per day. Fluid is also removed from the amniotic cavity by absorption back into the mother's bloodstream and as a result of swallowing by the baby.

The functions of the amniotic fluid are to keep the baby at an even temperature, to cushion against injury, to provide a space in which the baby can move easily, and to provide fluid to drink. Just before or during labor the amniotic sac usually bursts and the fluid drains out of the vagina, a process often referred to as the 'waters breaking'.

The amniotic fluid also contains cells and other substances shed from the baby's mouth, nose and skin and these can be very useful for making the prenatal diagnosis of abnormalities involving disorders of chromosomes, or cellular enzymes, and for confirming the diagnosis of spina bifida when the screening blood test suggests this. In the latter situation a protein (alpha feto protein or AFP), which is present in all babies, leaks through the area of the baby's back which is uncovered by skin and is found in abnormally large quantities in the amniotic fluid. Amniocentesis is used to test for such abnormalities (see p. 27), although AFP is also present in the maternal bloodstream and may also be measured through a blood sample.

HORMONES IN EARLY PREGNANCY

Hormones are substances secreted by various organs in the body which are transported in the blood and produce their effects at distant sites. As we have already seen, the sex hormones estrogen,

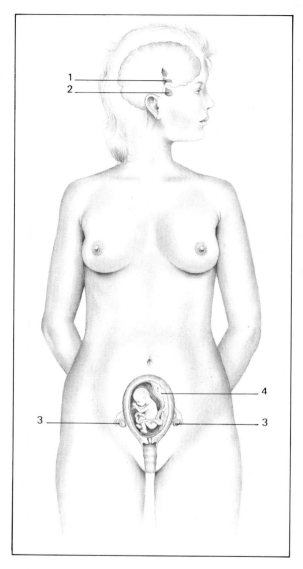

Hormonal activity of reproduction and pregnancy
1 *Hypothalamus (controls the pituitary gland)*
2 *Pituitary gland (secretes LH, FSH and prolactin)*
3 *Ovary (corpus luteum – secretes progesterone and estrogen at start of pregnancy)* 4 *Placenta (secretes HCG at start of pregnancy, then progesterone and estrogen in the form of estriol)*

progesterone and testosterone, secreted by the ovary and testis, play a fundamental role in sexual function and reproduction. Hormones also have a vital role in the implantation and maintenance of the pregnancy itself and in the preparation of the body to meet the increasing demands of the growing baby. Later in this chapter reference is made to the many profound physical changes that take place in women's bodies in anticipation of these demands – these are brought about mainly by the influence of three important hormones, estrogen and progesterone, which are present in pregnancy, and human chorionic gonadotrophin.

Human chorionic gonadotrophin (or HCG for short) is a special hormone produced by the developing placenta almost from the moment of implantation, and its role is to maintain the function of the corpus luteum in the ovary (see p. 10). At this time the corpus luteum is actively involved in producing the estrogen and progesterone which maintain the endometrium (lining of the uterus) in a suitable state to nourish and sustain the developing baby. It continues to do this until the placenta is mature enough to take over this function at about twelve to fourteen weeks.

During pregnancy the levels of estrogen and progesterone rise steadily until just before labor starts. As well as their effects on maintaining the pregnancy, they produce many changes elsewhere in the body. Estrogen, for example, is very important in preparing the breasts for the production of milk and progesterone relaxes smooth muscle in all parts of the body including that in the uterus, dampening down its activity and inhibiting premature delivery. Because these hormones are produced by the placenta, their measurement is sometimes used as a check on how well the placenta is working but since the amount of hormone produced can be very variable even in healthy pregnancies, this sort of test does have its limitations.

The hormone HCG does not have the same pattern of production as estrogen and progesterone, since its most important role is in the early stages of pregnancy. It reaches peak levels about eight weeks after the last period and then falls to much lower levels by the end of the first twelve weeks. This hormone can be detected in the blood from very early on, often as soon as the time of the first missed period, and is a very accurate method of diagnosing pregnancy. Blood testing at this early stage is only performed if there is a special medical indication. Sophisticated immunological tests for HCG in the urine have also recently become available, whereby it is possible to diagnose pregnancy within a few days of the missed period and several of such kits are commercially available, although rather expensive. The standard pregnancy tests are however less sensitive and do not give a positive result until five or six weeks.

The mechanism of the test is rather complicated but practically it consists of mixing a small amount of urine – preferably the first passed in the day since this will contain the greatest concentration of hormone – with some specially prepared reagents, and observing what happens. The result is entirely dependent on the amount of hormone present in the specimen tested so if it is negative and yet you definitely think you are pregnant, it may be you have done the test too early, before there is sufficient HCG present. A repeat test a week or so later will give a more reliable reading.

PHYSICAL CHANGES IN EARLY PREGNANCY

To accommodate the changing needs of mother and developing baby, major changes take place which affect almost every system in your body. Many of these alterations start in early pregnancy, and some may reach their full development during this period, thus anticipating the demands the baby will make. Some of these changes are likely to pass unnoticed, but others are more obvious.

BLOOD CIRCULATION AND HEART RATE

The increased blood circulation required to sustain the pregnancy produces a mild degree of apparent anemia in early pregnancy, and there are also changes in lung and kidney function, but these are not obvious to most people. However, you may be well aware of your increased heart rate, and the increased blood flow through your hands and feet, which tends to make them warm and moist. This may also make you less tolerant to heat – pregnant women often find they need to wear fewer clothes than usual in cold weather.

WATER RETENTION AND URINE

The body's handling of fluids is also altered in pregnancy, with large amounts being retained. In early pregnancy the readjustment to this new state is the probable explanation for the frequent need to pass urine (frequency of micturition) noticed by so many women at this time. In later pregnancy water retention may be noticed as slight puffiness, particularly around the ankles (see p. 70).

THE EFFECT OF HORMONES

The hormone progesterone, present in high levels from early pregnancy onwards, causes relaxation of smooth muscle. This produces a variety of effects, contributing to the development of hemorrhoids (piles) and varicose veins, heartburn and constipation. The thyroid gland in the neck becomes enlarged and the general rate at which your body works (metabolism) increases.

Under the influence of the hormones estrogen

and progesterone, the uterus and cervix become soft, and because of an increase in the local blood supply, the cervix takes on a bluish appearance. Similar changes occur in the vagina and you will notice an increase in normal secretions in this area. However, if these secretions are smelly, accompanied by soreness or itching, or are bloodstained, you should see your doctor at once (see p. 62).

THE BREASTS

The breasts also undergo marked changes from a very early stage; in fact for some women, this may be their first inkling of pregnancy since breast tenderness, tingling and enlargement often precede the first missed period. These changes in the breast are also the result of hormonal stimulation, in particular estrogen, causing proliferation of the milk producing tissue, which continues throughout pregnancy (see p. 149). However the acute feeling of discomfort experienced in early pregnancy does diminish after the first three months.

THE SKIN

Another physical change you may notice is an alteration in the pigmentation (coloring) in your skin. Pregnancy induces extra production of melanocyte stimulating hormone (MSH) from the pituitary gland in the brain. This hormone activates cells called melanocytes to produce the pigment melanin – the same pigment that develops with a suntan. In pregnancy the pigmentation is localized to specific areas, and you will notice it particularly around the nipples, along your cheek bones (chloasma) and along a vertical line from your umbilicus (navel) to your pubic bone – the so-called linea nigra.

You may also notice the development of small red spots, particularly on your upper body and face, which are formed by tiny spreading blood vessels visible just under the skin. These are called spider nevi and are caused by the high level of circulating estrogen. Both these and the pigmentation fade once the pregnancy is over, but the darkening of the nipples and the linea nigra never disappear completely, although the latter is scarely noticeable when you are not pregnant.

FATIGUE

These profound physical changes which take over almost from the moment of conception are also responsible for the feelings of intense fatigue, faintness and weariness so often experienced in early pregnancy. It seems a curious paradox that just when you feel you would like to celebrate your potential parenthood your body feels exhausted – but you can be reassured these symptoms are only temporary and by the third or fourth month you will feel much better.

Try to rest when you feel tired – either sleep on a bed or sofa for a while, or just drop your head on your arms at a desk or table. If you notice a tendency to feel faint, try not to stand or sit in one position without moving for too long, and get up slowly and steadily rather than suddenly. If you feel faint, just lie down or drop your head between your knees for a minute or two until you feel better.

If you are working and you want to keep the pregnancy quiet for a while, bear in mind that fainting is likely to alert people to the fact that something is amiss. To prevent unnecessary alarm, it might be worth taking someone into your confidence so that he or she can reassure your colleagues that all is well until such time as you want your pregnancy to be common knowledge.

MINOR PROBLEMS OF EARLY PREGNANCY

Although they are so important to the well-being of the baby, the physical and hormonal changes of early pregnancy can and do produce some unwelcome effects in you, the mother. Some of these have already been indicated – increased vaginal secretions, for instance, or breast tenderness. Others are more inconvenient and irritating, but there are ways you can minimize their effect, and they need not worry you, provided you are reassured about the cause. If you have any anxieties that all may not be normal, it is best to consult your doctor or midwife. It is also helpful to know that most do pass within the first twelve to fourteen weeks.

NAUSEA AND VOMITING

Perhaps the most common disorders of early pregnancy are nausea and vomiting. It is estimated that feelings of nausea will be noticed by three-quarters of all pregnant women, and although the symptoms tend to be worst around the middle of the first twelve weeks, in one in ten they start before the first period has even been missed. As with breast tenderness, feelings of nausea may be one of the earliest indications that you are pregnant.

The common belief that this sickness is confined to the morning is not true for most sufferers and the more usual pattern is for symptoms to persist throughout the day. Fortunately these feelings do not last throughout pregnancy and in nine out of ten women they will have settled and virtually disappeared by fourteen to sixteen weeks.

The reason why women should so commonly feel sick at this time is not known. It was once believed to be related to the hormone HCG, but this is no longer thought to be the case. It is almost certainly related to hormonal changes of some kind, however, and is seen much more commonly in pregnancies where excess hormones are being produced, such as twins (see p. 65). In later pregnancy sickness may be associated with heartburn (see p. 53) but this symptom is uncommon in the early weeks.

There are various ways which have been suggested to help you cope with nausea and vomiting, including eating small amounts often rather than two or three large meals each day; avoiding foods and smells that upset you; getting plenty of fresh air and avoiding stuffy atmospheres; wearing loose fitting clothes; and having a dry cracker or toast before getting up in the morning. It is worth trying each of these until you find something that works for you.

If you feel very ill or are vomiting so much that nothing is staying down then you should see your doctor. You may be developing a serious complication of pregnancy called hyperemesis which will need special management. For less severe cases however it is nowadays very unusual for your doctor to advise medication, as the risks to the baby may far outweigh the benefits to you.

EXCESSIVE SALIVATION

For some women, nausea and vomiting is not as much of a problem as excessive production of saliva. This can happen to such an extent that it is difficult to keep pace with swallowing. Again the reason for this is not known but it tends to disappear in the later part of pregnancy in the same way as sickness. Keeping a good supply of paper tissues handy to spit into will help avoid embarrassment until the problem fades.

FOOD CRAVINGS AND TASTE ALTERATIONS

Sometimes in pregnancy you may experience other symptoms related to eating and drinking. Cravings for particular sorts of food (pica) are very common, and may even extend to other things which would not normally be part of your diet, such as coal or wood! These cravings are not usually dangerous unless they prevent you from eating a healthy diet or contain some harmful substances, in which case you need to seek professional advice.

Another common complaint of pregnant women is a metallic taste in the mouth which can persist throughout pregnancy and alter your enjoyment of

particular foods. The reason for these phenomena are not known but may have something to do with meeting the nutritional needs of the baby.

CONSTIPATION AND HEMORRHOIDS

Another irritating feature of early pregnancy is a tendency to constipation – this is caused by progesterone, which relaxes the smooth muscle of the bowel wall, slowing down the normal elimination of feces. Unfortunately, it is likely to last all through pregnancy but may be helped by altering your diet so that it contains plenty of fiber, fruit and vegetables. Constipation, like nausea and vomiting, may be made worse by iron pills and if this seems to be a problem it is worth discussing with your doctor as to whether these are really necessary or if an alternative type could be prescribed.

Straining to open your bowels, particularly if you are constipated, will also encourage the development of hemorrhoids. These are varicose veins of the anus (back passage) which occur commonly in pregnancy because of the congestion caused by the pressure of the enlarging uterus. If the hemorrhoids cause a lot of problems, such as bleeding, itching or discomfort then your doctor can prescribe something for them. Always consult your doctor rather than buying a preparation over the counter at the drug store, since it is important that you use one that is safe during pregnancy.

VARICOSE VEINS

Pressure from the uterus can also cause congestion in the veins of the legs and those around the vulva, an effect that is exacerbated by the relaxant effect of progesterone. For some women this will lead to the development of varicose veins which may result in the legs becoming swollen and uncomfortable, particularly by the end of the day. Support hose and elevation of the legs in the evening will offer some relief. The symptoms tend to get worse as pregnancy progresses, but there is a marked improvement after delivery.

VAGINAL DISCHARGE AND BLEEDING

An extra amount of normal discharge is common in pregnancy as already mentioned, but pregnancy does predispose to certain infections, particularly candida (thrush). In this condition you would notice some itching and irritation as well as a cheesy sort of discharge. Candida can be easily treated by the use of suppositories and will not harm your baby in any way.

Bleeding from the vagina should never be considered as a normal part of pregnancy and if noticed you should consult your doctor as soon as possible. Occasionally slight spotting may occur at the time when a period would have been due, but other causes for the bleeding, such as the start of a miscarriage, would need to be excluded (see p. 58). So-called 'withdrawal bleeding' may be due to insufficient hormonal support in early pregnancy so it, too, must be taken seriously.

KEEPING HEALTHY IN EARLY PREGNANCY

A great deal of the advice which is offered in early pregnancy is a natural extension of that discussed in the prepregnancy section (see p. 12). It is very important to review your lifestyle and dietary habits in order to minimize the risk of harm to your baby.

SMOKING AND ALCOHOL

Medically there is no doubt that your baby stands a better chance of being healthy and well nourished if you do not smoke during pregnancy. You may well 'go off' cigarettes at this time anyway because of feelings of nausea, which may make it easier for you to establish the initial break. In the same way many develop a distaste for alcohol and if you can give it up completely then you are minimizing the risk of harm. The evidence about the effects of alcohol in small amounts however is far less clear than for smoking and so you need not feel guilty if you enjoy an occasional drink once or twice a week, but more than this should be avoided.

DRUGS, MEDICATION AND X-RAYS

It is best to avoid all medication in early pregnancy. Most drugs do cross the placenta and potentially could affect the baby, which is developing very rapidly at this stage and is therefore particularly vulnerable. Having said this, most drugs will not harm your baby and if you need any medication, let your doctor know you are pregnant so that a safe preparation can be prescribed. If you have inadvertently taken pills or medicines and you are anxious about possible effects then it is wise to consult your doctor. Illicit or 'recreational' drugs should always be avoided.

It is wise to be cautious about exposure to other potentially harmful agents, particularly x-rays. If for any reason it is suggested that you should have an x-ray and you think you might be pregnant tell the doctor or the radiographer that this is the case. Some hospitals will not perform x-rays on any woman of childbearing age unless she is in the first ten days of her menstrual cycle.

HAZARDS AT WORK

It is also worth checking whether there are any hazards associated with your place of work – this should be done before pregnancy if at all possible. Particular note should be made of work with chemicals, toxic metals and radiation. Publicity has recently been given to the possible harmful effects of working with VDUs (visual display units) but there is no medical evidence to support this. If you are a nurse or a teacher or work in any profession which takes you into contact with small children, then it is especially important to make sure you have checked your immunity to rubella *before* you get pregnant (see p. 13).

DIET AND WEIGHT

The same guidelines for diet that were given in Chapter 1 for pre-pregnancy fitness apply during pregnancy itself (see p. 13). In particular, this is not a time to diet – it is just as important to put on enough weight as not to put on too much. Don't 'eat for two', but eat sensibly and include lots of high-fiber foods like wholemeal bread, beans and fresh vegetables, which will have the added benefit of helping avoid problems with constipation.

The average weight gain during pregnancy is about 28 pounds. You do not usually put on much weight in the first twelve weeks or so, especially if you are suffering from nausea, but after that a gain of about 1 pound per week is about right. You will probably notice your shape changing (apart from the obvious protuberance in front!) as fat is laid down to help milk production after the birth (see p. 149). This fat is often distributed round the hip bones, buttocks and thighs. Breastfeeding uses it up quite rapidly and many women find they are actually thinner after breastfeeding for a few months than they were before they were pregnant.

EXERCISE IN PREGNANCY

On the positive side pregnancy is not an illness, and this is a time to enjoy life and prepare for your new baby. If you are used to being active and taking regular exercise there is no need to stop. Athletes, dancers and women who are used to regular exercise can usually continue to 'work out' during pregnancy, as long as you don't push yourself to maintain your pre-pregnancy standard. Warm up before vigorous exercise (which shouldn't be attempted in hot, humid weather or if you yourself have a temperature), and a period of declining activity is advisable to cool off afterwards. Bouncy, jerky movements should be avoided, and dangerous

If all is going normally, swimming is an excellent way to keep your body fit and healthy throughout your pregnancy.

sports such as horse riding and skiing should not be attempted. Stretching exercises and positions should be gentle and joints shouldn't be forced or overstretched – due to the action of progesterone, all the ligaments of the body have softened and relaxed; they can easily be damaged by over-enthusiastic exercise.

Many women who don't normally exercise, decide that they would like to do something during their pregnancy to improve their fitness, suppleness, strength and endurance. Yoga and swimming are two particularly safe and suitable forms of exercise and can be continued up until the very late stages. Special classes for pregnant women are commonly available. It may be wise to consult your doctor first, however, and if you embark on yoga for the first time, make sure your instructor is qualified and understands the needs of pregnant women.

SEXUAL INTERCOURSE

Having sexual intercourse during pregnancy is very much a personal decision, but there is no reason why you should not continue with this until late in pregnancy provided everything is normal. Sex during the first few months may be inhibited not by your physical shape but by how you feel. Intermittent nausea and extreme tiredness are not the best of sexual stimulants for many women, and some men may also be anxious in case deep penetration harms the baby. This is quite definitely not the case in the majority of pregnancies.

If you have any worries, or really feel that the physical discomforts of pregnancy are getting in the way of your sex life, talk to your doctor about it, but more especially discuss it with each other. Remember that there are other ways apart from conventional intercourse that you can use to achieve sexual satisfaction. Sometimes the conventional positions adopted for intercourse become too difficult, particularly as pregnancy advances and alternative ways of love-making may need to be explored.

If you have had problems with miscarriages or premature deliveries in the past, or have had complications in your current pregnancy, then these may be reasons why you should avoid intercourse. Again you should be guided by your doctor on this matter. If you are advised to avoid penetrative sexual intercourse for any of the reasons already mentioned, do remember that the seven or eight months involved is not really a long time when the safety of a much-wanted baby is at stake.

CHAPTER FOUR

LATER PREGNANCY

Your baby's development from twenty weeks to full term and its effect on your body

The second half of pregnancy, from 20 to 40 weeks, is the time when the growth of the fetus is outwardly noticeable and when the baby develops the necessary maturity of body and organs to be able to thrive in the world outside the uterus after birth.

LANDMARKS OF FETAL DEVELOPMENT

As we have already seen, between sixteen and 20 weeks, growth of the fetus is very rapid. The head becomes more proportional to the body length and movements can be felt by the mother. It is during this period that detailed growth and differentiation of the parts of the body take place. Measurement of

the fetus is usually taken as the 'crown-rump length', in other words the 'sitting' length of the baby, from the top of the head to the seat. If you have an ultrasound to measure your baby's growth rate it may be this measurement, along with the diameter of the head, that the ultrasonographer will be plotting on the visual display unit. The rate of growth is highest between the twenty-eighth and thirty-sixth week (see the table, opposite).

TWENTY TO TWENTY-FOUR WEEKS

At 20 weeks, the vernix caseosa (the cheesy covering which protects the baby in the uterus)

Fetal development from 24 weeks to full term
From 24 weeks the size of the growing baby and uterus has its most direct effect on the mother's body. At 24 weeks the baby is fully formed but very thin. At 28 weeks upward pressure on the stomach can cause indigestion and heartburn. By 32 weeks the baby is beginning to lay down body fat. At 36 weeks the size of the uterus can cause breathlessness as it presses on the diaphragm, but by 40 weeks this may ease as the baby drops deeper into the pelvis, putting pressure on the bladder and groin instead.

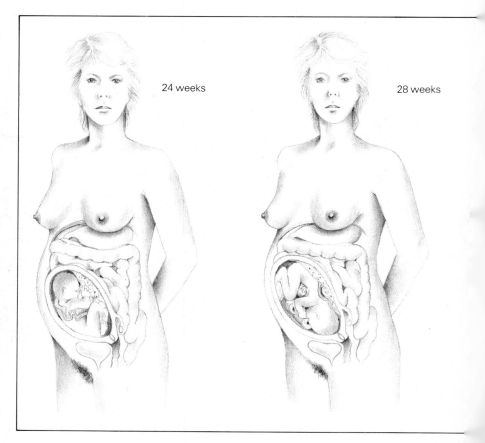

24 weeks

28 weeks

FETAL GROWTH FROM 16 TO 40 WEEKS		
Weeks (after last period)	Size cm. C-R length	Weight g
16	16	110
20	19	315
24	23	620
28	36	1050
32	42	1700
36	46	2500
40	50	3400

TWENTY-FOUR TO TWENTY-EIGHT WEEKS

At 24 weeks, the fetus overtakes the placenta in weight, but the placenta continues to increase in efficiency. Hearing is well developed and creases and fingerprints develop on the hands and feet. At 28 weeks the eyes are open and eyebrows and eyelashes have grown. At this stage the skin is wrinkled and quite red. The lungs are not fully developed, but if born at this stage the baby would be able to breathe with difficulty, cry weakly and move his limbs. The enlargement of the abdomen becomes obvious and appears high; the fetus is often in a breech position and movements are vigorous.

collects on the skin. Body hair (lanugo) is present and the nose develops. From 20 weeks the organs are fully developed and simply grow thereafter. By 24 weeks, the fingernails have grown and the head and body become proportional in size. The nostrils open. The fetus moves freely in the amniotic fluid, which is recycled every three hours via the fetus's mouth, kidneys and urethra. Parts of the fetus, especially the head, can be felt when the abdomen is felt (palpated), and the fetal heart can be heard with the help of a portable ultrasound at 20 weeks, and with a fetal stethoscope about two weeks later.

TWENTY-EIGHT TO THIRTY-TWO WEEKS

The baby is very skinny at 28 weeks, but by 32 weeks body fat has started to collect, essential to keep the baby warm once born, and the body begins to fill out, beginning to grow slightly faster than the head. The skin is smoother, the fingernails reach the finger tips, and in boys, the testes usually descend from the groin into the scrotum.

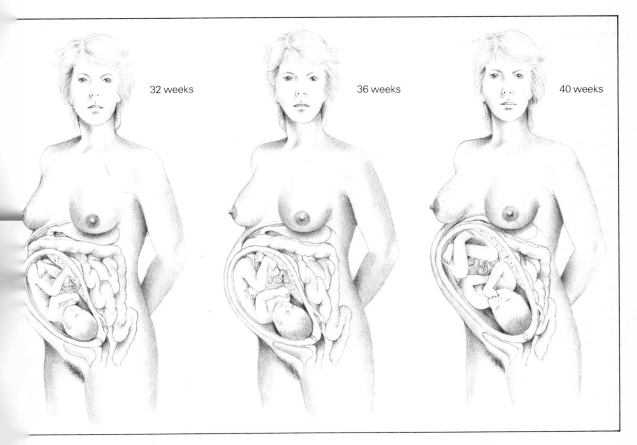

32 weeks   36 weeks   40 weeks

By 36 weeks the lanugo hair which is so characteristic of preterm babies is beginning to disappear, while the hair on the head thickens. The development of the brain, kidneys, lungs and gastro-intestinal tract is now completed after growing progressively from 24 weeks. About 90 per cent of fetuses will have turned to the cephalic (head down) position.

THIRTY-SIX TO FORTY WEEKS

Although the fundus (top of the uterus) will have reached its maximum height by about 36 weeks and be pressing against the diaphragm, the head may engage in the pelvis during the last two or three weeks of pregnancy, especially in women having their first babies. Engagement tends to make the weight of the uterus drop, relieving such problems as heartburn and breathlessness. At 38 weeks, the fetus's mammary glands protrude, the finger nails grow beyond the finger tips and the soft, immature bones are beginning to ossify. The suck and swallow reflexes have developed. The placenta reaches its maximum efficiency at about 38 weeks, maintaining the fetus satisfactorily for another two weeks, after which it ages rapidly. At 40 weeks (term), the baby will be able to breathe without artificial aids, all the reflexes will be fully developed and the lanugo usually has disappeared except on the shoulders. The baby is ready to be born.

FETAL VIABILITY

When a baby is capable of surviving outside the mother's uterus, it is termed viable. With rapidly increasing pediatric expertise, babies of gestation as little as 24 weeks can with adequate support survive and develop normally. The immature lung is the problem, so such an early baby would have to be nursed in intensive care surroundings with mechanical aids to breathing (see p. 116).

The correct definition of a premature baby is, incidentally, taken irrespective of weight (unlike previously when under 5 pounds was the weight limit), and is a baby born before 37 weeks. In terms of a baby's ability to survive, maturity and viability are obviously two very different things.

PHYSICAL CHANGES AND PROBLEMS

Between 20 and 40 weeks the growth of the uterus starts to put pressure on the other organs of your body, and although you will probably feel well, from 20 weeks onward you are likely to experience some minor discomforts. Consult your doctor if you are at all worried, however.

WEIGHT GAIN

Gaining weight may distress some figure and weight conscious women but is both inevitable and desirable as the uterus and its contents grow. As has already been mentioned, the average weight gain in pregnancy is 28 pounds, most of which goes on in between 20 and 30 weeks, but during this time a weight gain of under 1 pound per week is desirable. But the only real reason for being concerned about excessive weight gain is that it is difficult to lose it after pregnancy. Excessive weight gain has not got the profound medical significance which doctors used to believe it had.

Greater weight gain may be associated with edema – swelling of hands and feet caused by the retention of fluid – and although this is commonly seen in otherwise normal pregnancies, it may be associated with pre-eclampsia. It then becomes of significance (see p. 70).

Static weight or even loss of weight may occur where the baby is growing unsatisfactorily – 'intra-uterine growth retardation'. Here again the mother's weight is a useful piece of monitoring information, which is why it is part of the routine assessment at each prenatal visit.

STRETCH MARKS

Stretch marks (striae gravidarum) are scar-like marks on the skin of the abdomen and sometimes the upper thighs. They are often a rather unsightly red or purple when they first appear, later becoming white. They do not always occur in pregnancy, but when they do they leave permanent marks, although these are not as pronounced as during pregnancy itself. Unfortunately oils, lanolins and other preparations rubbed into the skin do not prevent them.

VEIN DISTENSION

All the surface veins of the body become more prominent as pregnancy progresses. Veins can often be clearly seen under the skin of the abdomen and over the breasts. Actual varicose veins are not uncommon and are most often seen in the legs; as a result of the weight and compressing effect of the growing uterus on the major draining veins of the pelvis, the more peripheral blood vessels become engorged.

Support hose can be of considerable help in minimizing the discomfort of varicose veins but they will not cure or prevent them. If the varicosity is very

Later pregnancy is a time for gentle exercise and lots of rest. Try to take maternity leave or give up work a few weeks before the due date, and it helps if fathers can share the heavier chores.

severe, they can be injected, but as the weight of the pregnancy continues to exert its pressure from above, the varicosities may, unfortunately, return after this treatment. Surgeons would be very reluctant to operate on varicose veins during pregnancy for the same reason. However, there is no reason why you should not seek treatment once the baby is born.

Varicose veins can emerge on the vulva and cause quite a lot of heaviness and discomfort. Because of their awkward site they are difficult to treat. Sometimes raising the buttocks on a pillow when resting in bed during the day can give a measure of relief. They tend to disappear quickly after pregnancy.

Hemorrhoids – varicose veins in the rectum – are discussed, along with the often accompanying problem of constipation on page 45.

EDEMA

Edema means swelling, and in pregnancy usually involves the hands, feet and lower legs. Sometimes you may notice your face getting puffy. It need not

51

indicate that anything is going wrong – as has already been mentioned it can happen in a perfectly normal pregnancy. Rings may become tight and may have to be removed for the duration of the pregnancy. The longer you are on your feet, the more swollen your feet may become, especially in hot weather. However, since edema is also a prominent feature of pre-eclampsia, it is looked for routinely at prenatal checks especially in the second half of pregnancy.

There is no specific treatment for edema, although resting with your feet up as often as possible helps to relieve it in the legs, ankles and feet. 'Water pills' (diuretics), used in other circumstances to help the kidneys to secrete more fluid, are not advisable in pregnancy because of their possible adverse effect on the fetus. It is not necessary to reduce your intake of fluids by drinking less, and salt reduction is now also known to make no difference.

NOSE BLEEDS

Vascularity – the number and dilatation of the blood vessels – increases in pregnancy, and the blood vessels of the nasal septum (the fleshy structure inside the nose which divides the nostril cavities) are no exception. Nose bleeds (epistaxis) are very common among pregnant women, occurring to a greater or lesser extent – some women never experience them, others have them frequently.

Nose bleeds can be alarming, but are normally stopped by the usual simple measures such as pressure on the bridge of the nose (see p. 278). Contrary to belief, they are not associated with hypertension (high blood pressure) in pregnancy, nor will they produce anemia unless they are very frequent and very heavy.

ANEMIA

This is a common problem in pregnancy and particularly in communities where nutrition is poor and there is little if any prenatal care. Physiological or 'natural' anemia occurs as a result of the normal changes of pregnancy. The red blood cells become 'diluted' and it is normal for the hemoglobin to fall in the middle third of pregnancy. (Hemoglobin is a pigment of the red blood cells and its measurement is used to tell whether someone is anemic or not.) Routine checking of hemoglobin is carried out at the first visit and again at 30 to 32 weeks and at 36 to 38 weeks (see p. 22).

Iron deficiency anemia is the most common form of anemia in pregnant women, which may be due to a diet deficient in iron adding to the physiological changes already mentioned. Foods containing iron are liver, other meats, fish and most green vegetables, so you should study your diet during pregnancy with this in mind. Most obstetricians will give an iron supplement to pregnant women. Unfortunately iron pills occasionally have a constipating effect, so that including plenty of fiber in your diet is an important 'back up' to the avoidance of anemia.

There are also two vitamins involved in anemia – folic acid and Vitamin B12. Folate deficiency is more common in Asia, but the practice of giving a small folate supplement with iron has made it uncommon in pregnant women in the West. Vitamin B12 deficiency is not common among younger women, unless they are vegans who eat no animal products at all. It is therefore not seen so often in pregnancy.

If you are anemic you will feel much more tired during your pregnancy, and will be more prone to infections such as urinary infections. It has been suggested that severe anemia may have an influence on the onset of premature labor. Obviously the effect of any bleeding will be more profound if you are anemic than if you have a good level of hemoglobin. It is therefore important that anemia should be detected and treated adequately during pregnancy and before labor.

HEADACHES

Many pregnant women seem to have a particular propensity for headaches. This may be a hormonal effect, but the actual mechanism is not entirely clear. Analgesics in the form of acetaminophen (Tytenol, Datril, Panadol, etc), for example, are safe in pregnancy, but if you are experiencing headaches so frequently that you need repeated doses of pain relief, seek the help of your doctor.

The severe headache of imminent eclampsia (see p. 71) is something which every obstetrician is aware of and it may provide a valuable warning sign. Fortunately it is rare.

SCIATICA

Some women experience pain and tingling down the leg due to pressure on the sciatic nerve during pregnancy, although it is usually not more than an annoying discomfort. It may also be associated with the pelvic joint pains described on page 55. It seems to be due to direct pressure of the baby's head on the mother's sciatic nerve, and although there is no specific cure, the discomfort is relieved as the baby's head moves downwards. Rest, heat and analgesics may give some relief.

FAINTING

Fainting is not at all an uncommon phenomenon during pregnancy. In literature, a woman is traditionally recognized as being pregnant by becoming faint in crowded places! Standing too long with the blood pooling in the legs is likely to make you feel faint while you are pregnant, so try to avoid it.

About ten per cent of pregnant women experience a condition known as the 'supine hypotension syndrome'. In this situation, they may feel faint or even lose consciousness for a few moments while lying flat on the back. If the blood pressure was taken at this time, it would be found to be low. The effect is due to the pregnant uterus pressing on the major blood vessels of the abdomen (the aorta and the inferior vena cava) which run behind the uterus.

Try to avoid lying flat on your back for too long during late pregnancy. However, if you do feel faint in this position, roll over on to your side to relieve the pressure on the blood vessels, so that your blood pressure can rise again, and the feeling of faintness will pass.

HEARTBURN AND NAUSEA

Nausea is a common problem in early pregnancy (see p. 44), which usually clears as pregnancy advances. Occasionally, however, it returns, accompanied by vomiting, in the last few weeks of pregnancy. When this happens it is often associated with 'heartburn' (which has nothing to do with the heart), which usually precedes the vomiting.

The unpleasant burning sensation of heartburn occurs when acid from the stomach is regurgitated into the esophagus (the tube connecting the mouth to the stomach). It is once again a result of hormone action which causes laxity of the stomach sphincter – the tight muscle which blocks the contents of the stomach off from the esophagus. During pregnancy it takes longer to empty your stomach after eating, which contributes to the problem.

If you suffer from heartburn, take small, frequent and bland meals, avoiding highly spiced or fatty foods, and use an antacid recommended by your midwife or doctor. The problem is often worse at night but can be helped if you sleep well propped up with pillows.

FATIGUE

As pregnancy progresses and your size increases, it is natural that you should feel more tired than usual. Where there are other young children to look after, or if you are working, it is not surprising that you should tire more easily, and if you are anemic, the situation will be made worse.

It isn't advisable to work right up until the last minute during pregnancy, unless there are good facilities for rest at your place of work and you don't have to travel far to get there. Take advantage of your rights to maternity leave and pay if available (see pp. 294-295), so that you can leave work well before the baby is due.

Resting for an hour or so in the middle of the day whenever possible, and going to bed early at night will help. If you have young children try to persuade them to play quietly with you when you rest with your feet up, or take your rest when your child is having a nap – don't be tempted to use this time to catch up with the chores. If you are found to be anemic, a good nourishing diet perhaps supplemented with iron pills will help.

VAGINAL DISCHARGE

Glands in the cervix normally secrete mucus to keep the area moist. During pregnancy these natural secretions increase, so you will notice more vaginal discharge. This should not be a problem, although the dampness can cause irritation, so attention to personal hygiene and wearing underwear made of cotton rather than an artificial fiber can help avoid this. If soreness or irritation persists, you should consult the doctor who will see if you have an infection in the area (see p. 56).

STRESS INCONTINENCE

Many women who are pregnant experience a slight leakage of urine when they cough, sneeze, laugh or do exercises. This leakage of urine is known as stress incontinence, and during pregnancy it is very common because of the pressure of the uterus on the bladder, and the general laxity of the pelvic floor muscles due to the action of progesterone. Pelvic floor exercises done regularly from the start of pregnancy can help to control this rather embarrassing problem. However, if you do suffer from it, you will probably continue to do so for a little while after the birth as the pelvic floor muscles are extremely stretched. Pelvic floor exercises begun immediately after the birth will strengthen the muscles and the problem should disappear within a few weeks (see p. 140).

INSOMNIA

Difficulty in sleeping can be quite distressing in later pregnancy, when the sheer discomfort of your heavy uterus makes it difficult to settle down

These positions can help relieve sacro-iliac and low back pain.

1 Pelvic twist: *Lie flat on your back on the floor. Bend the knee on your painful side, twist that foot round the calf of the opposite leg, then roll your pelvis away from the pain, keeping your shoulders flat on the floor. Gently rock your pelvis back and forth, then carefully return to your starting position.*

2 Leg up: *Lie flat on your back on the floor, bend the leg on your painful side right up, taking the knee towards your shoulder and holding it there with your hand. With your other hand, grasp your foot and draw it towards your opposite groin. Gently pull and release your knee and foot several times before carefully putting your leg down.*

To get up after either of these exercises, bend your knees up high, roll on to your side (keeping your knees pressed tightly together), and push yourself up with your hands.

comfortably in bed at night. Your natural worries and apprehensions play a part, and it doesn't help if you find you need to get up to go to the lavatory several times during the night as well.

Simple measures can help you: avoid drinking late at night so you are less likely to need to pass urine; not eating too late; not drinking stimulating fluids like coffee; using extra pillows to give more comfort and minimize the problem of heartburn (see earlier), and practicing the relaxation technique described on page 33 or recommended by your prenatal class instructor.

If you are really becoming exhausted from lack of sleep, discuss it with your doctor, who may be able to prescribe mild sleeping pills to help reintroduce the 'habit' of sleep.

JOINT PAINS

Aches and pains in pregnancy are common; this is not at all surprising when one considers the rate and extent of growth of the uterus. Joints may suffer simply because of the action of the hormone progesterone, loosening the ligaments which normally hold them in a position of stability. The particular joints affected in this way are the sacro-iliac joints, the lumbo-sacral joint which is the joint between the last lumbar vertebra and the sacrum, and the pubic symphysis in front. In the much rarer, more extreme form of involvement of the pelvic joints – pelvic arthropathy – the woman may be totally incapacitated and hospitalization required.

It is difficult to do much to relieve sacro-iliac and lower back pain apart from heat treatment in the form of hot baths and compresses, and simple analgesia. You can help to avoid back trouble by being careful about your posture – try not to allow yourself to lean back to compensate for the weight of the baby in front – and if you need to lift something heavy from a low position, always bend the knees and use the strong muscles of the thighs rather than bending from the waist. When getting up from the floor or the bed, always roll over on to your side and push yourself up with your hands and arms (see the illustrations opposite).

If you do suffer from severe lumbo-sacral or sacro-iliac pain, seek the help of the obstetric physiotherapist in your hospital. She may be able to help with manipulation and heat treatment, and can give you a special supporting corset to wear during your pregnancy. In the meantime the positions given in the illustrations opposite can be very effective in relieving this type of pain. Although the effect of progesterone on the ligaments continues for some weeks after the birth, and you should continue to be careful about posture and lifting,

whether it is your baby or anything heavy, the problem does begin to resolve with the end of pregnancy.

CRAMP

Muscle cramps, especially of the feet and legs, are another troublesome discomfort of late pregnancy. Their actual cause is not known and there is no evidence that extra calcium will help. Since cramp often seems to occur when stretching the legs with the toes pointed down, a simple trick to avoid cramp is always to stretch with your toes pointing up, so that your feet are at right angles to your shins.

If a spasm of cramp wakes you at night, it can be nipped in the bud by pulling your feet up so that the Achilles tendon above your heel and your calf muscles are well stretched. Follow this with some deep massage and vigorous foot pumping and you should escape the painful bruised feeling that bad calf or in-step cramp can leave behind.

SKIN IRRITATION

Pimples, acne, soreness in the folds of the groin or the arm pits may develop – but all these fade after pregnancy. Skin rashes are common, although once more the cause is not known. The rashes frequently involve the abdomen and the back. Treating the itching caused by the rash with a mild lotion such as calamine is all that is possible. If you suffer from this type of rash, you should avoid using perfume, talcum powder and other cosmetic body or bath preparations as they make the rash worse. It is best not to use detergents for your clothes, as well. If you are suffering from a more widespread rash, then your doctor might want to look for a specific allergy.

In some severe cases of skin irritation (not always, incidentally, associated with a rash), antihistamine tablets may be required, but their use during pregnancy must be supervised by the doctor.

CARPAL TUNNEL SYNDROME

The main nerves supplying the fingers and hand pass under a fibrous sheath at the wrist known as the carpal tunnel. This can become swollen during late pregnancy, causing a severe 'pins and needles' discomfort in your fingers, and even numbness and clumsiness of the hand. It is often worse at night.

If you suffer from carpal tunnel syndrome, your doctor may suggest splinting the hand and wrist, which can bring some relief. Sometimes it may be suggested that the sheath is injected with cortisone, but this isn't used frequently during pregnancy because of the high chance of the syndrome recurring. However, it does get better once pregnancy is over, so surgery is not required.

MATERNAL INFECTIONS

There are, needless to say, a very large number of infections which may occur during pregnancy. These are usually coincidental to pregnancy, but every mother who develops an infection of one kind or another is naturally concerned as to whether it will have an effect on her pregnancy.

GENITAL TRACT INFECTIONS

There are two main types of vaginal infection; 'thrush' (Candida albicans or monilia) is discussed on page 45, and is very common throughout pregnancy. The pregnancy is not affected either by the condition or by the treatment for it. Another infection is Trichomonas vaginalis, which produces a thin, yellow, smelly discharge and soreness rather than itching. Treatment is by tablets containing metronidazole (Flagyl). This drug is better avoided in the first three months of pregnancy but thereafter is safe. In both forms of local vaginal infection both the mother and her partner must be treated.

A common organism found in the vagina is the 'Group B' streptococcus. Its presence is not usually associated with excess discharge, so you may be unaware of its presence. However, as it can cause infection in the newborn baby, it is common practice now in many maternity units to take a vaginal swab and send it to the laboratory to check for the organism's presence as a routine in late pregnancy. If it is found, a course of safe antibiotics is given before labor so that the way is clear, so to speak, for the baby during delivery.

Sexually transmitted diseases such as gonorrhea may also occur in pregnancy. Fortunately this is almost always responsive to treatment by the penicillin group of antibiotics.

Herpes is a problem which has come into prominence in recent years. Genital herpes is common and treatment less than satisfactory. The baby may become affected if he passes through a herpes-infected birth canal, so if the virus is found, then delivery by cesarean section is advisable.

URINARY TRACT INFECTIONS

These are not uncommon in pregnancy. The effect of the hormone changes in pregnancy means that the tissues of the kidneys and ureters (the tubes that lead from the kidneys to the bladder) expand and become lax, and urine tends to 'pool' in the area,

rendering it more liable to infection.

Routine checking of urine at prenatal appointments, by sending it for culture in the laboratory, will screen for excess numbers of organisms. If such are found, even if you don't have any symptoms, a course of antibiotics will be given. As in all such situations, the antibiotics used are chosen specifically for their safety in pregnancy. Some antibiotics used for urinary tract infections are suspect, so if you think you have an infection early in pregnancy, make sure you tell your doctor (if you haven't already) that you think you may be pregnant.

A full blown urinary tract infection may bring pain, fever, frequency of passing urine and the risk of premature labor. Here again laboratory testing will indicate which antibiotic to use. In such a case, you must be followed up after pregnancy to make sure the infection is completely eradicated and to check the function of the kidneys.

GENERALIZED INFECTIONS

Quite apart from pregnancy, a mother may develop an infection anywhere in the body – skin, eyes, chest and so on. The same overall rules apply in pregnancy – locate the organism causing the infection, test its sensitivity to antibiotics in the laboratory and treat using of course an antibiotic with no known adverse effects on the baby.

The group of infections which worry mothers most of course, because of their possible effect on the baby, are the common infectious diseases, such as measles, mumps, chicken pox or rubella (German measles). In all these illnesses, if a high fever develops in early pregnancy, then there may be an increased possibility of miscarriage. Mumps has no proven effect; polio virus and measles may give an increased chance of miscarriage or premature delivery; and chicken pox is rarely associated with serious effects in pregnancy, except at the time of delivery.

Rubella is the problem which is now well identified (see p. 13). If the mother develops rubella in the first three months of pregnancy then fetal abnormalities can develop in as high a proportion as 20 per cent. The abnormalities affect eyes (blindness), ears (deafness), brain, heart or limbs. Termination of pregnancy is clearly justifiable in these circumstances. Between thirteen and sixteen weeks the risk is down to four per cent, and thereafter to one per cent or less.

Laboratory testing of a blood sample will tell you whether you are protected if you come into contact with the disease or, if there is no sign of protection, repeat testing will indicate whether significant infection has recently occurred. You and your

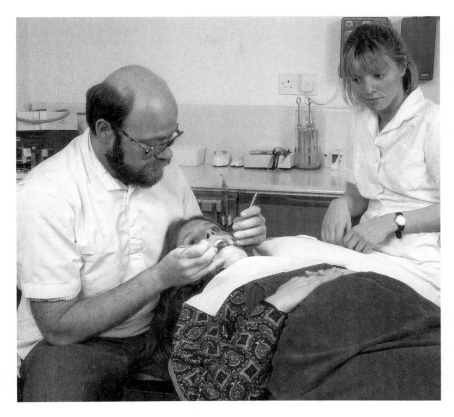

Dental care during pregnancy is important since the increase in the volume of your blood supply can lead to bleeding and gum disease. It makes sense to have regular check-ups at this time.

partner can then be counseled accordingly, depending when in pregnancy this occurs.

If you aren't immune you will be offered rubella vaccination after pregnancy. You should use careful contraception to avoid pregnancy for three months after the vaccination (see p. 143).

KEEPING HEALTHY IN LATE PREGNANCY

The minor discomforts of pregnancy, and the extra burden of the growing baby, inevitably limit your movements somewhat during later pregnancy. In any case, you will probably find that you are becoming more 'home-based' by choice since your thoughts will be focused on preparing for the birth.

There aren't any special rules about keeping healthy in later pregnancy. A sensible diet, eating little and often if you suffer from indigestion or heartburn, and resting as much as possible have already been discussed. It is useful to keep as active as possible within limits – walking and swimming are good forms of exercise.

Sexual intercourse may be continued as long as you feel like it, although there may be physical restraints in the last weeks. Deep penetration may become difficult, but it won't harm the baby unless you have been specifically advised to avoid it.

DENTAL CARE

It is advisable to ensure that your teeth are in good condition during pregnancy. The gums become spongy with the extra blood supply, which may enhance any existing gum infections. Dental hygiene and advice on the care of your teeth and gums become particularly important so you should be sure to visit your dentist regularly at this time.

TRAVEL DURING PREGNANCY

Traveling long distances can be rather uncomfortable during late pregnancy, and the length of an automobile journey may have to be planned to accommodate more stops than usual. Take a cushion to tuck into the small of your back to avoid backache. It is probably sensible not to travel too far from your home and hospital after 37 weeks, as there is always the possibility you may go into labor unexpectedly early. Air travel is not advisable in late pregnancy – many airlines are reluctant to take pregnant women after 32 weeks or so. If it is necessary for you to travel by air after about this stage of pregnancy, you should check with the airline beforehand and let them know that you are pregnant.

PROBLEM PREGNANCIES

A reassuring guide to unexpected or unusual medical
conditions that may arise during your pregnancy

Most pregnancies proceed without any problems at all beyond the minor discomforts and irritations that have already been described in the previous chapter. However, some do not, and it is because they can occur unexpectedly that regular prenatal check-ups are so important. Midwives and obstetricians are on the look-out for problems which even the mother may not suspect, and will do all they can to help your pregnancy proceed to a successful conclusion – that is, the birth of a healthy baby.

MISCARRIAGE

It is unfortunate that a chapter on problem pregnancies has to start with a description of miscarriage, which implies the loss of a pregnancy, but most of these do occur in the first trimester. Fortunately, however, though it is distressing, a miscarriage does not usually mean that you will not have a normal, full-term pregnancy next time.

When a pregnancy does not continue for its full time and is lost before the twenty-eighth week, it is described popularly as a miscarriage, although the medical term is 'spontaneous abortion'. This can occasionally cause confusion, since the word 'abortion' is also popularly used to mean the surgical termination of pregnancy. Medically this is actually called an induced abortion, but to avoid confusion doctors and midwives prefer to call it therapeutic abortion or TAB.

EARLY MISCARRIAGE

By far the commonest time for miscarriages to occur is in the first three months, and it is thought that perhaps as many as one in four or five pregnancies end in this way, although many women may not even have realized they were pregnant. The reasons for this very high wastage are not fully understood, but when one considers the complex mechanisms of fertilization and implantation discussed in Chapter 3, it is perhaps not so surprising that all pregnancies are not successful.

Sometimes there is a problem with the chromosome make up of the embryo – not every ovum and sperm are perfectly manufactured – and sometimes there is a problem with the implantation of the embryo into the wall of the uterus. In such cases the pregnancy will fail to develop and eventually will be rejected by the uterus. Miscarriages at this stage are not caused by physical injury, despite the belief of popular novelists, nor are they usually precipitated by sexual intercourse.

The symptoms associated with a miscarriage can vary but in the typical situation you would have noticed all the usual signs of pregnancy – a missed period or two, feelings of nausea, breast tenderness and possibly even a positive pregnancy test – and then you would notice vaginal bleeding and cramp-like pains in your lower abdomen.

If the bleeding is very slight and the pain mild or non-existent then this may not be too serious and the pregnancy may well continue normally – this is what is known medically as a threatened abortion or miscarriage. However, it is something that can only be diagnosed by your doctor, so if you have any vaginal bleeding, however little, you should seek professional advice. An ultrasound scan may be necessary to confirm the viability of the pregnancy. If this is normal then you need not worry about the future, the bleeding will not have harmed the baby.

If you experience much heavier bleeding (this can sometimes be very profuse and make you feel weak and faint), with moderate to severe stomach cramps, then it is most likely that you are miscarrying – you may even pass small pieces of material, which are portions of the placenta. This is a medical emergency and you will probably need immediate admission to hospital for a minor operation to evacuate the uterus and make sure it is empty, otherwise further bleeding or infection may result. This operation is often referred to as a 'scrape of the womb' or a 'D&C' (dilatation and curettage) and usually involves an overnight stay in hospital.

You will probably be very concerned to know why you have lost the baby, but it is often difficult to be any more specific than the reasons stated above, and examination of the products of conception is usually unhelpful. At this stage of pregnancy it is sadly not possible to tell very much about the baby,

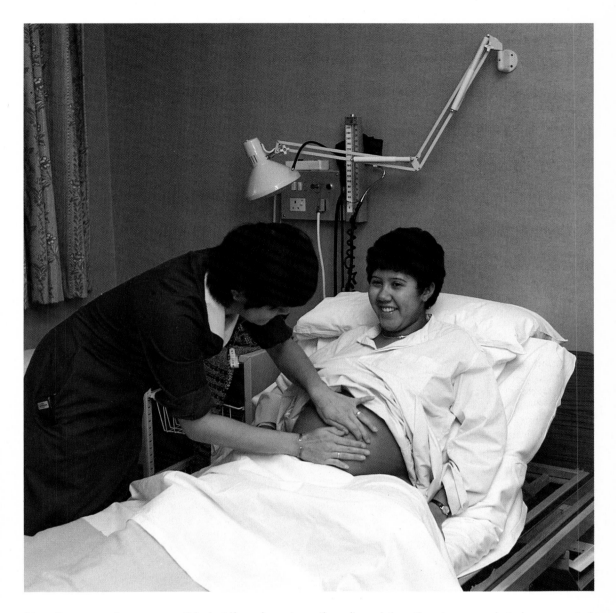

Not all pregnancies run smoothly, but if you have to spend time in the maternity ward, you know that it is best for both you and your baby.

which is so small it is usually not identified.

Occasionally a pregnancy can cease to continue but will not be miscarried in the way described above. Instead the products are retained in the uterus without further development. This situation is known medically as a missed abortion or miscarriage. The only symptoms here may be a disappearance of the feelings of pregnancy and a little vaginal bleeding or brown discharge. Diagnosis can be made conclusively by ultrasound and if confirmed then the uterus needs to be evacuated.

Having a miscarriage does not mean you will be unable to have children and it is only when a couple have had three miscarriages in a row that special medical investigations are thought to be necessary. Even in that circumstance there is a 40-50 per cent chance of a successful pregnancy in the future. We now recognize that many women experience considerable grief for a long time after a miscarriage. Often it makes good sense to seek counseling for a while to talk about the sense of loss and to help cope. Your doctor will be happy to discuss with you any special precautions for the next pregnancy and how long you should wait before trying again.

LATE MISCARRIAGE

In much rarer circumstances pregnancies can be miscarried in the second three months. Again there can be several explanations for this, some of which, such as premature separation of the placenta and intrauterine death, are covered elsewhere.

Miscarriage at this time can also be caused by what is known as cervical incompetence. In this situation the cervix (neck of the womb) is weak and opens up without warning usually around 20 weeks, allowing the contents of the uterus to pass through – resulting in a very rapid miscarriage, sometimes associated with spontaneous rupture of the membranes. Cervical incompetence may be something you are born with, but is more usually associated with cervical damage following surgery or vaginal termination of pregnancy.

If your obstetrician thinks from your medical history that you may have this problem it may be recommended that you have a stitch (known as a Shirodkar or McDonald's cerclage) placed around the cervix to close it. This is performed under anesthesia about fourteen weeks into the pregnancy. The stitch is removed again around the thirty-eighth week or when labor starts if this is sooner. You do not need an anesthetic to have it removed.

ECTOPIC PREGNANCY

Sometimes a pregnancy never gets as far as implanting in the uterus and imbeds itself somewhere along the way. Usually this is in the Fallopian tube, and is more likely to happen if the tubes have been damaged by infection or surgery or if there is an intrauterine device preventing implantation in the womb. Symptoms of pregnancy start but the pregnancy cannot develop for long in this environment and so after only a few weeks will be passed out of the tube or rupture through its wall. When this happens there is usually severe pain on that side of the abdomen with a small amount of vaginal bleeding. Severe hemorrhage may occur internally leading to fainting and collapse.

An ectopic pregnancy is a serious medical emergency and will need to be dealt with in hospital. If you think you could have this condition contact your doctor immediately. If examination and further tests confirm the diagnosis then an abdominal operation will be required to remove the pregnancy and usually the damaged tube with it.

Having an ectopic pregnancy does not necessarily mean you cannot conceive again. Your chances will depend on the cause of the ectopic pregnancy and the state of your remaining Fallopian tube.

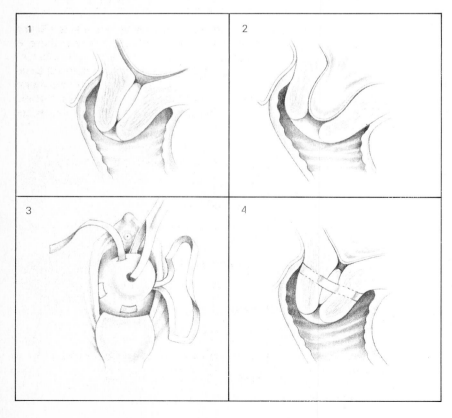

Incompetent cervix
1 *In the normal cervix, the cervical os (canal) is tightly closed and sealed with a plug of mucus during pregnancy.*
2 *In cervical incompetence, the cervix opens, allowing the membranes and amniotic fluid to bulge through the cervical canal, eventually leading to miscarriage.*
3 *An incompetent cervix can be closed surgically at about fourteen weeks using a 'purse string' suture (cerclage).*
4 *The suture shown in cross-section, holding the cervix closed. It is removed at about 38 weeks of pregnancy.*

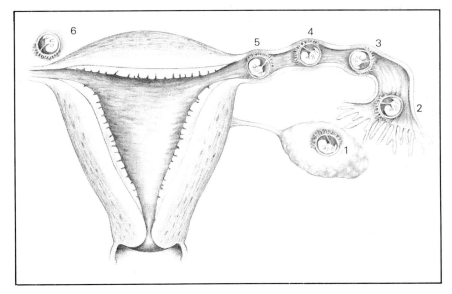

An ectopic pregnancy is one where the embryo does not reach the uterus but imbeds itself elsewhere. This is usually somewhere in the Fallopian tube (2-5), but more rarely the embryo imbeds in the ovary (1) or outside the uterus within the abdominal cavity (6). An ectopic pregnancy usually fails and has to be removed surgically.

THE RISK OF PREMATURE LABOR

Arguably the problem of prematurity exercises the minds of obstetrician and pediatrician more than any other single problem in obstetrics. The aim of every obstetrician and midwife is to give to the mother and father a healthy mature baby undamaged by pregnancy or delivery. Prematurity is a threat to this aim.

A premature labor is one that starts after the twenty-eighth week of pregnancy. Before that it would constitute a miscarriage if the fetus is born dead, although in practice many babies born nowadays as early as 24 weeks of gestation can survive with the support of an up-to-date neonatal intensive care unit (see p. 116). In most cases, the basic cause of the onset of premature labor, or premature rupture of the membranes, is not known, but certain background factors, listed in the table right, are well defined, and should alert your obstetrician so that extra monitoring of your pregnancy can be arranged.

To stop premature labor in its tracks would seem the obvious thing to do, but that is not always possible. Certain drugs are available which act to inhibit the uterus from contracting. They can be given initially by intravenous tube and subsequently in pill form, but these cannot be used under all circumstances, such as when there has been an obstetric hemorrhage, and they are not without some unpleasant side-effects to the mother, such as dizziness and rapid pulse. However this is a small price to pay for improving the prospects for the baby.

Although this treatment can be administered for several weeks in some cases, the most important function for these drugs is in delaying labor for 24 for 48 hours. This is to enable the mother to be given steroid injections which can help to improve the baby's lung maturity, by apparently increasing lung surfactant (see p. 118).

ALLOWING PREMATURE LABOR TO PROCEED

In some circumstances it may be sensible to allow a premature labor to proceed, especially if there is a neonatal intensive care unit in the hospital or nearby (see p. 116). If the membranes have ruptured it may not be advisable to attempt long-term inhibition of labor because of the risk of infection. If the cervix is already dilated more than 1½ inches

FACTORS ASSOCIATED WITH PREMATURE LABOR

☐ Multiple pregnancy

☐ Antepartum hemorrhage

☐ Intrauterine growth retardation (fetus 'small for dates')

☐ Cervical incompetence

☐ Congenital abnormality of the uterus

☐ Diabetes

☐ Excess amniotic liquor

☐ Generalized infections, e.g. kidney infection

☐ Previous history of premature labor

labor will progress anyway. Labor should be allowed to progress also if the estimated weight of the baby is over 5 pounds or the definite gestational age is more than 34 weeks.

If such a premature labor takes place in a hospital without neonatal intensive care facilities, then urgent transfer of the mother to such a unit has to be arranged, before labor progresses to any extent. A premature labor has to be very carefully managed and this is discussed in Chapter 7.

RECOGNIZING PREMATURE LABOR

It is often difficult, especially for a first-time mother, to recognize the signs of premature labor. Braxton Hicks contractions (see p. 76) can be quite cramping and regular. However if regular pain is accompanied by hardening of the uterus, a 'show' and certainly if your membranes rupture, you should go to hospital immediately.

If you are in any doubt, telephone your obstetrician for help and advice. Because everyone is so aware of the problems of prematurity, it is more than likely that the advice will be to come to hospital at once for admission, to be rested, observed and monitored to show exactly what is happening to your uterus and the condition of the baby. The information gained, plus the results of a clinical examination, will then guide the obstetrician as to what action to take, based on the factors discussed above.

Quite often, a mother may stay in the maternity ward for some time after a threatened premature labor, and the pregnancy is conserved for as long as possible. Rest is the key, and mothers become very bored in this situation, but there is the compensation of knowing that every day nearer to full term that the baby can be maintained in the uterus increases his chances of survival.

BLEEDING DURING LATER PREGNANCY

When bleeding occurs from the vagina after the twenty-eighth week of pregnancy and before the birth of the baby, it is called an 'obstetric hemorrhage'. It is important to realize that the bleeding need not be heavy, in spite of the implications of the word 'hemorrhage'. Blood loss may be quite slight, but you should always treat it seriously and contact your doctor at once, since slight loss can herald a much bigger loss, and the sooner everyone is alerted the better.

There can be several possible sources of obstetric hemorrhage. Sometimes the bleeding may be accompanied by other symptoms, although this is not always the case.

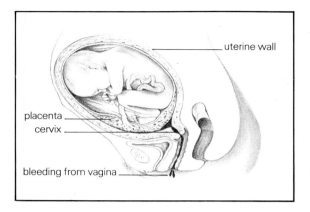

Placenta previa means that the placenta is very low, partially or wholly covering the exit from the uterus. It is a major cause of painless bleeding during pregnancy.

PLACENTA PREVIA

Placenta previa is a major cause of obstetric hemorrhage – probably accounting for between 20 and 40 per cent of all cases. Placenta previa – which literally translates as 'placenta first' – means that instead of being positioned somewhere toward the top of the uterine wall, the placenta is partly or completely attached to the lower segment of the uterus. This usually results in part or all of its mass covering the area of the internal os, or opening, of the cervix. The internal os is a tight ring of muscle at the top of the cervix which is pulled up into the lower uterine segment as pregnancy progresses and during labor will become part of the lower uterine segment as the whole cervix is dilated (see p. 76).

Depending on how low is the site of the placenta, the condition is classified into four types, ranging from type 1, where it does not quite reach the opening of the uterus, to the 'complete' type 4, where the placenta totally covers the cervix. Placenta previa is frequently diagnosed during early ultrasound examination. Often no bleeding results; this is because as the lower segment of the uterus is formed as the uterus grows, the placental insertion site is 'pulled up' away from the cervix. What appears as a low-lying placenta at sixteen to eighteen weeks may be seen on a repeat ultrasound at 30 to 32 weeks to be a normally situated placenta.

Placenta previa is thought to occur in about half a per cent of all pregnancies. The cause of such an abnormal site for the placenta is not known, but in a multiple pregnancy (twins, for example), it is more common simply because a larger placenta, or even two placentas may be involved, thereby covering a larger area of the uterine wall.

The features of a placenta previa are quite typical. You may experience a sudden painless loss of blood which is very often slight at first. If it recurs, which it is likely to do, and if there is a major degree of placenta previa, the bleeding may become heavy. When you are examined, the doctor may well find that the baby is lying transversely or obliquely across the uterus, simply because the placenta is preventing the head from getting into the lower segment of the uterus.

Bleeding occurs as the internal os region of the cervix is pulled up into the lower segment of the uterus during pregnancy. The placenta becomes dislodged from its site and a tiny area is exposed, and it is surprising how much bleeding can come from such a small area. However, unless the quantity of blood loss is such as to affect you adversely (with a sudden drop of blood pressure and rapid pulse – in other words, the onset of 'shock'), the fetus remains undisturbed. Although you may be alarmed by the amount of blood you lose, you can be reassured that your baby will be quite safe, in contrast to other causes of obstetric hemorrhage. However, once placenta previa has been diagnosed, the well-being of the fetus will be checked by electronic monitoring to get a trace of the fetal heart rate (see p. 81).

Bleeding from a placenta previa tends to occur quite late in pregnancy; 60 per cent occurs after the thirty-sixth week. As a result, it is a golden rule among obstetricians never to give a mother with bleeding in later pregnancy an internal examination. If you suffer from bleeding at this time, your doctor will suspect placenta previa and will be anxious not to touch the low lying placenta, thus precipitating further bleeding. Instead, you will be given an abdominal examination, looking first for areas of tenderness (see placental abruption, overleaf), and for the lie of the baby – transverse or oblique, or perhaps longitudinal but with an unusually high presenting part (head or breech). You will be given an ultrasound scan as well which can accurately detect the position of both the placenta and the baby.

TREATING PLACENTA PREVIA

If you experience slight bleeding, and your doctor suspects placenta previa, you will be referred without delay to the hospital or to the nearest large maternity unit if you had been planning a home delivery. If the bleeding is so bad that an ambulance has to be called, the paramedics will check your health and the baby's heart rate, and will put an intravenous tube into your arm to maintain fluids. You will then be transferred to hospital as quickly as possible.

Once in hospital a more detailed history will be taken and your notes will be checked. You will also be asked some relevant questions: Have you had an ultrasound scan earlier in pregnancy? Was there pain when you bled? How much have you lost – a cupful, a jug-full? What were you doing when it started? For example, sexual intercourse with deep penetration could precipitate bleeding from a placenta previa of major degree.

Your pulse rate, blood pressure and temperature will be checked, and you will be given an abdominal examination. The fetal heart rate will also be checked again. You will almost certainly be given an ultrasound scan at this stage to check the site of the placenta. The doctor may also take a blood sample to double-check for cross-matching in case of more severe hemorrhage and the need for blood transfusion.

Although you won't be given an internal examination, the doctor may decide to pass a speculum into your vagina – this is an instrument which will allow examination of the cervix, which is commonly used for taking cervical smears. The doctor will want to rule out the possibility that a polyp of the cervix is the cause of bleeding, especially if it was disturbed during intercourse, so it is worth having a look at the appearance and condition of the cervix. (A polyp is a small 'tag' of tissue, full of blood vessels, which bleeds readily to touch. It is quite harmless and can be removed easily by a simple operation after pregnancy.)

The treatment in hospital following the initial investigation once again depends on how severe the bleeding is, and what stage the pregnancy has reached. If the bleeding is severe, a maternal shock has to be corrected by blood transfusion or equivalent treatment and the baby must be delivered at once regardless of maturity. Severe bleeding usually means that there is a major degree of placenta previa which would prevent a vaginal delivery, so for the sake of speed an emergency cesarean section would be carried out (see p. 96).

In mild bleeding, however, the object would be to conserve the pregnancy. You are admitted to hospital for observation, but nothing further would be done until an ultrasound scan confirms the degree of placenta previa. If the placenta is found to be very low an elective cesarean section will be arranged. This is because in a major degree of placenta previa bleeding is likely to recur and the position of the placenta would again prevent a vaginal delivery. 'Elective' simply means that a convenient date and time will be pre-arranged and these will be determined particularly by the maturity of your pregnancy. Your doctor will try to wait until

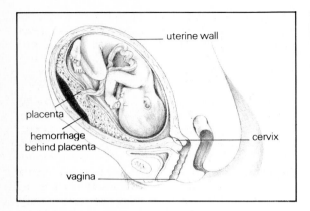

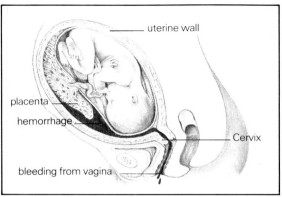

Placental abruption means that part of the placenta becomes detached from the uterine wall and bleeding occurs behind it, associated with pain. The

abruption may be 'revealed' (above) with vaginal bleeding, or 'concealed' (left), where the blood collects at the placental site but does not escape.

you are at least 37 weeks pregnant, so you may have to stay in hospital for several weeks.

If the diagnosis is in any doubt or the degree of placenta previa appears to be minimal then your doctor might want to carry out a vaginal examination first, although this is rarely necessary nowadays with the sophistication of ultrasound scanning techniques. However if it is thought necessary, a vaginal examination will be done under general anesthetic with everything prepared for an immediate cesarean section, in case the doctor 'hits oil' and precipitates bleeding during the examination. However this examination is only done if it seems possible that the placenta is *not* previa and therefore vaginal delivery could be allowed.

THE RISK TO MOTHER AND BABY

It must be emphasized that the risk to mother and baby from placenta previa is nowadays very slight, provided that warning signs are acted upon at once. Even if bleeding is severe, the maternal blood pressure can be maintained by adequate transfusion and adequate facilities can be made ready for an emergency cesarean delivery.

Placenta previa is not a problem that need necessarily recur in a subsequent pregnancy. If you have to have a cesarean because of this problem, there is no reason why you should not have a vaginal delivery next time, if all else is normal.

PLACENTAL ABRUPTION

One of the commonest causes of vaginal bleeding after the twenty-eighth week of pregnancy is abruption of the placenta, or abruptio placentae, to give it its classical title. Placental abruption needs swift

treatment by specialists in the hospital, since it is potentially dangerous to the health of both mother and baby.

In placental abruption, the placenta is situated normally in the uterus, in the upper segment, and either on the front or back wall or across the top (the fundus). The bleeding occurs behind the placenta, shearing it off from its attachment to the uterus. This may be slight, or it may extend to a much greater degree, even occasionally lifting the placenta off its attachment to the uterine wall altogether. Placental abruption occurs in as many as two per cent of all pregnancies and is thought to account for 60 per cent of all cases of obstetric hemorrhage.

Like placenta previa, the actual reason for a placental abruption is not known, but there are several recognized associated factors. For example, it is more common in women who have had several children, and it may complicate a pregnancy already complicated by high blood pressure. Trauma – in the form of some accidental external damage – plays a small part, but it can follow a blow on the stomach, such as experienced in a car accident, for example.

The fundamental difference between the obstetric hemorrhage associated with placental abruption, as opposed to that experienced in placenta previa, is pain. The amount of visible bleeding is usually slight, but the amount of bleeding behind the disrupted placenta can be quite considerable and pain results from the tension produced by the trapped blood.

Pain may also be accompanied by tenderness and irritability of the uterus, and indeed labor may ensue. Finally, and most importantly, the oxygen supply to the fetus is interrupted to some extent, fetal distress may result and prompt action may be required on behalf of the baby. Apart from these serious problems, the situation may be complicated by maternal shock caused by loss of blood, failure of her blood to clot in severe cases, and, rarely, temporary kidney failure, also in severe cases.

TREATING PLACENTAL ABRUPTION

When you are initially examined by your doctor, placental abruption will probably be diagnosed if you have had bleeding with associated pain; if your uterus is generally rather hard, tender and irritable or has an area of marked tenderness on examination; and especially if the fetal heart rate is fast or slow or showing 'dips' in association with the activity of the uterus. You will be admitted immediately into hospital in the same way as described for placenta previa, above, but how you are treated subsequently depends on the severity of the abruption. You will probably be given an ultrasound scan which may show evidence of a blood clot behind an area of uterus. However, in major degrees of abruption there will be no time for scanning.

In a mild case of placental abruption before 37 weeks of pregnancy, where there was only slight blood loss, with no distress of the baby and the mother's condition is good, you would be scanned to confirm the diagnosis and then advised to rest in bed in hospital. Yours and your baby's condition would be monitored carefully to try and conserve the pregnancy as long as possible. If the abruption occurs after 37 weeks, then your membranes would be ruptured and labor induced (see p. 87). Rupturing the membranes appears to 'clamp down' the uterus on the bleeding spot, preventing further extension of the abruption. Obviously the baby's condition would be closely monitored during the ensuing labor.

Moderate placental abruption might consist of more loss of blood – say 1-2 pints – although not all would be visible and measurable, a raised pulse and lowered blood pressure, much pain, a very irritable, tender uterus and probably evidence of fetal distress.

Here the baby would have to be delivered urgently and an emergency cesarean section is required. Your condition would have to be corrected by blood transfusion and special steps taken to correct the inability of your blood to clot (if this has happened) and to preserve kidney function.

Severe abruption is a rare but extremely important obstetric emergency. The mother would be profoundly shocked, her uterus tense and very tender, and unfortunately the baby, who has had his life-line cut, does not usually survive. In such a

life-threatening situation, the labor would be induced as soon as possible, with adequate transfusion and close monitoring of the mother.

OTHER REASONS FOR BLEEDING

It has already been mentioned that a polyp of the cervix may cause a small loss of blood, which, after 28 weeks, must be classified as obstetric hemorrhage, although it is not serious. Other rare local conditions causing bleeding may be severe inflammation of the vagina due to infection, a cervical ectropian (cervical erosion), which sometimes occurs during pregnancy, or even more rarely, cervical cancer. All these conditions would be borne in mind by the obstetrician when examining the mother through a speculum in the vagina, following a small obstetric hemorrhage.

Apart from the extremely rare case of invasive cervical cancer, no active treatment would be given to any of these local conditions during pregnancy. Your doctor would probably arrange for an ultrasound scan to be done as well to make quite sure that a low lying placenta was not after all the cause of the bleeding, and the local condition simply coincidence.

Quite a large number of women are admitted into hospital with a slight bleed which has to be classified as of 'unknown cause'. A scan excludes placenta previa, there is no evidence of placental abruption and no local condition can be found.

Even so most obstetricians would prefer to regard such cases as probably mild abruptions, and although the treatment would be to conserve the pregnancy, they would want to monitor mother and baby, probably with a few days in hospital, for the rest of the pregnancy.

MULTIPLE PREGNANCIES

A multiple pregnancy of course means more than one baby in a pregnancy – twins, most commonly (1 in 80 pregnancies), triplets less commonly (1 in 80 × 80), and still less commonly, quadruplets or more.

It seems a pity that the topic has to be put into a chapter entitled 'problem' pregnancies. It would be nice to think that the mother with twins would not look on her pregnancy as a problem, but rather as an exciting, if challenging, prospect. Hopefully the description and explanation which follows will help to emphasize the latter rather than the former.

We talk about twins simply because that is the most common form of multiple pregnancy. Any additional points on triplets (or more) will be made where relevant.

TYPES OF TWINS

Twins are described as dizygotic (non-identical) or monozygotic (identical), which means that they either develop from two separate eggs or from the one fertilized egg dividing into two at an early stage. In dizygotic twins each fetus is separate, with a separate placenta and two sets of membranes (amnion and chorion). In monozygotic twins there is a single placenta and one chorion but each fetus usually has a separate amniotic sac. Monozygotic twins are always the same sex, but dizygotic twins may not be. Dizygotic twins are no more alike than any other brothers or sisters from the same family. The proportion of dizygotic to monozygotic twins is approximately 60:40. At birth it is sometimes quite difficult to tell whether twins are identical or not, but parents obviously want to know this. The placenta has to be examined by a pathologist, but even so, the diagnosis might have to be confirmed by special blood tests.

DIAGNOSING MULTIPLE PREGNANCY

How do we recognize if you are going to have twins? First of all your uterus would be bigger than would be expected for the calculated dates. As the pregnancy grows there seems to be an excess of fetal parts when your abdomen is examined and often two heads can clearly be felt. If there is a family history of twins (it is an hereditary trait) then

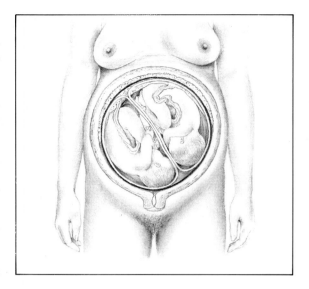

In many twin pregnancies, both babies adopt a cephalic (head down) presentation. These twins have a separate placenta and amnion (inner membrane) but share a single chorion (outer membrane).

the diagnosis seems highly likely.

Confirmation of the diagnosis will nowadays be made by ultrasound scan; it is then that a 'head count' shows whether there are two or more babies present. In the absence of ultrasound a single x-ray picture will also give the diagnosis, but this cannot be done until quite late in pregnancy to avoid damaging the fetus (or fetuses). An ultrasound picture can diagnose the situation as early as eight weeks of pregnancy.

PROBLEMS IN A TWIN PREGNANCY

Increased nausea may be experienced in early pregnancy, and may lead to actual vomiting, often well into the second trimester. Ask your doctor's advice if this becomes incapacitating. In later pregnancy all the minor discomforts of pregnancy may be exaggerated – hemorrhoids, varicose veins, ankle swelling, heartburn and so on – all made more troublesome as a result of the extra size of the uterus. There is more amniotic fluid – especially with monozygotic twins – and the uterus is considerably distended, so it is not surprising that these discomforts appear. This is especially so in triplets or quadruplets where the uterus can become enormously distended. When the babies begin to move, you may find it very uncomfortable and they may make sleeping difficult. Use extra pillows to take the pressure off your abdomen, and don't be

WHY DO TWINS OCCUR?

As is so often the case the reason for twinning is not really known, but several associated factors are recognized which are listed below.

Family history	There is a strong familial tendency to twins
Older age groups	The chances of twins increase over the age of 35
High parity	The more babies a woman has the more likely she is to have twins
Racial factors	Twinning is more common in Africa and Asia (except the Far East) than in Western countries
Fertility drugs	Nowadays this is a recognized 'risk' factor in twin pregnancies (or more). The use of fertility drugs has certainly increased the chances of a multiple pregnancy simply by increasing the number of eggs available for fertilization.

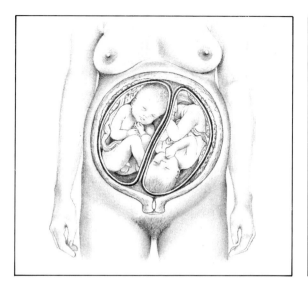

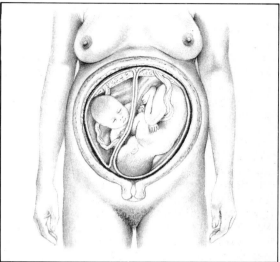

Another common twin presentation is for one baby to be cephalic, the other breech. As shown here, most non-identical twins have separate amnions, chorions and placenta.

If one twin is smaller than the other, the baby may be forced to adopt a transverse lie. The safest form of delivery for these babies would probably be by cesarean section.

afraid to ask your doctor for a mild sedative. Try to avoid sleeping on your back as this may cause faintness. If you are working, you should expect to give up at least twelve weeks before the expected date of delivery.

Other problems are associated with multiple pregnancies. Pre-eclampsia (see p. 70) is one, anemia is another (see p. 52) and the bigger placental area in a twin pregnancy may mean the chance of a placenta previa (see above). The onset of premature labor is a risk that is recognized and steps will be taken to avoid it.

Premature labor is a direct result of the over-distension of the uterus.

PRENATAL CARE FOR THE TWIN MOTHER

Bearing these points in mind it makes sense to take special care of you prenatally to minimize your discomfort and make sure the pregnancy continues for as long as possible.

Once twins (or more) have been diagnosed, you will be advised to have all your prenatal check-ups at the hospital and your progress will be closely monitored by the senior members of the obstetric team. If you are found to be anemic, you will be given iron pills to correct this, and it is important to pay particular attention to maintaining a good balanced diet.

Your blood pressure will be closely monitored, and you will be advised to take extra rest. A twin pregnancy is very tiring and you will probably need to give up work earlier than most pregnant women. Indeed some obstetricians will recommend that you are admitted to hospital for a period of rest between, say, 26 and 32 weeks.

The babies' growth will be maintained by regular ultrasound scanning. Twin babies tend to be individually smaller and one may be much smaller than the other, so that it is valuable to watch their growth in the uterus. The babies commonly lie in one of the positions illustrated, which can make a difference to the way labor is managed, and many twins are eventually delivered by cesarean section. Twin births are discussed in Chapter 7, but need not necessarily be problematic.

THE PHYSICALLY HANDICAPPED MOTHER

We see many more handicapped mothers nowadays in the prenatal clinic. There are probably two reasons for this. One is that advances in medical care are such that women, born disabled, are helped to lead a much more complete life including in many instances marriage and child bearing. The other is that road accidents are increasing, leading to 'acquired' handicap and these women may, with care, go on to bear children.

There are many types of handicap, from deafness or blindness which may cause a problem of adjustment when caring for the newborn baby, to major handicaps such as paraplegia.

PARAPLEGIA (PARALYSIS)

This severe disability may have been present since birth or it may have been acquired through trauma – an automobile accident for example. It is of the utmost importance that you get thorough pre-pregnancy counseling if you are in this position, so that together, the doctor, you and your partner can map out a picture of how things will be during pregnancy and particularly how you are going to cope after the birth of the baby.

Associated medical conditions such as kidney problems have to be assessed, as well as how much extra nursing care you yourself require as a result of your disability (such as impaired bowel and bladder control). Then everyone must consider the help you will have with the new baby from your family, friends, social services or voluntary organizations.

If you have become paraplegic as a result of an automobile accident it is obviously necessary to check the size and shape of your pelvis in case it was significantly damaged at the time of the accident. There is no reason why such a paraplegic mother should not have a vaginal delivery but if any pelvic abnormality exists then cesarean section will be necessary. In any case help with forceps is likely to be required in the second stage of labor since you will not have the power to push and deliver the baby yourself (see p. 92).

Help with the care of the baby afterwards is essential but paraplegic mothers are quick to adapt, and devise methods to overcome their disability.

MULTIPLE SCLEROSIS

The cause of this neurological disease is still unknown. Cruelly, it tends to manifest itself in women in their late twenties or early thirties, when they may already have started a family, or are just starting to plan for it. In its more advanced stages multiple sclerosis causes paraplegia, so careful counseling before pregnancy is essential. There is some evidence, for example, that there is an hereditary element in the disease and this fact alone may deter many such couples from contemplating pregnancy. However, many MS sufferers have fairly mild symptoms and feel able to contemplate childbirth for the sake of their partners', and their own, fulfillment.

Pregnancy seems to have no effect on the long term outlook for the patient with multiple sclerosis but unfortunately the patient who is already pregnant before the disease reveals itself, seems to develop a greater degree of disability.

Pregnancy and labor may be normal but again delivery may have to be by forceps.

PELVIC DEFORMITIES

These may result from accident or disease or to be present from birth. Basically the degree of deformity must be assessed by x-ray so that a decision can be made as to whether a vaginal delivery is possible or whether a cesarean section will be required. If there is any real doubt then, for the safety of the baby, the latter course will be chosen.

EXISTING MEDICAL PROBLEMS

If you already suffer from an existing medical condition, such as heart disease or diabetes, it does not necessarily mean you should not have a baby. However, it is clear that your pregnancy is not going to be as straightforward as that of someone who doesn't suffer from any of these conditions, and you can expect to have more medical monitoring and more intervention during your delivery for the safety and health of yourself and your baby.

HEART DISEASE

We do not see severe heart disease nearly so often nowadays. This is because congenital (developmental) heart conditions are detected early in life and with the advanced techniques of cardiac surgery now available, are corrected well before childbearing age. Rheumatic heart disease is also much less common nowadays.

However, women do still suffer from heart disease, and also have babies. Occasionally, the problem may not be discovered until the woman is pregnant, so it is essential that the doctor examining a pregnant woman listens carefully to her heart. If an abnormality is discovered then the opinion of a heart specialist is sought; in fact it is crucial to the success of the care of a pregnant woman with a heart problem that her case is shared between her obstetrician and her cardiologist.

During pregnancy, adequate rest is essential, and may involve a stay in the maternity ward for observation at any time during pregnancy, but especially in later pregnancy – if the condition is severe enough to warrant it. It is important, of course, to avoid anemia and to treat any infections promptly. If dental treatment is required it must be covered by antibiotics.

DIABETES MELLITUS

Although pregnancy worsens a diabetic's condition and is equally dangerous for mother and baby, this somewhat alarming statement does not mean that a diabetic woman should not undertake a pregnancy.

What it does mean, however, is that the care of a diabetic pregnant woman must be in the hands of experts – preferably as mentioned for the cardiac mother, the combined team of specialist, in this case a diabetologist, and obstetrician – and that the control of her diabetes must be as strict as possible, sometimes needing a special pump for insulin.

DIAGNOSIS

If you are already diabetic when you become pregnant, you will be well aware of the management of your own condition. Occasionally however pregnancy induces a condition known as gestational diabetes, in which the ability of the body to handle sugar becomes abnormal only during a pregnancy. There are particular signs which may point to this possibility, such as previous large babies (over 9 pounds); an unexplained still-birth; a family history of diabetes; obesity; and repeated sugar in the urine during pregnancy.

One of the changes that takes place in the function of the body during pregnancy allows the kidneys to spill sugar over into the urine. But when this occurs repeatedly in a pregnancy, further investigation must be carried out. This consists of a glucose tolerance test. First of all you will have a sample of blood taken when you have had nothing to eat for a certain length of time, and your blood sugar level will be measured. You then drink 2 ounces of glucose in solution and further blood sugars are measured half hourly for the next 2½ hours. A normal glucose tolerance 'curve' is shown at the top of the graph on this page; a diabetic one in the center and one which suggests gestational (pregnancy only) diabetes at the bottom.

PROBLEMS OF DIABETES IN PREGNANCY

During pregnancy, it is important that you control the diabetes very strictly because pregnancy does make it worse, bringing with it other complications. Before diabetes was properly understood and controlled, the picture for diabetic mothers and their babies was a rather depressing one. They were likely to suffer distension from excessive amniotic fluid and pre-eclampsia (with high blood pressure) was often associated with it. The diabetic mother was also more prone to various infections. Diabetes could cause the baby to grow very large in the uterus, with consequent difficulty in labor and with delivery.

Diabetes also brought with it an increased chance of abnormalities in the baby, and the likelihood of premature labor was increased. If the baby was very large he or she might suffer the trauma of a

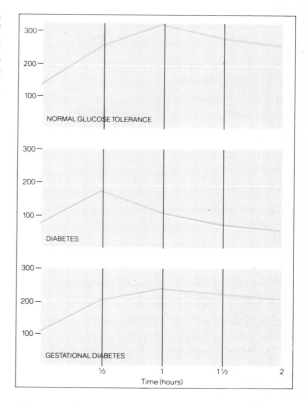

Glucose tolerance curves. **Top:** *In a normal pregnant woman.* **Center:** *In a previously diagnosed diabetic.* **Above:** *In a woman with gestational diabetes (diabetes of pregnancy).*

difficult delivery. There was also a higher risk of stillbirth if the mother's diabetes was not controlled, and in the neonatal period, babies of diabetic mothers often suffered respiratory difficulties, low blood sugar, and infections. But these risks are minimized nowadays by strict control of the diabetes. With increasing understanding of the implications of diabetes on the pregnancy – and vice versa – and increased expertise in the control of diabetes the outlook for the diabetic mother and her baby is nowadays greatly improved and almost all diabetic women can plan two or three pregnancies confidently provided they are prepared to cooperate with the strict medical supervision which is required for the sake of mother and baby.

THE MOTHER WITH DIABETES

If your diabetes is already being treated, your obstetrician will work closely with your physician throughout pregnancy. Your diet will be controlled at 1500-2400 calories per day with 6-8 ounces of carbohydrate and 4 ounces of protein.

If you were using oral agents for the treatment of your diabetes this will be changed to insulin by injection so as to maintain stricter control over blood sugar levels, and you may be admitted to hospital as often as necessary to supervise that control. However, you may be taught to monitor your own blood sugar at home, especially if the diabetes has only appeared in pregnancy.

In many centers you can phone the hospital diabetic unit and discuss these results directly to assess any alteration of insulin requirements. If diabetes is only seen as a potential threat, only your diet need be controlled, but your pregnancy will be strictly monitored.

Nowadays there should be no need for intervention in a normal vaginal delivery unless there are complicating features such as hypertension or fetal distress, when a cesarean section would be carried out. Needless to say, great care in the control of blood sugars during labor, delivery and postpartum must be maintained.

HYPERTENSION AND PRE-ECLAMPSIA

First of all a definition. The left side of the heart (the left ventricle) pumps blood through the arteries and smaller vessels of the circulation and the blood returns to the right side of the heart via the veins. There is a higher 'head' of pressure stemming from the left ventricle than from the right, which means that the flow of blood will be maintained. This is known as the arterial blood pressure or simply the blood pressure, and it varies between 120 and 80mm mercury above atmospheric pressure.

At the beginning of pregnancy the level measured represents your non-pregnant level. This is one reason why it is important to be seen by a doctor as early as possible. However, in the middle third of pregnancy (the second trimester) the blood pressure drops slightly.

High blood pressure or hypertension (which has *nothing* to do with nervousness) can be a problem in pregnancy and can have all the potential for disaster. But if it is recognized and managed with skill and care, both mother and baby should emerge from the pregnancy fit and well.

To simplify what is quite a difficult and complex subject, women suffering from hypertension in pregnancy can be considered in two groups. In the first group, there is pre-existing hypertension, that is a significantly high level of blood pressure (more than 140/90) known to be present before pregnancy begins or, as so often happens, discovered early in pregnancy (before 20 weeks). This is one of the reasons why it is so important for a mother to start prenatal check-ups early in pregnancy, for the blood pressure reading recorded at the first visit represents her non-pregnant level of blood pressure (see p. 21).

The second group suffers from a condition peculiar to pregnancy called pre-eclampsia (also known as pregnancy-induced hypertension). No one yet knows the cause of this condition, which is characterized typically by a rise in blood pressure, swelling of hands and legs (edema), and (in the more severe forms) protein in the urine.

CAUSES OF HYPERTENSION

There may be no known cause for pre-existing hypertension (in this case called essential hypertension), or the raised blood pressure may be due to other conditions such as kidney diseases, diabetes or other rarer conditions.

Although, as has already been mentioned, the cause of pre-eclampsia is unknown, there are several associated background factors which make it easier to identify the woman at risk. These include a first pregnancy or a pregnancy following one which was severely affected; women with a family history of hypertension especially involving pregnancies; women who are hypertensive before pregnancy (referred to as 'superimposed pre-eclampsia'); women with diabetes or kidney diseases; multiple pregnancies; and poor socio-economic backgrounds. It is interesting to note that for some reason the incidence of pre-eclampsia in women who smoke is lower, but for smokers who do develop the condition, the outlook for the baby is not at all hopeful.

PROBLEMS WITH HYPERTENSION AND PRE-ECLAMPSIA

There is no doubt that if hypertension is at all marked and certainly if there is pre-eclampsia, a pregnancy does not fare so well. The mother may be at risk of kidney problems and in severe uncontrolled cases, there is the chance of eclampsia developing (see later).

So far as the baby is concerned, the environment within the uterus in either of these conditions is not at all favorable. The placenta functions less well and the baby grows more slowly than one would expect for the dates, leading to a 'small for dates' or 'growth retarded' baby (see p. 72). In severe cases, abruption of the placenta may occur with associated heavy bleeding (see p. 64) and death of the baby is an increased risk.

Essential or pre-existing hypertension may get worse as pregnancy progresses. If you are already having treatment for the condition, the dosage of the drug used may need to be increased, or you may need to start treatment for the first time in pregnancy. So far as pre-eclampsia is concerned, left alone the condition almost always deteriorates as pregnancy progresses.

TREATING HYPERTENSION AND PRE-ECLAMPSIA

It is obvious that hypertension in pregnancy is taken very seriously indeed. The problem is that there are no symptoms to help you realize that an important situation has arisen. This is especially true of pre-eclampsia where you may have known nothing of hypertension previously, and feel perfectly well. It is therefore often difficult to accept the restrictions suddenly placed on you by the doctors – the need for extra rest, for example, and even the need to come into hospital for closer observation of your blood pressure.

However it is important to take your midwife or doctor seriously if you are informed that your blood pressure has risen to an unacceptably high level, compared to your pre-pregnancy level. In point of fact, pre-existing hypertension of a mild degree may not require any treatment. The only important feature of management is to keep a very close eye on you, so you will be seen more frequently for prenatal checks and may be admitted to hospital, if necessary, to monitor for either deterioration of the blood pressure or for the appearance of pre-eclampsia.

More severe degrees of hypertension however, will require drug therapy. The drugs will be chosen for their safety in pregnancy and again in consultation with a physician specializing in this area. Close monitoring will be of great importance. The aim of your care if suffering from hypertension will be to keep your blood pressure at acceptable levels, compatible with your safety and the healthy growth of the baby. This will be done until the baby is mature enough to be born – ideally at term, but often at 36 to 38 weeks.

There is no cure for pre-eclampsia, either, except to deliver the baby, so the aim is to control your blood pressure, monitor fetal well-being and to step in and deliver the baby preferably when he is mature and conditions are favorable for induction of labor (at around 38 weeks).

If the environment for the baby within the uterus is clearly no longer ideal (shown by worsening blood pressure levels, increasing protein in the urine, and evidence of fetal distress shown on a heart-rate tracing), the situation calls for prompt action. It may arise well before term, sometimes as early as 26 to 28 weeks, and certainly before 38 weeks, so cesarean section may be necessary and the baby may need special care.

ECLAMPSIA

Eclampsia is also associated with high blood pressure and is a very serious condition which only affects pregnant women. It can occur prenatally, as early as 26 to 28 weeks in rare cases, and it also occurs during labor or in the immediate postpartum period (up to 48 hours after the birth). Eclampsia is typified by convulsive seizures which occasionally happen out of the blue, but mostly in women already suffering from pre-eclampsia (see p. 70). Although much rarer than pre-eclampsia, eclampsia poses a very high risk for the mother, and equally for the baby if it occurs before the birth.

Eclamptic fits are like the convulsive fits of epilepsy and are handled in the same way. First of all the fit is treated. The airways are cleared to ensure that the patient has a good supply of oxygen, then a sedative such as diazepam (Valium) is given intravenously to control the convulsions, as well as a hypotensive drug to lower the blood pressure.

During eclampsia the mother runs the risk of kidney failure, brain hemorrhage and an associated condition called 'disseminated vascular coagulation' (DIC). In this the blood fails to clot and the risk of uncontrollable hemorrhage develops, unless the situation is recognized and treated.

If eclampsia occurs during labor, the birth is speeded up, and unless labor is already far advanced an emergency cesarean section will be required. Both mother and baby will need intensive care for some days after the event.

EPILEPSY

Epilepsy is a common condition and many women who are epileptics have children. Pregnancy may cause an increase in the number of seizures but this is by no means always the case and often epileptic women remain in the same state of control as before pregnancy.

Provided that control of seizures is good, pregnancy does not present many problems. However, severe, repeated seizures, known as 'status epilepticus', can be disastrous for both mother and baby unless treated promptly and adequately.

Some drugs used to control epilepsy, such as Phenytroin or Dilantin, are thought to cause developmental abnormalities in the fetus so these are best avoided. But others – such as carbamazepine – appear to be safe for use in pregnancy.

Frequent monitoring of the drugs used is essential in order to maintain just enough in the blood to control seizures. The levels seem to fall more quickly in pregnancy so that adjustment of dosage may be required from time to time.

RHESUS ISO-IMMUNIZATION

The problem of rhesus (Rh) iso-immunization is described and its effect on the baby discussed on pages 22 and 122. The condition is now rare, thanks to the 'Anti-D' injection which can be given to rhesus negative mothers, but even so, occasional cases do slip through. If a mother is found to have antibodies present in her bloodstream which would in effect be attacking her baby's red blood cells, then careful supervision of her pregnancy preferably in a specialized rhesus clinic is essential if her baby is not to be severely affected.

If you are found to have antibodies, a careful history is taken regarding previous pregnancies, miscarriages and so on, and both yours and your partner's blood is checked. After this, the level of antibodies in your blood is measured every month or more often if necessary.

It may be necessary to carry out repeated amniocentesis to sample the amniotic fluid and measure its bilirubin content. The amount of this substance indicates the rate at which fetal red blood cells are being broken down, and therefore the degree to which a baby is affected. A severely affected fetus may be given an intrauterine transfusion of a small amount of rhesus negative blood direct into the abdominal cavity under ultrasound control to allow the fetus to remain in the uterus until mature enough to be born. Even so, early induction of labor – or even delivery by cesarean section – may be necessary, and the affected baby will require special neonatal care (see p. 122).

THROMBO-EMBOLISM

The risk of deep vein thrombosis (clotting) is something of which the public is well aware because of the publicized connection with the contraceptive pill. It usually occurs in the leg, and may be associated with pain. It is equally well known that a piece of clot may occasionally break off and travel to the lung, with potentially fatal results. Such an event is tragic in any age group, but in a young mother is profoundly so. There are factors which predispose some women to this problem. The older mother is at greater risk, as is one who has had several children. Obesity is a factor, and so is long confinement to bed, for instance, following surgery. Knowing this, doctors are on the look-out for 'at risk' women and take precautions – early mobilization after surgery, special 'pressure' stockings to wear in bed, dietary restriction to reduce weight and so on.

The treatment for deep vein thrombosis is with anti-coagulant drugs which act to 'thin' the blood. It is a fairly rare occurrence in pregnancy but when it happens anti-coagulant pills would have to be replaced by injections of a drug called heparin; mothers can be taught to administer this to themselves. Treatment would almost certainly have to be continued for a minimum of six weeks after delivery.

Pulmonary embolus – that is, when a piece of clot lodges in the lung – may follow a deep vein thrombosis or may occur out of the blue. It causes chest pain, breathlessness and a little blood may be coughed up. Confirmation of the diagnosis is made on x-ray or by a lung scan, and the treatment – which is urgent – is with anti-coagulants.

THYROID DISEASE

Occasionally a woman who is already on treatment for an over-active thyroid gland becomes pregnant. Treatment must be continued during pregnancy and careful supervision and regulation of these drugs maintained throughout. Sometimes the problem is an underactive thyroid and the same principle of treatment applies.

Breastfeeding may or may not be allowed depending on the drugs being used and in all cases the baby must be tested for over or under-activity of his thyroid.

PROBLEMS OF FETAL GROWTH

Fetal growth can cause concern during pregnancy, either because the fetus is too small or too big. Of course there is a wide range of normal birth weights (see graph opposite), but babies born below the 10th percentile are classified as small for gestational age (small for dates) and above the 90th percentile, large for dates.

Small babies may be premature (born early but an appropriate weight for their period of gestation) or simply small (but mature) or small for their dates – sometimes called 'growth retarded'. This last situation has been increasingly recognized in recent years and requires expert care if the outcome of pregnancy is to be successful.

CAUSES OF GROWTH RETARDATION

The actual cause is obscure but several background factors are recognized. One of the most important is poor placental function – and this happens where high blood pressure, pre-eclampsia, kidney disease or diabetes exist in the mother. It may occur following partial placental abruption and possibly in prolonged pregnancy (beyond 42 weeks).

Twins and higher multiples are often smaller than

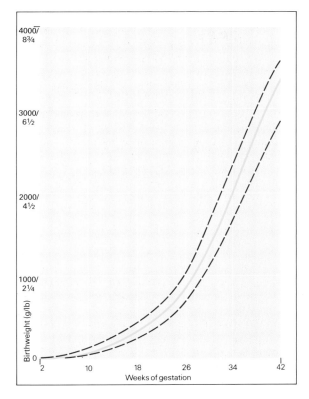

Birthweight (g/lb)

4000/
8¾

3000/
6½

2000/
4½

1000/
2¼

0

2   10   18   26   34   42

Weeks of gestation

The range of normal fetal birth weights according to the weeks of gestation. Weights below the lower centile may indicate a 'small for dates' baby.

average – this is not surprising since they have less room and the mother may have fewer resources, but occasionally one baby may be considerably smaller than the others.

Another rare cause may be due to infection, for example by rubella (German measles), and chromosome abnormalities may be associated with small-for-dates babies. Poor maternal nutrition is a contributing factor. but more importantly, smoking has a highly significant relationship to the incidence of growth retardation in pregnancy. It has been proved conclusively that mothers who smoke during pregnancy have smaller babies than those who do not. Smoking constricts the blood vessels and restricts the passage of blood carrying oxygen and nutrients to the baby.

DISCOVERING GROWTH RETARDATION

Suspicions are aroused that the baby may not be growing well when the uterus appears to be small for the dates. Measuring from the pubic bone (pubis symphysis) to the top of the uterus (the fundus) gives a fair estimate of the duration

of pregnancy. If the gestational age has been confirmed by early ultrasound scan and a discrepancy develops between it and the symphysis-fundal measurement, then the doctor will suspect growth retardation.

Repeated scanning (every two weeks) will show a discrepancy between the measurement of the head (nature seems to watch over the brain, and the head measurement grows), and the circumference of the abdomen (which grows poorly). Meanwhile, other simple clinical features become apparent. The mother's weight, for instance, remains static or even drops; the measurement of her girth likewise.

Growth retardation may arise in the absence of other complications but not infrequently a mother may have high blood pressure, which would alert the doctor to the possibility of a growth retarded baby. Dealing with the problem in this situation can be difficult, as a decision has to be made as to when the environment within the uterus is actually *less* favorable to the baby than the environment in a special care unit would be. The mother and baby have to be monitored by frequent visits (weekly or even more often) to the obstetrician, for routine weighing, examination and clinical assessment of the growth of the baby, and by frequent scanning.

Many doctors would want to monitor the baby's health daily or two or three times a week by repeated cardiograms – tracings of the baby's heart beat pattern, or 'biophysical profiles'. This is a bit like phoning in to the fetus to ask how he is, and getting a beat-by-beat reply!

The mother would also be monitored by other tests which indicate how well the placenta is functioning. This is done by measuring levels of the hormone estriol, for example, in the mother's blood or urine. These tests tend not to be as useful nowadays in the face of our ability to 'phone in' and get an immediate answer from the baby, but are still used by some doctors as a method of 'tracking' the function of the placenta.

When it is obvious that the baby has, in a sense, outgrown his placenta – or has simply stopped growing – then delivery is the only answer. Induction of labor may be the choice under favorable circumstances, especially if the mother has had a previous baby, the cervix is ripe, and there is no immediate fetal distress. But if the baby seems to be seriously affected, then cesarean section will be chosen as the safest method of delivery.

The care of a mother carrying a baby which is growth retarded must be intensive, so it is often sensible and necessary that care is provided within the hospital, so that moment by moment supervision can be offered. Resting can help to increase oxygen

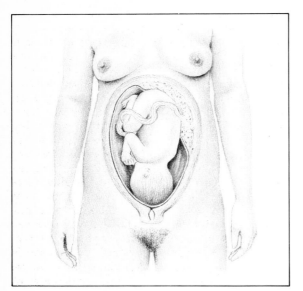

The normal position for a baby at term. The lie is vertical, the presentation is cephalic (head down) with occiput anterior (the baby facing the mother's back).

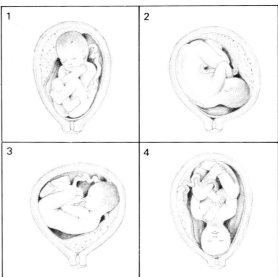

Some abnormal positions which may lead to difficulty at the delivery. 1 Breech presentation 2 Oblique lie 3 Transverse lie due to placenta previa 4 Occiput posterior (face to pubis).

flow to the baby. In other cases it will be sufficient to see the mother twice a week, say, in the obstetric clinic and to attach her to the electronic fetal monitor at those times to assess directly the well-being of the baby.

THE LARGE-FOR-DATES BABY

The opposite problem is the 'large for dates' baby. As we have seen this means that the birth weight exceeds the 90th percentile for the gestational age. The background to such a situation may simply be inheritance – the parents may both be big. It has already been mentioned that diabetes causes larger-than-average babies, but it is as well to remember that the 'dates' may be wrong – women are quite often unsure of the date of their last menstrual period – and that the size of the baby may seem big but is actually appropriate for the true dates.

The management of a diabetic mother's pregnancy has already been described. In other situations if the baby seems unduly large (and this is confirmed on ultrasound scan) then cesarean section may have to be carried out or, if there is a possibility of a vaginal delivery, a trial of labor will be conducted. This means that the doctor will allow labor to proceed to see if the baby can be delivered. The progress of labor is watched very carefully, and the well-being of both mother and baby are monitored. If there seems to be a difficulty, the doctor

can then be ready to intervene with cesarean section, if necessary.

ABNORMAL LIE

By about 36 weeks the lie of the baby has become stabilized within the uterus and is normally vertical (straight up and down) most commonly with the head presenting. In certain abnormal circumstances the position of the baby in relation to the uterus may be oblique, or even directly transverse. If a baby's lie is oblique on one examination, then changes on a subsequent examination to transverse, it is described as an 'unstable lie'.

CAUSES OF ABNORMAL LIE

There are several causes for unstable, oblique or transverse lies. A uterus which has borne several babies becomes 'floppy', loses tone and the maintenance of a vertical lie is more difficult. Excess amniotic fluid may allow the baby to 'float around' even to a late stage in pregnancy. This may be caused by such conditions as diabetes, rhesus iso-immunization, or some abnormality of the baby.

It is quite common for at least one of the babies in a multiple pregnancy to lie abnormally, because of space problems in the uterus. Similarly a low lying placenta 'blocks' the way for the baby to take up his normal vertical lie, while a pelvic brim of small size has the same effect of 'blocking' the baby. Finally, and rarely, abnormalities of the shape of the uterus may restrict the way the baby lies.

DIAGNOSIS

The midwife or doctor will discover an abnormal lie on palpating the abdomen. If necessary it will be confirmed by ultrasound scan or x-ray. The reason will be looked for at the same time, scanning to locate the placenta, or x-ray to measure the pelvis, and so on. One of the fundamental points must be to re-check the dates and the maturity of the baby – after all, although a 36 week baby may be expected to have stabilized the lie, a 32 week one may not have, so the doctor will want to make sure that he or she is not dealing with 'wrong dates'.

DEALING WITH AN ABNORMAL LIE

If an oblique or transverse lie is found between 32 and 35 weeks, then it can be left but you will be seen frequently to monitor the baby's position. After 36 weeks, the cause must be looked for as above.

By 38 weeks, you would be safer in hospital in case the membranes should rupture. This is more likely in this situation, as neither the head nor the breech are positioned to 'plug' the lower segment. As a result the membranes bulge against the internal os of the cervix and may rupture early, allowing the cord or an arm to prolapse (protrude).

If this happens, an emergency cesarean section may be required to rescue the baby.

If labor begins and the lie can be converted into a vertical one and maintained there by enhancing the contractions with an intravenous infusion of Pitocin (see p. 86), then a vaginal delivery may be possible, but obviously a close watch has to be maintained to ensure that the lie does not revert to oblique or even transverse.

THE MATERNITY WARD

In the previous pages, the possibility of hospitalization during a difficult pregnancy has frequently been mentioned. There are of course many reasons for admission to the maternity ward. Some of these have already been mentioned, such as hypertension and pre-eclampsia, or where the baby is growing poorly – 'light for dates'. Simple surgical procedures, like inserting a cerclage for cervical incompetence, are dealt with through the maternity ward, and where there has been a previous history of premature labor, a mother may be admitted to hospital for rest and observation round about the time of the previous onset of premature labor.

Obstetric hemorrhage, for whatever reason, may require a stay in hospital, and women suffering from diabetes or some cases of rhesus iso-immunization may be hospitalized. An acute urinary tract infection may need treatment in hospital, as indeed may many other abnormal situations in the pregnancy.

Fundamentally admission to the maternity ward will be for observation of both mother and baby more frequently and more closely than is possible in a single, even weekly, visit to the obstetrician. It is often said that a mother is being admitted 'for rest'. It must be admitted that the amount of rest you can obtain in a busy maternity ward which in many units is shared with postpartum mothers – and their babies! – is somewhat limited, although for a tired mother with other children at home it does offer rest and care, especially if you can have your own room. And rest is particularly important if your baby is thought to be growth retarded. But in the main the reason for admission is for intensive monitoring of both mother and baby.

ON THE WARD

What can you expect in the maternity ward? First, and perhaps most important of all, visiting times are usually very generous. There are usually periods of rest when visitors are not admitted, but otherwise partners, parents and families are allowed to come and go fairly freely.

Rarely, it could be that you may have to face admission to hospital for an extended period of time – up to six or eight weeks for example. If you are admitted for a period of rest however, if both yours and your baby's condition seem stable, you may be allowed to go home for weekends to break the monotony and boost your morale. It is essential however that your partner or someone else reliable is also at home and able to look after you. On Monday you would return to hospital so that close monitoring of your condition can start again. Some units have established a day ward where mothers suffering from hypertension for example, or with a growth retarded baby, can come and spend the day resting, having their blood pressure taken and the baby's heart monitored at intervals, returning home in the evening.

There is no doubt that where other young children are involved, considerable distress and disruption to a family unit can occur if the mother has to come in to hospital for an extended period. This is where grandparents, family and friends can play such an important supportive role. The hospital's Social Service Department can be alerted too and every help will be given to the mother so she can rest in hospital with some peace of mind.

LABOR AND BIRTH

A moment-by-moment guide for both parents to the
progress of labor and normal birth of your baby

Labor is the name given to the process during which the uterus contracts repeatedly, the cervix opens and is pulled up over the baby's head. The baby and placenta are then expelled through the vagina. Labor is divided into three stages: during the first stage the uterine muscles thin the cervix, then pull it up and open so that the baby's head can pass through. The second stage pushes the baby down the birth canal and out through the vagina, and the third stage consists of the expulsion of the placenta and membranes, often called the afterbirth.

WHAT HAPPENS DURING LABOR

The uterus is a large muscular bag closed at the bottom by the cervix, the ring of muscle which normally dips into the vagina. Throughout your pregnancy the muscle contracts regularly with painless Braxton Hicks contractions (so-called after the doctor who first observed them). As you approach full term you may be able to feel these contractions quite strongly as the uterine wall hardens. They are quite often mistaken for actual labor pains (see later). Braxton Hicks contractions do not usually have an effect on your cervix during the first and second trimesters. As you approach term your cervix will have softened due to the action of progesterone and as labor begins the muscle fibers of the uterus shorten, pulling the cervix up into the lower uterine segment.

THE FIRST STAGE

At first the cervix is simply being thinned (effaced) and during this time the contractions are often not particularly noticeable. In second and subsequent labors, many women are not aware of this process at all and may only realize they are in labor when the cervix is already dilating. Once the cervix is fully effaced it begins to dilate (open) and the uterine contractions become more efficient. The cervix dilates slowly at first, then dilatation becomes quicker and quicker, in response to stronger, longer and more frequent contractions.

The cervix has to dilate to about 4 inches in diameter to allow the baby's head to pass through. You may hear your midwife or doctor refer to your cervix being ½ inch dilated during internal examinations in labor; once it is 1 inch dilated it is referred to as half dilated and the midwife would feel a rim of cervix all round the baby's head. At three-quarters dilated the cervix can only be felt at the front and sides of the baby's head, and the last part of the cervix to be taken up is the front edge. When the cervix is fully dilated labor enters the second stage. The membranes usually rupture by the end of the first stage, if they had not done so before labor really started.

THE SECOND STAGE

While the cervix has been dilating the baby's head comes lower and lower inside your pelvis. During the second stage, the muscular effort is expulsive; in other words it is pushing your baby down through the vagina (the birth canal). The skin inside the vagina is normally folded and crinkly; as the baby's head descends, the vaginal walls stretch and become smooth to allow the baby to pass through. As the baby's head descends it rotates so that it is facing the back as it emerges. It then rotates to allow the shoulders and body to be born.

THE THIRD STAGE

The third stage of labor often passes without mothers really taking much notice. After a pause of five to ten minutes the uterus contracts to expel the placenta and membranes; alternatively you may be given an injection to speed the contraction and the doctor will gently ease the afterbirth out by pulling on the cord. The midwife or doctor will check to make sure that the placenta has come away cleanly.

HOW LABOR STARTS

Labor starts in different ways, but remember that with the first baby labor may take longer than you expect. Most first labors last at least twelve hours

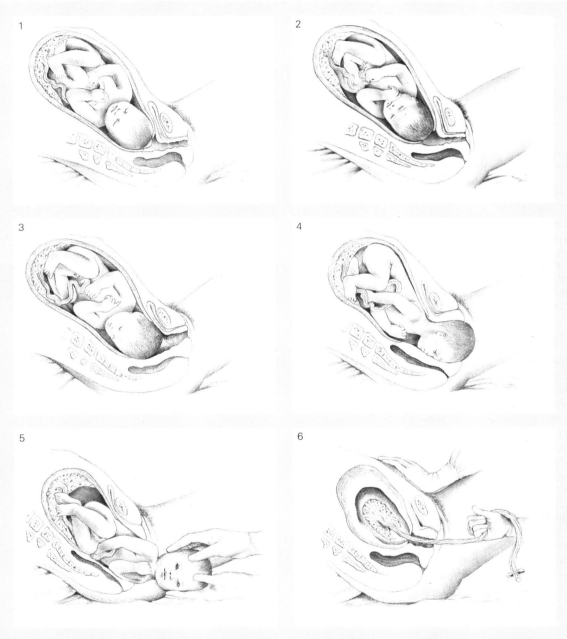

The normal birth

1 *During the first stage of labor, the uterine contractions gradually thin and open the cervix.* 2 *Toward the end of the first stage, the cervix is almost dilated, and the membranes usually have ruptured.* 3 *In the second stage, the cervix is fully dilated and the uterus produces strong, expulsive contractions.* 4 *The baby's head rotates to face the back and presses against the* perineum, *stretching the tissues as it emerges through the vagina. This is known as crowning.* 5 *Once the head has been delivered, the baby rotates again to the side, gently guided by the doctor, to allow the shoulders, then the body, to emerge.* 6 *The third stage is the delivery of the placenta and membranes. The doctor presses one hand on the abdomen to keep the uterus in place, and gently pulls the cord with the other.*

from start to finish and sometimes longer. There are women who have their first babies in an hour or two but they are extremely rare. Women are often surprised by just how long, tedious and painful labor can be.

A couple of days before labor starts, many women experience a bout of diarrhea, and many others have a 'show' as the plug of mucus that has been keeping the cervix closed and protecting the uterus from infection comes away. This plug of mucus is gelatinous in texture and may be slightly blood-stained. It comes away painlessly, often when you go to the toilet. These are signs that labor may be approaching, but they may occur several days before anything concrete happens – or they may not happen at all.

FALSE ALARMS

Some people experience quite strong contractions for a few hours, which then cease, and others think that the strong Braxton Hicks contractions of late pregnancy are in fact the onset of labor. This can be very disappointing after the long weeks and months of pregnancy, and partners and friends may have to find things for the mother to do to keep her mind off it! Stress incontinence (a small gush of urine on sneezing or coughing) can also sometimes lead mothers to think their waters may have broken. The temptation in this situation, especially if you are at full term or even later, is to go to hospital or call the obstetrician or midwife. But it can be very embarrassing to have told your parents and neighbors that you are off to hospital only to come home again after a false alarm.

If this happens to you don't worry too much – it can even happen to pregnant midwives! The nurses in the maternity ward are very sympathetic about false alarms – if you turn up they will probably monitor you for a while to make sure that you really aren't in labor, and maybe suggest you stay overnight if there is a bed. If you are having the baby at home it isn't so bad, as your midwife can come to you to check and reassure you either way.

COPING WITH EARLY FIRST STAGE

When your labor really starts you will have painful contractions of the uterus, which often feel like menstrual pains, or stomach cramps, or back-ache; they come regularly so that you can time them – perhaps every ten or fifteen minutes; and they don't go away. The pains become stronger and stronger and the space between them gets shorter. Some women can actually feel the cervix being pulled open as the baby's head pushes down against it and the uterine muscle pulls it up.

It is much more comfortable during this early stage to be at home. You have all the things around you that you like; you can do what you like – watch television, have light food and drink, arrange for other children to be looked after, call your partner if he is at work, go for a walk in the park or to the local shops. You can check that you have everything packed and ready for the hospital as well.

During this early stage of labor it is sensible to keep your bladder as empty as possible by passing urine every hour and a half or so.

WHEN TO GO TO HOSPITAL OR CALL THE DOCTOR

There will come a time when the uterine contractions are very painful and strong and seem to be coming very quickly – every five minutes or even less. The pain comes in waves, of about 30 seconds duration to start with, rising to 90 seconds or even two minutes toward the end of first stage. At this point you will probably need to stop what you are doing and try to relax through the pain – many women find it helpful to vocalize in some way at the height of the contraction. At this stage however there are still spaces in between the contractions when you can rest and relax.

Now is the time to go to hospital, either by calling an ambulance or by getting your partner or a friend to drive you there. Do not try to drive yourself. Call the obstetrician's office before you leave, so they can collect your chart and notify the hospital for you.

If you are having your baby at home this is also the time to call your midwife and doctor, although many independent midwives like to be informed right at the beginning of labor, even if they do not come to you straight away. You will have to ask your midwife what she prefers.

IF YOUR MEMBRANES RUPTURE

If you experience a sudden gush of warm, clear fluid from your vagina, then it is essential for you to call your obstetrician or go to the hospital directly. This can happen quite unexpectedly, even though you have not felt any contractions at all. It means that the membranes have ruptured and that the amniotic fluid has escaped.

It is important to be examined immediately if this happens. In very rare cases the umbilical cord can drop down (prolapse) in front of the baby's head when the waters gush out. The cord could be pinched by the pressure of the head, depriving the baby of oxygen. Although it is almost impossible for prolapse to happen when the baby's head is deep in

WHAT YOU WILL NEED IN HOSPITAL			
2-3 nightdresses	Front fastening nightdresses in light material are best, particularly if you are going to breastfeed.	Magazines and books	To read in the maternity ward.
Nursing bras	You will need at least two, and possibly one a larger size to support you during the engorged stage two or three days after the birth.	Writing things	To write letters to your family and friends. Some people like to record a 'labor and birth diary'.
Breast pads	One box, to protect your clothes from milk leakage.	A natural sponge	To wipe your face – it is also nice to suck cold water from when your mouth is dry.
Cotton underpants	These can be more comfortable than belts to wear with sanitary pads.	Something to wear during labor	It is more comforting to wear your own dressing gown, nightdress or comfortable maternity dress during labor than a hospital gown. Many people prefer to wear nothing when it comes to giving birth.
Maternity strength sanitary pads	Take at least two packets.	Change for the telephone	There will be pay phones in the hospital so that you can contact your family and friends after the birth. A collect call will probably be accepted however by anxious grandparents!
Towels	Most hospitals expect you to bring your own towels.	A photo or picture	Something to look at during labor – a beautiful scented flower would do as well.
Toilet articles	A sponge bag containing soap, talc and other articles for washing and bathing, plus toothbrush and paste.	A camera	For pictures of baby and parents immediately after the birth.
Pillows and pillowcases	Two or three of your own pillows are more homely than hospital pillows which tend to be covered with polythene and are therefore very hot.	Honey	Many women find spoonfuls of honey nourishing and easy to digest during labor.
A dark-colored face cloth	To have over your face during labor to exclude light.	Sandwiches and a thermos of coffee or tea	For your partner or birth assistant – it can be a long time before he can get to the cafeteria, and anyway he might miss something!
Sweets	To suck during labor; pastilles are nice and comforting and provide a little sugar to keep your blood sugar level up. Mints sometimes help to keep your mouth fresh and help avoid nausea.	Baby clothes	For your baby's use.
Cassette player or radio	To listen to during labor.	Salt	Ordinary cooking salt is soothing and healing in the bath.

the pelvis (known as engaged), it is important to have it checked. Most first babies' heads are engaged before labor starts, but the heads of second and subsequent babies may not engage until you are in labor, so if the waters break a few days early the danger of cord prolapse is greater. The membranes also protect the baby from infection through the vagina, which, though unlikely, could occur if labor has not started after about 48 hours. However, for most women labor will start within 24 hours of their waters breaking.

If the amniotic fluid is green, and it can be as dark as cooked spinach, it means that there is meconium present in it. Meconium is the contents of the fetal bowel, and a baby who is distressed in the uterus may have a bowel movement, passing meconium into the amniotic fluid. This is very serious and you should go to hospital at once, even if your waters have only leaked a little.

If you think your waters are leaking a little when your baby is due, it is worth being checked by your doctor. Often when the waters are just leaking slightly the small hole in your membranes will heal over and the leaking will stop. If your waters leak

In order to assess the progress of your labor when you arrive at the hospital, your labor nurse may ask you where you can feel the pains, how long they last and how frequently they are occurring.

and it is still several weeks before your baby is due, then you should always go to hospital or call your doctor (see p. 61).

WHAT HAPPENS IN HOSPITAL

When you go to hospital you will go straight to the maternity ward, no matter what time of day or night it is. The baby's father is always welcome – nowadays most fathers witness the birth of their babies, and it is often remembered by them as one of the most exciting and moving events of their lives. It is also extremely helpful and supportive for the mother to have her partner or someone else close to her throughout labor, especially in hospital, where a long labor may mean a change of nurse at some stage.

The initial procedures may vary a little from unit to unit, but what follows is typical. Your community or independent midwife will probably follow much the same procedures when she comes to you for a home delivery. In the hospital, a labor nurse will be assigned to you and you will be shown into one of the rooms. Some hospitals allow you to labor and give birth in the same room, others will move you into a special delivery room for second stage.

The nurse will ask you what is happening and why you felt it was time to come (or to call her, if you are at home). She will want to know if the

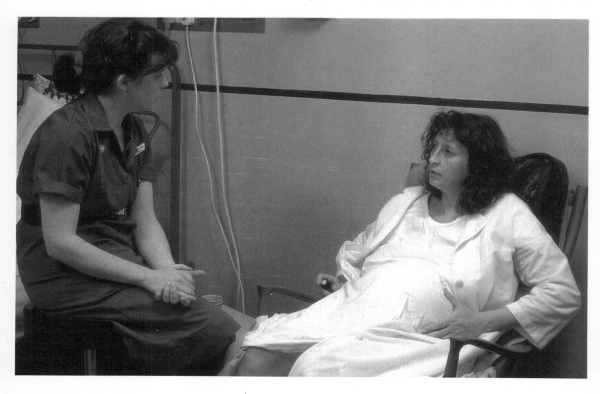

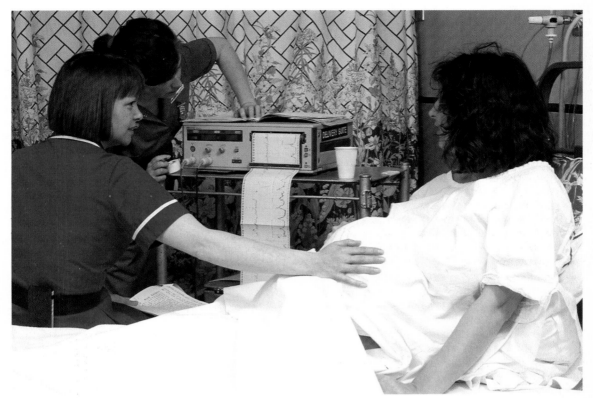

ELECTRONIC MONITORING

Most large maternity units will suggest monitoring you electronically for a period of about twenty minutes in early labor, using a machine called a fetal monitor. Small pads strapped to your abdomen pick up the baby's heart beat by ultrasound and measure the strength of your contractions onto a continuous graph.

waters have broken, how much the baby is moving, how you are feeling in yourself and what each contraction feels like and how long it lasts. She will then check your general health – your temperature, pulse and blood pressure will all be measured. She will ask you to give a specimen of urine for testing. She may time your contractions and will feel your abdomen to check which way the baby is lying and whether the baby's head is engaged. She may also listen to the baby's heart with a little ear trumpet or an electronic stethoscope (doptone).

The doctor will then do an internal examination. She will be feeling for your cervix to work out whether you are in established labor and how far advanced it is. She will also be feeling for the baby's head to see how low down it is lying and how deep inside the pelvis it is. If your baby is breech (see p. 98) she will be checking to see how far down the baby's bottom is and whether any limbs are descending first.

Some units suggest that mothers spend about 20 minutes being electronically monitored, which gives a very accurate picture on a moving graph of the strength and timing of your contractions and their effect on the baby's heart beat. When you have settled in and before contractions have become too painful the midwife may ask you if you would mind doing this. Straightforward monitoring is done by strapping electrodes round your abdomen with belts. This can be quite uncomfortable if you have to lie on the bed so ask if possible to be monitored while sitting in a chair. You will feel more in control of the situation if you can keep upright during labor and the ability to keep moving can be a great help in coping with contractions (see p. 82).

Some modern units may have remote control monitors available which feed the information being picked up by the electrodes into a small apparatus rather like a personal stereo, which you wear on a strap round your neck. This then transmits the data to a larger, fixed unit which prints out the graph. It still entails a certain amount of paraphernalia, but is much easier to cope with as you are able to move around.

If the midwife or obstetrician suggests that you should be monitored throughout your labor, it is

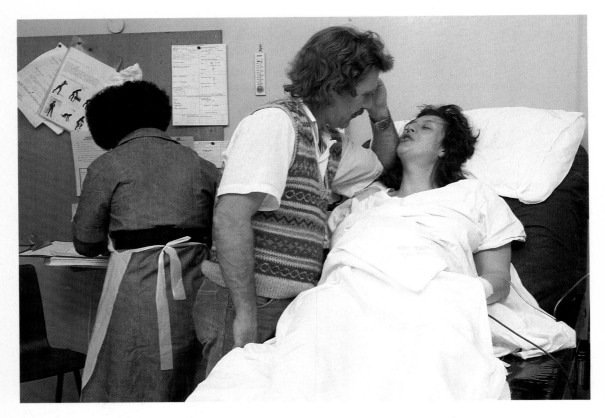

Toward the end of first stage, when the contractions are at their height, you may feel the need for quiet, dim lights, and the reassurance of your partner's presence to support you.

worth asking whether this is really necessary. The technology is very sophisticated and the medical staff are often very interested in the information that is being recorded. However, monitoring is restricting, which makes it difficult for you to cope with the pain of labor in the way that suits you best. Monitoring should not really be necessary throughout labor unless there are signs of fetal distress, your contractions are found to be abnormal (irregular or weak), or if you are having an epidural anesthetic. These situations are discussed later and in the next chapter. Monitoring is sometimes also used if you are being induced or your labor is being accelerated, or if you have an existing medical condition which means that your own and your baby's condition need to be closely watched throughout labor.

If you are at all anxious about electronic monitoring, it might be wise to talk about it during one of your prenatal check-ups toward the end of your pregnancy and have your wishes written into your chart. Alternatively your partner or birth assistant could discuss the situation with the nurse for you in the maternity ward so that you can concentrate on the contractions.

COPING WITH LATER FIRST STAGE

Once monitoring has been completed, it is a good idea to try to keep moving, walking about, leaning on whatever is handy during each contraction. The positions discussed on page 35 may be helpful. Some women find it very comforting to lie in a bath of warm to hot water, others just want to lounge on the bed, or on a bean-bag. Others find kneeling on all fours is comforting, or perhaps leaning on a chair seat supported by cushions. Only you can decide at the time what is right for you, which is why it is so important to have available all the different mats, surfaces and other equipment in the labor ward.

As labor progresses, you will need to pass urine frequently in order to keep your bladder empty so that it does not impede the baby's progress through your pelvis. Drink refreshing and nourishing drinks, and keep yourself fresh with a face cloth or soft sponge wiped over your face from time to time. Cologne can be refreshing too. You can keep your spirits up by thinking that each contraction is one less to be had, each contraction is one nearer to being able to see and hold your baby. Like any other long, muscular effort, such as running a marathon or climbing a mountain, labor is an endurance test; it goes on for a long time and takes a lot of energy and dogged determination. You just need to keep at it and realize that this is really only a short time in the whole of your life, and that millions of women would be envious of you at that moment. It is particularly helpful if your partner can be encouraging you in this way, too.

As the contractions become stronger and closer together – lasting for up to two minutes and with what seems no pause between them, you will become more and more self-absorbed, going deeper and deeper inside yourself. You won't want to chat to the labor nurse or your partner, and you may find you are irritated by interruptions such as the nurse wanting to see what is happening to the baby, because you will just want to concentrate on what is happening inside your body.

Perhaps the best way of coping with the contractions of labor is to relax and surrender to their sensation. They are very painful, but you may be able to cope with the pain if you can just let yourself be carried along with it. The body releases natural analgesics (endorphins) to deaden pain when it is relaxed and allowed to do what it needs to do.

THE TRANSITIONAL PHASE

There comes a point when time becomes irrelevant, the contractions are really strong and close and you try every method to get comfortable: standing, leaning against your partner, lying in the bath, lying on the bed, leaning forward on to a work surface or a chair, wriggling your hips, rocking, crawling, walking about. Nothing seems to help – and at this point many women have a crisis: 'I can't bear it any longer, I've had enough, I want to go home, when will it stop, give me an epidural, anything!'

Labor nurses are very used to seeing women reach this point in labor, which is known as the transitional phase. It means that very soon your cervix will be fully dilated and you will be ready to push your baby out. Your nurse will try to distract you – she may send you off to the lavatory to pass urine, for instance, and just going for a little walk to the lavatory may make you feel more on top of things again.

PAIN RELIEF

The obstetrician will probably examine you internally at this point to see how far your cervix is dilated. If you still have quite a while to go he or she may sugget that now is the time for you to try some analgesia (pain relief) if you haven't done so already. It is up to you – many women can go through labor without any analgesics, but different people have different pain thresholds, and if your labor is very long and you are getting very fed up you may feel that you would like something to help the pain. The important thing is not feel that you are a failure if you accept some pain relief, nor to feel that you are being forced into having it if you don't want it. It is your choice.

MEPERIDINE (DEMEROL)

Meperidine (Demerol) is given as an injection intravenously or into your thigh or buttock. It is a strong analgesic and also seems to help your cervix to relax and dilate more quickly. If you have Demerol you will have to stay on the bed unless the dose is very small as it makes you feel very sleepy. Often doctors mix in another drug, either phenergan or hydroxyzine (Vistaril), to stop you feeling sick. However this also has the side-effect of making you forget your labor, so if you don't want this to happen you might want to suggest that phenergan isn't added to your Demerol injection.

Some women find Demerol very helpful as it gives them a little 'time out' when they can doze between contractions – although the pain isn't completely deadened, the drug seems to help women to detach themselves from it. Other women, however, complain that they just feel drunk and out of control, and that it doesn't really help the pain at all. It is a difficult decision to make, especially if you don't know how it is going to affect you.

Demerol passes across the placenta and can make the baby very sleepy and slow to breathe after the birth. The baby may need to be given an antidote by injection after the birth, which fortunately works very quickly.

NISENTIL

Nisentil (properly alphaprodine hydrochloride) is often used for brief pain relief. Usually it is administered by injection under the skin, and acts rather promptly. However, the duration of action is short; fortunately Nisentil generally has less of a depressant effect on the baby than Demerol.

NITROUS OXIDE AND OXYGEN

The use of nitrous oxide and oxygen gas for pain relief has declined greatly. Occasionally this combination is administered through a face mask from which you breathe it in. After about four deep

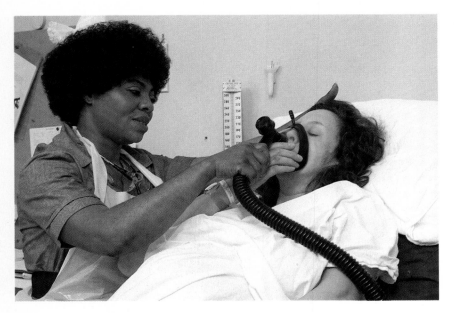

Both pain relief and induction of anesthesia (for cesarean section) can be accomplished by inhalation of oxygen mixed with anesthetic gas. You breathe them in via a mask held over the mouth and nose.

breaths, the analgesic effect begins to take hold. Generally, nitrous oxide is used today in combination with other drugs for induction of general anesthesia, usually before cesarean section.

EPIDURAL ANESTHESIA

An epidural anesthetic (or block) consists of a quantity of local anesthetic injected into the epidural space in your spinal column, which deadens all sensation in your lower trunk. Before you have it you will need to sign a form giving your consent. This is a reasonable request on behalf of the hospital administration, as giving an epidural is a skilled procedure which like all such procedures does involve a tiny element of risk. However if you are asked at any point to sign a permission form for 'any procedures necessary for childbirth' it is worth thinking twice about it. These forms are very questionable and probably have no legal validity at all: you can't sign your rights away for a whole period of time, each procedure should be negotiated separately. If you are faced with one of these forms you can either sign it and realize that it is not valid, or not sign it at all.

To administer the anesthetic, a very fine tube (catheter) is passed through a needle into the epidural space around the spinal cord. The needle is then removed. The anesthetic drug is injected through the catheter, and all subsequent 'top-up' injections are given down the plastic tube which is secured to your back with adhesive tape. You will be asked by the anesthesiologist to curl into a tight ball so that your chin is right down on your chest –

this position separates the bones (vertebrae) of your spine. The anesthesiologist will then numb the skin of your back with an injection of local anesthetic before inserting the needle and catheter carefully between the third and fourth lumbar vertebrae.

One dose lasts about two hours and it can be topped up as labor progresses. The catheter is inserted in the lumbar region just above the point where the nerves connected to the uterus enter the spinal cord, anesthetizing you below that point, but you remain awake and alert throughout labor and the birth of your baby, and usually require no other form of pain relief.

If you have an epidural you will need to have an intravenous tube put into your arm. This introduces glucose water and salt to keep you fresh. Your baby's heart will also need to be monitored continuously with the electronic fetal monitor, and as there is sometimes a tendency for a woman's blood pressure to drop during an epidural this will be monitored regularly as well.

Obviously the use of all this equipment is going to mean that you will be confined to the bed for most of your labor, which can be very boring. However, chances are that having an epidural is something you will have considered carefully before labor, so you can be prepared for your time confined to the bed. Occasionally epidurals don't work very well, or only partly anesthetize you, which can be very trying. There is also a higher incidence of forceps deliveries associated with epidurals because the anesthetic has a very relaxing effect on your pelvic floor which can mean that the baby's head does not rotate into a good position for birth.

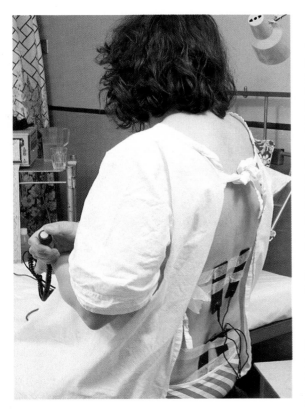

Transcutaneous nerve stimulation (TNS) is a relatively new form of pain relief during labor. A hand-operated stimulator activates the nerves that lead to the uterus to produce natural pain-relieving substances called endorphins.

TRANSCUTANEOUS NERVE STIMULATION (TNS)

TNS is an analgesic technique that is used in the treatment of acute or chronic pain, and which is now being introduced during labor. It is produced by a small battery-powered electronic stimulator. Four electrodes (rubber pads) are taped to your back over the nerve roots which supply the uterus. The tingly, throbbing 'pins and needles' sensation can be very soothing during a contraction and has the effect of blocking some of the pain messages going to your brain. It also stimulates your body to produce some of its own pain-relieving chemicals – endorphins. TNS can be very helpful if you have back pain in labor – if your pain is in the front, massaging your abdomen at the same time can be very soothing.

Many women like this form of pain relief if it is available; it doesn't restrict you at all, and you remain in charge of it at all times.

SIMPLE AIDS TO PAIN RELIEF

If you think about how you usually cope with pain you will find that you already know quite a lot about analgesia. Some people like to curl up in a ball and let the pain flow over them. Others like to massage the hurting part, either with very firm strokes on your back, or smooth and gentle, almost stroking movements, over your abdomen. Deep massage may be helpful for back pain; your partner could try kneading your back with both fists. Some women feel associated pain in their thighs and find it helpful to have them massaged deeply.

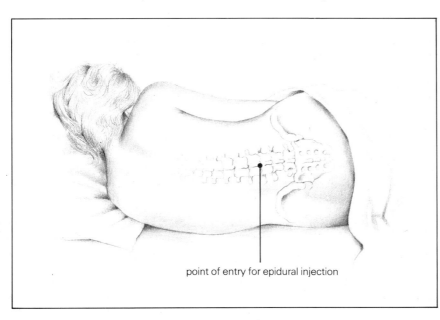

point of entry for epidural injection

The epidural anesthetic is injected into the epidural space around the spinal column through a small gap between the third and fourth lumbar vertebrae (back bones). When the catheter is inserted the mother curls up on her side with her knees bent to widen the gap between the vertebrae as much as possible. An epidural anesthetic completely numbs the uterus, lower back and pelvic floor for about two hours per injection.

Heat and cold help pain too – a hot water bottle or an ice pack pressed against the part that hurts, both bring relief in their different ways. Baths have already been mentioned – some women stay in the bath for six or seven hours, just having the water filled up now and then, and women have even given birth in the bath.

Many women like to walk around or lean against a piece of furniture while rotating their hips or rocking gently from side to side. This can also help to rotate the baby into an advantageous position. It is soothing too, if everyone is silent and the room is darkened, or if you lay a dark face cloth over your face for a while.

FATHERS DURING LABOR

Some men become quite distressed when they see their partners in pain, especially if like many women, you decide you need to vocalize during contractions. It is very good to hear a noise when you are in strong labor, even if it is you who has to provide it. If you feel relaxed and at ease with the nurse you will feel less inhibited about making a noise, and partners need to be warned about this tendency to grumble, moan and groan, so that they realize what a tremendous help it can be to a woman.

However fathers can also play a very supportive role in helping with massage, holding and comforting their partners, giving drinks and wiping brows. A father can also discuss medical procedures with the nurse or doctor when they are suggested, especially if it is something he knows may worry you.

MEDICAL INTERVENTION DURING LABOR

Throughout the first stage your midwife will be doing regular checks on your health and the condition of the baby in the uterus. In hospital an obstetrician will probably come in to see you from time to time and to ask the nurse how things are progressing. He will almost certainly examine you himself, especially if an internal examination is required, and it is he who will arrange for pain relief, such as an epidural, if you want it.

Every now and then the midwife will take your pulse, your blood pressure and occasionally your temperature. She will listen to the baby's heart during and between contractions with a fetal stethoscope or a portable ultrasound, or may ask if you would mind being monitored by the electronic fetal monitor again. It has already been mentioned that continuous monitoring should not be necessary unless there is concern about your baby's health, in which case a clip may be attached to your baby's scalp to monitor the baby directly. If it is felt that your baby needs monitoring in this way, your membranes will probably have been broken already to check for the presence of meconium (see p. 120).

ARTIFICIAL RUPTURE OF THE MEMBRANES (AROM)

Breaking the bag of waters round the baby is known as artificial rupture of the membranes (AROM). It is a completely painless procedure in itself, and is done to speed labor up or to examine the amniotic fluid for the presence of meconium (see above) if there are concerns about the health of the baby.

There are several disadvantages in having your membranes ruptured. This action often makes contractions much more painful and thus harder to cope with. It creates a passage for infection to enter the uterus, which means that you will need to give birth within the next 24 to 48 hours. If your labor is not really established and the contractions cease, the risk of having a cesarean section is increased if your membranes have already been ruptured. However, AROM is a very effective means of speeding up labor if it is dragging on very slowly and you are becoming tired.

ACCELERATION OF LABOR

If your labor seems to be prolonged, the doctor may suggest accelerating it artificially. There are good reasons for this. A labor that becomes prolonged (more than about eighteen hours) can lead to infection and dehydration in the mother, and infection and hypoxia (lack of oxygen) for the baby. If your progress is going more slowly than that indicated on a graph of average cervical dilatation, then the situation may be becoming abnormal and there are probably good grounds for speeding things up.

The first step would be to rupture your membranes, as described above. In most cases the doctor or midwife would wait for up to four hours before intervening further, in the hopes that normal progress of labor can be restored by the AROM alone. However, if nothing much seems to be happening and your contractions are still weak, irregular, or the cervix is not dilating more quickly, then synthetic oxytocin will be introduced through an IV into your arm. Oxytocin (Pitocin) is the natural hormone which initiates the contractions of labor.

Oxytocin speeds up contractions and makes them more regular and efficient, but they are more painful than normal contractions and most women need to have an epidural to cope with them. On the other hand, with the nurse and your partner supporting you through every contraction you may

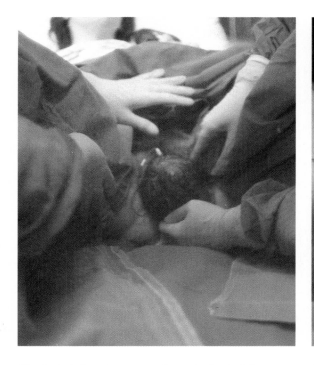

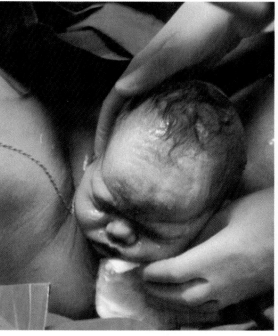

The baby's head appears through the bulging perineum (known as crowning), stretching the vagina open. The head is molded and elongated as it is squeezed through the birth canal.

The head is delivered and the baby begins to breathe. At this point the nurse may insert a bulb syringe to suck out fluid from the baby's mouth, while the baby rotates and the body emerges.

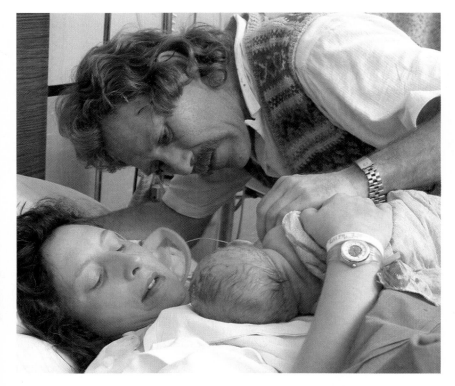

The cord is clamped and cut and if all is well the baby is wrapped and given immediately to the parents. This is always an emotional moment, even for the practitioners who deliver several babies every day of the year!

knees wide apart to ensure that your pelvis is as wide open as possible. Some mothers push their babies out sitting upright on the bed, supported by lots of pillows; others lie down; others squat with support from their partners and midwives or supported on a birthing stool or special bed; others stand with legs bent and apart or lie on their sides with one leg held up. Other women kneel on all fours and push from this position. Once again do what feels right at the time, but it is helpful to know that being upright or on all fours allows gravity to help the baby's descent.

'CROWNING'

The vagina is soft and stretchy due to the action of progesterone and it opens out with the advancing head. On inspection by the obstetrician, first of all only a small amount of the baby's head is seen. Each time you push, the baby's head descends further and further until it is said to be 'crowning' – pressing against the perineum and stretching it wide apart – as the widest part of the baby's head begins to move through the vaginal opening and the crown of his head becomes visible.

The sensation of stretching can be quite alarming and many women feel they are literally splitting. However the skin becomes so stretched that it is completely numb, and although some women do 'give way' and the skin tears a little, you don't feel it at the time.

EPISIOTOMY

Sometimes the skin around the vagina is quite firm and is impeding the baby's entrance into the world, or the midwife may be worried about the baby's

An episiotomy incision may be postero-lateral (1), J-shaped (2) or median (3), depending on the circumstances when it is needed.

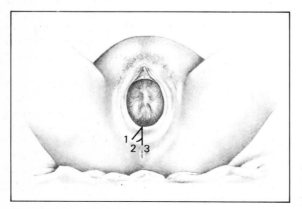

heart beat so may want to speed things up. In this case she or the doctor may ask you if she can perform an episiotomy – a small cut to enlarge the opening of your vagina. Before doing it you will be injected with local anesthetic to make you completely numb.

An episiotomy has to be stitched after the birth, whereas some 'tears' or superficial grazing may not need to be. There is some evidence to suggest that natural tears heal better than episiotomies although this is disputed. It is very common to be given an episiotomy for a forceps delivery, but if you have an epidural it may not be necessary because of the perineal relaxation caused by the epidural. But in other circumstances, try to make sure you understand the reason for suggesting it, and if you feel strongly that you don't want to have an episiotomy, have this recorded in your chart beforehand.

THE BIRTH

Most babies' heads are facing downwards at birth so if you look down you will see the back of your baby's head emerging. Some women like to touch the baby's head at this point. If you can't see what is going on, the nurse might be able to hold a mirror for you. When the head has emerged the doctor or midwife will run her fingers round the baby's neck to make sure the cord isn't tightly round it. Then the baby's head turns to the side so that the first shoulder slips out, followed by the second shoulder, and then with a quick, smooth motion the rest of your baby's body slides out and the midwife will probably lay her immediately on your abdomen while she clamps the cord.

Many midwives use a small, soft bulb syringe to suck out any moisture from your baby's mouth and throat at this stage, although not all babies need this. If a baby does still have a mouthful of amniotic fluid or an accumulation of mucus, 'sucking out' can help breathing to be established more easily and quickly. Some babies cry quite lustily at this point; others make little noise at all. This is perfectly all right so long as the baby is breathing normally and 'pinks up' without difficulty (see p. 102).

DELIVERY OF THE PLACENTA

Once the baby is born or just as she is emerging, it is common for you to be given an injection of oxytocin (Pitocin), which helps the uterus to contract strongly. This helps to dislodge the placenta because the part of the uterine wall where it was embedded shrinks down, sloughing the placenta off. The cord is usually clamped immediately the baby is born so that the oxytocin does

After the birth, when mother, father and baby have all had a chance to relax, there is usually a reviving hot drink to enjoy while you get to know the baby.

not have a chance to get into the baby's circulation. The obstetrician will then place one hand on your abdomen and gently pull the placenta out with the other. This process takes about three minutes.

Some women choose not to have oxytocin, preferring to wait for the placenta to come out naturally and for the cord to stop pulsating of its own accord. This means that the time after the baby is born is conducted at a more leisurely pace. It usually takes about 20 minutes for the placenta to be delivered naturally, but can take longer – up to an hour or more. Putting your baby to the breast and letting her suckle can help deliver the placenta and to make the uterus involute more rapidly, so many women do this immediately after the birth (see p. 104).

The other reason that oxytocin injections are given is that doctors believe that it prevents women from bleeding dangerously after the birth. The original studies which indicated the need for this injection were done some time ago when women were less well nourished and had more children, so there may not be the same necessity to use oxytocin today. This is being researched at the moment, but in the meantime doctors and midwives prefer to be on the safe side and give the injection, with your permission.

Occasionally, the baby may need further sucking out or warming. The nurse will take her to the resuscitation table that will already have been prepared in the delivery room, and sometimes a pediatrician will be called in to help, or in some circumstances may be on hand at the birth (see p. 102).

Once the baby is born and the afterbirth delivered, the doctor will stitch up a tear or episiotomy if necessary. The area will be thoroughly numbed again with local anesthetic and you will be asked to lift your legs into the lithotomy position, resting them on two slings fixed to the end of the bed for the purpose. Stitching can take up to 30 minutes to complete, but it is important that it is done carefully so that the area heals with as little subsequent discomfort as possible.

You may be offered a cup of tea, and the nurse may offer you a blanket bath, so you can change into a clean nightdress if you need to. If your partner is with you, you will probably be given an opportunity to spend a little time alone together with your baby while the midwife writes up your chart. If all is well with the baby, both of you will be wheeled up to the maternity ward within an hour or so, and you will be able to get some rest.

CHAPTER SEVEN

THE ASSISTED BIRTH

The types of medical assistance that may be
needed to help with the safe delivery of your baby

A spontaneous delivery, as described in the previous chapter, happens when the mother delivers her baby through the vagina virtually unaided – 'virtually', because, of course, some help is almost always necessary from the obstetrician, even if it is only to lift the baby out. An assisted delivery, however, is one where the medical staff take over most or all of the work in delivering the baby – with forceps, for example, or by cesarean section.

A breech delivery, where the baby is born bottom first, is also 'assisted', in that however nearly spontaneous it may be, a doctor is almost always required to bring out the baby's legs and arms, and then to supervise the controlled delivery of the head. Similarly the birth of twins, although usually a perfectly normal delivery, may require the active assistance of the midwife or doctor, and if a mother suffers from some existing medical condition, such as heart disease, she will probably need assistance to avoid exacerbating her condition. It is these situations which are described in this chapter. Stillbirth and perinatal death are also covered, to help parents face this tragic situation.

FORCEPS DELIVERY

Forceps are instruments designed to cradle the baby's head in a rigid metal frame so that the baby can be pulled out of the pelvis without compression on the head. They were first introduced into midwifery practice in England in the seventeenth century, by the Chamberlen family. There is quite a variety of types of forceps, ranging from small, very light ones designed to lift out the baby when it is on the floor of the pelvis, to long flat ones (Kielland's forceps) which are designed to rotate the baby's head into the favorable occiput anterior position (face to mother's back) for delivery.

Most mothers are naturally nervous about having to be delivered by forceps but it must be emphasized again that the blades act as a 'cage' to protect your baby's head during the delivery – they do not harm the baby in themselves – and their use is always in the hands of someone fully trained in their application or under close supervision.

THE NEED FOR FORCEPS

There are a number of situations where forceps may be necessary. One of the most common is a prolonged second stage, where the baby's head is not moving down the birth canal in spite of strong pushing by the mother. Alternatively, the second stage may need to be curtailed, if the mother has high blood pressure or there are signs of fetal distress on the electronic monitor. It is important also to ensure the controlled delivery of the baby's head in a breech birth.

However, forceps delivery will only be undertaken if certain conditions exist. Normally forceps will not be used to help bring the baby out in a breech birth which is delayed, as the forceps cannot fit round the buttocks. (However, the forceps can be used in the latter part of a normal breech delivery – see below.)

It is clearly most convenient if the baby's head is presenting normally, with the crown of the head (occiput) in front; abnormal presentations, like face or chin are more difficult to manage (see below). The head must also be at or below the ischial spines of the pelvis (see p. 11). If the baby's head was above this level, this used to involve a procedure known as 'high forceps' but as it is known to be dangerous to the baby it is never undertaken nowadays; in these circumstances an emergency cesarean section would be performed instead.

Forceps cannot be used either if there is any disproportion between the mother's pelvis and the size of the baby's head. If this turns out to be the reason for a delayed second stage, then once again a cesarean section would be performed.

Forceps cannot be used if the cervix isn't fully dilated, so the medical staff would wait until this happened, or again may decide that it is safer to perform an emergency cesarean, depending on

The baby's father is almost always allowed to stay with his partner for an epidural cesarean, even if the operation is unexpected. Both parents can then see and hold their baby while the mother is being sutured (stitched).

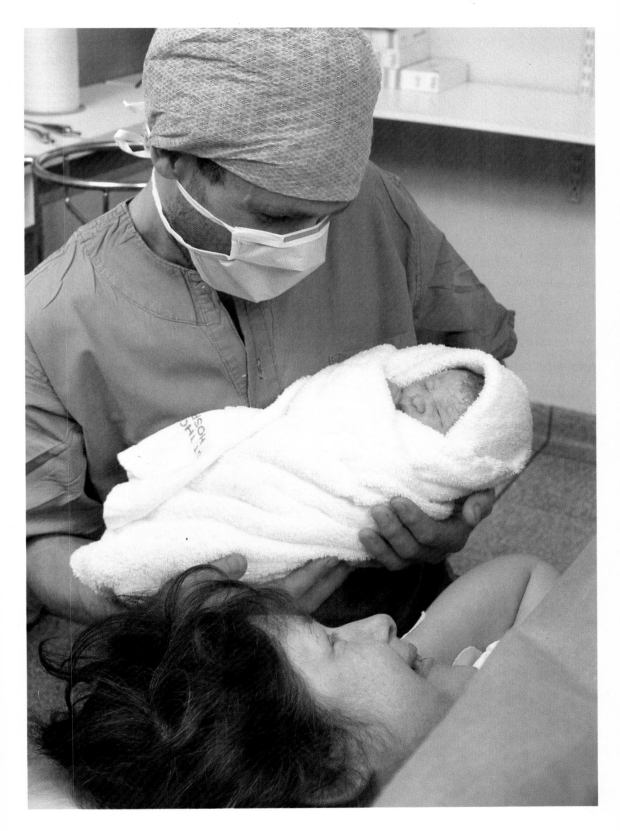

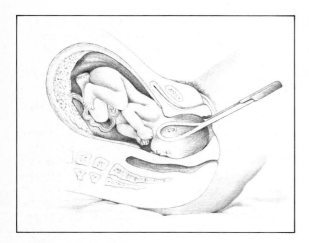

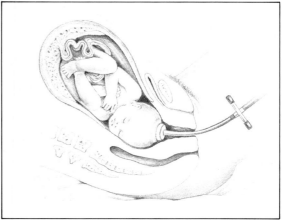

For a forceps assisted delivery, the blades of the forceps are inserted carefully one at a time on each side of the baby's head, then locked together before gentle traction is applied.

For a vacuum assisted delivery, the suction cup is slipped into the vagina sideways, then applied to the top of the baby's head by means of a vacuum. Gentle traction is then applied.

the circumstances. Above all, there must be adequate anesthesia for the mother. Many forceps deliveries are performed with an epidural in place (indeed the epidural anesthetic may unfortunately be the reason for the need for forceps); otherwise the perineum is completely numbed with an injection of local anesthetic.

USING FORCEPS

If you are found to need the help of forceps, the doctor will make sure that a pediatrician is on hand at the birth. The baby may need help in clearing his airways of fluid, and may need oxygen as well, especially if forceps have been required because of fetal distress.

For the delivery, you will be placed in the lithotomy position – with legs bent and held up and open by resting in stirrups on poles fixed to the bed. Your legs and perineum are draped with sterile towels and the whole procedure is carried out like a surgical operation, with full sterile precautions. If you are having an epidural already, the doctor will proceed; otherwise you will be given an injection of local anesthetic. Once you are completely anesthetized in the area, your bladder will be emptied by catheter and you may need an episiotomy, if you haven't had one already. Depending on the reasons for needing a forceps delivery, it takes on average three to five minutes to deliver the baby.

As has already been mentioned, a forceps delivery is not dangerous to the baby, especially now that the practice of high forceps delivery has been abandoned. However it is not uncommon for

marks from one or other of the blades to be left on the side of the baby's face. These may look quite worrying, but they fade within a day or two.

VACUUM EXTRACTION

The vacuum extractor consists of a metal or plastic cup which is placed over the baby's head and attached by a rubber tube to a machine which creates a vacuum. A chain also runs down from the cup; when a vacuum is produced under the cup, an area of the baby's head is sucked into it, giving it a firm grip on the scalp. Traction can be applied via the chain so that the baby's head can gently be pulled down the birth canal.

This method is used in very similar circumstances to forceps, and some obstetricians simply prefer to use it. It can also be used to rotate the head to a more favorable position for delivery, and in theory at least, it can be applied to the baby's head before the cervix is fully dilated.

It is very unlikely to damage the baby in any way, but it does produce a characteristic puffy, rounded area on the baby's head after delivery. This is the part of the scalp that was sucked into the cup by the vacuum. It is prominent at first, but subsides within a day or two.

CESAREAN SECTION

The cesarean section is a historic operation for the delivery of a baby; it is the surgical technique whereby a baby is delivered through an incision in the uterus and lifted out through the abdomen. The present rate of deliveries by cesarean section averages 20 per cent, including elective and emergency cesareans.

ELECTIVE AND EMERGENCY CESAREANS

There are many reasons for delivering a baby in this way, some of which have already been mentioned. Cesareans are usually referred to as 'elective' or 'emergency'. An elective cesarean is one that is planned beforehand because it is clear that a normal vaginal delivery will not be possible, while an emergency cesarean is one that has to be performed without prior warning because of some unforeseen circumstances once labor has started, or because the health of mother or baby suddenly deteriorates during late pregnancy.

An elective cesarean may be planned several weeks in advance, or only a day or two, but you will know exactly when the operation is going to be performed and will be admitted to hospital the day before. For healthy mothers, there is often the opportunity to have the operation performed under epidural anesthesia, which means that you will be awake throughout and can see your baby as soon as he is born. Of course, you won't feel any pain and you won't be able to see anything during the operation as the area of the incision will be masked by sterile towels.

Sometimes, your partner may be allowed to come into the operating room with you in these circumstances and provided the baby is healthy when delivered, he will be able to hold the baby and talk to you while you are being stitched. It is particularly comforting to have your partner with you while the epidural anesthetic is being injected and during the time it takes effect. This may be anything from 30 minutes to an hour, and you may become quite apprehensive during this waiting time.

The birth of the baby only takes a few minutes, but the 'tidying up' afterwards can take about 25 minutes. Your own recovery after the operation is

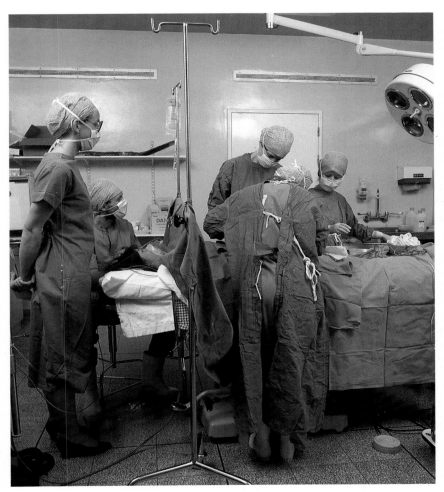

A cesarean section performed under epidural anesthetic takes place in an operating room, sometimes in the delivery suite, or else in the general hospital operating area. It is performed under full sterile conditions and everyone present, including the baby's father, wears gowns, hats and masks. Towels are carefully draped across the operating table so that the surgical procedures are masked from the parents' view.

usually much more rapid after an epidural cesarean as you do not have to cope with the trauma of a general anesthetic.

An emergency cesarean may be required without warning at any stage of labor. If you are already having epidural anesthesia it may be possible to perform the operation as described above, with you awake throughout, or there may be time to set up an epidural before the operation is performed. However if speed is essential or there is serious doubt about yours or your baby's health, then a general anesthetic will be required and you will be fully asleep during the delivery.

REASONS FOR CESAREAN SECTION

You will need an elective cesarean if your pelvis is too small or the wrong shape to allow the baby's head to pass through it safely. This is usually discovered during a first labor, which results in an emergency cesarean, and elective cesareans would be arranged for subsequent births. Most obstetri-

Being awake during a cesarean section can be a nerve-wracking experience, even though the incision is hidden from your view, but it does mean that you can see your baby at the very moment of birth.

cians suggest cesarean section for breech presentation, although some allow you to go into labor, letting it proceed normally probably under epidural anesthetic, but being ready to step in if the baby shows signs of getting stuck. If you have had more than one cesarean section in the past, you will generally need a cesarean for any subsequent babies as the scar tissue can weaken the uterine wall. However, obstetricians increasingly are willing to try for vaginal birth after cesarean (V-BAC), depending on the original reason for the cesarean.

An elective cesarean will be performed also for most cases of placenta previa, even if the amount of bleeding has been small, partly because the placenta is impeding the baby's exit from the uterus, but also to avoid excessive hemorrhage during the birth. The obstetrician would be unlikely, however, to allow an epidural anesthetic in this case. Certain cases of premature delivery would be performed by elective cesarean too, for instance for triplets.

Depending on the circumstances, a mother with hypertension (high blood pressure) or pre-eclampsia may be delivered by elective cesarean, or an emergency cesarean may be required. Severe fetal distress during labor and certain cases of placental abruption would mean that the baby should be delivered by cesarean.

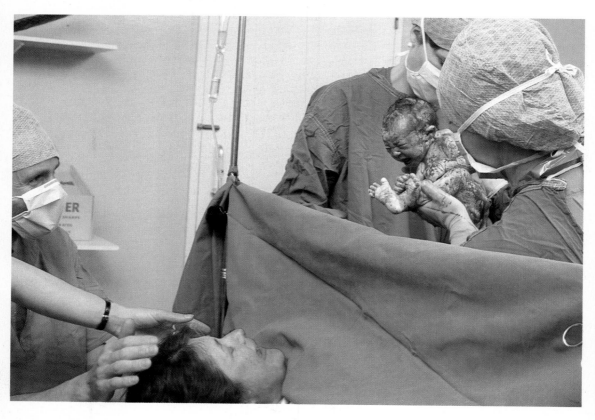

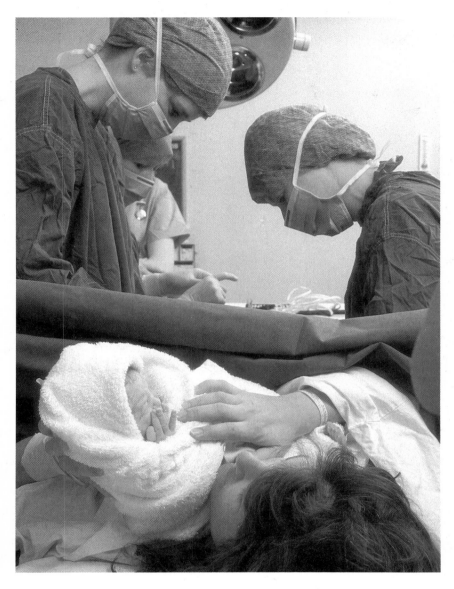

One of the main advantages of a cesarean section performed under epidural anesthesia is that if all goes well you can actually hold your baby after the birth. Stitching the uterus and abdominal wall is the longest part of the operation, but it is always masked off from the mother's view by carefully positioned drapes.

THE OPERATION

A cesarean takes place in an operating room under full sterile conditions – it is a major piece of abdominal surgery, like the removal of an appendix or any other internal organ. The classic cesarean incision used to be a vertical one in the upper part of the uterus, but nowadays the obstetric surgeon usually uses a transverse incision in the lower uterine segment, using the so-called 'bikini' incision through the abdomen for cosmetic reasons.

The skin incision is deepened through the layers of the abdomen to reach the abdominal cavity. The uterus is then opened through its lower part also by a transverse incision. The membranes bulging through the incision are opened and the baby is lifted out – head first if he is presenting that way or, if it is a breech presentation, gently extricated by grasping round the baby's ankles and pulling him from the uterine cavity.

The cord is clamped and divided, the placenta is then extracted and finally the uterus and abdominal wall are sutured (stitched) layer by layer so as to restore the normal anatomy. The entire procedure usually takes about 30 minutes.

Recovery from cesarean section is slower than for a spontaneous delivery but nowadays you need only be in hospital for about five days. The discomfort from the abdominal wound makes progress slower, but with better modern techniques

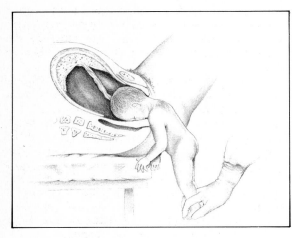 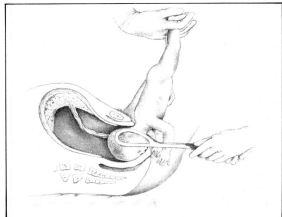

For a breech delivery, the baby's legs, body and arms are delivered first (above). As the baby's head is the largest part, an episiotomy is usually recommended. Then the obstetrician lifts the baby's legs and body out of the way to enable the doctor to apply forceps to protect the baby's head during its delivery (above right).

of suturing (stitching), even this is less of a problem than it used to be. The wound takes about two to three weeks to heal completely and it is best to arrange for your partner or someone else to help you as much as possible at home until you are fully recovered (see p. 138).

For the future, it is worth knowing that if you have a baby delivered by cesarean section it does not necessarily mean that every other delivery will have to be the same way, unless the reason for it is one that does not change, such as a small pelvis. It is perfectly possible for your next baby to be delivered vaginally as normal.

BREECH PRESENTATION

A breech presentation occurs when the baby's buttocks (or breech) is the lowermost part, rather than the head. Most babies will have turned into the cephalic (head down) position by the last few weeks of pregnancy; in four per cent of cases they do not. The baby may have both legs and hips flexed so that he is curled up and only his seat is presenting – this is known as a complete breech. If both legs are extended at the knee, so that the baby's heels are at the level of his ears, it is known as a frank breech; if one or both of the baby's feet are tucked under the buttocks, thereby becoming the presenting part, it is called a footling breech.

If your baby is breech, it may be possible to have a vaginal delivery, but your doctor will want to be satisfied that certain criteria have been fulfilled before allowing it. Your pelvis must be of adequate size and shape so that there is no delay in the delivery of the baby's head. (As it is the largest part of the baby, but will be delivered last, the head is obviously the most crucial part of the delivery.) The baby himself should not be too big, which would mean of an estimated weight not greater than 7½ pounds. If he was thought to be bigger then a cesarean section would probably be suggested instead. Similarly, if there were complicating factors like hypertension, diabetes and so on, then a cesarean section would again be safer, as it would be for a baby that was small for dates or premature. Most obstetricians think that a complete or footling breech presentation are also more safely delivered by cesarean, because of the risk of cord prolapse.

EXTERNAL VERSION

It is possible for a breech to be converted to a cephalic presentation by swivelling the baby round in the uterus, a maneuver known as 'external cephalic version.' However nowadays obstetricians rarely attempt this, and there is no purpose at all in trying it until 34 weeks, since many babies will revert spontaneously to the breech position before then. At the end of the day the number of breech deliveries carried out by an average maternity unit remains much the same whether external version is carried out or not. As it is not without some small risk, of disrupting the placenta, for instance, it is rarely used.

DELIVERING A BREECH BABY

It goes without saying that a full team of doctors and nurses must be present for the breech delivery, and a pediatrician will be present to receive the baby to check and stabilize his condition if necessary. The first stage of a breech labor proceeds more or less as normal, although you are likely to be monitored frequently, if not continuously. You will probably be advised to have an epidural as forceps may be required to help the delivery of the head, and it is useful to have it in place in the event of an emergency cesarean. An episiotomy is almost always performed for a breech delivery, as the perineum is unlikely to be stretched enough by the baby's buttocks and body to allow the head, which is the widest part, to pass through.

In second stage, the baby's buttocks are allowed to deliver as spontaneously as possible, after which the doctor will lift out the legs. Then the shoulders are rotated so the arms can gently be brought down and the head is allowed to descend on to the perineum. This part of the delivery is done quickly, with the fetal heart being monitored continuously. The delivery of the head is then carefully controlled by the obstetrician, either by hand or with the help of forceps.

Some authorities feel that there is no place for a vaginal breech delivery and that cesarean section should be the method for all such deliveries. But some obstetricians consider that providing the prenatal assessment of both mother and baby is carried out scrupulously there is no reason why a vaginal delivery should not be permitted.

THE BIRTH OF TWINS

Although a twin birth need not necessarily be assisted, very many are because difficulties can arise with the delivery of the second twin. This is usually due to some form of malpresentation (see p. 66), or possibly because of fetal distress, especially if one twin is much smaller than the other, which is frequently the case. Preterm labor is also a likely complication with twins, although steps will be taken to try to prevent it (see p. 61). Naturally a full team of medical experts will be on hand, including pediatricians to look after the two babies. Triplets or higher multiples are always delivered by cesarean section.

The birth of the first twin is usually straightforward if the presentation is cephalic, and may even be quite trouble-free if breech, since twins are usually smaller than average babies. Reasonably enough, parents of twins want a birth with the minimum of intervention, but if the second twin is to be delivered safely there must be a minimal delay between the two babies.

Once the first twin is delivered your abdomen is examined to check the lie of the second twin, and to correct it if possible. There is often a pause in the contractions, but they usually pick up again quite quickly or can be stimulated with oxytocin (Pitocin) in an intravenous drip. The membranes of the second sac are then ruptured, if they haven't already done so.

If the baby's presentation allows it, a vaginal delivery follows, although a breech presentation (which is quite common in the second twin) may require the help of forceps in delivering the head, especially if the baby is small or preterm. If the second baby shows any signs of distress, due perhaps to cord prolapse, he will be delivered immediately with the help of the vacuum extractor (see p. 94) if the head is presenting, by forceps if the head is low enough, or by breech extraction, which simply means the deliberate extraction of the baby from the pelvis by the obstetrician.

Since the uterus is greatly distended by twins, there is an increased risk of hemorrhage following delivery, so special precautions will be taken to avoid it. If you have an intravenous tube (IV) in place the Pitocin dose will be increased, if not you will be given an injection of Pitocin to speed up the delivery of the afterbirth, and you will be examined to make sure nothing is retained in the uterus.

Twins are tiring to look after the first few weeks and months so it is a good idea to take the opportunity if offered to spend as long as possible in hospital getting used to caring for them. If they are premature, they may anyway have to spend some time in the Special Care Unit (see p. 116).

DELIVERING A PREMATURE BABY

The fundamental point to remember about a premature delivery is that the baby is particularly fragile and immature and great care has to be taken throughout. Whether to allow a vaginal delivery or perform a cesarean section is a difficult decision.

If labor is progressing fast, which is likely to be the case if you have had children before, then a vaginal delivery is best, but with your baby's heart rate being monitored continuously. Extreme care with the delivery of the head is necessary – it must have a controlled, gentle exit from the birth canal, so a wide episiotomy may be necessary.

If the labor is very premature, or the baby needs to be delivered early because of some problem, such as high blood pressure or placental abruption, then a cesarean section would be the safest form of delivery, and this is certainly the case with a premature breech presentation or a multiple pregnancy.

Delivering a premature baby is a highly skilled operation, requiring a full team of experts. There will also be senior pediatricians and nursing staff from the Special Care Unit present, with mobile incubators ready to ensure the baby's survival, especially if he is very immature.

DELIVERIES REQUIRING INTERVENTION

No two labors are the same, and unfortunately, a labor that starts perfectly normally may well require intervention by the medical staff in order to effect a safe delivery. Fetal distress is one such problem – if your baby shows signs of asphyxia during either first or second stage the doctor or midwife may want to speed up the delivery with oxytocin, help the birth with forceps or vacuum extractor, or it may even necessitate an emergency cesarean (see above).

DELAY IN LABOR

A frequent cause of unexpected intervention is delay in the progress of labor. One very important potential reason for this is the occiput posterior position. Here the crown of the baby's head (occiput) is at the back instead of the front, and the baby's face is turned toward your front. Almost inevitably the head is thrown back slightly, presenting a longer diameter to the pelvis, so there will be less room for the head to pass through. Not only that: to rotate to the anterior position the baby has to turn 180°, which takes time.

This is probably the most common cause of delay in the first stage of labor, particularly in the first-time (primigravid) mother; not infrequently it leads to a cesarean delivery. In the second stage, the midwife or doctor may be able to rotate the head by hand, or by using Kielland's forceps.

Other, rarer, reasons for delay are a brow presentation, where the head is markedly hyper-extended, or a face presentation. In both of these, cesarean section will be necessary unless, in the case of a face presentation, the chin is already lying to the front, when a spontaneous delivery is possible.

HYPERTENSION AND LABOR

If you suffer from any pre-existing medical condition, such as diabetes or heart disease, your labor will of course be very closely monitored and you will be given all the help you need to maintain your own well-being and that of your baby (see p.68). The medical staff will be equally vigilant if you are suffering from high blood pressure (hypertension) or pre-eclampsia, which are generally caused by the pregnancy rather than predating it (see p. 70).

An epidural anesthetic is particularly helpful in lowering the blood pressure, and you may be asked to accept this for the sake of your baby. Your blood pressure may also be controlled during labor, using drugs usually given in an intravenous drip. Equally, monitoring the baby's heart rate throughout labor is imperative, along with frequent, or continuous, recording of your blood pressure level. Naturally, this will be very restricting, but you know that your baby's safety is the over-riding concern.

Provided that your blood pressure remains satisfactory throughout labor and that the baby's condition does not give rise to concern, a spontaneous delivery should be possible. It may, however, be necessary to curtail the second stage of labor, using forceps if any delay occurs.

After the birth and for the first few days postpartum (see p. 132), your blood pressure will continue to be measured at frequent intervals, and treatment with drugs will be continued if necessary. If you were found to be hypertensive from the early stages of pregnancy, further investigation as to its cause will be continued postpartum. If you suffered from high blood pressure or pre-eclampsia you should make sure you attend your six-week postpartum check-up at the hospital (see p. 139) so that the implications for future pregnancies and your own health can be discussed and you can be referred to a specialist physician if necessary.

LOSING YOUR BABY

Sadly not all pregnancies end in the birth of a perfectly formed and healthy baby. For some parents the tragedy will be that their baby is born dead, medically known as stillbirth, for others that the baby will die shortly after birth, a neonatal death. (If the fetus dies before 28 weeks, it is deemed to be a miscarriage, or 'spontaneous abortion' – see page 58.)

The period of time around birth and the week which follows it are known as the perinatal period and statistics are collected annually on the numbers of baby deaths during this time. From these we know that over the years the perinatal death rates has been steadily falling and, at present, it is just over one in a hundred.

THE CAUSE OF DEATH

There are three major reasons why a baby may die at this time. The oxygen supply to the baby in the uterus may be reduced, sometimes because of problems with the placenta or umbilical cord, and the baby may die of asphyxia before it is born or shortly afterwards; the baby may be born with a major physical abnormality which cannot be corrected; or the baby may be born very much too early and die because of his immaturity.

Sometimes it is very difficult to be precise about the exact cause of a baby's death, but should this happen to your pregnancy then it will probably be the most important question you want answered. The doctors attending you will want to help you all they can and may well ask for your permission to perform a post mortem examination. This examination not only gives very important information sometimes on the cause of death, but just as importantly can exclude a number of other problems which may otherwise have been relevant, although it does not always provide the answer.

COPING WITH THE LOSS

If you have the misfortune to lose your baby then the intensity of your feelings and the expression of your grief often make it very difficult for you to take in all that is happening. The medical and nursing staff will also be distressed, so this may not be the best time for lengthy explanations. You will be offered the opportunity to see and hold your baby, perhaps to give him or her a name, and to have some private moments together. Baptism can be arranged if this is your wish. Most units will also take a photograph of the baby which you may like to keep. Do not worry if you cannot accept this when it is first offered to you – the hospital retain it in your chart for you till you are ready for it.

As with any death there are certain legal formalities which must be dealt with. The hospital medical staff will complete the appropriate death certificate for a stillbirth, and both a birth and death certificate for a neonatal death. (Previable miscarriages do not require either certificate.)

This is a desperately difficult time for decision-making but you will be faced with one more choice, once the legal formalities have been dealt with, as to whether you would prefer a hospital or private funeral. In the former circumstance the hospital will take all the arrangements off your hands. If a private funeral is preferred then you can make arrangements with an undertaker according to your own wishes. A member of the hospital staff familiar with the local situation can help here.

You may feel that you want to leave hospital quickly, but unfortunately immediate discharge is not always possible, for example if your own physical condition calls for supervision or treatment. You can choose whether you would prefer to be in a room to yourself or whether you would welcome the company of other mothers. Quite often it is possible for your partner to stay with you, through the night as well as during the day, and this can be very comforting to you both.

AT HOME WITH THE FAMILY

When you do go home you may find it difficult to talk to your relatives and particularly to other children in your family, who often feel that their thoughts or actions may have had something to do with the baby's death. Meeting other pregnant women or those with young babies may also be difficult. Your obstetrician can advise you on practical problems such as lactation, and put you in touch with local self-help groups, if the hospital have not already done so. Talking to other parents who have had a similar experience can be very consoling and a helpful book titled *Surviving Pregnancy Loss* by Friedman and Gradstein is worth reading as you attempt to cope with the grief. (See Appendix.)

THE POSTPARTUM CHECK

Before you leave the hospital you will be checked by the obstetrician who looked after your pregnancy, and an appointment will have been made for you to come back and discuss your case in detail once all the results are available. This could be anytime from two to six weeks from the time of the baby's death and may also be attended by a pediatrician if your baby received special care after birth. It is helpful if you have listed all the questions you would like to ask beforehand. In this interview the doctors should give you as precise an explanation of what happened as is possible and discuss its implications for the future. A tremendous increase in knowledge related to fetal death and stillbirth has occurred in the last several years. Particularly in the field of genetics, we know a great deal about both overt and inapparent abnormalities in the fetus that can contribute to a fatal outcome. Occasionally, it may be even necessary to test parents for genetic problems as the information may be quite important to planning the next pregnancy. You may like to ask about the timing of another pregnancy, and any special tests or management that might be advised. If the doctor thinks that specialist genetic or other medical opinions are necessary then these can be arranged.

An invitation to return at some time in the future, perhaps when considering another pregnancy, is often offered but do not hesitate to ask for a further appointment if, on reflection, you have further questions. The process of grieving will take a long time to work through and you must not feel guilty about this. Even though you may not have known your baby for very long, his or her loss is no less painful for you and your partner than losing a close relative or friend.

CHAPTER EIGHT

THE NEWBORN BABY

**Getting to know your newborn baby during the first
few hours and days after the birth**

For new parents, the first view of your baby immediately after the birth is often an extremely emotional occasion, especially with your first child. But this emotional feeling is almost always accompanied by a feeling of apprehension about the baby's condition, his apparent fragility, and whether you will be able to look after him properly. And if the birth has been at all difficult or prolonged for the mother, you may not feel particularly drawn to your baby at all and may feel guilty about whether you can ever learn to love him (see p. 137). But a normal newborn baby is an extremely resilient being, and although not designed like a calf or foal to struggle to his feet within minutes of the birth, the newborn baby has instincts and reflexes which are designed to help him survive.

IN THE LABOR WARD

Most full term babies who are born normally require no special attention at birth and you are likely to be able to touch your baby as he is born and let him lie on your stomach before the cord is cut, after which he will be given to you to hold (see Chapter 6).

If you need a cesarean section or forceps delivery, if there is any anxiety about the baby's condition or indeed if you are having twins then the obstetrician will have arranged for a pediatrician or neonatologist to be present at the delivery. You are likely to be so absorbed in the labor that you will probably not notice his arrival. In many instances his presence is merely a precaution and his service is not required. However, you may find that once the cord is cut, instead of being given to you, the baby is taken to the pediatrician who will be waiting by the resuscitation cart at the side of the room. In the great majority of cases this does not preface a serious problem.

It is very common for babies to have a lot of mucus and fluid in the airways at birth and to require suction to clear them, or to be a little slow to start breathing regularly and to remain a bluish color. Sometimes this is because they have been a little asphyxiated during the delivery or it is a side effect of analgesics such as Demerol during the

labor. In this case the pediatrician might give the baby some extra oxygen for a few minutes or he may even need to help the respiration either with a mask over the baby's face or by inserting a tube into the airways. Usually the baby will be breathing well within a few minutes and remains pink without extra oxygen. The pediatrician will probably remain for another few minutes just to check that all is well before confirming that the baby will be able to go with you to the maternity ward.

Sometimes the baby is a little slow to breathe in the first few minutes even when there has been no problem identified during the labor. In this case the pediatrician will not have been informed and the delivery room nurses, who are specially trained in techniques of resuscitation, will do what is necessary while the pediatrician is called.

Even if there are no particular problems at this time you will find that the staff are most concerned to ensure that your baby does not become cold. Newborn babies are particularly inclined to lose heat because they are wet and naked and have a relatively large surface area. Even if you have been able to deliver the baby on to your own abdomen and he is crying vigorously the staff will be anxious to dry him and wrap him in warm towels and blankets. It is most important that they are able to do this. They will feel, rightly, that they have failed in their duties to your baby if his temperature drops.

THE APGAR SCORE

As soon as the baby is born, the midwife or doctor will be observing his condition closely and assessing it in terms of the Apgar score, so called after the doctor who first described it. Five features – the heart rate, the respiratory rate, color, activity and response to stimulation – are assigned a score between zero and ten, so that a baby who is pink and very active and responsive will be given a score of ten, while a baby who fails to breathe and is limp, needing resuscitation, will get a low score. The score is usually calculated at one and five minutes after birth and only later if resuscitative measures are still required. Many babies who have very low

APGAR TABLE

Sign	Points		
	0	1	2
Appearance (color)	Pale or blue	Body pink, extremities blue	Pink
Pulse (heartbeat)	Not detectible	Below 100	Over 100
Grimace (reflex irritability)	No response to stimulation	Grimace	Lusty cry
Activity (muscle tone)	Flaccid (no or weak activity)	Some movement of extremities	A lot of activity
Respiration (breathing)	None	Slow, irregular	Good (crying)

Apgar scores respond very well to resuscitation and may not even require admission to the Special Care Unit (see Chapter 9).

You will probably not even realize that the obstetrician is calculating the score because she will be doing it by observation while she is busy delivering the afterbirth and attending to you and the baby. When things have quieted down a little later, she will write the scores into your chart. Many professionals are sceptical about the actual usefulness of the Apgar score system, but it is very widely used and remains the most efficient shorthand way of describing the baby's state of health in the minutes immediately after the birth.

WEIGHING AND MEASURING

If you are able to hold the baby immediately after delivery the delivery room staff will probably leave him with you while they tidy everything else up. They will then ask you if they can just borrow the baby for a few minutes to have a quick check that all is well, or they will have a quick look at him during any resuscitation that is required. It is part of the nurse's duty to weigh, measure and to examine the baby at this time to ensure that there are no major congenital abnormalities. While this is being done they will also attend to the umbilical cord; a light plastic clamp will be put about an inch from the umbilicus itself and the cord cut just beyond this.

In the majority of maternity units the babies are also given some Vitamin K at this time. This is in order to prevent a rare bleeding illness, known as hemorrhagic disease of the newborn, which very occasionally affects even completely fit full term babies. The Vitamin K may be given by mouth but if the baby is at all premature or if there has been any problem necessitating cesarean section or forceps delivery, it may be given by injection into the thigh.

In addition to Vitamin K, babies routinely receive prophylactic eye care to prevent the potentially destructive effects of undiagnosed gonorrhea on the newborn eye. Silver nitrate drops, or ethromycin ointment, are placed in both eyes, thereby averting any risk of infection. The silver nitrate may irritate the eyes for a day, causing some reddening and swelling of the eyelids. This side effect is quite harmless and passes quickly.

PUTTING THE BABY TO THE BREAST

If you are intending to breastfeed your baby you will probably want to feed him as soon as possible after the birth. You may still be relatively immobile because of an epidural anesthetic or because of stitches and you will need some help either from your partner or one of the nursing staff. Most babies are very alert at this time and suck well. As the baby begins to suck you will experience not only the sensation of the 'let down' reflex within the

Many parents are surprised by how alert their babies are immediately after the birth, if pain-relieving drugs such as Demerol have not been used and the baby is well.

breast (see page 150), but often a fairly strong contraction of the uterus. This arises because oxytocin, the hormone released during suckling, acts upon the uterine muscle as well as on the muscle in the milk ducts in the breast. This contraction helps to deliver the placenta and minimizes bleeding from the uterus.

THE BABY IN THE FIRST FEW HOURS

While the nurses will be keen to dry the baby to prevent his becoming cold they will not go to any great lengths to clean him while you are still on the labor ward, apart from wiping his face, so he is still likely to have dried blood and occasionally meconium (fetal bowel contents) on him. If the baby is at all early you may find that he has a thick creamy material known as vernix on the skin. There is no hurry to clean away any of these substances, as it is much more important for you and your partner to hold and admire your child.

It is often a great surprise to new parents to see how wide-eyed their baby is in the first few hours after delivery, often staring up at his mother or father or gazing around the room and appearing to explore his surroundings. It has been shown that many babies spend the greater part of the first twelve hours after delivery awake and in the second twelve hours they are more likely to sleep.

Before you leave for the maternity ward, usually an hour or so after delivery, the nurses will check the baby's temperature and color and that there are no problems with breathing.

It is common, especially after a cesarean section or forceps delivery, for women to get as far as the maternity ward without having been able to have a good look at the baby without clothes on. You will have been reassured by the staff in the delivery room that all appears to be well and it is a great excitement to be able to inspect the baby yourself. Sometimes the appearance of the baby is rather a surprise. Newborn babies are often not the rather red, wrinkled creatures we would be led to believe.

THE HEAD AND HAIR

One of the things that often first strikes the parents is the shape of the head. If you have had an elective cesarean section or a breech delivery then the head is likely to be round, but if you have had a normal delivery the head will have 'molded' in order to aid its passage through the birth canal, and may be tall and elongated. If the labor has been long this may be very marked and the appearance further complicated because of swelling of the scalp

known as 'caput'. Caput arises because of the pressure on the scalp during contractions, but it resolves rapidly over the first day or so of the baby's life.

The bones of the baby's head are of course mobile and just as they have moved to enable the head to 'mold', so over the next few days they will return to a normal position, the caput will subside and the head will become a normal shape.

To facilitate the molding of the baby's head during birth, the four bones of the skull are not fused and there are areas at the top and at the back of the head which are covered only with a tough membrane – these are the fontanels or 'soft spots'. The posterior fontanel is usually closed before birth, and if not will have closed within a very short time afterwards. The anterior fontanel, or 'soft spot', with its characteristic diamond shape, is probably one of the most worrying things for first-time parents – the baby's head seems so vulnerable, especially as you may notice the fontanel pulsating, particularly when the baby cries. However the membrane is very tough and it does not matter if you touch it, when you are washing the baby's hair for instance. The anterior fontanel takes quite a long time to close completely – twelve to eighteen months is quite normal.

Occasionally, the baby may have an area of swelling on the head which is caused by bleeding over one of the bones of the skull (cephalohematoma). There may be more than one of these swellings, which, although not serious, are much slower to resolve than a caput, and may not disappear for several weeks. They can be rather unsightly and as they settle you may notice as you run your finger over them that there is a depression in the centre. This will gradually extend outwards as the collection of blood becomes liquid and disperses. All this can be worrying, but it does not cause any subsequent problems.

Within a few days of birth you may notice a blister or patch of thick white skin appearing centrally on the inside of the lips. This is related to sucking and is quite normal.

The amount of hair on your baby's head at birth does not bear any relation to how thick it will be subsequently. Some babies are born with a great deal of hair; unfortunately most of it usually falls out by about three months of age.

If the baby is premature there may be some downy hair (lanugo) over the body, especially on the shoulders. This has usually disappeared in white, Afro-Caribbean and oriental babies at full term, but it is quite normal for Asian babies often to be born with a considerable amount of body hair.

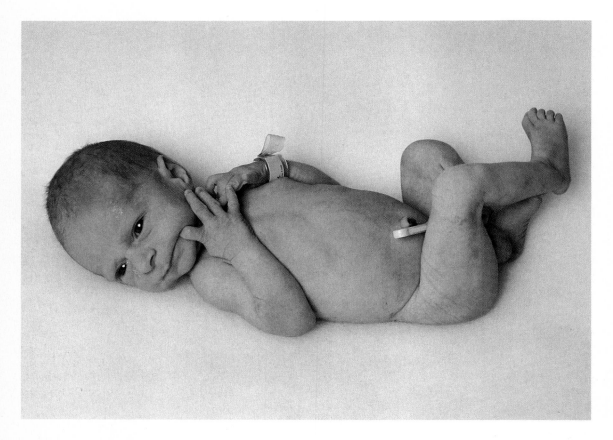

A normal newborn baby, photographed within 24 hours of the birth. The cord clamp is not removed for four or five days, when the remains of the umbilicus have dried to a leathery stump.

EYES AND EARS

The white of the baby's eyes is often not as clear as in older children and the color of the eye tends to be a deep blue. True eye color develops over the first year.

Occasionally little red areas are visible on the white of the eye to either side of the colored iris. These are small hemorrhages which arise because of the high pressure placed on the head as it comes through the birth canal. They will resolve over the first week or so and will not cause any permanent damage.

The ears of the newborn baby are often more striking than in the adult because they are disproportionately large and less likely to be hidden by hair. If your baby is a little early the cartilage inside the ear may not extend right out to the edge at birth and you may find the ears lying forward. Don't worry, they will soon stiffen up so don't feel that you need to coax them back by sticking them down!

THE SKIN

The texture of the skin in the first few days is very variable and you must not be dismayed if your baby doesn't, from the outset, have the peachy skin of the magazine advertisements.

If the baby is a little early the skin is likely to be a pinkish to red color and to be smooth. If your baby is at term or a bit late you may find that the skin is rather dry at delivery and seems to be peeling off, especially on the fingers. This peeling can be very dramatic, with apparently very dry skin coming off over the whole body in the first few days. The nurses may rub some baby oil on to the skin to soften it during this time. It is only a temporary phase and when the peeling has stopped the skin will be softer.

If the delivery is a bit late or if there has been some fetal distress, the baby may have had his bowels open (passed meconium) while still in the uterus. This may result in yellow or brownish staining of the skin and of the umbilical cord, which will gradually disappear over the first few days.

Afro-Caribbean parents are often surprised because their baby's skin is relatively fair at delivery. You will find however, that the pigmentation increases rapidly over the first few weeks.

Between about the third day and the end of the first week, you may notice small white spots with a red wheal around them appearing over your baby's body and sometimes extending over the limbs and face. This characteristic rash, known as toxic erythema, is usually easily distinguished from infected spots. It is not serious and requires no treatment.

Another common and totally innocuous rash appears in the form of small pearly spots known as milia, which are present over the nose and cheeks. These are often seen in great numbers during the first few days and though harmless sometimes persist for weeks before subsiding.

After the second day you may notice your baby's previously normal pink skin becomes yellow because of jaundice. This is very common even in healthy full term babies (see page 121).

BIRTH MARKS

The majority of pigmented birth marks and the common raised strawberry marks seen on the skin of babies are not present at birth. However, you may notice flat red marks of various shapes and sizes over the eyelids, on the centre of the forehead and at the nape of the neck. These are the well known 'stork marks'. The ones on the face disappear in the first year, while those at the back of the neck tend to persist but are usually well hidden by hair. If present at birth, flat red marks on either side of the face are more likely to persist. The pediatrician will advise you about this.

Another common birth mark is the 'mongolian blue spot'. This is a flat blue-grey mark, usually found on the buttocks or lower back. They are often small, single marks, but can be multiple and extend all over the back. They are particularly common in babies with pigmented skin and become less apparent as the pigmentation of the surrounding skin increases.

THE NAILS

At full term the finger nails are often rather long and they may be stained brown with meconium. This fades within a week or so.

Long nails need cutting. If they are not cut you may find that your baby scratches himself quite badly. Some people suggest putting mitts on a baby when this happens, but they rarely stay on for long. Keeping your baby's nails short is more effective. The easiest way to cut your baby's nails is with a pair of small nail scissors. This is a two person job; one holds, the other clips.

THE BREASTS

You may be rather taken aback by the development of your baby's breast tissue which may be marked in either sex, greatly in excess of the breasts of older children. The nipple may be well formed with a well developed pad of breast tissue. In extreme cases you may even notice a slight milky discharge on the nipple. This is because the baby has been exposed to high circulating levels of female hormones while in the uterus and the activity in the breast will gradually subside after birth. Sometimes this effect is greater on one side than the other.

THE UMBILICUS

The umbilical cord itself is a clear gelatinous structure through which the umbilical blood vessels which carry blood between the baby and the placenta can be seen. The cord is usually about ½ inch in diameter but can vary greatly. About 1 inch of cord will remain at the umbilicus, clamped with a plastic clamp. It dries up very quickly in the few days after birth so that by about the fourth day it looks thin and leathery. The nurse will remove the clamp before discharge, after which the cord needs no special attention other than to be kept clean (see p. 109).

THE GENITALS

Another frequent source of surprise is the prominence of the baby's genitals. Male babies have a well developed scrotum and penis, large in proportion to the size of the body, and Afro-Caribbean and Asian babies will have a pigmented scrotum even if the rest of the skin is still pale.

The labia (lips of the vulva) of female babies often appear to be rather swollen and there is very commonly a mucusy vaginal discharge which may very occasionally be slightly blood-stained. This is another effect of the mother's high hormone levels on the baby and diminishes after delivery.

THE LEGS AND FEET

You may be concerned that your baby's legs are abnormal because the thigh, the lower leg and the feet do not seem to be properly aligned, and the lower part of the legs is often bowed inwards. Occasionally of course there is a genuine abnormality but usually these funny postures are purely positional – a newborn baby is naturally curled up – and the nurses or the pediatrician will demonstrate to you that the leg can easily be brought into a normal position. Minor abnormalities of position and over-riding toes nearly always correct during the first year as the baby begins to bear weight. Breech babies often have very tightly flexed legs, at the hip, which take months to return to normal.

SEEING AND HEARING

As you watch your baby you will see that there is lots of normal movement of all his limbs and you will notice that he is looking around and sometimes seems to be staring in a particular direction, often towards a sunlit window or lamp. It is surprising how many new mothers have been led to believe that their babies will not be able to see straight away but simple observation of the baby's activity will soon dispel this misconception.

If you catch your baby wide awake and not crying and hold him so that your faces are about 10 inches apart you may find that he is gazing at you intently, and if you then move your head from side to side he may follow you with his eyes. You can play similar games with simple objects such as a brightly colored brick or a ball of about 3 inches diameter. Don't worry if your baby goes cross-eyed at this time. This is very common and is because the baby does not yet have good control over the muscles around the eye which determine the direction in which it is looking.

Formal testing of hearing is complex in the newborn but it is often clear that the baby can hear when he is seen to startle in response to a bang close by, or to quiet down in response to a reassuring sound close to him, such as a musical toy, or his parent's voice.

THE NURSERY

It is not long since babies spent most of their time in a side nursery and were only with their mothers at the regular feeding times. Now nurseries are largely reserved for bathing babies, and babies remain in a bassinet at the bedside throughout the day and night. This practice is known as 'rooming in'.

The nurses may suggest that your baby goes to the nursery for the first night so that you are able to sleep. You should only agree to this if you feel quite happy about it and you should discuss plans for night feeding so that the nurses are quite clear as to whether you want to be woken.

After the first night it will almost certainly be assumed that you will have your baby with you and that you will feed him yourself through the night. Even though you may feel tired, this is particularly important if you are breastfeeding as it helps to establish feeding as quickly as possible.

FEEDING

Provided your baby is full term and well grown he will be fed 'on demand', although you may be advised not to let him sleep for more than six hours at any one time until feeding is established.

If you are breastfeeding you will need help with getting the baby on to the breast for the first few feedings (see p. 152). Your milk flow will become established more quickly as you put the baby to the breast each time he cries for the first few days. Don't be worried if you find you are feeding very frequently, even up to about fifteen times a day for a few days; provided that the baby is getting on to the breasts properly they shouldn't become sore.

If the baby cries frequently this is most unlikely to be because you don't have enough milk and there is no need to supplement with a bottle after the feeding. If the baby cries just put him back on the breast.

If you are bottle feeding you will be provided with pre-packed bottles while you are in hospital. Bottle fed babies will probably demand feeding less frequently than breastfed babies for the first few days. Milk is all they need; clear fluids should not be necessary.

Full term babies are weighed at birth and are then not usually weighed again until the third day. You should expect your baby to have lost some weight at this time. Breastfed babies often lose more than bottle fed babies because they obtain fewer calories in the first few days. This weight loss is absolutely normal and is not going to put your baby at any long term disadvantage: full term babies who have grown well in the uterus will have stores of fat beneath the skin and carbohydrate in the liver which they can use in the first few days, both to help keep themselves warm and to keep their blood sugar at the right level.

Nurses have a rule of thumb by which they calculate the amount of weight loss they consider acceptable (usually up to ten per cent of the birth weight), and they will probably show concern only if the loss exceeds this figure or the baby seems otherwise to be unwell. When your baby is next weighed a few days later he will probably be gaining and most babies have regained their birth weight by the tenth day.

DAILY CARE

The purpose of keeping you and your baby in hospital for a few days after delivery is not just to ensure your health prior to discharge but also to help you learn how to care for your baby. In many hospitals the baby does not receive a bath until about the third day but you will be shown how to keep the baby clean without resorting to a full scale bath (see p. 169). If the baby is not having a bath the neck area and armpits should be cleaned carefully with cotton wool balls and water. Only water should be used on the face and a clean piece of cotton wool must be used for each of the eyes.

The diaper area is best cleaned with cotton wool balls dipped in tepid water. Always clean in the folds of the groin and upper thigh. Clean a baby girl from the front to back to avoid germs from the anus reaching the vagina. The whole area should then be smeared liberally with a barrier cream, either a zinc and castor oil mixture or petroleum jelly, before the diaper is put on.

Particular attention is paid to the area around the cord (umbilicus) until it has dropped off, usually toward the end of the first week, and its base dried up, usually at about ten days. Various techniques of cord care are available but the most satisfactory and widely used is probably to clean the cord with a small alcohol swab. At first the nurse may do this for you, but you will be encouraged to take over as soon as possible. Alternatively, simply keep the cord stump clean and dry until it falls off.

The cord is inspected carefully every day until it has dried up and dropped off as it is a common site of infection. If the cord, or the area around it, looks inflamed, this may indicate an infection, so ask the advice of your pediatrician.

THE FIRST BATH

Your baby will probably receive his first bath just after the cord has dropped off. A nursery nurse will show you how to bathe the baby and then the next day you will probably do it yourself with a member of staff close by in case you are in difficulties. This is when your baby will receive his first hair wash and finally get rid of all those little bits of debris which have been present since delivery.

You have the choice of using a cake of non-scented baby soap and soaping the baby prior to putting him into the water or using a liquid baby soap added to the bath. In terms of cleanliness there is probably nothing to choose between the methods but do remember that once soaped your baby will be very slippery.

Most babies enjoy their bath but some clearly don't until they are a little older. You can keep your baby perfectly clean without a bath so don't feel that you have to perform this ritual daily (see p. 169).

BOWELS

The great majority of babies move their bowels

within the first 24 hours and the remainder before 48 hours. If a baby has not moved his bowels by this time the pediatrician will be informed.

Meconium, which is present in the baby's bowel at birth, is a sticky greenish-black substance often passed in copious amounts on the first day, necessitating a premature first bath! By two or three days the color of the stool will be lightening, a 'transition stool', so that by four or five days the normal soft yellow stool of the milk fed baby will be passed.

The frequency with which babies move their bowels and the texture of the stools is very variable and can surprise parents, causing unnecessary anxiety. Breastfed babies' stools are very soft, usually light yellow and virtually odorless. Some babies may have dirty diapers with runny stools at every change, while other babies may only move their bowels every two or three days or even once a week! Any of these is perfectly normal – what you need to find out is what is normal for your baby; you should only become concerned if the bowel habit changes or if the baby seems unwell.

Bottle fed babies usually move their bowels two to four times a day, although it is not uncommon for them to go much more frequently. The stools are usually a yellowish color and are soft. Occasionally the baby's stools may be green, but provided they are not runny or frequent this is probably normal for your baby. If you have any doubts it is worth showing a little sample of the stool to your pediatrician.

Parents are often distressed because of the tremendous straining and redness of the face which might go on for some time before their baby passes what turns out to be a perfectly ordinary, soft stool. This is absolutely normal behavior in young babies and you only need to seek guidance if the stool becomes hard (see p. 192).

URINE

Urine is frequently passed at the time of delivery and then not very often during the first 48 hours. Thereafter the baby will have a wet diaper at most feeds. It is most important that you don't leave your baby for too long in a wet diaper as this will lead to a rash (see p. 192).

SLEEPING, WAKING AND CRYING

Babies do not settle straight into a routine from the first day. In fact it is likely that no two days in the first week will be the same. Breastfed babies may feed many times a day in the early weeks and they may sleep for variable lengths of time, ranging

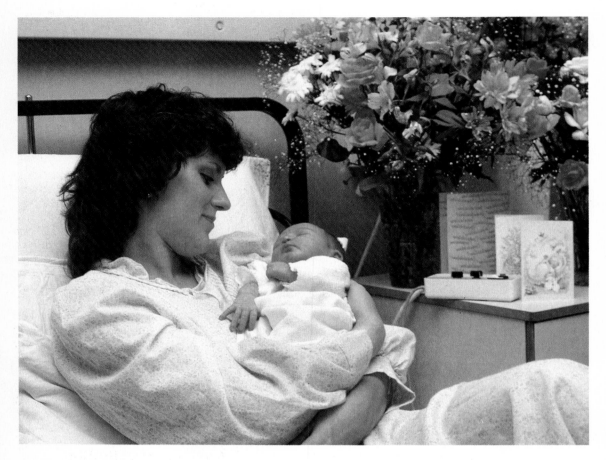

The practice of 'rooming-in' – having your baby's bassinet by your bed in the maternity ward at all times – is now almost universal in modern maternity units. It helps you get to know your baby more quickly, and means that you can feed your baby whenever he needs it, which helps to establish breastfeeding.

between about half an hour and six hours. Similarly the length of time that they are awake varies, some babies commonly lying wide eyed in their cribs for prolonged periods. The baby bottle fed on demand is less likely to feed so frequently in the first few days but you will find that the length of time taken between feeds varies.

You may find that your baby varies greatly from the one in the adjoining bed in terms of the amount of noise that he makes. Most babies do not really cry very much in the first few days but perhaps your baby will be the exception. Why some cry so much is often difficult to explain. The cause seems to be hunger on some occasions while in many others it can be stopped just by picking the baby up or simply by wrapping him up well in the blanket and

tucking it into the bassinet. In the early days a wet or dirty diaper does not seem to upset the baby. You may worry that your baby is crying because he is unwell but this is unlikely to be the case; quietness and lethargy are much more common signs of problems in the newborn. If your baby does cry a lot at the beginning, it doesn't necessarily mean that he is going to continue in this manner.

VISITING ON THE MATERNITY WARD

Visiting hours will vary between different hospitals but you are likely to find quite firm restrictions and there are often periods when only fathers are allowed to visit.

One of the reasons for staying in hospital for a few days after the delivery is to ensure that you have some time when you can concentrate wholly on yourself and your baby without the distractions of household problems. This is just as important with a subsequent baby as it is with the first. If you are swamped with visits from well-meaning family and friends it can sometimes be difficult to relax and enjoy the new rituals of feeding and changing. It can be very tiring to feel you have to be polite to a constant stream of visitors, and your partner should tactfully try to cut down the numbers on any one day.

It is equally important that you are able to have time alone with your partner and the baby, so that the father feels fully involved in this unique experience. The first dirty diaper, the first bath, the early feedings are all great milestones which both mother and father should be able to share.

PERSONNEL ON THE MATERNITY WARD

The care of mother and normal baby in the days after birth is traditionally the responsibility of the nurses. Within a hospital unit the doctors will have a considerable influence over patterns of care although in practical terms they will concentrate on the problems and leave the care of normal babies to the nurses.

LENGTH OF STAY

It is not long since it was standard practice for women to stay in hospital for ten days after delivery. Now it is usually only women who have had complications who stay this long and even after a cesarean section many women go home after only five days.

Your length of stay will have been discussed with you prenatally and you will probably stay for 48 hours. If you are particularly eager to be at home you may even have arranged with your obstetrician and midwife to go home as soon as six hours after the delivery (see p. 19).

If you are well supported at home and everything has been straightforward, then it is lovely to be able to leave hospital, but for many women a few days on the maternity ward is a blessing even if it is rather noisy at night and the daytime is a bit regimented.

While you are obviously not eager to upset plans, do remember that a decision to take a 48-hour discharge is not binding and if you feel uneasy about handling or feeding your baby you should ask to stay a little longer.

EXAMINATION OF THE NEWBORN

Your baby will receive several examinations while in hospital. The first of these is performed by the nurse in the delivery room (see above), and is performed to rule out obvious malformations, such as wrong numbers of fingers and toes, club feet (talipes), and the like. Thereafter the nursery nurse will check the baby daily looking for any signs of minor infections such as rashes and sticky eyes, or common problems such as jaundice. They will pass on any problems they cannot solve to the pediatrician. He or she will make a routine daily visit to the nursery.

In addition to the daily nursing checks, your baby will be thoroughly examined by a doctor. If you are staying for more than 48 hours there will probably be two such examinations, the first at about 24 hours and the second within 24 hours of your discharge. If you are being discharged at 48 hours the baby will probably only be examined once by the pediatrician.

The purpose of these medical examinations is threefold; firstly, to identify any congenital abnormalities that may have been missed or which were not apparent in the delivery room; secondly, to ensure that the baby is feeding adequately and that the systems such as bowels are functioning normally; and thirdly to give you, the parents, an opportunity to discuss any anxieties of your own. From this it is clear that the examination is best done in your presence.

Before proceeding to examine your baby, your pediatrician will review the birth records for both of you. He will search through your chart for any entries which may suggest possible problems for the baby. For example, if the amniotic fluid was stained dark brown-green, the pediatrician will be concerned that the baby experienced distress in utero, and will be alert for any manifestations of the problem in the newborn.

THE PHYSICAL EXAMINATION

The pediatrician may ask you to undress the baby yourself and will examine the baby either in his bassinet or in a nearby examination room. He is likely to watch the baby's general level of activity and alertness briefly while also noticing the color of the skin and any obvious abnormalities, before proceeding to the more thorough examination.

When you yourself are examined by a doctor, he will usually look systematically at the heart and lungs, then the abdomen, then the nervous system, and so on. Examining a baby is rather different, as co-operation cannot be guaranteed! Things like listening to the heart and feeling the pulse which need to be done while the baby is quiet and relaxed are done first, while maneuvers such as checking for congenital dislocation of the hip, which might make the baby cry, are kept till the end.

THE HEAD

After watching the baby, the pediatrician will probably run his hand over the head, feeling the soft spot (fontanel) on the top, which is of variable size, and checking that there are no obvious abnormalities of the head, or swellings such as cephalohematoma which relate to the delivery.

THE HEART, PULSES AND ABDOMEN

The heart is listened to both at the front and the back, as some cardiac murmurs (extra heart sounds) are more easily heard at the back between the shoulder blades. You will also notice the pediatrician feeling in your baby's groin; this is to check the pulses in the arteries to the legs, which are difficult to feel if there is a narrowing (coarctation) of the aorta, the main artery coming from the heart.

The doctor will gently feel your baby's abdomen while the baby is still relaxed to ensure that there are no masses or lumps felt; such positive findings are extremely unusual but may represent one of the very rare neonatal tumors, or a congenital abnormality of one of the abdominal organs.

MUSCLE TONE

At this stage the doctor may lift the baby up, checking that there are no obvious abnormalities of the spine, and feeling the 'tone' of the muscles. Tone is really a description of the normal tension in the muscles; some babies who have suffered from asphyxia or babies with Down syndrome tend to be floppy, rather like a rag doll, while other asphyxiated babies are more than usually stiff. Normally babies offer some, but not excessive, resistance as the limbs are moved to and fro.

REFLEXES

The pediatrician may then demonstrate some of the primitive reflexes which are present in normal babies at birth, such as the grasp reflex, when the baby grips a finger or pencil passed across the palm of the hand; or the stepping reflex, when the baby makes a stepping up movement when held upright and the top of the foot touches a surface, such as the rim of the bassinet. Other reflexes include the 'Moro response', when the baby throws out his arms and legs when startled; the walking reflex, when the baby 'walks' along a flat surface if held upright with feet touching it; and the 'rooting' reflex, which is important for feeding (see p. 152).

SPECIFIC AREAS

After this the doctor will look at specific areas more carefully. He may need to hold your baby's eyes open gently and shine a light into them, looking

particularly for the rare cataracts which are sometimes visible as white specks in the lens of the eye. The roof of the mouth is felt with a finger and also examined with a flashlight to check there is no cleft palate.

Your baby's genitalia will be examined, ensuring in a girl that the vagina and the urethral opening are normally positioned, and in a boy that the penis is normal and that the testes are present in the scrotum. If one of the testes is not descended, this will be checked again at six weeks and later if necessary. Most testes come down by three months. Occasionally your doctor may suggest hormone injections to stimulate the descent, but if the testis has not come down by twelve months, an operation will be performed to bring it into the scrotum. This operation would take place in the hospital (see p. 258 for advice about this).

LEGS AND FEET

Attention now passes to the lower limbs and the position of the feet will be checked. A newborn baby's feet are often held in an unusual position, with the soles either inwards or outwards. This probably relates to the position of the feet while in the uterus and frequently causes anxiety in new parents. In the great majority of babies the feet are very mobile and the pediatrician will demonstrate to you how easily they return to a normal position. Only a very few have true deformities requiring referral to an orthopedic surgeon.

EXAMINATION OF THE HIPS

Finally the hips are examined, either separately or together. You will see the pediatrician holding the leg with the knee bent as far as it will go, with the doctor's thumb in front and fingers behind the hip. With the baby lying flat on his back, the doctor will turn the leg outwards so that it comes to lie almost flat on the bed. The doctor is testing to ensure that the top of the thigh bone (the head of the femur) is within the socket of the hip joint (the acetabulum). If the joint is not correctly in place he will be unable to turn the leg out. This disorder is known as congenital dislocation of the hip.

Having ensured that the hip is in place a second maneuver is performed to check that it is stable and remains in place when gentle pressure is applied. It is common for slight 'clicking' of the ligaments around the hip to be noted during the first week or so and the pediatrician may comment upon this. This is thought to arise because the ligaments are relaxed as a result of the hormones of pregnancy crossing the placenta. These clicks are

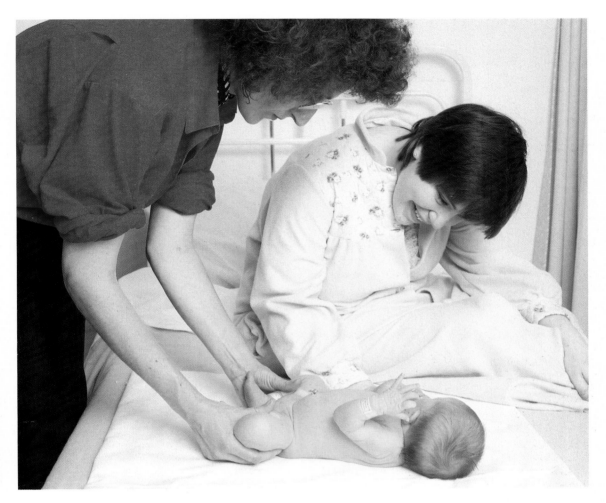

Testing for congenital hip dislocation is one of the most important elements of the careful medical check made on your newborn baby by the pediatrician.

not serious. Genuine instability of the hip joint is much less common. If there is any concern about your baby's hips he will probably be referred fairly quickly to an orthopedic surgeon. Congenital hip dislocation can be corrected over the first few months of life with the help of a special brace or plaster cast.

The examination of the hips is rather uncomfortable; not surprisingly, many babies object to this and may cry, so at this point in the examination you should be able to wrap him up and give him a comforting cuddle. Indeed, you yourself may find the hip maneuvers rather distressing to watch. However it only takes a few seconds and helps to diagnose a problem which could lead to disability later in life if not treated.

NURSERY PROBLEMS

Occasionally babies who are well grown and who cause no anxiety immediately after delivery develop problems during their stay in the nursery. The most common of these is jaundice, which does not usually appear until the latter part of the second day (see p. 121). Another frequent finding is that the baby makes repeated, quick, jittery movements of the limbs and startles a lot, which can be a sign that he has low blood sugar or calcium.

Similarly you or the nurses may notice a change in your baby's pattern of behavior over the first few days in that he becomes sleepy or irritable and vomits, or has difficulty feeding. Any of these signs may herald a problem such as an infection which, if not detected early, may become serious. In this case the nurses will quickly alert the pediatrician who will rapidly organize tests to try to find the cause of the problem. These will usually consist of blood tests together with the collection of a urine sample and frequently a lumbar puncture (removal of fluid from around the spinal cord) to exclude the very unlikely but important possibility of meningitis.

You may be fortunate enough to be in a hospital where these tests can be performed in the maternity ward, so that you and the baby can stay together, but usually it will be necessary to move the baby to the Special Care Unit. You may also find that if the staff are sufficiently concerned they will want to start treatment with antibiotics before all the results of the tests are available. In the newborn, it is not satisfactory to give antibiotics by mouth as they are not reliably taken up into the blood stream and so they have to be given into a vein. This too will probably mean that your baby has to be admitted to a Special Care Unit (see p. 116).

Many of the common early problems such as jaundice or the frequently heard but usually insignificant heart murmurs in young babies are often not apparent until after the first 48 hours. With increasing numbers of women choosing to go home early the responsibility for identifying and managing these problems is being removed from the hospital staff and put on to your pediatrician. This is why most doctors schedule a first baby visit within two weeks.

TESTS ON BABIES

In addition to the examinations of your baby performed during the first few days of your baby's life, which are designed to detect anatomical abnormalities, other tests may be carried out during this time. These are designed to discover certain disorders not apparent on examination, or simply to monitor the extent of problems such as jaundice.

TESTS PERFORMED ON ALL BABIES

It is only justifiable to impose mass screening for a disorder if the diagnosis is not apparent upon routine physical examination and if there are advantages to be gained for the baby from early treatment. The disorders for which all babies are screened currently are a very rare disease known as phenylketonuria, and the less uncommon condition of under-activity of the thyroid gland (hypothyroidism).

Babies with phenylketonuria are unable to use one of the amino acids (protein components) present in milk; as a consequence the level of this amino acid in the blood rises and can cause damage to the brain. This problem is excluded by a test which will be performed on your baby several days after starting to nurse, or bottle feed, probably when you are back at home.

The baby's heel will be pricked and spots of blood collected on to absorbent paper. These papers are then sent to a reference laboratory where the blood is extracted from them and analyzed. In the unlikely event of your baby's test being thought to be abnormal you will be contacted very quickly and a repeat sample of blood obtained for confirmation, before further evaluation.

Some blood collected at the same time is used for detection of under-activity of the thyroid gland. A few babies with thyroid problems will be detectable on physical examination but others with less severe impairment, which may none the less affect their later development, cannot be detected without a blood test and will benefit from early treatment with thyroid hormone.

SELECTIVE SCREENING TESTS

It is well known that some inherited disorders are more likely to occur in specific groups of people, and it is obviously helpful to detect them early in life. The most notable example of such a disorder is sickle cell anemia which occurs predominantly in black and Afro-Caribbean people.

If you are black you will probably have had a special blood test during pregnancy (see p. 26) and if you are known to be a sickle cell carrier, your partner will have been checked too. This will enable the doctors to find out if your baby is at particular risk and a blood sample can be collected from the vessels in the umbilical cord after delivery. This blood is the baby's rather than yours, and it can be tested to determine whether or not your baby has sickle cell anemia, and if so a course of treatment can be planned immediately.

There are inherited disorders of hemoglobin (the red pigment in the blood) other than sickle cell disease and if you live in an area with a population affected by a disorder of this kind, you may find that all babies have blood collected from the umbilical cord in order to screen for these conditions.

The most common, serious inherited disorder among white children in this country is cystic fibrosis. This chronic disease results in chest infection, failure to digest food and reduced life expectancy. There are probably some advantages for diagnosing this condition early and it may be suspected after examination of the protein content of the baby's first bowel movement or by analysis of blood collected on to absorbent paper. Unfortunately, neither of these tests is totally reliable and they are not widely applied. If there is real anxiety about the possibility of cystic fibrosis a formal 'sweat test' is necessary and will be carried out when the baby is about six weeks of age.

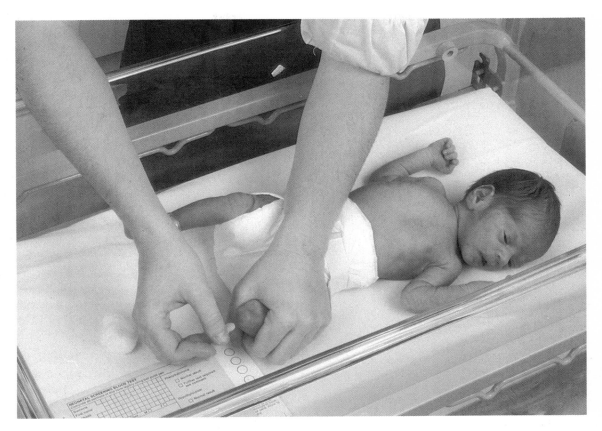

Your baby's blood will be collected by a heel prick a few days after the establishment of feeding, to be analyzed for a rare metabolic disorder and for an under-active thyroid gland.

OTHER TESTS IN THE FIRST WEEK

The only reliable method by which to assess the severity of the very common problem of jaundice seen in the first week is to take a blood sample and to measure the amount of the yellow pigment, bilirubin, in it (see p. 121). Only a very small quantity of blood is required and it will usually be collected into a narrow capillary tube from a prick on the side of your baby's heel. The nursery nurses will often perform such routine tests themselves and will only inform the doctor if there is a problem.

Similarly the nursery nurses are ever vigilant for signs of infection and if your baby's umbilicus does not look completely clean, if his eyes are sticky or if there are any suspicious spots or red areas they will take swabs to look for bacteria, often before the doctors have examined the baby. If you are discharged early from hospital your doctor will take responsibility for organizing the routine screening procedures.

GOING HOME

Hopefully you will have been able to prepare home for the arrival of the baby during the late stages of your pregnancy. If your baby is delivered prematurely and you have been unable to make these preparations it may be a good idea to go home for one or two afternoons before the baby's discharge to make sure that everything is all ready so that you are able to relax with your partner during the first few days and concentrate on looking after the baby.

You will be bringing the baby home from the hospital in his own clothes so if possible you should remember to put these out before you go into hospital.

It is a good idea to give your baby a feeding shortly before leaving the hospital and then if you are lucky you will have time to get things straight before you have to feed for the first time at home.

When you leave the maternity ward your baby will be carried by one of the nurses and will be given to you at the hospital entrance, as they have responsibility for his safety until you leave the hospital. In the automobile the baby should be carried only in an infant automobile seat. Some hospitals refuse to send a baby home in an automobile without one!

CHAPTER NINE

THE SPECIAL CARE UNIT

The technology of the modern Special Care Unit
and how it helps low birth-weight babies

Having a baby taken into special care can be extremely worrying for parents. In many ways it is easier to understand if your baby is born very prematurely – and many special care units regularly care for tiny babies born at 24 or 25 weeks' gestation. Having a basic idea of the likely reasons can help to allay fears, but more importantly you should talk to the pediatrician in charge of the unit who will explain exactly why your baby needs special care and what the treatments are likely to be.

Most maternity units now have a ward dedicated to the care of babies with problems. Wards which offer full support for extremely tiny premature babies are increasingly referred to as 'Neonatal Intensive Care Units' (NICU), while the previously widespread title of 'Special Care Unit' (SCU) tends to be applied to units which, while able to support extremely ill infants for short lengths of time, usually refer more complex or long term problems to a more specialized unit.

The majority of health regions support at least one referral unit offering neonatal intensive care. The level of care offered in other regional maternity units will depend to a considerable extent upon local levels of pediatric medical and nursing staff. If your obstetrician has reason to believe that an extremely premature birth or a serious medical problem in the baby is likely (see p. 61), you may be advised to transfer to the maternity unit with the NICU during your pregnancy. This may well necessitate a stay on the maternity ward. Alternatively, if this is not possible or if unexpected problems arise after the birth, a team comprising a doctor and a nurse trained in neonatal intensive care (a 'transport team'), will come with their equipment in a special ambulance to take the baby to the referral unit.

WHICH BABIES GO TO SCU/NICU?

Admission to a special care unit depends largely on how much care is possible in the nursery in terms of monitoring and attending to minor neonatal problems. The proportion of babies being admitted to SCUs in recent years has tended to fall as blanket rules have been abandoned, such as the admission of all babies delivered by a cesarean section or all infants of diabetic mothers and babies in the 4½ to 5 pound birth weight bracket. This enables the skills of the staff on the SCU to be reserved for those babies most needing them. However, the pressure on these units remains very high and there has been a move in a few larger maternity units to establish 'intermediate care units' within nurseries. Babies requiring traditional 'special care' procedures, such as phototherapy treatment for jaundice (see p. 121), or tube feeding (see p. 127), can be looked after in intermediate care, usually in close proximity to their mothers, thus avoiding unnecessary separation. This also enables the SCU/NICU to concentrate increasingly on the most vulnerable babies.

The reasons for admission of babies to areas providing these different levels of care are summarized in the table overleaf, but it is important to emphasize that great local variations will be found in the interpretation of these ground rules.

PREMATURITY AND LOW BIRTH WEIGHT

The most common reasons for admission to SCU/NICU are prematurity and low birth weight. These conditions often, but not always, co-exist. Some babies born at the expected time will have grown poorly in the uterus and be of low birth weight ('small for dates'); the baby of a woman with poorly controlled diabetes may be premature but large. Slightly premature babies and those of low birth weight can usually stay with their mothers on the maternity ward, but if the gestational age is below 35 full weeks or the birth weight is below 4½ pounds, they will probably be taken into special care. The distinction between a small baby who is premature but well grown and a baby of the same weight who is mature and 'growth retarded' is important in terms of expected postpartum problems and prognosis.

The sophisticated technology of the Special Care Unit continuously monitors the progress of the tiny babies in its care.

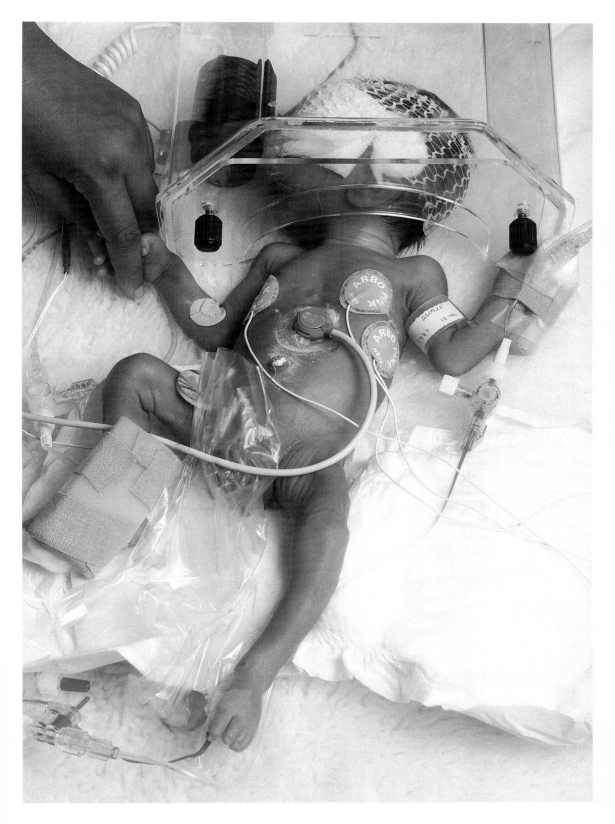

NICU ADMISSION	INTERMEDIATE ADMISSION
Birth weight less than 1.5 kgs (3 lbs)	Birth weight 1.5-2 kgs (3-4½ lbs)
Prematurity less than 34 weeks	Prematurity 34-35 weeks
Severe respiratory problems	Moderate respiratory problems
Severe birth asphyxia	
Heart disease	
Severe infections	Minor infections
Convulsions	Low blood sugar
Severe jaundice requiring exchange transfusion	Moderate jaundice requiring phototherapy
Drug withdrawal	
Serious surgical problems	

PROBLEMS OF PREMATURITY

A baby who is born before the expected time suffers from immaturity of several systems, which leads to a variety of medical and management problems.

TEMPERATURE CONTROL

All babies are at risk of becoming cold. This risk is increased in the premature baby because of the comparatively large surface area in relation to body weight, and decreased amount of body fat for insulation. If babies are to grow properly they need to be able to put most of the energy from their food to that purpose and not to have to expend it on generating heat in order to preserve body temperature. Consequently one of the most important elements in their care is to minimize heat loss. Most premature babies are nursed inside incubators whose temperatures are adjusted according to the size and age of the baby and according to whether or not the baby is wearing clothes. As soon as it is practicable babies are dressed in ordinary baby clothes and usually wear a hat or bonnet. This not only brings pleasure to parents and staff but usefully helps reduce heat loss (see p. 130).

THE LUNGS

In the extremely premature baby, below 26 weeks' gestation, the airways within the lungs are very primitive, and actually create a barrier to the effective transfer of oxygen and carbon dioxide, essential if the baby is to survive outside the uterus. As the baby becomes more mature the airways become more fully developed in structure but often remain functionally immature. This means that they do not produce sufficient amounts of the substance surfactant, which enables the lungs to expand adequately for breathing. This produces the problem known as hyaline membrane disease or respiratory distress syndrome, which is the most serious respiratory problem in the premature baby. While this illness becomes less common with increasing gestational age, it can still occur in a baby born up to 36 weeks' gestation. Babies with this problem need help with their breathing in order to survive (see p. 126).

THE CENTRAL NERVOUS SYSTEM

Many aspects of the brain and nervous system are immature in the premature baby. The most important effects of this are upon control of breathing and the ability to suck. Many premature babies experience frequent pauses in their breathing (apneic attacks), and may require help with breathing as a result, even if they do not have hyaline membrane disease.

While many very premature babies demonstrate sucking movements, very few babies below 35 weeks' gestation can feed effectively and many babies up to 37 weeks' gestation will not manage all their feedings themselves. This means the baby will have to be 'tube fed' – the administration of milk feeds via a tube passed either through the mouth or nostril into the stomach (see p. 127).

THE IMMUNE SYSTEM

The immune system, which comprises the white blood cells and the lymphoid tissue in the body, helps us to combat infection. During the last part of pregnancy some antibodies are transferred from the mother across the placenta (see p. 41), which help to protect the baby against a wide range of infections, including several months' protection against many of the common viral illnesses which the mother may have suffered, such as chicken pox. Nonetheless, even the well grown, full term infant is not as good as an adult at mounting an attack against infection and this problem is accentuated in the premature baby who has a very poor immunological response and who has not had the full benefit of placental antibody transfer.

As a result the premature baby is particularly susceptible to infection from a wide variety of organisms and may rapidly become extremely ill. Adult patients are usually persuaded that they do not need antibiotics unless there is definite proof of bacterial infection. However, a newborn baby, especially when premature, is so vulnerable that doctors leave nothing to chance and if infection is suspected, antibiotic treatment is often started immediately. Meanwhile the baby will be screened for infection by sending samples of blood, urine and cerebrospinal fluid, together with swabs from the baby's throat, umbilicus and rectum, to the laboratory for detailed analysis at the first suggestion that anything might be wrong.

THE SMALL-FOR-DATES BABY

The full term baby who is mature but small because of poor growth before birth has particular problems related to inadequate nutrition – the baby has literally been starved in the uterus. This may be due to a number of causes, such as poor placental function, or heavy smoking during pregnancy (see p. 73), but the most notable results are poor temperature control and blood sugar maintenance as well as feeding difficulty.

TEMPERATURE CONTROL

During the last part of pregnancy the well grown baby accumulates 'brown fat' within the body, fat which, when put to use, generates significant amounts of heat. This tissue is lacking in small-for-dates babies, a deficiency which contributes to their tendency to become cold in comparison with normal babies. Even at full term a severely growth retarded baby might need to be nursed in an incubator as a result. Babies with lesser degrees of growth retardation will be nursed either on the SCU or on the nursery in cribs with extra blankets, but their temperature will still be monitored by frequent checks.

BLOOD SUGAR

Full term normally grown babies who are totally breastfed obtain comparatively little nutrition from the breast in the first few days and maintain their blood sugar by using up food stores laid down during pregnancy (see p. 49). The small-for-dates baby has failed to accumulate enough nutritional reserves and is liable to develop low blood sugar (hypoglycemia) which if not attended to, can lead to convulsions that might damage the baby's brain cells. To prevent it, small-for-dates babies are usually fed more than their well-grown counterparts and are given feeds more frequently. The blood sugar is usually checked regularly to ensure that the feeding regime is adequate. A tiny prick is made in the heel, similar to the test for phenylketonuria (see p. 114) and a single drop of blood squeezed out for testing in the laboratory.

SPECIAL CARE OF THE FULL TERM BABY

Your baby may be taken to the SCU for many other reasons even though he or she may be more mature. This can be bewildering if you have just given birth at the expected time, especially if you are still a bit groggy from drugs or very tired after a long labor. Your baby may need extra help on the resuscitator in the labor ward, and may be taken to the SCU, the nursery or intermediate care unit for observation. It is difficult not to worry even though you should be trying to rest. Ask the staff on duty to make sure the pediatrician in charge comes to explain the problem as soon as possible; if your partner is with you he can make the necessary inquiries or find out for you later if you are still worried about anything.

RESPIRATORY PROBLEMS

The common respiratory problems in the premature baby, respiratory distress syndrome and apnea, have already been described. However, there are many other causes of breathing problems which occur in more mature babies. Occasionally babies develop breathing problems because of a structural abnormality. Such defects are comparatively rare but early diagnosis is important as they may require surgery. These abnormalities can usually be ruled out by obtaining a chest x-ray.

Some babies develop an illness in the first few hours of life which is known as transient tachypnea of the newborn. It is characterized by rapid breathing which may persist for several days. It is especially common in babies born after elective cesarean section and is thought to be due to slow clearance from the lungs of the fluid which fills them when in the uterus. It is a less serious condition than hyaline membrane disease.

MECONIUM ASPIRATION

Meconium is the substance inside the bowel while the baby is in the uterus (see p. 109). If the baby is asphyxiated (deprived of oxygen) during labor, meconium may be passed before delivery as a sign of fetal distress, and there is a risk that the baby might inhale some at the time of delivery. If fresh meconium has been noticed in the amniotic fluid during labor a pediatrician will probably have been called to be present at the delivery, who will try to clear any meconium from the airways. However it is sometimes impossible to prevent some of this material being taken into the lungs, and if this happens the airways become plugged so that parts of the lungs fail to expand. Minor degrees of meconium aspiration do not usually create major problems but larger aspirations are serious as they impede breathing and may result in the death of the

A premature baby aged four weeks and born nine weeks early (left), compared with a 'small for dates' baby aged two weeks, weighing only 2lb 10oz at full term (center), and a normal newborn baby of only two days, weighing 8lb 4oz.

baby. Meconium aspiration is the commonest serious breathing problem in full term babies.

PNEUMONIA

A baby may suffer from pneumonia soon after birth, especially if the membranes have ruptured several hours prior to delivery, enabling bacteria to invade the amniotic fluid and cause an infection (see p. 78). It is also possible for the baby to develop pneumonia during the early neonatal period either as a primary disease or as a complication of other lung problems.

BIRTH ASPHYXIA

Birth asphyxia arises when the baby is short of oxygen around the time of delivery and is frequently predicted by the signs of fetal distress. The baby is liable to be born very limp with a slow heart rate and may not begin breathing without help. All labor ward staff are trained to resuscitate such babies – indeed it is one of their most important roles. The aim of neotatal resuscitation is to oxygenate the baby so that he or she becomes a normal pink color with a normal heart rate, and to achieve this without letting the baby become cold.

Many babies who do not cry immediately at birth only require a little stimulation to start them

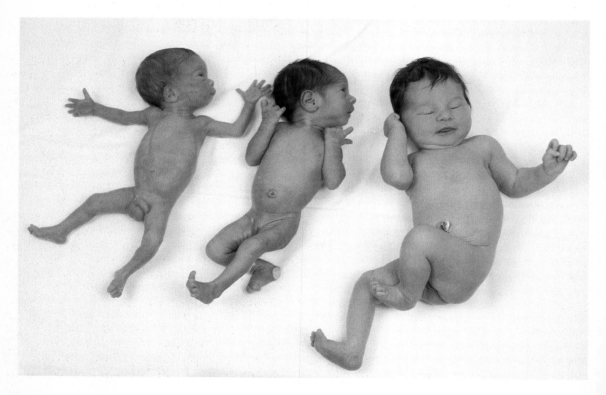

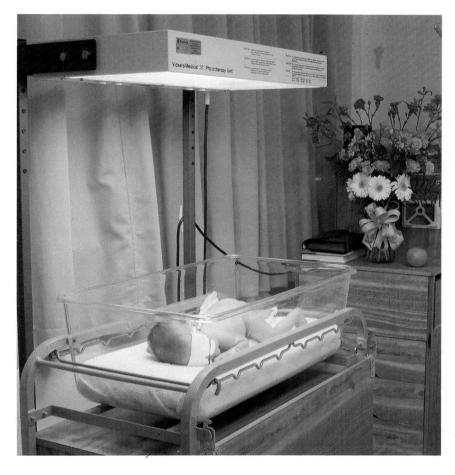

Babies with jaundice are treated with ultraviolet light, which changes the yellow pigment in their skin into a form which is more easily dispersed. Although severe cases may need to be taken to the special care unit, nowadays light therapy is often available either in an intermediate care unit or beside the mother's own bed on the nursery.

breathing, such as a suction catheter being passed into the upper airway, after which they rapidly 'pink up' (see p. 102). However, babies who are severely asphyxiated will need more active intervention in the form of cardiac massage, and ventilation with oxygen either through a mask held over the face or through a tube passed into the trachea (wind pipe). This is obviously a situation which causes great anxiety to parents because of the possibility of brain damage. If the heart rate rises rapidly and the baby takes over his or her own breathing in the first fifteen to twenty minutes then the outlook is usually good, but if the baby fails to breathe on his own during this time even if he has become pink, then a more senior pediatrician is likely to be called to advise on the cause of the asphyxia and its likely result. He or she may want to discuss whether to continue resuscitation (see p. 100).

Babies who have been severely asphyxiated but successfully resuscitated are likely to be transferred to the NICU. While asphyxiated the blood pressure is often low, which, combined with oxygen deprivation, may lead to a temporary failure of oxygen

supply to crucial organs. This could result in swelling of the brain so that the baby may become semi-conscious, have difficulty in breathing properly or suffer from convulsions. It is also common to see a failure of urine production during the first few days. These problems require meticulous monitoring and treatment if adverse long term damage is to be kept to a minimum.

JAUNDICE

Jaundice is yellow discoloration of the skin and is extremely common during the first week of life. The characteristic yellow color, which in mild form makes a fair-skinned baby look as if he has a sun tan, is due to the presence of a pigment known as bilirubin which is formed from the breakdown of hemoglobin within red blood cells. In adults, bilirubin is carried to the liver where it is converted into a form which dissolves in water, and is passed through the bile duct into the intestine to be excreted in the stool. Even at full term, the livers of newborn babies are immature and do not convert the bilirubin into a soluble form very efficiently. Since newborn babies also have an increased rate of red cell breakdown, a minor degree of jaundice occurs frequently in normal full term babies, but usually disperses without special treatment.

In the normal baby jaundice does not appear until at least the second day. It peaks at a modest level at about the fourth day and has disappeared by the eighth day. If the baby is well and the jaundice conforms to this pattern then no investigations or treatment are needed. In premature babies, it is common for jaundice to persist into the third week but in the absence of other worrying features this is usually regarded as normal.

Jaundice which deviates from these well recognized patterns needs investigation, because the level of bilirubin itself may be dangerous and the underlying cause may be significantly different from the description above. Before its conversion in the liver, bilirubin exists in a form which can cross into the brain and be deposited there. This does not occur to any significant extent in healthy full term babies, but if the bilirubin level becomes high in an ill baby then the amount being deposited in the brain is likely to be increased. This deposition in the brain is known as 'kernicterus' and may lead to a sudden and severe neurological illness. Previously this was most commonly seen in association with severe rhesus disease (see p. 22). If the baby survived, it often led to a severe form of cerebral palsy with associated mental retardation and deafness. However, severe rhesus disease is now mercifully rare, as is this particular form of cerebral palsy.

Some very low birth weight babies do develop deafness, although it is unclear whether this is attributable to jaundice. Even so, it is customary to treat jaundice once it has risen above certain levels or when its rate of rise suggests that it will reach high levels.

If your baby develops jaundice on the first day, your blood group and your baby's will be checked to exclude a blood group incompatibility. Injections of anti-D immunoglobulin ('RhoGam') to rhesus negative women before or after delivery have led to a dramatic reduction in the incidence of this problem but occasional cases do occur. Nowadays, incompatibility of the ABO blood groups is a more common problem – unlike rhesus disease it may arise in first pregnancies, and cannot be prevented by immunization.

If the bilirubin level rises very much then the baby will be examined closely for signs of infection and a urine sample will probably be collected to see if there is an infection of the urinary tract and to rule out certain very rare metabolic diseases. If jaundice has not disappeared by the eighth day the baby will be examined again and a blood test done to look for rare causes of prolonged jaundice such as structural abnormalities of the bile duct or hypothyroidism (an under-active thyroid gland).

TREATING JAUNDICE

Jaundice is usually treated by phototherapy (light treatment). The baby remains naked under a special ultra-violet light which changes the chemical structure of the yellow pigment in the skin so that it can be excreted. As a precaution the baby's eyes are covered with a pad during this procedure so that there is no possibility of their being damaged. Babies under phototherapy usually pass rather runny, greenish stools and they may need extra water to drink. In many hospitals phototherapy for full term babies can be given in the nursery or in the intermediate care unit, so that mother and baby do not need to be separated, important for both reassurance and convenience. Jaundiced babies are often very sleepy but need frequent feeding (perhaps even every two hours) which may be difficult and time-consuming. If your baby does need phototherapy, at least if it is taking place close by, you will not have to keep going to the special care unit to feed.

A severely jaundiced baby may require an exchange transfusion, which means that literally all the baby's blood has to be replaced with new blood. This is usually only necessary if the baby has rhesus disease, although it is occasionally required for other forms of blood group incompatibility. The blood is usually exchanged through a catheter in the umbilical vein (through the navel), although other blood vessels may be used. This is a slow procedure which can take up to two hours, and may need to be carried out again.

PROBLEMS WITH FEEDING

Failure to suck may simply be a sign of prematurity, but some of the drugs commonly used for pain relief during labor have a sedative effect upon the fetus and may cause early suppression of sucking in a full term baby. If a baby who has been feeding well goes off his feeds, the pediatrician is likely to consider infection. A baby who is not feeding well may require admission to SCU if tube feeds cannot be given on the maternity ward.

A little vomiting during the first few days is common and provided the baby is otherwise well is unlikely to cause much concern. If however the vomit is green (bile stained), if it is associated with distention of the abdomen or the baby is otherwise unwell it is possible that there is an obstruction in the intestine and the baby will require admission to SCU for investigations, including x-rays of the abdomen. Obstruction usually arises as a result of a structural abnormality of the bowel such as a narrow segment, a twisted bowel or a hernia in the groin, the latter being especially common in premature babies. If the x-ray suggests that there is a blockage the baby will probably need to have an operation to clear it, which in many areas may involve transferring the baby to a referral NICU. Neonatal surgery is highly skilled, requiring the services of a specialist pediatric surgeon and of an anesthetist experienced in treating the newborn.

The great majority of normal babies open their bowels for the first time ('pass meconium') in the first 24 hours (see p. 109). This may be delayed in premature or ill babies. If there is no obvious cause for delay then the pediatrician will want to find out if there is an obstruction in the lower intestine such as an abnormal anus or a congenital abnormality of the large bowel which again may require surgery.

INTENSIVE CARE OF THE NEW BORN

Certain categories of ill babies are defined as requiring 'intensive' as opposed to 'special' care and they will be cared for in 'beds' (usually incubators) in the special care unit specially designated for this purpose. These have a higher level of equipment and staffing. Included in this group will be babies with severe lung disease requiring mechanical ventilatory support or who, although breathing on their own, are requiring constant attention, and babies requiring special procedures such as exchange transfusion. The majority of these babies will be premature, though not exclusively.

When a baby comes into intensive care, he or she will be looked after in an area of the ward where the lights are full on round the clock and the air temperature is between 77° and 82°F. The baby will probably have monitoring electrodes stuck on his or her chest and abdomen within minutes of arriving on the ward, and is likely to have tubes passed into the stomach through the nose or mouth. The baby will probably have an intravenous tube put into an artery and another into a vein. These various leads and tubes will go into a variety of monitoring machines with 'beeping' alarms and flashing lights, and visual display units showing circulatory and respiratory wave forms. Large portable x-ray machines and ultrasound scanners will be moved in and out of the intensive care area during the often frenetic first hours while the support systems are established and the baby stabilized.

This activity is a thrill to the medical and nursing staff, many of whom will have a particular interest in the technology and it is too easy for them to forget that for the parents whose pregnancy has just abruptly and prematurely ended it is a catastrophic nightmare. Once the initial flurry of activity is over and the baby is stabilized in the incubator, the staff are careful to introduce you to the ward and its routines, and will explain the various pieces of apparatus. It is important to understand that the equipment is not actually doing anything to the baby, but rather it is collecting and displaying information so that the staff can assess the baby's clinical conditions without constant handling.

MONITORING BABIES IN INTENSIVE CARE

The baby's temperature will be monitored continuously by a probe on the baby's skin. The recorded temperature may be shown continuously on a digital display. Heart rate and respiration are usually recorded from three small electrodes stuck on the baby's chest. Most monitors display the electrocardiograph (usually abbreviated to ECG) and the respiratory wave form on a visual display unit and usually give a numerical value for the heart and respiratory rates.

The oxygen and carbon dioxide in the baby's arterial blood are monitored carefully to ensure that the baby is being adequately but not over treated. (The level of oxygen and carbon dioxide indicate how well the lungs and heart are operating.) Blood for this purpose can be obtained intermittently by inserting a needle into an artery, usually at the wrist or behind the ankle. This is painful for the baby and causes disturbance, so in the first few days when the baby is at greatest risk most people choose to insert a tube permanently into an artery (catheterization) so that samples of blood can be taken without handling the baby. The most common place to insert such a tube ('A-line') in the first few days is into an artery at the umbilicus, where the line can then be threaded through so that it lies in the aorta, the main artery coming from the heart. After a few days the umbilical arteries close and become impossible to enter and if a line then needs to be inserted it is usually put into the artery at the wrist.

In recent years it has become possible to monitor the blood gases through the skin using 'transcutaneous' electrodes. These warm the skin beneath the electrode so that the tiny blood capillaries expand. The oxygen and carbon dioxide in the blood pass through the skin and can be measured at the surface. Transcutaneous electrodes may be unreliable in babies who are very sick but they have reduced the number of babies who need to have

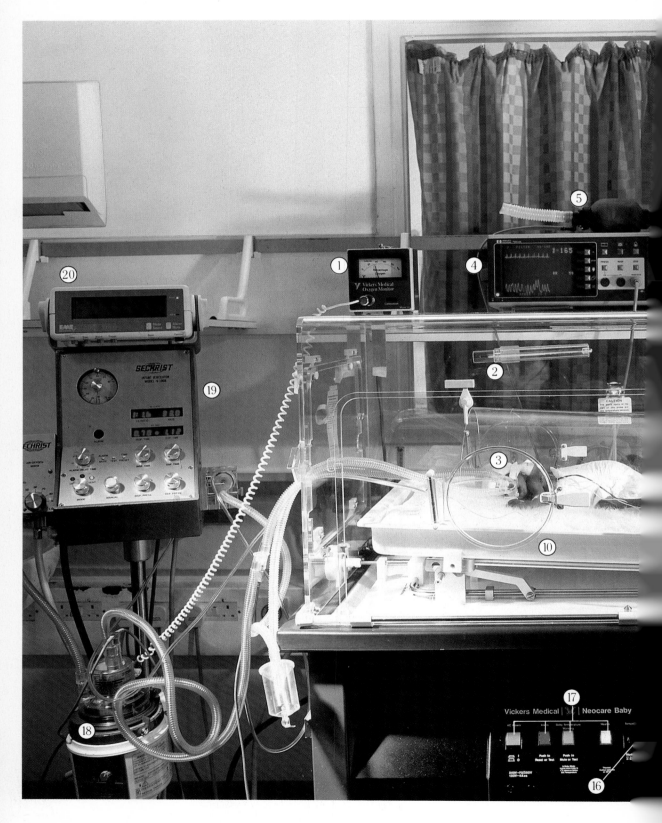

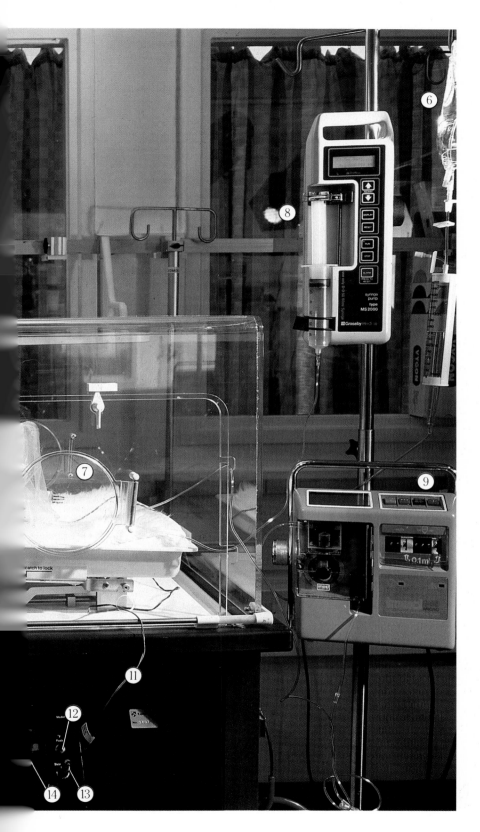

1 Oxygen monitor (monitoring oxygen concentration that baby breathes).
2 Thermometers, measuring air temperature in incubator.
3 Mouthpiece, connecting baby to ventilator.
4 Monitor display, showing heart rate and respiratory trace, can also show blood pressure waveform, temperature and transcutaneous oxygen and carbon dioxide in digital form.
5 Bag and mask, for hand ventilation.
6 Bag of intravenous fluid, with dextrose, sodium and potassium.
7 Porthole, for access to baby.
8 Syringe pump, for intravenous fluids, can also be used for giving continuous feedings.
9 Volumeter pump, for intravenous fluids.
10 Tilting tray, which can be pulled out for access to baby.
11 Skin temperature probe.
12 Conversion to fahrenheit.
13 Skin probe attachment.
14 Display of baby's skin temperature or air temperature.
15 Digital display control button.
16 Control to set air or baby's skin temperature.
17 Control and alarm buttons.
18 Humidifier, for moistening gases in ventilator.
19 Ventilator.
20 Display of pressure wave from ventilator.

arterial lines inserted and have shortened the time for which those lines need to be left in.

Blood pressure gives a very important guide as to the baby's general condition and helps the medical staff monitor the effects of various treatments. Blood pressure can be monitored directly if there is an arterial line and the blood pressure trace may be displayed with the heart rate and respiration on the video screen. If there is no line it is possible to monitor the blood pressure with a small cuff around the upper arm which can be attached to an automatic inflation device, similar to that used for adults during surgical operations, which measures the blood pressure at regular intervals.

APNEA AND BRADYCARDIA

Apneic attacks are periods when the baby fails to breathe. They are particularly common in very premature babies but may occur in any baby as a sign that there is something wrong. Apneic attacks may be very brief, with the baby starting to breathe again on his own, or they may be prolonged, requiring intervention by the staff. The baby is resuscitated in the same way as a baby who does not establish breathing immediately at delivery, either by stimulation or by ventilating through a face mask or a tube in the airway (intubation).

Apneic attacks are important to prevent as they can be associated with a fall in the blood oxygen content and with circulatory disturbances which may occasionally lead to a long term handicap. If the attacks become frequent the medical staff will try to prevent them either by administering drugs which stimulate the baby's respiration, or by supporting the baby's ventilation either with 'continuous positive airway pressure' (CPAP), or 'intermittent positive pressure breathing' (IPPB). Either of these techniques may involve the insertion of a tube (known as an endotracheal tube) either through a nostril or through the mouth, which is firmly held in position by taping.

Continuous positive airway pressure is a technique which involves the continuous application of low pressure to the airway. This may be applied either through an endotracheal tube, through a soft prong inserted in a nostril or via a face mask. It has the effect of helping to hold the baby's lungs open and of stimulating the baby's respiration and is very useful in the treatment of hyaline membrane disease and apneic attacks.

For intermittent positive pressure breathing, a ventilator is actually inflating the baby's lungs. If the baby is very sick total ventilation can be used, inflating the baby's lungs many times a minute. As the baby improves the ventilator rate is turned down so that the baby is mostly responsible for his own breathing, receiving just occasional help.

Bradycardia is slowing of the heart rate, and is often seen in association with apneic attacks. Premature babies quite often suffer brief bradycardic attacks. The causes and implications are similar to those of apneic attacks and they will probably be investigated and treated in the same way.

PNEUMOTHORAX

Pneumothorax arises when a portion of the lung 'bursts' and a leak of air from the lung leads to an accumulation of air in the space between the lung and the chest wall. If the leak is only small this may not affect breathing significantly, but if there is an increase in the accumulation of air, the lung is unable to expand against the surrounding air pressure, and will collapse. In the most serious case ('tension pneumothorax'), structures of the midline, such as the heart, are pushed over toward the other side and the lung on the opposite side is unable to expand properly. Large pneumothoraces can very quickly lead to cardio-respiratory failure, with the baby becoming blue (cyanozed) from poor circulation. The treatment then is an emergency.

Pneumothorax occasionally arises around the time of delivery in otherwise completely well babies. It is, however, more common in babies with lung disease especially when ventilation is required. The treatment is life saving and involves draining the air which has collected between the lung and the chest wall by putting in a tube (a chest drain) through the chest wall. This tube connects to a valve system so that if any further air collects it is drained to the atmosphere, but it is impossible for air to go back the other way.

CEREBRAL HEMORRHAGE

Some of the blood vessels in the brains of babies born before 32 weeks' gestation seem to be rather primitive in comparison with those in more mature babies. In older babies and adults the blood flow through the brain is controlled in such a way that the brain tissue is protected against the effects of sudden surges and reductions of blood flow. The physiological processes affecting this control are less well developed in the premature baby so there may be sudden changes of blood flow through the primitive vessels, causing them to burst. The result is a cerebral (brain) hemorrhage. The parts of the brain where such bleeding is most likely to start are those around the cerebral ventricles, the fluid filled chambers in the center of the brain. This is known as periventricular hemorrhage. If the bleeding continues, the hemorrhage may burst into the ventricles themselves (intraventricular hemorrhage) or into the surrounding cerebral tissue.

Such bleeding may occasionally occur in otherwise well premature babies but it is more likely to happen in those who have other problems, particularly lung disease with complications such as pneumothorax.

Hemorrhages are usually diagnosed by an ultrasound scan of the brain. Ultrasound scanning has become very much a part of the ordinary routine of neonatal care. The equipment is very similar to that used during pregnancy to look at the baby in the uterus, and the technique is both painless and safe. The images are obtained by placing the scanner over the anterior fontanel, the soft part on the top of the baby's head.

A small hemorrhage is usually of no great consequence but more extensive bleeding is a serious event. In the short term the bleeding can lead to a drop in the baby's blood pressure and further deterioration of his general condition. Over the next days and weeks, particularly if blood has escaped into the cerebral ventricle, the fluid filled ventricles may progressively increase in size (hydrocephalus). This happens because the presence of blood within the ventricles interferes with the normal circulation of the cerebro-spinal fluid (CSF). As the size of the cerebral ventricles increases the pressure within may rise, preventing normal development of the surrounding brain tissue. Often this process corrects itself, but if not, the fluid has to be removed to relieve the pressure. This can usually be done by performing a lumbar puncture, which involves inserting a needle into the back and draining the fluid from around the spinal cord. (The fluid in and around the brain is continuous with that around the cord.) While this may sound a difficult procedure, it is easy and safe in a new-born baby and is commonly done while looking for infection.

The more extensive the hemorrhage and the more ventricles have been distended, the greater is the chance that the baby may develop some later neurological handicap, such as a problem with walking. This is a situation which causes concern both to parents and staff. It is extremely difficult at this early stage, when the brain is still growing, to predict what the long term prospects might be for a baby who has suffered cerebral hemorrhage and doctors are usually rather guarded in their advice to parents at this stage. If this happens to your baby, he or she will be monitored closely in the hospital newborn followup program, where the picture will only become clear over the first few years. You will be offered all possible help if necessary (see p. 280).

The ductus arteriosus is a blood vessel passing between the pulmonary arteries, which come from the right side of the heart, and the aorta, on the left. Before birth the fetus obtains oxygen via the placenta rather than the lungs so it is not essential for all the blood to pass through the lungs. The ductus arteriosus is important before delivery as it enables most of the blood coming from the right side of the heart to by-pass the lungs and to flow into the aorta and hence to the placenta.

The ductus usually closes within minutes of birth as the blood flow to the lungs increases and the baby becomes pink. It is however some time before the ductus becomes permanently closed; if the baby has respiratory disease and has a low blood oxygen level the ductus may re-open, a condition known as patent ductus arteriosus (PDA).

The doctor can diagnose this condition by hearing a typical heart murmur. The presence of PDA can lead to heart failure and may delay improvement in the baby's respiratory condition. If this is judged to be the case the medical staff may attempt to close the ductus by the use of drugs; if this fails, they might operate on the baby, to tie off the ductus.

FEEDING THE PREMATURE BABY

Although extremely premature babies often make sucking movements, your baby is unlikely to take a whole feeding by mouth much before 33 weeks' gestation, and unlikely to be taking all his feedings that way until after 35 to 36 weeks. In fact some babies do not do so until 38 to 40 weeks. Delay in establishing total oral feeding can often be the sole reason for keeping a healthy premature baby in hospital, and is often frustrating for parents.

TUBE FEEDING

The most common way to feed a small premature baby is to put the milk down a narrow tube, which is passed through the nose into the stomach. This feeding tube will probably be secured to the face with some sticky tape and left in place between feedings.

The milk feed is drawn into a syringe connected to the tube and held above the baby so that it flows slowly down by gravity. The amount of milk depends on the weight of the baby and his age – most units start with about 1 ounce per pound body weight on the first day, 1½ ounces per pound on the second, rising to about 2½ ounces per pound over the first five days.

You may be able to hold the syringe and give the feed yourself. Depending on your baby's general condition, this can be done within the incubator or the baby may be cradled in your arms.

FEEDING BREAST MILK

If you want to breastfeed your baby, you will be encouraged to express milk regularly from birth (see p. 154), and your own milk will be put down the tube. Any milk you produce in excess of the baby's needs can be stored in the freezer.

Maintaining milk production while the baby is too small to go to the breast can be difficult. Regular expression is the key, but even so you may find you cannot produce adequate milk and the baby might need supplementing with formula. Remember that, even if your milk dries up before the baby is able to feed orally, the breast milk he has received will have been given to him at the time he most needed it.

PROGRESSING TO ORAL FEEDINGS

As the baby grows older and stronger and begins to suck more vigorously, the number of feedings which he is offered orally will be increased. If he tires during a feeding it can always be completed by putting the rest of the milk down the tube. The manner in which the sucking feedings are increased will to some extent depend on whether you want to breast or bottle feed. If you are keen to breastfeed then the staff may be reluctant to offer bottles at all. This is obviously a problem if you go home before the baby, and around this time you may find yourself being encouraged to come back into hospital for a while. If this is not possible you should try to increase your day time visiting so that the baby can be offered the breast during the day and be tube fed at night. Certainly before you take the baby home the staff will need to ensure that you can breastfeed successfully right round the clock.

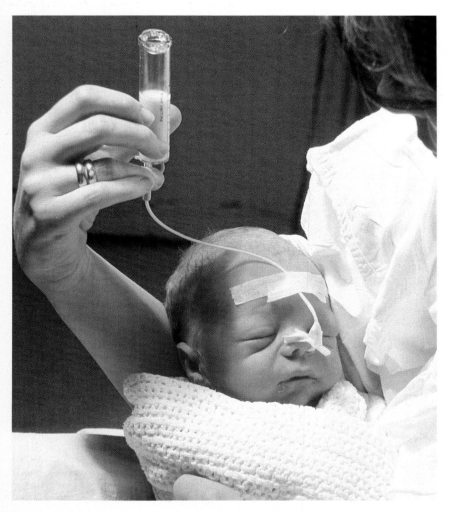

Even though your premature baby may still be being tube fed, and his heart rate, temperature and respiration monitored, if he is otherwise well you may be able to take him out of the incubator to hold.

If you intend to bottle feed, the organization is more straightforward and the baby will probably progress steadily through being offered a bottle on alternate feedings to total bottle feeding. If you are at home, the staff will try to arrange the feeding so that bottles can be offered at visiting times and you can feed your baby yourself. This is obviously much easier to arrange if you can let the staff know when you are going to visit. It can be very upsetting to arrive on the ward to discover that the nurses have already had to give your baby his one feeding of the afternoon.

Healthy babies of 32 or 33 weeks' gestation often appear eager to suck, and parents may be distressed that the staff do not push the feeding along faster. The reason for sometimes holding back a bit is that very few babies can achieve total sucking feedings before 35 weeks. Trying to increase the number of feedings before this will not bring foward the time when total feeding is achieved or the date of the baby's discharge from hospital, and occasionally results in setting the entire process back, with the baby tiring and the number of tube feedings having to be increased again.

FEEDING IN INTENSIVE CARE

If your premature baby needs intensive care he may not absorb milk passed down a feeding tube. In this situation fluids will probably be given as a dilute solution of dextrose by intravenous tube. However, such solutions do not provide a significant number of calories, so if after a few days there is still no likelihood of establishing milk feedings, your pediatrician may choose to feed the baby by IV, with solutions of fat, amino acids and carbohydrate together with minerals and vitamins – a process known as 'total parenteral nutrition' (TPN). The nutrition is often administered via a 'long line', a very fine tube which is inserted under special sterile conditions into a vein in an arm or leg and then passed into one of the great veins in the chest. This way weight loss is minimized and the baby can begin to grow.

The proportion of very low birth weight babies fed intravenously varies between different units. Some pediatricians prefer to withhold milk until the baby is entirely stable and no longer requires intensive care, while others will begin to feed with milk while the baby is still requiring respiratory support from a ventilator.

TYPES OF MILK

When milk is to be introduced there is some dispute as to what type it should be. Many pediatricians favor using the mother's own breast milk, expressed and given straight to the baby. It is believed that the fine tuning of the content of such pre-term milk is ideal nutrition for the premature baby, that it is easily digested and that it contains immunological factors which are not available in any of the formulas. On the other hand, babies fed even with their own mother's milk do not regain their birth weight as quickly as babies fed on the formula specially prepared for premature babies which is now available and which has a higher calorie content. As has already been mentioned, premature babies do not have the nutritional reserves which tide a full-term baby over the few days before his mother's milk comes in, and a premature baby may lose a dangerous amount of weight without these extra calories. However, premature babies fed on breast milk can have their growth rate increased by adding small amounts of carbohydrate and/or fat to the milk.

The long term significance of early rates of weight gain is very difficult to assess, which accounts for the variation in feeding regimes from place to place. The feeding regime should be fully explained to you and your feelings taken into account, especially if you have been keen to breastfeed. If you are not sure, ask the staff and make sure you understand their reasons. A mother can feel frustrated and powerless to help her tiny premature baby, so expressing milk is a way of positively contributing to her baby's care. If you want to express milk but your pediatrician thinks a special premature formula is more suitable for a while, you can always continue to express milk and freeze it. On the other hand, many mothers find continuous milk expressing tedious and tiring, especially if a baby is very premature and may be in special care for three or four months. There are other ways you can care for your baby to compensate for not being able to feed him yourself (see below) and if you can see the benefits of formula feeding in rapid weight gain it is easier to accept.

CARING FOR THE PREMATURE BABY

The days of excluding parents from neonatal wards have gone and it is most unusual for a SCU or NICU ward not to allow free visiting by the parents. Usually you will be asked to put on a gown and to wash your hands before entering the nursery. Units vary as to whether or not they ask people to wear gowns all the time but you are likely to be asked to do so whenever handling the baby. Even when your baby is at his most ill you will usually be encouraged to touch him, since research has shown the benefit of this sort of contact in promoting growth, and at the earliest opportunity you will be able to hold him, maybe even while the baby still has many attachments in terms of tubes and electrodes. The degree of parental involvement is however at the discretion of the medical and nursing staff and occasionally if they are worried about the baby or if another baby in the same room is critical and requires urgent attention, parents may be asked to wait outside. There will probably be a sitting room within the unit for this purpose, where families can relax and spend time with their other children and prepare hot drinks for themselves.

Most purpose-built neonatal wards have the clinical area divided up so that there is a room which will be reserved for babies requiring intensive care, with a series of other rooms for babies requiring different levels of care, probably including some single cubicles for babies who are known to be infected with problem organisms which may be resistant to common antibiotics.

STAFF ON THE SCU/NICU

The problem for parents in identifying staff within the ward is often complicated by the wearing of operating room clothes because of the heat. Some units have a helpful photograph at the entrance to the ward identifying the permanent members of the medical, nursing and support staff, and the staff often wear identifying badges as well. The nursing staff on the ward will have done special courses training them in the care of ill newborn babies.

On the medical side there is likely to be a Neonatologist with overall responsibility for the running of the ward with a team of pediatric Residents and Neonatology Fellows, whose duties may be divided between the neonatal ward and general pediatric wards.

Having a baby on such a ward for many weeks and often at a significant distance from the family home can impose terrible emotional and financial strains. There will be a social worker available who may be able to help with some of these problems. Ask the nurse how to contact the social worker if you need support of any kind, whether financial or otherwise.

There will be other people working on the ward, such as a clerk and cleaners with whom parents often strike up relationships because they may not seem as busy or remote as the medical staff. In addition there are representatives of the support services, such as pharmacists and physiotherapists skilled in working with babies, who will have a commitment to the ward and who are likely to become familiar faces to parents whose babies have a long stay.

INVOLVING THE PARENTS

The nurses will be glad to teach you to take over much of the day-to-day care of your baby when you are able to visit the ward, even if he is still in the incubator. He will probably wear a diaper and be clothed in a stretchsuit or nightie – small babies usually wear hats as well to reduce heat loss through the head. First size baby clothes are far too big for premature babies and look ridiculous. Some people use doll's clothes for their babies and there are now specialist suppliers of tiny baby clothes specially designed for premature babies.

The skin on a premature baby's elbows and knees is very thin and sometimes active babies can rub it until it is quite sore. For this reason babies in some units are nursed on a sheepskin mat rather than on a sheet, which is liable to chafe the skin however soft it is.

You should always wash your hands before handling the baby; you can then open the portholes of the incubator to look after him. You will soon become quite adept at changing and dressing your baby in this confined space. Your baby will seem very small and fragile at first but in fact you will soon discover he is quite resilient.

At the equivalent of about 35 weeks' gestation, a healthy premature will be transferred from an incubator into an ordinary bassinet. From this point onwards his care is very little different from that of a full term newborn baby, except that he will usually be kept in a warmer room.

In the early days the baby is unlikely to have a bath as this is a great disturbance and may make him cold. Instead, he will be cleaned with cotton wool balls dipped in warm tap water. At about 35 weeks, however, he may receive an occasional bath. This is a great thrill for parents and staff, and is always seen as a significant landmark towards going home.

OTHER VISITORS

There is considerable variation as to who, apart from the parents, is allowed to visit the baby. Some units have observation corridors through which the babies can be seen, which eases the problem. Most departments are becoming more flexible in their visiting guidelines and whereas brothers and sisters used to be excluded universally, it is now very common for them to be allowed to come to see the baby and often to touch him. The extension of visiting to grandparents and other friends and family is often limited simply because the presence of large numbers of people makes the ordinary work of the unit very difficult.

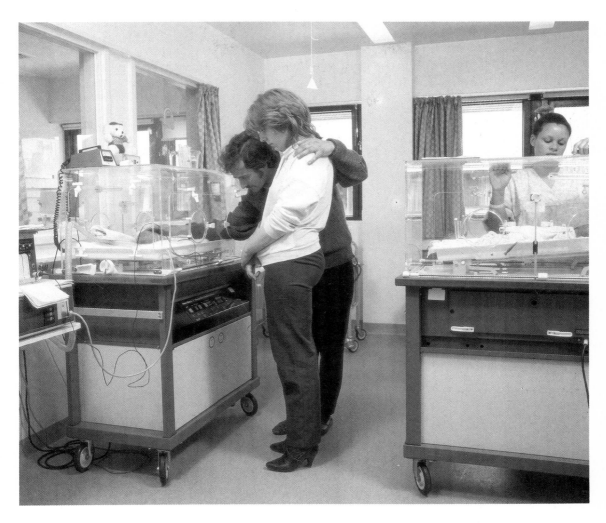

The special care unit often seems frightening to parents because of the amount of sophisticated technology used in the care of tiny and vulnerable babies. However most units now allow parents and sometimes other members of the family to visit as much as they like and encourage parents to help in the care of their babies as much as possible.

GOING HOME

One of the questions you will most want to ask about your premature baby after the birth is how long will it be before he is able to go home. The answer you are likely to be given is that he will be discharged at around the time you expected him to be born, so that if your baby was born at, say, 33 weeks, he will probably have been in hospital for about seven weeks. This sort of example is true in most cases, although if he has no complications at all he will probably be home a little earlier. Twins usually go home together, but if you have more babies you might want to stagger their discharge.

You will almost certainly have gone home yourself long before your premature baby is ready to be discharged, so it may be helpful to come back into the hospital to room in with the baby for a few days before going home together. Most units have so-called 'mother and baby' rooms for this purpose on or close to the special care ward. This is particularly helpful if you live some distance away and have been unable to visit very regularly.

It used to be the case that strict criteria of age and weight were applied before premature babies were allowed home. Now things are much more relaxed. Most units prefer babies to be about 4½ pounds before discharge. Sometimes babies who are mature and feeding well go home sooner. Most units do not apply rules in terms of gestational age but simply want to be sure the baby is feeding satisfactorily.

CHAPTER TEN

BACK TO NORMAL

**Restoring your health and fitness during the six
weeks after your baby's birth**

For the first few hours after your baby is born, you may find it difficult to grasp the fact that you are now a mother – you may be elated, dropping with fatigue, eager to talk to your partner, family and friends, or just want to be left alone with your baby. However you feel, your body is immediately working hard to return itself to its normal non-pregnant condition.

For women, the postpartum period, known as the puerperium, is a time of adjustment after pregnancy, labor and delivery, during which there is a gradual return to normality in bodily functions. It can conveniently be divided into the immediate postpartum period – the first 24 hours after delivery; the early postpartum period – the first ten days during which supervision is usually undertaken by your obstetrician; and the late postpartum period, which lasts until six weeks after delivery, at the end of which the postpartum examination is usually performed. The effects of pregnancy can, of course, continue after this time, but the involution of the genital tract – the uterus, cervix and vagina – will have been completed.

THE MATERNITY WARD

If you had your baby in hospital, your stay could be anything between a few hours for a vaginal delivery, to four or five days for cesarean section. The average stay for a first baby is three days, depending on your own and your baby's progress. When you go home you will continue to be looked after by your own doctor.

Use your time in the maternity ward to rest and to get to know your baby in the knowledge that there is help at hand whenever you need it. Most units nowadays prefer you to keep your baby with you at all times, and visiting is usually open for fathers and family members apart from a rest period in the afternoon. The number of other visitors and visiting times are very much at the discretion of the individual unit – too many visitors can be extremely tiring.

You will be examined by an obstetrician every day, a pediatrician will check your baby's progress

(see p. 111) and the nursing staff will advise you about postpartum exercises and pain relieving techniques (see p. 139).

EARLY POSTPARTUM CHANGES

While still in the labor ward, like most women, you may put your hands on your abdomen and be surprised and delighted by its softness and 'flatness'. However, this delight is often short-lived – in fact when you examine it properly your body will look saggy and stretched, and you will still look five or six months pregnant. This is a temporary state which improves rapidly as the uterus contracts and you begin to regain the strength of the abdominal muscles. You can regain your figure more quickly by following the exercises recommended by the nursing staff.

THE UTERUS

By the end of your pregnancy the uterus will have increased in size till it weighs just over 2 pounds. Immediately after delivery the uterus will begin to decrease in size (involute) rapidly. This reduction is brought about by contraction of the muscle fibers, and by reduction in the number of muscle cells, but because of the stretching action of pregnancy the uterus never quite reduces to the size it was before your first pregnancy. On the first day after the birth, the uterus can be felt at about the level of your navel; after about the tenth or twelfth day of delivery it is no longer possible to feel its position in your abdomen.

THE LOCHIA

The vaginal discharge that follows delivery is known as the lochia. For the first three to four days this is red and may contain some tiny clots. Subsequently it becomes brown, then yellow, before disappearing altogether. The duration of the lochia is very variable – in some women the brownish discharge can last for five to six weeks, in others it can cease after two to three weeks.

If you are breastfeeding, you may notice that the lochial discharge becomes heavier during feeding. This is because oxytocin, the hormone which causes the 'let down' reflex (see p. 150), also causes the uterus to contract.

Heavy bleeding with clots and abdominal pain is not normal, particularly if it happens after the lochia has turned brown, and should be reported to your doctor at once. It may mean that a small piece of placenta or membrane has been retained in the uterus and this may necessitate a small operation to empty the womb – an 'evacuation of retained products of conception' (ERPC).

THE BREASTS

Lactation begins about 48 to 72 hours after delivery, with engorgement of the breasts as the milk comes in (see p. 154). Before this time the breasts produce a thin yellowish substance called colostrum. Milk production is controlled by the hormone prolactin, and the release of the milk, stimulated by suckling, is regulated by oxytocin, as mentioned above. Both these hormones are produced by the pituitary gland in the brain. The mechanisms of milk production and breastfeeding in general are covered in detail in Chapter 11.

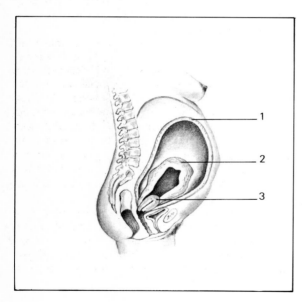

The uterus involutes (shrinks back) to its pre-pregnancy, normal size during the six weeks of the postpartum period. 1 *The uterus just before delivery.* 2 *Immediately after delivery; the uterus has shrunk down to about the level of the navel.* 3 *The uterus six weeks after delivery.*

SUPPRESSION OF LACTATION

Some mothers may not wish to breastfeed, or may be unable to for medical reasons – either to do with themselves or their babies. Once the suckling stimulus has been removed then milk production will cease, but the breasts will still go through a period of being painful and engorged. Wearing a good supporting bra and the use of mild painkillers are usually the only treatments required for the few days that this process takes, and this natural suppression of lactation is generally preferred.

It is possible to assist the process with medication, and nowadays the usual treatment would be with the drug bromocriptine, which inhibits the production of prolactin, the hormone associated with milk production. It has to be taken for about fourteen days and tailed off slowly, otherwise lactation can start up again immediately the drug is withdrawn. It can also cause nausea, particularly on an empty stomach. If nausea becomes a problem for you, ask the advice of your doctor or midwife.

GENERAL PHYSICAL CHANGES

Following delivery the average woman loses about 9 pounds in weight just as a result of the excretion of accumulated fluid – so you will notice a great increase in urine output. The circulation returns to normal, but the blood clotting mechanism is exaggerated, which accounts for the increased likelihood of thrombosis (a clot being trapped in a vein) at this time (see p. 72). Hormonal changes are abrupt – estrogen and progesterone levels fall to non-pregnant amounts within a week.

ABDOMINAL AND PELVIC FLOOR MUSCLES

The abdominal muscles will have been greatly stretched during pregnancy – the waist measurement of the average woman increases from about 28 inches to as much as 50 inches! At first the muscles and their connective tissues stretch easily – but after a while the ½ inch strip of tissue which holds together the two straight abdominal muscles (the recti abdominis) begins to split and the two sides of the abdominal 'corset' separate, leaving a gap which may be as much as 4-5 inches wide. This is known as diastasis. The muscles will never again join, but muscle tone can be regained, particularly with the help of special postpartum exercises (see p.140).

The pelvic floor muscles will also have been stretched during your delivery and you will probably notice a distinct weakness in your perineal area. It is important to begin exercising these muscles as

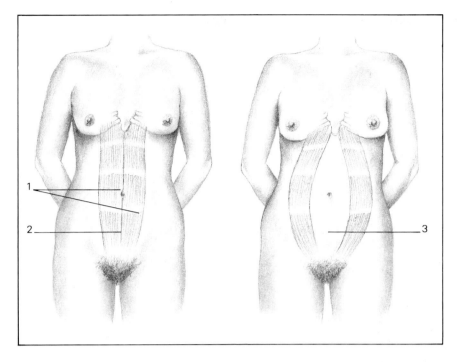

Far left: *The recti abdominis (straight abdominal muscles) before pregnancy (1).* Left: *The recti immediately after delivery showing how they have been stretched apart at the middle (linea alba) (2). The resulting gap (3) is known as the diastasis recti.*

soon as possible after the birth (see p. 140) – because they are invisible, the pelvic floor muscles are unfortunately often forgotten and are not exercised as vigorously as the abdominal muscles although they perform an equally vital function.

COMMON POSTPARTUM PROBLEMS

Even the most straightforward normal delivery can leave a woman feeling drained and tired, and few new mothers escape all the rather annoying physical problems associated with the postpartum period. If you have had to have stitches, or your labor was long and your baby quite big, you will probably have some discomfort to contend with after the birth. However, there are ways these problems can be alleviated – one of the most important being adequate rest!

PERINEAL DISCOMFORT

You may experience discomfort in the perineum (the pelvic floor area) even if you have no stitches, because of bruising, swelling and tiny lacerations caused by the passage of the baby. Usually the more stitches that were required the more the discomfort, but there are various ways of relieving it. The most obvious is of course analgesia – your doctor or nurse can give you pain-relieving drugs which will not harm your baby if you are breastfeeding.

Although you may be nervous because of the pain, try to begin your pelvic floor exercising – four tightenings held for a count of four at least every half hour (see p. 32) – as soon as possible. It will help disperse the bruising and swelling and help to speed the healing process.

A short relaxing soak in a comfortably warm salt bath (a couple of handfuls of salt is sufficient) is very soothing, and cleansing the perineal area with a sitz bath, if available, is also extremely helpful. Ice packs applied to the area are also soothing, and you may be able to obtain an anti-inflammatory foam which you spray on to your sanitary towel. Ask your nurse about this. Most hospitals can supply an inflatable rubber ring to sit on so that you are not putting direct pressure on the painful area, but it is also a good idea to try to lie flat as much as possible, even for feeding (see p. 153).

If you are badly affected, infrared heat is a soothing technique which can be used if stitches become infected or are slow to heal. Stitches are usually of material which dissolves in ten to twelve days and so do not have to be removed. They may float away in the bath.

HEMORRHOIDS AND CONSTIPATION

The action of progesterone on smooth muscle gives many women a predisposition to hemorrhoids (piles) during pregnancy, but they are also a particular nuisance after delivery. They often protrude through the anus as a result of the expulsive efforts of the second stage of labor and become engorged and painful. Your doctor may prescribe an ointment for local treatment plus pain-killers, and ice packs pressed against the affected area are also helpful. Try also to avoid constipation.

During the early postpartum period you will probably be experiencing a change in your diet with hospital food, and may also need to take iron pills which tend to make the constipation worse. Try to eat high-fiber food, and a gentle laxative may be prescribed, although it may affect your baby if you are breastfeeding.

Perineal discomfort or hemorrhoids (or both) may inhibit you from trying to move your bowels at first, and some women worry that they may tear their stitches. Try supporting your perineal area with a spare sanitary towel or soft pad of toilet paper as you sit on the toilet – your stitches won't come apart and the support will give you confidence by making the first bowel movement much more comfortable.

'AFTER PAINS'

'After pains' are the cramping pains caused by contractions of the uterus after delivery. They are usually worse after second and subsequent pregnancies and are often most severe during breast-feeding, due to the release of oxytocin (see above). They can be relieved by mild analgesics and usually disappear within a few days of the birth.

BLADDER PROBLEMS

It is not uncommon to have difficulty in passing urine in the first day or two after delivery, particularly if you have had a long labor and a complicated delivery requiring forceps or a cesarean section, possibly with epidural anesthesia. This problem is caused by bruising to the bladder and urethra, and it usually resolves itself once you are up and about. Soaking in a warm bath often helps. Very rarely a urinary catheter may be necessary to drain the bladder for a short time.

Sometimes women have difficulty in controlling their urine flow and will notice leakage of urine on coughing and laughing – so-called stress incontinence. This is usually due to weakness of the pelvic floor muscles and can be considerably helped by pelvic floor exercises and other stimulative treatments.

ANEMIA

If you lost blood during your delivery, had a cesarean section or were known to be anemic before the birth, your hemoglobin levels will be tested on the postnatal ward and you may be given iron pills. Rarely a very anemic mother may require a blood transfusion.

Anemia is quite difficult to diagnose without a blood test, although severely anemic women look pale and often complain of fatigue, which improves dramatically when the anemia is treated. Most women are given a blood test routinely on about the fourth day after the birth from which any unsuspected anemia can be detected. If you are found to be anemic it is important to continue to take your iron pills at least until your postpartum check-up, when your blood will be tested again. This is specially important if you are breastfeeding. If iron pills make you feel sick, or you are constipated, talk to your doctor or nurse.

BACK PAIN

Backache can be troublesome and is often related to bad posture, exacerbated by ligaments loosened by the hormonal changes of pregnancy. Postpartum back pain is not restricted to any one part of the back and can range from upper back and neck pain, to lumbar or sacro-iliac pain, with very many women complaining of pain between their shoulder blades in the early days as well. If you have had an epidural anesthetic, you may occasionally experience a little discomfort in your back over the site of its insertion – this is caused by slight bruising around the area and will disappear gradually in the same way that any bruising does.

Even women who did not have sacro-iliac pain prenatally may suffer it following the birth of their babies. It can be triggered by the movement of your legs into and out of the lithotomy position (the position required for forceps delivery or stitching). Try to make sure your legs are lifted into and out of the stirrups simultaneously.

If you experience sacro-iliac pain, your physical therapist or nurse may be able to supply a simple elastic support for your back; an old girdle may be helpful. The positions shown for the relief of sacro-iliac pain on page 54 may be necessary. If the pain fails to respond to these measures, your doctor can help with a referral.

The stabbing ache between your shoulder blades which comes on after a few days can almost always be traced to a bad feeding position such as sitting on the edge of your bed or chair and leaning forward over the baby. It's always worth an extra 30 seconds of your baby's crying to make sure you are properly supported (see p. 152) before you begin feeding. Remember that it is going to take four to five months for your ligaments to return to normal and they are easily strained until then.

Low back pain can also be caused by bad posture. Bending over a low crib or changing table can cause intense pain in the lumbar region which can be aggravated by physical fatigue. Try to avoid this sort of bending, and always squat down rather than bending at the waist to pick up something from floor level.

FATIGUE AND MOOD CHANGES

You may feel exhausted after having your baby, so try to get as much rest as you can during the day. Enlist as much help as you can from your partner, friends and relatives.

Mood swings are very common after having a baby, and you may find yourself feeling miserable and crying for no obvious reason. This is particularly likely around the third postpartum day and is probably much influenced by the profound hormonal changes which are taking place around this time. It quickly resolves itself and needs no special treatment, except of course sympathy and understanding, especially from your partner and visitors.

Rarely, a very much more prolonged period of depression will occur after childbirth, with physical as well as mental symptoms, such as a disturbance of sleep pattern and loss of appetite as well as lack of interest in your baby and things around you. This is a serious problem and needs advice and treatment from your doctor. Indeed you may not realize yourself that it is happening – your partner however may be more vigilant and notice the signs of listlessness, fatigue and general inability to cope which may not be relieved by a reasonable period of rest. If a father does notice this in his partner, he should talk to the doctor about it.

THE FATHER AND THE NEW FAMILY UNIT

One of the benefits of a home birth is that after the midwife and doctor have gone home, mother, father and baby can be together. It can be hard for the newly delivered father to have to leave his family in the hospital and go home to an empty house. The past few hours have been a time of stress for him too and he may well feel in need of support.

Pregnancy is a time for emotional as well as physical growth and maturation for both parents. But it would be an odd father who didn't at some stage worry about the impending changes in his life and in the relationship between his partner and himself. Here he is, his family unit suddenly increased by as much as 50 per cent (the first baby makes the most impact) and his whole way of life is about to change for ever. Any man who thinks things will return to exactly the way they were before his partner was pregnant is deluding himself and is going to be disappointed.

A new father finds the task of getting to know and cherish his newborn baby is just as thrilling and emotional as it is for the mother who actually gave birth.

The mature and understanding father will be prepared for tiredness, turmoil and disorganization – he can be a great source of strength and support during what can be a trying and exhausting time for both partners. He may have to show his caring and love in different ways for a while and accept that his partner's sexual desire is at a very low ebb.

AFTER A CESAREAN SECTION

The most important thing to remember if the baby was delivered by cesarean section is that you have had a major abdominal operation which will restrict your mobility and require the administration of post-operative analgesia (pain relief). You will need help with feeding and changing your baby every time for at least the first 48 hours, and it may be worth asking if your partner, mother or a friend can stay with you in the hospital to help you during that time.

The nurse will show you the most comfortable way to get in and out of bed and how to support your wound if you need to sneeze, cough, laugh or move. She will show you the early breathing, foot and leg exercises which are routine following any form of abdominal surgery. Having a cesarean section doesn't mean that you can't breastfeed, although this may be slightly more difficult. If you support the baby on a pillow so that he is not resting directly on your wound, or feed him lying down (see p. 153), you will find that breastfeeding can proceed quite successfully.

Common problems after cesarean section are difficulty in passing urine and abdominal gas, which tends to be worst on the second or third day after delivery. Deep breathing while pulling your abdominal muscles in firmly and gentle pelvic rocking (see p. 32) are both helpful.

You are likely to be in hospital for five to six days after a cesarean section. Many women are grateful that modern birth technology has given them a healthy undamaged baby, but others may feel very disappointed after a cesarean, especially if they had been hoping for a normal delivery until the last minute. It is helpful to talk to your obstetrician before you are discharged and go over again the reasons for your cesarean operation to clarify whether this is something that might need to be repeated in a subsequent pregnancy.

POSTPARTUM COMPLICATIONS

After delivery, most women experience little more than the minor disorders that have already been mentioned above. However there are a few more serious complications which can occur in a few cases.

HEMORRHAGE

During the immediate postpartum period there is a danger of hemorrhage from the site of the placenta within the uterus (see p. 91). After the first 24 hours, the likelihood of severe hemorrhage lessens but may still occur if a small piece of placental tissue or membrane is retained. This is called a secondary postpartum hemorrhage; if it happens after you have been discharged from hospital you will have to be readmitted at once and usually have an ERPC (evacuation of retained products of conception).

INFECTION

The genital and urinary tracts are particularly susceptible to infection after childbirth. Urinary infections are likely if you have a long labor or repeated bladder catheterizations. The genital tract is vulnerable because the cervix is open, the tissues are bruised and the lochia neutralizes the normal acidity of the vagina. Other common sites for infection are the breasts, the sites of perineal lacerations or episiotomy and a cesarean section wound.

If your temperature rises at all, it will be taken seriously by the medical staff as a sign of infection and will be fully investigated. Once the source of the infection has been found you will be given suitable antibiotics to clear it up.

THROMBOSIS

Blood clotting mechanisms are enhanced after delivery, causing a predisposition to thrombosis (blocked circulation caused by a clot in a vein). If this occurs, it is usually in the deep veins of the lower leg, causing pain and stiffness in the calf muscle. Thrombosis in the pelvic veins is also possible, although this usually does not have any symptoms. It usually occurs about ten days after delivery.

Thrombosis is a rare but very serious complication of the postpartum period as blood clots can travel to the lungs to cause a pulmonary embolus. Risk factors for thrombosis include a past history of thrombosis, obesity, smoking, age over 35 years, operative delivery especially by cesarean section, a prolonged labor and dehydration. Superficial varicose veins do *not* predispose to this condition however.

The risk of thrombosis can be reduced by early mobilization, so the nurses will be eager to see you up and out of bed within hours of the delivery. Leg exercises also help (see p. 31), and certain mothers may be given anticoagulant treatment.

PSYCHIATRIC PROBLEMS

Postpartum depression has already been mentioned, but it is worth bearing in mind that it can have an insidious onset and only become manifest weeks or even months after delivery. There is also a very rare complication of the postpartum period known as postpartum psychosis, which is characterized by hallucinations, restlessness, insomnia and sometimes expressions of harm toward the baby. This condition needs expert psychiatric help and usually involves in-patient treatment.

BEFORE YOU LEAVE HOSPITAL

While you are in hospital (or are under the care of the doctor at home) you will have daily checks of temperature, blood pressure, involution of the uterus and inspection of your stitches. The baby's general progress will also be monitored (see p. 111).

RHESUS NEGATIVE MOTHERS

If your blood group is Rhesus (Rh) negative (see p. 22) then the blood group of your baby will also have been checked by taking a blood sample from the umbilical cord at delivery. If the baby is Rhesus positive then you will be given an injection of Anti-D immunoglobulin ('Rho Gam') within 72 hours of the delivery to prevent you forming antibodies against rhesus positive cells which could cause severe anemia and jaundice in your next baby.

RUBELLA IMMUNIZATION

If you were not immune to rubella when routinely tested at the start of this pregnancy (see p. 22) then you will be offered immunization by injection. You should avoid pregnancy for three months after this has been given.

THE POSTPARTUM EXAMINATION

When you leave hospital you will be given an appointment six weeks after delivery for a postpartum check-up. It is frequently seen as the 'signing-off' consultation, whether it is with your own doctor or the hospital obstetrician. Although this check is primarily concerned with the physical aspects, most good doctors will be equally interested in you as a person; remember that the postpartum check is to establish *your* state of health, not to find out how your baby is progressing, which is done separately by the pediatrician or hospital pediatric clinic (see p. 189).

It is important to keep this appointment – in the flurry of looking after a newborn baby it is easy to ignore your own state of health, but ultimately both yours and your baby's well-being may depend on it. Use the check-up to discuss any concerns you have about yourself, no matter how small they may seem. Write them down beforehand as you did at prenatal visits in case you forget anything when the time comes.

THE PHYSICAL EXAMINATION

The postpartum check is very like your early prenatal visits. Blood pressure, weight and urine are all checked and you may have a blood test as well if you were anemic immediately after the birth. Your breasts will be examined, whether you are breast-feeding or not, and the doctor will check your abdomen to see that the muscles are returning to normal.

You will be given an internal examination to check the uterus, cervix and vagina, ensuring that any stitches or laceration have healed and that the vaginal walls are neither too tight nor too lax. The doctor will also take a cervical smear for testing if this was not done prenatally. If you have resumed intercourse let the doctor know if you have experienced any discomfort and he or she will advise you on the best course of action.

The doctor will also want to know when the lochia ceased and if you have had any subsequent bleeding or discharge. He or she will also want to know if menstruation has begun and will probably discuss contraception with you or refer you to the family planning clinic.

The doctor will also want to know how you are feeling about your baby, whether you are eating properly and getting enough rest, and how the rest of the family have reacted to the new baby. If any problems, physical or emotional, remain, make sure that a further appointment is made to assess your progress. There is no need to put up with backache, perineal discomfort, pain during intercourse, stress incontinence or a feeling of constant fatigue or depression. Your doctor is there to help you return to physical and emotional comfort and strength, so don't feel that you are bothering him with your anxieties.

POSTPARTUM EXERCISES

Most women will find that quite a lot of regular exercising will be necessary to firm and strengthen weak stretched muscles – and during the first few postpartum weeks this may be the very last thing you feel like doing or have time for. However, one of the causes of fatigue following your baby's birth is the fact that your abdominal and pelvic floor muscles aren't able to carry out their normal role of supporting your internal organs properly. Nor are they able to give proper support to your spine, which, together with the softened state of its ligaments, makes it much more vulnerable to injury.

Apart from the immediate aims of reducing fatigue and the risk of back damage, the long term aims of postpartum exercises are also important. Every woman wants to regain her figure or even improve on the shape she had before pregnancy – the tape measure and her old clothes are cruel critics of the state her body is in. If she looks good, the chances are she'll feel good too. So much for the exterior figure; but there is an interior 'figure' as well – the shape and strength of the pelvic floor muscles, the vagina and all the connective tissue and ligaments which go to make up this incredibly important part of the female body. Even when clothes fit and visible muscles are firm and strong again, because the pelvic floor area is out of sight it is often out of mind, too, and a woman can be storing up long term trouble for herself in terms of stress incontinence, prolapse and sexual dissatisfaction if the pelvic floor remains lax.

EARLY DAYS

Unless you have been following a rigorous exercise program during the whole of pregnancy your motto for postpartum exercising must be 'slowly but surely'. A sudden return to the aerobic workout of a year ago is ill advised and foolhardy.

For the first few days concentrate on foot exercises and pelvic tilting (see page 32), which you should now do lying on your back with both knees bent, standing up, or sitting on a chair. (Omit pelvic tilting on all fours until your vaginal loss is no longer red or brown.) Pelvic floor tightening and relaxing (see page 32) can be started while you are still in the maternity ward. Some women will have reasonably normal sensation in this area, while others may find it difficult to control these muscles at all during the first few days!

'Little and often' is the best way of dealing with the early postpartum exercises. Pelvic floor and abdominal muscle work can easily be carried out while you're feeding, day or night. Progress the strengthening effect of these gentle exercises by holding your tummy muscles in while you count slowly – first up to six – then eight, ten, and finally twelve. Vary your pelvic floor work too; sometimes draw the muscles inwards and upwards, then relax at once; other times, contract the muscles – count up to four and then release slowly.

Postpartum exercises
1 Curl ups

Lie on your back with your knees bent up high. Draw your abdominal muscles in, lift your head and shoulders from the floor and curl up as high as you can, reaching your hands toward your feet. Try not to jerk upward, and don't tuck your toes under something heavy or hold on to your legs. Hold the position for a moment, without holding your breath, then lie back slowly.
Increase the strength of this exercise by staying curled up for longer each time – up to 30 seconds.

2 Curl downs

Sit on the floor with your knees bent up high, your ribs lifted, abdomen pulled in and your arms stretched out in front of you. Gradually round your back and curl down slowly; stop when you reach half way – hold the position a moment then return to your starting position without holding your breath. Increase the time you hold the position gradually to 30 seconds.

3 Side bends

Lie on the floor with your knees bent up high. Draw your abdomen in firmly and stretch your right hand towards your right foot, bending sideways – then return to the middle. Repeat to the left. At first, bend to one side and then rest in the starting position; as you get stronger move from side to side like a clock's pendulum, but make sure your abdominal muscles are held in firmly all the time.

4 Twisters

Once again, lie on the floor with bent knees and abdomen well drawn in. This time stretch your right hand towards your left foot, twisting your body from the waist – then return to the floor. Repeat to the other side.

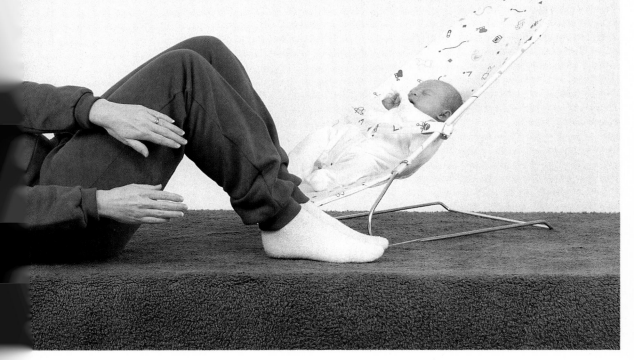

POSTURE

The way you sit and stand after birth can reduce the size of your waist by as much as 4-5 inches! Slump in your chair or walk about with rounded back, drooping breasts and sagging abdomen and it will take you much longer to regain your normal shape. Sit well in to the back of your chair, with a cushion behind your waist and bosom lifted, and you'll be two inches 'thinner'; stand and walk 'tall' – breast and ribs lifted, bottom tilted under – and inches drop off your waist measurement! Your body has forgotten its normal upright posture after months of adapting to an increasing abdominal bulge, so make use of mirrors and shop windows constantly to check on your posture. It is important, too, to choose a stroller with handles that are not too low for you (see p. 176).

STRONGER EXERCISES

While still on the maternity ward, you can ask the nursing staff to help you begin the rehabilitation of your muscles, and also seek their advice regarding perineal and back pain. There are exercises to do regularly at home which will strengthen your abdominal and pelvic floor muscles and close the gaping space in front (see page 135). The width of the gap between the recti abdominis muscles varies from woman to woman – a lot depends on her height and pelvic shape and the size and number of babies is important too. Also, there are many exercise classes available in the community specifically geared to postpartum women. Joining them not only helps restore your body to well-being but also offers a chance to meet other women who have also just come home with new babies.

To check your own abdomen, lie on your back with your knees bent up high. Put two or three fingers in the midline just below your umbilicus and press them into your abdomen. Then draw your abdominal muscles in firmly, curl your head and shoulders up from the floor and reach for your feet with your other hand. You will feel your two recti come together as you lift up and then move out sideways again as you lower back. Some women may have a wide gap – as much as four inches or more to start with. Others will find that the space is only a couple of fingers wide.

Eventually, the two recti muscles should lie side by side, about ½ inch apart, and should feel firm and strong when they work.

WHEN TO EXERCISE

The amount of spare time for exercises will be strictly limited at first – there are many other demands on your time – so restrict yourself to the four illustrated on pages 140 and 141, and do them as often as possible. However, don't neglect your pelvic floor exercises (see p. 135) which can be done at any time.

Try to find three or four short periods during every day to lie down and do these exercises. Start by doing each one eight times and gradually increase to 20. Again, 'Little and often' is better than fifteen minutes once a week when you're feeling guilty because you haven't thought of exercising for days!

These exercises are designed gradually to improve your muscle control and strength so that when your baby is a few months old, you will be fit for whichever form of normal exercising you prefer. It can be dangerous to go to an intensive exercise class to get fit – only start when you are fit and your muscles are strong again. Make sure you tell your exercise teacher that you have recently had a baby when you do take up any new form of exercise.

RESUMING SEXUAL INTERCOURSE

There is no reason to wait until after your six-week postpartum check before resuming sexual intercourse, unless your doctor advises it because of a particular problem. Resumption of intercourse is very much a personal decision and most men these days understand that, physically and mentally, their partners may not feel like full coitus for quite a long time. Apprehension, the soreness from stitches or bruising and vaginal dryness may make the first attempt rather uncomfortable.

When sex becomes attractive again, it's worth bearing one or two points in mind to make things more relaxed. Use a smear of KY jelly or another lubricant just inside the vagina and vulva and forward to the clitoris. Postpartum dryness can sometimes be a transitory problem, but if you are breastfeeding your estrogen levels will be at a low level throughout that time which may make the vagina slightly inflamed and tender.

A nervous woman will feel more confident if she is on top so that she can control the amount of penetration. Both partners may be unable to relax for fear of waking the baby – if so, it will not do any harm to move the crib into another room for a while.

Ovulation does not normally resume until two or three months after delivery in mothers who are not breastfeeding, but can occur as early as six weeks, so contraception does need to be considered. In breastfeeding mothers the return of ovulation is delayed and menstrual periods may not return for many months. However it is important to remember that it is possible to conceive while breastfeeding.

CONTRACEPTION

Contraception may be the last thing on your mind when you have just had a baby, but if you want to space your family then it makes sense to consider various options at this time.

The midwife or doctor advising you on family planning will often start by discussing the method you used before becoming pregnant. In some circumstances it may be possible merely to return to this exactly as before, but in others certain modifications are needed because of changes brought about by the pregnancy.

THE PILL

If you are breastfeeding then the combined estrogen-progestogen pill is not usually recommended as it can reduce the amount of milk produced – the progesterone-only pill, sometimes known as the 'mini pill', is suggested instead as it has no effect on lactation. It is usually started around the twenty-first day after delivery and must be taken daily. It is not quite as effective as the combined pill and a change is generally recommended to alternative contraception once breastfeeding is discontinued. For non-breastfeeding mothers either pill is suitable.

THE INTRAUTERINE DEVICE (COIL)

If this is your chosen method of contraception then it can be fitted at your six-week postpartum check. Insertion before this time is not recommended because the uterus has not regained its normal size. The fitting of an intrauterine device is much easier once you have had a baby as the cervix has been stretched. This makes it a method worth considering even if, in the past, you may have rejected it.

THE DIAPHRAGM

Even if you have used this method in the past you will need to be fitted for a new diaphragm once you have had a baby. This is best done at the six-week postpartum visit, as by this time the genital tract should have returned to normal. The stretching of the vagina during delivery, however, will probably mean that you will need a slightly larger sized diaphragm than before.

THE CONDOM

This popular method of contraception is often a sensible choice for the early postpartum months. No preliminary fitting or insertion is required and it may be a relief to transfer the responsibility for contraception to your partner. This method is most effective in combination with spermicidal cream.

STERILIZATION

You may consider that after this pregnancy you do not want any more children and are looking for a permanent form of contraception. If you are thinking of sterilization then you should discuss this with your obstetrician before birth.

Nowadays, it is possible to undergo sterilization through a minor operation performed straight after you have delivered. Many obstetricians can arrange for this tubal ligation if notified promptly at delivery. Some obstetricians prefer to delay the procedure for six to eight weeks and to have the operation performed via a laparoscope – a telescopic instrument which is inserted just below the navel. This procedure usually is performed through outpatient surgery with minimal discomfort.

It may be that your partner has decided he will be sterilized, in which case he will undergo the operation of vasectomy and will need to discuss this with his doctor and the local hospital. Vasectomy operations are not immediately effective and so you will have to consider alternatives until the stored sperm supplies have been ejaculated.

Although the operations of both male and female sterilization are meant to be permanent and reversibility cannot be guaranteed, they are associated with a small failure rate. The real concern with sterilization operations is not the failure rate, but the finality. There is no guaranteed method to maintain frozen sperm in a viable state indefinitely. Many couples hesitate to consider either vasectomy or tubal ligation because they worry that some unforeseen twist of fate will make them regret cutting off the possibility of further procreation forever. If you do not feel perfectly comfortable with this finality, do not proceed. Furthermore, it is an issue that certainly warrants discussion with others (friends, clergy, family) if ambivalence persists. Some states may have laws mandating permission from a spouse before proceeding. Lastly, be sure your health insurance covers the procedure; most do not unless there is a medical indication.

THE RHYTHM, TEMPERATURE AND MUCUS METHODS

These rather unreliable methods of contraception are based on the avoidance of intercourse around the time of ovulation. Because regular ovulation may take some time to re-establish itself after delivery these methods are particularly inappropriate for use in the postpartum period.

FEEDING THE BABY

**The essentials of feeding for the young baby,
whether you choose breast or bottle**

Apart from the birth itself, feeding is probably the aspect of babycare that most preoccupies new parents. Feeding is fundamental to the well-being of a new baby and is a positive symbol of the love and care that parents can give to their child. Whether your baby is fed by breast or by bottle, if feeding is going well you can see the benefit to your baby by the way that he is thriving, and the pleasure he obviously derives from it.

You will probably be asked early in your visits to the obstetrician how you intend to feed your baby. Many women will have made the decision already; others may not like the idea of breastfeeding or may be undecided. The doctor will probably discuss the pros and cons of breast and bottle feeding with you during your pregnancy, and there is usually a session on feeding in preparation classes run by hospitals, clinics and others. If you haven't made up your mind early in your pregnancy, you still have plenty of time to think about it before the birth. The following guidelines may help you.

BREAST OR BOTTLE

Every woman is naturally equipped to feed her baby, yet as recently as twenty years ago, as many as 75 per cent of all babies in the West were bottle fed. This statistic is now changing, as the advantages of breastfeeding are being re-established, and women are being able to make informed decisions for themselves. The two most powerful reasons for favoring breastfeeding are the nutritional suitability of breast milk for the human baby, and the great psychological pleasure which successful breast-feeding brings to mother and child. But there are other factors which also need to be considered, such as allergy, medication, convenience and expense.

NUTRITIONAL FACTORS

Human milk is by definition precisely formulated for the nurturing of human babies, and, provided that breastfeeding is successfully established, is always completely satisfying. There is no doubt that un-treated cow's milk as delivered from the dairy is an unsuitable formula for human infants on several counts – not surprisingly, since it is perfectly formulated for calves!

It has a higher protein and lower carbohydrate content than does human breast milk, and although the contribution of fat to its overall calorie content is similar to that of breast milk, there is a higher proportion of saturated to polyunsaturated fat. Just how significant some of these differences are is still unclear, but there is no doubt that the high protein content makes it quite unsuitable.

Another great area of difference is in the mineral content. In contrast to other mammals, human milk has a particularly low sodium (salt) content. The young baby's kidneys have difficulty in dealing with too much sodium and in trying to get rid of it, the baby loses water as well, subsequently becoming dehydrated. This can be dangerous. Human milk has a fairly low iron content but iron is particularly well absorbed from it. Untreated cow's milk has an even lower iron content and far from being well absorbed, it provokes bleeding from the intestine. As a result a baby fed with cow's milk is likely to become anemic.

All the standard infant formulas are based on cow's milk, although they may have vegetable fats or products from other animals added. The formula manufacturers have paid meticulous attention to modifying cow's milk so that it more closely resembles human milk. The protein content has been reduced to the minimum levels recommended by the World Health Organization, although these still exceed the protein content of breast milk. The nature of the protein has been changed so that it is more easily digested. The carbohydrate content is increased, the ratio of polyunsaturated to saturated fats is adjusted and the sodium reduced. Iron is less well absorbed from formula feeds than from breast milk, so most have iron added, as well as other minerals and vitamins, usually having a higher level than human milk.

When looking at the crude values of protein, fat and carbohydrate in infant formula, it appears that there is little significant difference between formula

milk and breast milk. However, there are inevitably many more subtle differences that remain, simply because formulas are not based on human milk.

PSYCHOLOGICAL FACTORS

In recent years particular emphasis has been placed on the evidence that a stronger mother/child relationship is forged between mothers and breastfed babies, particularly when the baby is fed soon after delivery. This does not of course mean that the bottle fed baby is at a psychological disadvantage; in very many individual instances, this is clearly not the case. There is no doubt however that the great majority of women who breastfeed do enjoy the experience and feel especially close to their babies as a result. Once breastfeeding is established it can be the most simple, relaxing and pleasurable activity for both parties. Indeed, some women continue to breastfeed well beyond twelve months just because of the pleasure it brings, for in the West at least, by this age there is no nutritional advantage in continuing to breastfeed.

However, it would be wrong to ignore the fact that some women do not enjoy breastfeeding and that they suffer it out of a sense of duty which can easily turn to a feeling of guilt when they stop. It is difficult to see how this benefits the developing relationship; if you feel like this, formula feeding would probably be a better option, since you can still hold your baby close and cuddle him while feeding from a bottle, and the baby enjoys feeding from the bottle because that is what he is used to.

A small proportion of women who have a genuine desire to breastfeed find that they are not natural breastfeeders: they appear to have a poor supply, or they find the sensation of feeding unpleasant. Women like this often eventually change to the bottle with a significant feeling of sadness.

FATHERS AND BREASTFEEDING

Fathers, too, often have ambivalent feelings about breastfeeding. Rationally, they will agree that 'breast is best' when presented with the facts, but first time fathers especially, who have been used to thinking of their partners' breasts in terms of sex, may have difficulty in making the psychological shift to seeing them as much more functional objects. Some men also resent the closeness of breastfeeding, as their partners seem to be utterly absorbed in the baby to the exclusion of the father. Yet others miss the chance to be able to contribute to their baby's care in a positive way.

A surprising number of women worry about starting to breastfeed, or give it up, because of their partners' reaction. If this seems to be the situation when you are thinking about breastfeeding, or once you start, it is best to try to talk it through. Your doctor may be able to help if you feel that your relationship as a couple is suffering. Bottle feeding does sometimes solve this type of problem without doing any harm to the baby and being able to share the feeding can be a positive advantage (see below).

PROTECTION FROM INFECTION

It is worth bearing in mind that even breastfeeding for a few days can give your baby the benefit of antibodies in the milk that will protect him from dangerous infection. On the world scale, the overriding reason for advocating breastfeeding is the avoidance of gastro-enteritis. The breastfed baby has the advantage of receiving milk which is itself clean and contains specific factors which increase the baby's resistance to infections of this sort. These immunological factors are particularly abundant in the colostrum produced by the breast in the first few days after delivery; infant formulas obviously cannot contain these immunological factors, are themselves easily contaminated by bacteria and could be fed to babies in bottles which have not been properly cleaned.

In developed countries, however, which have good water supplies and sterilizing equipment readily available (see p. 158), it is easier to be sure that bottle feeds are not contaminated. While it is still true to say that infantile gastro-enteritis is more common in bottle than breastfed babies, babies in the West do not usually succumb to the problems of chronic infection.

ALLERGY

Within some families, there is a significant incidence of allergic problems, such as asthma, eczema and hay fever. Such families are known as 'atopic' (see p. 270). Mothers in this situation are often advised to breastfeed their babies, for while it does not offer total protection against the development of atopy, it might limit its severity. The evidence in this area is rather conflicting; some research seems to suggest that breastfeeding might actually predispose a baby to atopy. Certainly you shouldn't feel guilty if you are in this situation and you elect to bottle feed.

If young babies are fed ordinary cow's milk, a significant proportion are found to be allergic to the protein in it. A sign of this is if the baby passes blood-stained stools; less commonly, the baby may develop swelling round the mouth and throat which

146

Breastfeeding is very convenient as you can feed your baby more or less anywhere, helped by discreet use of a bulky sweater, coat or shawl. Even a trip to the local playground with older children need not be curtailed when your baby is hungry.

may lead to difficulty in breathing. These reactions were relatively common with early infant formulas, but as these have been improved, reactions like this have become very rare. Babies who are found to be sensitive to cow's milk protein should either be breastfed or given an alternative formula. Some doctors advise the use of a soy milk but this is not always the answer, as a significant proportion of babies who are sensitive to cow's milk are also sensitive to soy. In this case there are special milks available on prescription.

Babies often grow out of cow's milk sensitivity and in later childhood cow's milk products can be reintroduced. Your doctor will advise you about this. If one child of a couple has had this problem there is an increased chance that subsequent children will also be affected, and breastfeeding should be seriously considered.

MATERNAL MEDICATION

You may assume that any medicines that you are taking will appear in the breast milk. Often however the concentration of the drug in the milk is very low and will not cause any problems for the baby. If you

do have to take medicines you should discuss with the medical staff whether breastfeeding is advisable: the answer will usually be 'yes'. Once you have left hospital, if you have to go to the doctor for any reason while breastfeeding and he is likely to prescribe drugs, let him know that you are breastfeeding. There are often several alternatives which he could prescribe for a given condition, and he will choose one that is safe to take while breastfeeding.

CONVENIENCE

One of the great attractions of breastfeeding is its convenience. It needs no special preparation, and there is always enough available for your baby's needs. By contrast, bottle feeding needs organization and forethought; bottles have to be washed every day, feeds have to be made up in advance, or you have to make a hungry baby wait while the formula cools down.

If you breastfeed, you can feed your baby almost anywhere and at any time. But while many women will happily nurse their babies in public places and at social gatherings, it should be remembered that there are others who are more inhibited and who prefer privacy. For these women breastfeeding can be slightly more restricting. In addition, although it is probably becoming less common, it is also the case that many people still feel uncomfortable in the presence of breastfeeding women, and while this may seem preposterous, it should be respected.

Buildings such as airports and railway stations usually incorporate a room for feeding and changing babies, but the appearance of such facilities in the more traditional restaurants, cafés and shops frequented by nursing mothers is lamentably slow, even when the establishment specifically caters for babies and children. This is something worth campaigning for.

Even if you are breastfeeding, when you go out with your baby you do need a certain amount of paraphernalia with you in terms of changing equipment and clean clothes. However, the problem is greater if you are bottle feeding. You need enough bottles to cover the time you are going to be out and you need to be particularly careful about hygiene. In addition you may feel that you need to be able to warm the milk before giving it to your baby, although this is not strictly necessary (see p. 161).

Bottle feeding is convenient however in that it can be done by another person apart from the mother. In terms of cementing the family unit, it is a great help for the father to be able to give some of the feedings, especially in the middle of the night. Also, if you are going back to work within a few weeks of the birth or simply want to go out somewhere without the baby, his feeds can easily be arranged. Some women do organize their lives so that they are able to leave expressed milk to be bottle fed to their babies while they are out, but this requires very considerable motivation (see p. 154).

EXPENSE

It is interesting how rarely people bring the question of expense into the decision as to how to feed their babies. In fact the outlay on bottles and the continuing cost of formula is quite considerable, while breastfeeding is of course free.

OTHER FACTORS

The stools of a breastfed baby are usually soft and inoffensive, whereas some bottle fed babies' stools are occasionally rather smelly. It is also true that the stools of a breastfed baby are more acidic and that they tend to have fewer diaper rashes.

Although they probably rarely influence the decision on how to feed, some other important points are worth mentioning. Breastfeeding helps the uterus to contract efficiently in the days after delivery (see p. 132) and, as it uses up fat specifically laid down during pregnancy to promote the production of breast milk, breastfeeding speeds up the regaining of your figure.

THE CHOICE

The majority of women make the choice about feeding their babies not because of the finer points of protein concentration or stool acidity but as the result of attitudes which will have developed from those within their own families and environment. Many women who are currently of child bearing age will themselves have been bottle fed during the fifties and sixties when breastfeeding was at a low ebb, and they will never have contemplated feeding their own babies. Conversely, it will never have occurred to other women that they will do anything other than breastfeed. The choice must be your own but it is inevitable that in the present climate you will be encouraged to breastfeed. What is essential is that this encouragement does not turn into pressure, and that it is backed by helpful support during the first two or three weeks after the birth while breastfeeding is being established. It is worth remembering that modern infant formulas provide an excellent food and the choice of feeding method should not become a battle ground.

BREASTFEEDING

Breastfeeding is a natural part of the physiology of child bearing; women do not have to do anything to make their breasts produce milk once the baby is born. Babies are also born with the ability to suck (see p. 104). However bringing these two in-built processes together especially for the first time often needs some guidance. Understanding how breastfeeding works through some knowledge of simple anatomy and physiology is an important start.

THE STRUCTURE OF THE BREASTS

The breasts lie over the muscle on the front of the chest; before pregnancy they are largely composed of fatty tissue, formed into a roughly circular shape except where they extend up towards the armpits. Each breast is divided up into about eighteen segments. Within the fatty tissue of each segment is a series of tiny sacs, each of which has a lining of cells which are potentially milk-producing, surrounded by muscle cells which can squeeze the milk from the sacs. All the sacs within a segment drain into a milk duct which extends towards the nipple, so that there are about eighteen openings at the nipple. Just behind the nipple each of the milk

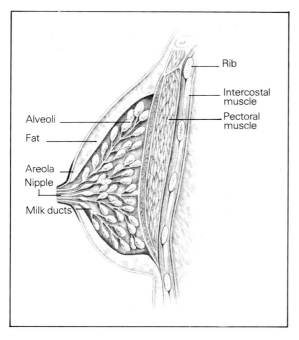

ducts has a slightly widened part where a limited amount of milk may collect.

The pigmented area around the nipple is known as the areola, upon which may be seen small raised areas, known as Montgomery's tubercles. These are thought to secrete lubricants which help to protect the skin of the nipple and keep it supple.

During pregnancy the breasts increase in size and the nipples tend to elongate under the influence of hormones, in particular the estrogens produced by the ovary and placenta which promote an enormous increase in the number of milk-producing sacs within each segment of the breast. During the last two or three months of pregnancy the sacs begin to produce colostrum, the 'pre-milk' which is produced until the baby is a few days old.

Once the baby has been born, the levels of estrogen fall dramatically and enable the main milk-producing hormone, prolactin, to make its presence felt so that the cells lining the sacs within the breast begin to manufacture milk. This happens even if the delivery is very premature.

The structure of the breast. During pregnancy, the number of milk-producing sacs increases. The breast is divided into eighteen segments, with milk draining from each to a separate duct.

HOW BREASTFEEDING WORKS

The more often the baby goes to the breast the more rapidly the prolactin levels rise and milk production is established. It is thought to be exceedingly rare

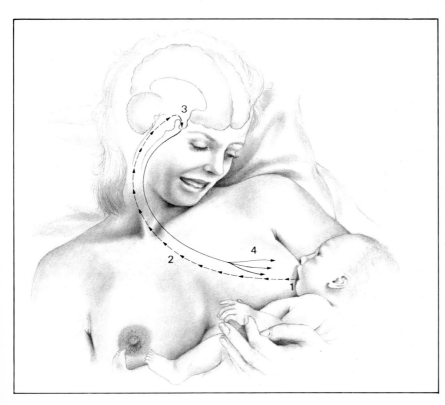

When the baby suckles on the areola (1), nerves send messages (2) to the pituitary gland in the brain (3) which secretes the hormone oxytocin. This causes the muscle cells of the sacs to contract (4), squeezing milk down into the ducts and out through the nipple.

for the breasts to fail to produce milk at all, but where some difficulties can arise is in the transportation of the milk from the sacs where it is made, down the ducts to the area behind the nipple from which the baby can suck it. This movement of milk is known as the 'let down' reflex, and can be felt as a tingling or prickling sensation.

The nipple area is richly supplied with nerve endings which are stimulated when the baby sucks upon the areola. Messages are carried along the nerves to the pituitary gland at the base of the brain which secretes a hormone called oxytocin (the same hormone which causes the uterus to contract during and after labor). There is a sharp increase in the concentration of this hormone in the blood stream and this causes the muscle cells around the milk producing sacs to contract and squeeze the milk down the ducts. (It also induces uterine contractions at the same time, which is why you may experience 'after pains' during breastfeeding in the early days after delivery – see p. 136).

The 'let down' reflex has well-defined neurological and hormonal components; however it does appear that it can easily be affected by the mother's mood. Many women do not actually need the baby to suckle directly on the breast to stimulate the reflex, but have merely to hear the baby cry or even to think about it for 'let down' to occur. A mother who is perhaps held up in traffic when hurrying home to feed her baby may find that her breasts are leaking quite involuntarily. Other women who are anxious about some aspect of feeding may find that the reflex is inhibited so that not enough milk comes down to satisfy the baby, despite his suckling and the presence of plenty of milk within the breast.

When a baby feeds he takes the whole nipple into his mouth until his gums are round the areola. Then he rhythmically squeezes it between the tongue and the roof of the mouth until he has obtained all the milk from behind the areola. He will then pause while more milk comes down the ducts, after which there will be another burst of sucking. Once feeding is established, the baby will get most of the milk in the first five or six minutes, although in practice most women feed their babies for about ten minutes on each side. Babies derive a great deal of pleasure just from suckling and being close, so this does nothing but good. After the feed the breasts will usually be full again within two or three hours.

CAN ANY WOMAN BREASTFEED?

It is probably true that any healthy woman can breastfeed, but it is clear that not everyone who sets out to do it is successful. In maternity units where there is particular energy put into the encouragement of breastfeeding and women are fully supported during the postpartum period, most women learn to breastfeed their babies successfully – but without this sort of support, breastfeeding rates fall away with regrettable speed. Breastfeeding comes easily and naturally to many women, but for others it can be a struggle to get it established.

In rural parts of underdeveloped countries where a baby's survival is dependent upon successful breastfeeding, virtually all women breastfeed with no problems. In the West, some women do genuinely seem to fail to feed. It seems unlikely that this is due to a simple organic failure; rather, it is probably due to doubts and anxieties within these particular women about their ability to produce adequate amounts of milk. These often have their roots in jibes about flat chests or flat nipples at school, and widespread talk of 'under-production' of milk, often by mothers and grandmothers who can insidiously undermine the efforts of midwives and others, and the confidence of the breastfeeding mother.

Small breasts are said to be more prevalent among twentieth century emancipated women, but there is no evidence that women with small breasts are poor milk producers. If anything the reverse is true. Similarly, a flat nipple should not be a problem as the feeding baby does not latch on to the nipple but fixes on to the areola. A true inverted nipple (see p. 157) can cause difficulties but it is a fairly rare condition that is much over-diagnosed, causing unnecessary worry.

BREAST CARE DURING PREGNANCY

Care of the breasts during pregnancy with a view to breastfeeding is one of the areas where you are likely to be given conflicting advice. Some people will advocate rolling the nipples regularly between the thumb and forefinger to help draw them out, and if you have rather flat nipples you may be encouraged to wear rubber shells inside your bra which are thought somehow to help this process. There is no scientific evidence that any of these activities help successful breastfeeding; pregnancy itself will prepare the nipples for feeding and it is quite possible that undue attention to the shape of the nipples may sow the seeds of anxiety, leading to later problems.

Another controversial question is whether colostrum should be actively expressed during the last week of pregnancy. Some people feel that this makes the milk flow more easily later on and that it ensures that the duct openings at the nipple are clear at the time of delivery. Again there is no evidence that this activity is of any benefit. It may worry you during your first pregnancy that you can't

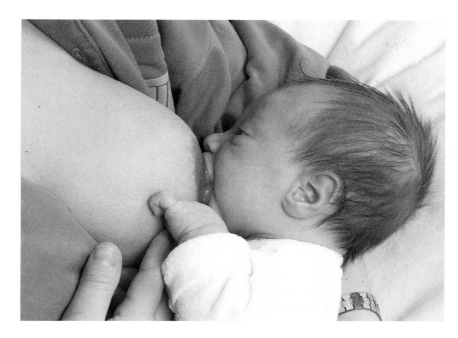

To establish breastfeeding successfully, make sure the baby has the whole nipple in his mouth and that his gums are firmly gripping the areola, the dark area that surrounds the nipple. This ensures that the 'let down' reflex is stimulated and helps to avoid sore or cracked nipples.

see the duct openings but you should rest assured that the openings are certainly there and that they will allow the milk through. There is no doubt that at the end of pregnancy the breasts will be full of milk-producing tissues and that as soon as delivery has occurred milk manufacture will accelerate at a great pace irrespective of whether you expressed colostrum prenatally or not.

It is sometimes thought that in order to prevent cracked nipples, moves should be made to toughen up the skin around the areola, especially if your skin is fair. Drying the breasts with a rough towel is a common suggestion and even more drastic abrasives have been encountered! Topless sunbathing is also advocated for this purpose, and for healing a cracked nipple. While there is probably something to be said for the latter in that fresh air probably aids healing, for the former it won't make any difference either way, while care should be taken as a sunburnt breast could be a disaster!

None of these measures is necessary – indeed they may have the opposite effect in that excessive dryness may make the skin more liable to cracking. Pregnancy prepares the breasts for breastfeeding and the cause of cracked nipples is not fair skin but the baby not being properly at the breast.

DIET

Most of the calories you require for breastfeeding will have been laid down during pregnancy. As has already been described, breastfeeding is of course the last part of the normal reproductive cycle and is the most physiological method of getting your figure back to its original dimensions.

You do not need to 'eat for two' while breastfeeding, any more than you did during pregnancy. However, it is obviously sensible to eat a normal, well-balanced diet and in particular to eat protein and iron-rich foods. If your doctor finds that you are anemic after the birth (see p. 136) you may need to take iron pills for a while as well. In terms of quantity you should just eat what you feel you need. Similarly you should only drink when you feel thirsty; indeed, excessive drinking sometimes seems to reduce milk production. Neither is it a good idea to drink large amounts of cow's milk as some of the protein might cross into the breast milk and can very occasionally lead to problems of cow's milk allergy.

ESTABLISHING FEEDING

It has been observed that female monkeys isolated in zoo cages do not feed instinctively and they have to be taught how to put their young to the breast. The same is true of women. In contrast to lower mammals such as the domestic cat, who feed by instinct, it appears that the higher order primates learn by watching and that women raised in small families who might never have seen other women breastfeed quite simply do not know what to do. This is fine provided that you are surrounded by skilled friends, relations or midwives to offer support. However, for women on maternity wards often short of nurses, whose families are scattered

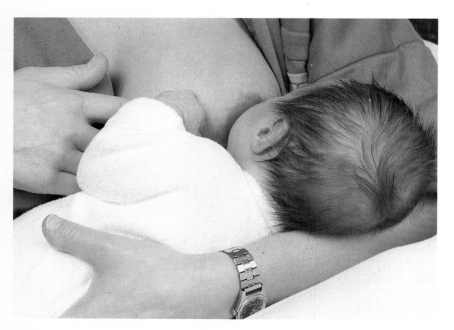

*This is the most
popular position for
breastfeeding, with the
baby's head cradled on
your arm and his body
across your chest.
To put the baby to the
breast, rest his head in
the crook of your arm
and turn his whole
body towards you. At
first it helps to guide
the nipple into his
mouth with your free
hand. Support your arm
and his body with a
pillow or cushion to
bring him up to the
level of your breast.*

and whose own mothers bottle fed, it is tragic how many who set out to breastfeed abandon their efforts in the first few weeks, demoralized by having to struggle behind curtains on the ward with painful nipples, and confused by conflicting advice.

It really need not be like this. With a little patience and good will, breastfeeding can be established with the minimum of fuss in most cases and it will not be long before you will be wondering why you ever thought it could be difficult in the first place. The most important thing is to make sure the baby is latched on to the breast properly, with his gums round the areola as described. This is best achieved if you are holding him properly and you are comfortable yourself.

HOLDING THE BABY

To start with, while everything is still new, it is often helpful to wrap your baby up in a receiving blanket so that his hands and arms aren't in the way. Later on, when breastfeeding is well established your baby will have his hands free and may hold the breast and play with it, while feeding.

Sit propped up in bed or in a good supporting chair with arms. The best position is to cradle your baby across the front so that he is almost horizontal, but his face is turned up and in so he can look at you. If you are right-handed you will probably feel most comfortable if the baby is lying along your left arm while feeding from the right breast, and vice versa. It is important however that you do find a comfortable way of holding the baby on both

breasts otherwise one of the breasts might not be regularly emptied of milk. To enable you to hold the baby comfortably close to the breast without having to lean forward, lay a pillow across your knee to raise him higher. Put a pillow behind the small of your back as well to avoid backache.

PUTTING THE BABY TO THE BREAST

It cannot be emphasized too strongly that the key to successful breastfeeding is putting the baby correctly to the breast. If the baby is not on properly the nipple is liable to become painful or even to crack. You will then dread the baby sucking on it, which will interfere with the 'let down' reflex, the baby will become frustrated and everyone will be in tears.

One of the first challenges for many mothers is to get the baby to open his mouth. However this is really simple since the baby will be ready to suck on anything if you take advantage of his 'rooting reflex'. If you tickle the side of the baby's mouth with the nipple or a finger he will turn in that direction and 'root' for the nipple by obligingly opening his mouth to receive it. He needs a little help at this stage; cradle his head in one hand, turning his whole face towards the breast while you hold the areola with the other to ensure that not just the end of the nipple but the whole of it plus part of the areola are in his mouth (see the illustration on p. 151). For the first few feedings it is a good idea to hold the baby's head and the breast in position; this is where an experienced helper and strategically placed pillows can provide invaluable assistance.

It is comfortable to breastfeed lying down in bed, with your baby lying alongside you. This position is useful for night feeding (don't worry if you both fall asleep in this position afterwards). It is particularly helpful to feed in this position after a cesarean section or if you had stitches after the birth, since it avoids putting any weight on the painful area.

You can avoid aching shoulders by breastfeeding with your baby tucked under your arm like a football, his head resting on a pillow by your side. If you have had a cesarean section, this is another useful position to avoid pressure on the wound during breastfeeding.

WHICH BREAST FIRST?

It is usually recommended that you offer both breasts to the baby every time, alternating the breast you offer first at each feed. In this way it seems likely that each breast is emptied at least at alternate feeds which will help milk production on each side to settle down to fit the demand.

LENGTH AND TIMING OF FEEDINGS

It used to be thought that if the baby stayed on the breast for too long in the first few days that the nipples were liable to crack, so strict guidelines for the number of minutes on each side were laid down. It is now felt that provided the baby is on the breast properly, the breast will not become painful and so the amount of time you have the baby on each breast is entirely up to you and your baby. Once milk production (lactation) is established, the milk flow is greatest in the first few minutes of the feed and if the baby feeds from the first side for eight to ten minutes, that side should be emptied. You may find that your baby often remains at the breast for much longer than he needs to for strictly nutritional purposes. He simply enjoys it, he is warm and comfortable and takes pleasure from the proximity of your body.

It was only relatively recently that strict feeding schedules were abandoned. There is now much evidence that if a baby is fed on demand, that is, put to the breast (or indeed, given the bottle) as often and for as long as mother and baby want, there are fewer problems with engorgement (see below) and that a feeding routine will be established more quickly.

When demand feeding was first advocated, it was argued that it was difficult to achieve on maternity wards because it made it impossible for the nurses to organize their time. In practice this has not been borne out, partly because in most hospitals the baby's bassinet remains by the mother's bed at all times, and partly because the adoption of demand feeding has drastically reduced the number of breast-related problems on the ward.

The length of time between feedings will gradually extend as the baby grows. However, whether he wakes up hungry after two, three or five hours depends on individual factors, and you cannot force a baby into a rigid routine – he will cry when he is hungry and if you leave him longer than about ten minutes he will become distressed. A distressed baby is more difficult to feed successfully.

During the first week of life he will want to feed very frequently which helps to build up the milk supply, but by the end of two weeks he may have settled down to a rough schedule of six to seven feedings in 24 hours. This will gradually decrease so that by three months many babies have dropped one late night feeding and most do not require feeding during the small hours of the night from about six months.

WHEN THE MILK COMES IN

At the time of delivery the breasts are large but soft, containing small amounts of colostrum. Under the influence of the hormone prolactin and increased blood supply, there is a speeding up of milk production during the first few days so that, around the third day if you have had your first baby, and a little earlier with subsequent babies, the breasts rapidly fill with milk, becoming stiff and engorged.

This can be uncomfortable as the breasts may feel very hard, lumpy, hot and tender. At this time it can be very difficult to get the baby on the breast because the nipple and areola become distended with milk. It is helpful to express a little of the milk by hand before putting the baby to the breast. This relieves the tension a little and allows the nipple to be manipulated into the baby's mouth.

Although it may be difficult, the best treatment for engorgement is frequent feeding. The discomfort in the breasts may be relieved by holding hot flannels on them or by lying in a warm bath. Ice packs are also helpful between feeds and discomfort is eased if you wear a supportive bra at all times. If your breasts are very uncomfortable your midwife or doctor may suggest a mild pain-killer. Mercifully

this stage does not last long; if you continue to feed regularly, within 24 hours the breasts will be softening again and it will be easier to feed once more.

BURPING

Breastfed babies usually have less problem with gas than bottle fed babies, although occasionally there is so much milk in the ducts at the start of a feed that it may cause the baby to splutter and choke, thereby swallowing some air. If you think your baby has gas, the simplest way to burp him is to set him on your knee with his back straight and his head supported under the chin with one hand, while you gently pat or rub his back with the other. Alternatively you can hold him against your shoulder. If no burp comes and he is comfortable, it is not worth pursuing it.

EXPRESSING MILK

At the time the milk is coming in it is often helpful to express a little milk at the beginning of the feeding prior to putting the baby on the breast (see above). You will probably find that the supply of milk settles very quickly to fit your baby's needs over the first ten days or so, but some women do seem to overproduce for a little longer than this and they find it helpful to use a pump to remove excess milk. Simple hand pumps are adequate for this purpose.

If your baby is ill and unable to feed but you anticipate being able to resume feeding when he is better, it is important that you express both breasts regularly, five or six times a day. If you don't do this your milk supply might begin to diminish. For total expression it is preferable to use an electric pump. These are expensive but they can often be rented from hospitals or voluntary organizations like the La Leche League.

CARE OF THE BREASTS AFTER DELIVERY

It is not necessary to wash the breasts with soap and water after every feed; if you do this you are likely to wash away the natural lubricating secretions which help to protect the nipple. Just wash your breasts normally in the bath or shower every day.

There are various sprays available which are said to protect the nipples from cracking and are mildly antiseptic. Some also have a light local anesthetic effect which may deaden the pain of a cracked nipple. However they are of no real benefit; in fact they tend to sting initially if your nipples are sore and they mask the natural smell of your breasts which is one of the ways in which your baby's instinct to suck is aroused.

Breastfeeding twins is best achieved by tucking a baby under each arm, with his head forward, in the 'football position' shown on page 153, and supported by as many pillows as possible.

BREASTFEEDING AFTER A CESAREAN

If your baby has been delivered by cesarean section you are likely to be uncomfortable for the first few days and you might not be able to cope with holding the baby horizontally as he may press on the wound (see p. 138). However there is no reason why you should not breastfeed successfully. You will need extra help from the nurses or from a friend but there are various tricks which might be helpful. Sometimes it is enough to put a pillow on your lap to support the baby as already described. Some mothers manage to feed comfortably lying on their side with the young baby lying beside them, as illustrated on page 153. Many mothers find this restful, whether they have had a cesarean section or not, and it is particularly useful at night. Another popular choice is to feed sitting up, well supported, with the baby lying on a pillow at the side from which he is feeding. You then tuck him under your arm with his head beneath the breast (see p. 153).

BREASTFEEDING TWINS

Breastfeeding twins is a practical possibility if you can feed them at the same time. This is usually achieved rather in the same way that you might feed after a cesarean section, with one baby at each side, their bodies tucked under your arms. You need to be well supported with pillows or cushions to achieve this and you will need lots of help while you are learning how to do it.

When breastfeeding is established some mothers of twins alternate between breast and bottle feeds, breastfeeding each twin in turn and letting the babies' father or another person give a bottle to the other baby. However many mothers of twins have successfully breastfed both babies for some months without recourse to supplementary bottles. Enough milk is produced because the babies create their own demand.

BREASTFEEDING A BABY WITH CLEFT PALATE

It is difficult for babies with cleft palate to breastfeed as they cannot suck with the nipple against the roof of the mouth and there is a tendency for milk to come back down the nose. It is sometimes possible to have a special plate made for the baby which makes breastfeeding easier. Special feeding tubes are available which also help to avoid regurgitating formula through the nose.

Alternatively some women in this situation express their milk and feed it to the baby on a spoon.

This sounds extremely tedious, but in fact babies cope very well. A cleft lip without a cleft palate is not usually a significant problem with breastfeeding.

COMMON BREASTFEEDING PROBLEMS

There are some common problems associated with breastfeeding which may be off-putting if you don't know how to deal with them. The nurses on the maternity ward are there to help you in the first few days, and your obstetrician will continue to advise you when you get home. Both will want to encourage you to continue breastfeeding and they are always available for continuing advice. An experienced friend or relation who has successfully breastfed can be just as good, if not better, since she will understand your doubts and fears and may seem more sympathetic than a professional health worker. Alternatively some organizations like the La Leche League have teams of volunteers who act as postpartum support and breastfeeding counselors able to visit you at home.

IS THERE ENOUGH MILK?

One of the things that most worries some women who are breastfeeding for the first time is that they cannot see the amount of milk that the baby is getting. During the first few days before the milk comes in the baby will only receive small amounts of colostrum, so during this time he uses some of the stores of carbohydrate that were laid down in his body during the last part of pregnancy. It is natural for him not to receive all his nutritional needs by mouth during this time; a normal full term baby should not need extra feeds. If he does not seem to be satisfied just put him back on the breast.

There is a great temptation during the early days of breastfeeding to offer the baby a bottle feed 'just in case he isn't getting enough milk' and 'would like a bit more'. It is very likely that he will drink it but it does not mean he really needs it and it will not help your supply of milk to settle down to match his needs. It can lead to confusion and the ultimate abandonment of breastfeeding.

The best way to prevent this situation is quite simply not to have any formula or bottles in the house. While you are in the hospital the nurses may offer to give your baby a bottle to let you rest, or if your nipples are sore. Try to resist this, for it is in these early days, when your baby may be coming to the breast as many as ten or twelve times during 24 hours, that milk production is established; supplementary bottles will simply fill your baby up so that he doesn't want to come to the breast.

CRACKED NIPPLES

Cracked nipples almost always arise because the baby has not had the areola properly in his mouth but has been chewing on the nipple itself. A cracked nipple is very painful and is a great disincentive to breastfeeding, so prevention is extremely important. Various sprays and lanolin based creams are available to help this problem, but they are of limited use.

You should be able to feed with a cracked nipple provided that the baby is properly latched on so that he is not actually gripping on the crack. The moment that the baby latches on is usually the worst, so it is worth trying to breathe through it as you may have done during labor, as the pain is transitory. Once the milk is flowing feeding is not painful. Be careful when removing the nipple from your baby's mouth – always insert your finger to release his grip as described earlier.

If it is really too painful to feed than it is worth trying to use a nipple shield for a few feeds. Your baby might not like this as it is sometimes quite difficult for a baby to suck efficiently on it. If all else fails, the solution is to express milk and to feed it to the baby on a spoon or in a bottle until the crack has healed. Mercifully, cracked nipples heal very quickly and are usually better within 24 hours.

BLOCKED DUCTS

Occasionally you will find that a segment or sometimes a larger section of the breast becomes locally firm and tender. The most likely reason for this is that the ducts leading from those segments have become blocked, so that when the 'let down' reflex occurs the milk collects in the ducts which become swollen and tender. As with many feeding problems this situation probably arises because the baby is not properly on the breast, so special attention should be paid to this.

The pain can sometimes be relieved by applying a warm face cloth to the breast and gently massaging in a downwards direction. It is most unusual for the blockage to persist for long. It is a good idea to put the baby to the affected breast first when he is hungry and sucks most vigorously as this encourages faster milk flow and helps clear the blockage.

MASTITIS

If a part of the breast becomes red and tender and you find that you have developed a temperature it is probable that you have an infection in the breast and you should contact your doctor as soon as possible, who will prescribe a suitable antibiotic.

This sort of infection is known as mastitis. It is particularly likely to occur if you have a cracked nipple which can act as an entry portal for bacteria or if you have a blocked duct in which the milk has stagnated. If the part of the breast which is infected is in the upper, outer quarter you may be aware that the tenderness is extending up towards your armpit, where you may feel inflamed glands.

Mastitis is not a reason to stop breastfeeding; in fact it is most important that feeding continues regularly so that the breast is emptied. The antibiotics prescribed will not affect the milk or harm your baby.

Rarely, mastitis develops into a full-blown breast abscess. In this situation, a part of the breast becomes very red, swollen and tender and it might be possible to express pus from the nipple. This might require admission to hospital for drainage of the abscess and antibiotic treatment. Again it is important that the breast is emptied of milk regularly but in this instance the milk from the infected breast has to be expressed and discarded until the infection has subsided, while the baby is just fed from the non-infected side.

INVERTED NIPPLES

If you have a true inverted nipple it is worth trying to encourage it to come out during pregnancy by rolling it between finger and thumb and wearing a nipple shell under your bra. The nurse at the prenatal clinic can advise you about this. If your nipples are still inverted after delivery (and this is very rare) you may still be able to feed, but if there are problems you could wear a nipple shield.

LEAKING

The extent to which different women leak milk from the breast varies. You may find that during feeding milk drips from the opposite side. At one time there was interest in collecting this milk for hospital milk banks, but in fact it is of low nutritional value. If you do drip in this manner you will need to wear a breast pad during feeds.

Leaking tends to be more of a problem in the first few weeks of lactation before the supply settles down to fit the baby's demands. You will quickly learn whether or not you do have a tendency to leak milk when the breasts are full or if you hear your baby crying, and if you know this is likely to happen it is worth always putting a pad inside your bra and keeping a few spares with you as they can quite quickly become saturated. Cup-shaped breast pads are more efficient than rectangular ones and fit more neatly inside your bra.

THE BABY THAT FIGHTS THE BREAST

Occasionally the first few days of breastfeeding are made particularly difficult because the baby appears to resist going on to the breast and becomes stiff and angry, sometimes arching his back and crying even though he is hungry. This is a curious phenomenon. One theory is that it may be due to the baby's nose having been restricted during feeding at some point so that his breathing was obstructed. The unpleasantness of this sensation may condition him to resist feeding. Whether this is true or not it really can be a most frustrating experience for mother and baby.

If your baby seems to be behaving in this way you need to make sure that his nose is free so that he can breathe and you need to seek some moral support as it can be a distressing time. Remember that it is not your fault, and your baby is not doing it because there is anything wrong with your milk. If your baby fights in this way it is a good idea to lift him off the breast and carry him about for a minute or two over your shoulder or cradled in your arms until he is calm again. If he has already shown an obvious preference for one side or the other, put him to the preferred side first for a while until the problem passes. Don't despair, this behavior is always temporary.

GOING OUT

Once you are home, going out with your baby while you are breastfeeding is not difficult, since in theory the baby can be fed anywhere. While your baby is still small it is usually easiest to take the baby with you if you are going to somebody's house. Make sure you wear something in which it is easy to feed – either front fastening or easy to lift from the waist. It can be very uncomfortable having to strip in order to produce a breast in a strange, possibly cold house!

Breastfeeding can be a hindrance while the baby is still feeding frequently if you want to go somewhere such as a theater or movie where you cannot take the baby, especially if it involves going out for longer than the period between two feeds. In the early weeks this time period may be difficult to predict anyway. In this situation it is important that you have some breast pads with you as you may well begin to leak at about the time the baby's feed is due.

Some women who are extremely well organized are able to express milk which can be left behind to be given to the baby from a bottle. If your feeding is going so well that this is no problem then it is probably the best thing to do, provided that the baby will take a bottle – and some breastfed babies are reluctant to do this once breastfeeding is established. Breast milk freezes well, and if you use bottles with disposable bags (see right) one of these can be defrosted and placed in the holder with the minimum of fuss. On the other hand, if your baby will take a bottle it really is not going to do any harm to give the occasional bottle of formula milk, and this is the preferred course of action for many women. If breastfeeding is well established, it is a myth that once the baby is offered a bottle he will no longer like the breast.

CHANGING FROM BREAST TO BOTTLE

If you want to wean your baby from the breast before six months you will need to use bottles. Usually this produces no problems, but some babies do take a little time to get used to them, so don't leave the change-over until the last minute if you have a deadline such as going back to work. You may need to experiment a bit with nipples before you find something he likes (see opposite).

If you breastfeed up to or beyond the age of about six months you may be able to wean your baby straight on to a cup with a spout and avoid ever having to use bottles. It is a surprise to many parents how well babies cope with these cups. It is probably best to continue on a formula until the age of about nine months, but if you do change to whole cow's milk, you must still pay great attention to hygiene. The cup needs washing as you would a bottle, paying special attention to cleaning the little holes in the spout.

It will be much more comfortable for you to effect the change-over to bottles gradually, stopping one or more breastfeeds every two or three days; this will help you not to become too engorged. If you have already started to introduce solid food into your baby's diet (see p. 200), it makes sense to start by dropping the breastfeed that accompanies the meal your baby is most enthusiastic about, such as breakfast or lunch. Some mothers manage to maintain the bedtime 'comfort feeding' for some weeks even when all other breastfeeds have been dropped.

If for some reason you do have to stop feeding suddenly you will probably need to express a little milk occasionally. Try not to do this more often than you need and within three or four days you will be through the worst.

BOTTLE FEEDING

Bottle feeding requires far more practical fore-thought than breastfeeding, whether you are intend-ing to bottle feed from the start or are changing from breast to bottle before your baby is six months old. You will need to decide on the type of formula you are going to use, which bottles and nipples you require and how many.

CHOOSING BOTTLES AND NIPPLES

While you are in hospital you will probably be provided with milk prepacked in small glass bottles. Once home, you have the choice between two main types of bottles. The traditional rigid bottle (now usually made of plastic) is still used by the majority of people with no problems. However, with these bottles the air pressure inside inevitably falls as the baby sucks, so that the nipple has to be released from time to time so that air can enter the bottle. Increasingly, however, women are using disposable plastic bags which are mounted on a plastic holder with a large latex nipple over the top. This type of 'bottle' has two advantages. First, the inside of the plastic bag is already sterile; secondly, the bag collapses as the baby sucks so that there is no vacuum to release and the baby holds the nipple in his mouth continuously as he would on the breast.

You have to buy the right nipple for the type of bottle you choose. Rubber nipples are larger and firmer than the human nipple and areola and it is generally easy for the baby to feed from them, but you may have to experiment to find the right hole size. For most newborn babies the size is right that allows a steady stream of drips when the bottle is held upside down. If the flow of milk is too slow the baby may become frustrated and angry during the feed, while a hole that is too large will produce a flow of milk so fast that the baby will splutter and choke.

CARE OF BOTTLES

Bacteria can easily grow in formula so clean preparation of bottles is essential. While we no longer sterilize infant formula bottles, the following steps are important in order to avoid feeding spoiled formula to your baby. The bottle should be rinsed out after every feeding, washed and scrubbed in soapy water and then rinsed thoroughly in running tap water. Great care must be taken to prevent stale milk from accumulating in the bottle, especially around the grooves at the neck. Latex nipples need gentle hand washing. If they become crusty, they can readily be cleaned by using a solution of dilute liquid laundry bleach and soaking them for a few hours. Very thorough rinsing after this treatment is important to avoid exposing the infant to any bleach residue. Running both plastic or glass bottles

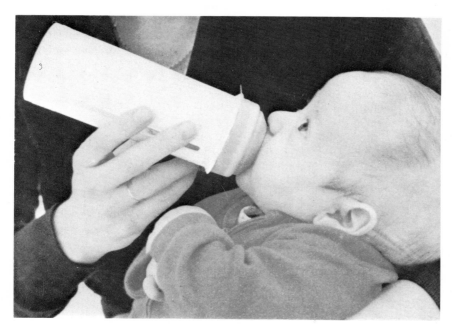

Bottles with disposable plastic bag liners have many advantages and you need never worry about bacteria in the liner, as it is always sterile. Never try reusing the liner, however, and pay attention to the latex nipple, being sure to rinse away all traces of stale milk every time you use the bottle.

through the dishwasher, setting the water temperature to very hot, is a good way to keep the bottles clean.

In many parts of the world, people still practice routine sterilization of all bottles and equipment. Both chemical solutions and boiling in air-tight pots are reliable methods. However, good attention to hygiene makes all this extra work unnecessary. Today, the commonest cause of spoiled formula is feeding a baby a bottle partially emptied at a previous feeding. At the first feeding, the baby introduces ordinary mouth germs into the bottle through the feeding action. When this bottle is set aside for four or five hours, these germs multiply, especially during the warm temperatures of summertime. Then, if this bottle is offered to the baby again, large numbers of these germs may enter the baby's digestive tract causing diarrhea and upset stomach. *Never* reuse a bottle of formula after it has been sitting around for more than one hour. Despite the reliability of home tap water, it is best to boil the water before using it to dilute canned concentrate.

MAKING UP FORMULA

If you choose to bottle feed from the time of the baby's birth your nursery nurse should teach you how to make up feedings. If you change from breast to bottle after going home and are uneasy about making up bottles contact your pediatrician for guidance. A feeding made up incorrectly can be dangerous.

In the United States, formula is sold ready made, in liquid concentrate (typically a 13oz can makes up 26oz of formula) and in powder form. Formula is available to you at most supermarkets, local food stores, and drug stores. If you qualify by income, the WIC (Women's, Infants, and Children's) Program pays for formula by issuing monthly food vouchers. Most local communities have a WIC Program which not only issues vouchers for formula but also for many other types of nutritious foods for pre-school children. By all means check to see if you qualify for this program as it can be a substantial saving.

You should always be careful to follow the manufacturer's instructions when making up formula. If you are at all confused ask for guidance from your pediatrician. Each powdered formula can is provided with its own scoop – only use the scoop provided for that particular brand.

As long as you have a refrigerator in which to store the bottles, it is sensible to make up the whole day's supply of bottles at one time. It is particularly useful to have bottles ready for night-time feeds so that you can feed the baby with the minimum of fuss. Some people suggest making up the day's supply in a large measuring jug and transferring it to the bottles, but you have to add a large number of scoops and it is very easy to lose count.

Boil the kettle and, while you allow the water to cool slightly, wash your hands thoroughly. Then stand the bottles on a firm, flat surface. While the boiled water is still hot, pour the required amount into the bottles. Most bottles are now calibrated with milliliters and fluid ounce measurements so there is no need to use a measuring jug. Then drop the required number of scoops of dry formula into the bottles. Each scoop should be full to the top but not pressed down – level it off with the edge of a knife to be sure. Cover the bottles then shake them vigorously to dissolve the powder. Allow them to cool and place them in the refrigerator if you don't need to feed immediately. If your baby doesn't finish the bottle at any one feed don't keep it for later, but throw it away and start afresh next time. You also should discard the milk in unused bottles at the end of 24 hours.

Only put in the number of scoops advised for the amount of water you are using – never be tempted to add an extra scoop because you think your baby may sleep better or because you think he isn't gaining weight fast enough. Seeing that your baby is growing well provides deep satisfaction, and some people have been led to believe that if a little more powder is to be added then the baby will become bigger and stronger. This is not the case; on the contrary, if the milk concentration is too high it is dangerous because of its high sodium content.

If you are making up formula from canned concentrate, the proportions are one can boiling water to one can concentrate. The total is usually 26oz and this fits nicely in a glass baking measuring cup. If you are using disposable insert bags, you can pour the formula directly into the plastic bag, as it is strong enough to withstand the temperature of boiling water. Do not reuse these bags as they are quite difficult to sterilize.

There has been some recent attention focused on the practice of using bottled mineral water instead of tap water for making up formula. This is not recommended. The powder contains all the minerals your baby requires and there are potential risks in increasing them by using mineral-rich water.

It is not advisable to take a bottle-fed baby to a part of the world where the water is liable to be contaminated and where you do not have free access to a kettle. If you have to travel to an area like this and bottled water is the only source of safe water, seek medical advice as to what type to use.

HOW MUCH TO OFFER

Some guidance as to how much milk to offer will be given on your can of formula, and your doctor can also help you here. To start with, during the course of the day your baby will take about 3 fluid ounces per pound body weight spread over several feedings during the day. He may take as little as 1 fluid ounce at any one feeding to start with, but by a week, a baby of average birth weight may be taking about 3 fluid ounces per feeding.

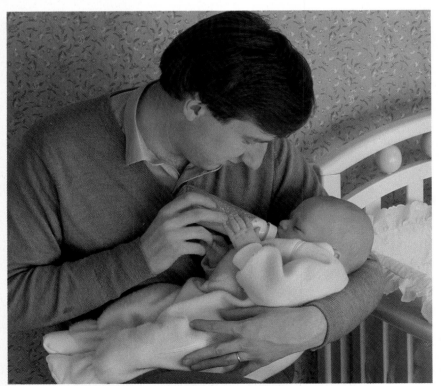

It is helpful and satisfying for both parents when a father is able to help with night feeds – usually only possible if you are bottle feeding your baby. Make sure the bottle is always held at enough of an angle to ensure that the nipple is full of milk. Never leave a baby alone with a propped bottle.

Making up a feed
To make up a feed, fill the bottle with the required amount of hot, boiled water.

Add the formula, a scoop at a time, levelling each scoop off with the back of a knife. Do not press the powder down and never put in more than the recommended number of scoops.

Put on the nipple and cover. Shake the bottle vigorously to make sure the formula is completely dissolved. Allow to cool before feeding, and store in the refrigerator if not needed immediately.

Don't try to force your baby to finish his bottle every time. If he fights the bottle while still obviously hungry, try burping him, make sure the nipple is not blocked or change position to settle him down again. The same principles of demand feeding should apply to bottle fed babies as have already been described for breastfed babies (see page 153). Provided he is growing normally you should not be too concerned about variation of intake between different feedings. He will probably settle down to six feedings a day till about eight weeks of age, and by the age of three months he will probably be taking about 8 fluid ounces per feeding – the equivalent of a full bottle – with about five feedings during 24 hours.

GIVING THE BOTTLE

Right-handed people usually feel most comfortable holding the baby in their left arm with the bottle in the right hand. The bottle should be held at an angle so that the nipple is always full of milk, otherwise the baby will tend to swallow air as well. If the milk is in a rigid bottle the baby will need to release the nipple periodically so that air can bubble back into the bottle to replace the milk he has drunk. If this doesn't happen it will become progressively more difficult for him to suck and he may become frustrated. Babies learn quite quickly to pause and release the nipple themselves, but in the early days you might find it helpful occasionally to remove the nipple from his mouth. This isn't necessary, however, if you use bottles with disposable bags, since the bag collapses as the milk is sucked from it.

BURPING

There is a tendency for bottle fed babies to have more gas than those fed on the breast. If your baby does seem to be swallowing a lot of air you should check that the bottle is always held at the right angle and pay attention to the size of the hole in the nipple.

It is customary to interrupt bottle feedings about half way through to burp, but this is only worth doing if you find that your baby does usually burp at that time. If not, he may become frustrated that his feed is being interrupted. When the feeding is finished he may need to be burped, so hold him like a breastfed baby, either sitting him on your knee with his head supported, or against your shoulder. A little milk often comes back with the gas so make sure you have a cloth handy. However, you can expect stained clothes occasionally!

Babies sometimes do seem to become very uncomfortable with gas and if you are having a lot of problems you should have a talk with your doctor (see p. 187). Sometimes changing from a rigid to a collapsible bottle can help.

THE TEMPERATURE OF THE MILK

When the milk is first made it is very hot and must not be given to the baby until it is cooled down at least to blood temperature. The temperature of the milk can be gauged by letting some drops of milk fall on to the back of the hand. The milk should feel neither hot nor cold.

In hospital bottles are usually given to babies at room temperature. At home most people warm the milk to blood heat by standing the bottles in a jug of hot water or a bottle warmer. Some people do this because it is believed that the baby is less likely to get colic. There is no real evidence to support this and if you find that your baby is happy with milk at room temperature there really is no point in wasting time heating it. If you do feel you want to warm it you must be careful not to let it get too hot.

CHAPTER TWELVE

THE YOUNG BABY

**Caring for your baby's physical and emotional
needs in the first three months of life**

Taking on the responsibility for a newborn baby is both exciting and unnerving. If the baby is your first, you will have all the usual apprehensions of anyone embarking on a new task, and even if he or she is not, there is always a certain amount of upheaval in introducing a new person into an existing family unit. Having a baby requires adjustment on all sides – mother, father and baby have to get to know each other – and if there are other children they also need to have it made clear that their needs and anxieties are taken into account too.

EARLY DAYS

If you had your baby in hospital, you will have had the security of knowing that there was always someone to call on if you were anxious about yourself or your baby. At the same time, you will probably be longing to come home to be in familiar surroundings and among your friends and family, so that you can begin to fit your new baby into your everyday life. Even so, you may feel lonely and frightened at first, particularly if you were on your own. In addition you may still be feeling physically uncomfortable as well as tired. The stress of coping with exhaustion from broken nights and constant emotional demands should not be underestimated. But mothers having their second babies will tell you how inexperienced they felt first time around, and how much more confident they felt about the second. They may tell you how they used to look in on their sleeping baby every few minutes just to check that he was still alive, and how worried they felt when he would not settle down.

All babies have different personalities – differences may even be apparent in late pregnancy – and they all have different rhythms of eating and sleeping. Some babies cry more than others, some sleep more than others, some are more contented than others. Your friends' babies will behave differently from yours; if they happen to be easier babies, that is just good luck, not better management, whatever your friends may say.

The early weeks are likely to be chaotic. There may be no pattern at all to your baby's needs for food and sleep and it is impossible to stick to a rigid timetable. Feeding and lack of sleep become the over-riding features of this period, and both parents need to recognize this and try to organize life to accommodate it. However, your baby will soon begin to settle into some kind of rhythm, although this is unlikely to be tailor-made to suit you. If you manage to satisfy his needs during the course of the day, feeding him when he is hungry, changing him when he is wet or soiled, comforting and cuddling him when he is upset or bored, you are doing very well indeed. Finding time for anything else at this stage may be impossible.

After a few weeks your baby's rhythms may become a little more predictable, and you might be able to start planning your routine around his needs. If he wakes you several times at night, you may be able to set aside an hour during the afternoon when he usually sleeps to have a rest yourself. The essential thing is to be flexible; your baby's requirements at this early age have to take priority over yours because he is unable to alter them to suit you. As the weeks pass you should be able to manipulate his routine to fit in with yours. Once he feels secure in the knowledge that you will always be there when he needs you, you might for example be able to lengthen the time between feeds, and to cut out the night feed. With luck, his timetable will gradually approach the one which suits you best, although this does not always seem to happen.

During the first few months – especially if you are breastfeeding – you may find it very difficult to concentrate on any intellectual activity. This is not a permanent loss of function but a normal feature of early motherhood, caused by a combination of your natural concentration on your baby and lack of sleep. It always gets better within a few months, so do not let it worry you.

FATHERS AT HOME

Fathers are sometimes able to get paternity leave or take a holiday for a week or two after the baby is born. It means that both partners can share the early

*Many fathers like to be at home in the early days
after the birth so that they can be with their new
family and take over the household chores to help
their partners recover fully from the birth.*

joys of your baby, and you can get to know your
baby together. It also means that he will be able to
take over the household chores to enable his
partner to rest properly.

A father often feels elated when his partner comes
home from the hospital with the baby, and needs to
be aware that she might not be feeling the same
way. She may be tired, weepy and irritable, or may
be totally absorbed with the baby to the exclusion of
everyone and everything else. In addition she may
not be feeling the expected surge of maternal
feelings and love for the newly arrived member of

the family, which can lead to feelings of guilt which
spill over into her relationships with others. These
feelings are normal – loving your child does not
always happen instantly but develops gradually as
you get to know him. In this situation it is not
surprising that some fathers feel rejected. A man
may feel that all his partner's affection and interest
has been transferred to the baby, or may worry that
his own feelings of love for the child are not fully
shared by the baby's mother. After a while things do
settle down and life begins to return to a familiar
pattern. Until then a father needs to be especially
tolerant and understanding. In turn, mothers need
to understand that their partners also may feel
overwhelmed by the changes in their lives.

With the understanding that perfect mothering
and fathering do not come instantly and automati-

cally (and are probably unattainable), and that the first weeks are always difficult, you will be able to experience together all aspects of your new baby – the rewards, the enjoyment and the fun, as well as the anxieties, tiredness and sheer hard work.

MAKING LIFE EASIER

During these early weeks when your life revolves totally around your baby's needs, any help you can get in running the home will make life easier for you and free you to concentrate on your baby. Friends, grandparents and other members of the family, or paid domestic help can all be valuable, depending on your circumstances.

With or without extra help, you should not feel bad about taking short cuts with cooking and housework. If you normally keep your home spotlessly clean and tidy, you may need to adjust to lower standards for a few weeks. Alternatively, if you can afford it, you may prefer to pay someone to keep your home as you like it. This is a worthwhile expense if you can budget for it, even if it is only for a couple of hours a week for the first few weeks. If you are a single parent, or have several other children and your partner cannot take time off, or if you have any other social problems at home, you may be able to get some help through the hospital social services department. If your local Visiting Nurse Association comes to see you for the first time, ask advice about this and they may be able to help you arrange it.

You may, however, feel that buying a large, labor-saving item like a washing machine, tumble drier, freezer or microwave would be more useful in the long run, if you don't have them already. Sometimes grandparents offer to buy large items of equipment for the baby to help out, so if they can afford it, suggest they contribute one of these to make your life easier, rather than some expensive item of baby furniture. As you will see from the next section, your baby's needs are few to start off with and you can build up the equipment gradually, much of which can be obtained secondhand.

Your priorities are attending to your baby and looking after yourself. Try to get some rest during the day and try to eat regular healthy meals in between feeding and changing – this will more than fill your day. If you can avoid being overtired you are more likely to be able to enjoy your baby to the full.

EQUIPMENT FOR YOUR BABY

Choosing clothes and equipment for your new baby can be a difficult task; the choice is vast and bewildering. There has been an enormous develop-ment in 'baby technology' in the past decade and the result has revolutionized the design of items such as buggies, strollers and high chairs. It has also resulted in the invention of a large number of attractive but expensive items which are not really necessary. For instance, a special changing table helps to confine the changing equipment to one area, but a simple changing mat on a convenient table or chest costs a fraction of the price.

Start looking round the shops several weeks before the baby is due, as you will feel increasingly tired as your pregnancy nears its end. Think very carefully about what you are likely to need before you spend any money. Your choice will depend on the time of year the baby is born and on your way of life, as well as on your budget. Do you usually drive a car, or do you walk to the shops or take a bus? Do you live in a house with stairs or an apartment with an elevator? Will your baby be born in winter or summer? Talk to friends with babies about what they found useful. Salespeople in some of the larger department stores can be helpful in guiding you around the market. Check all items for safety.

Equipment need not be expensive as many of the larger items can be bought secondhand. You can look at advertisements in the newspaper, or check in your local baby clinic where notices of items for sale are put up. Friends and relatives are often delighted to hand on a buggy or portacrib which has been taking up space in the attic, but do check especially carefully for safety on older models. Friends and family may like to give clothes as gifts for the baby; if they ask you what you would like, don't be afraid to tell them exactly what you need – this avoids duplication and helps your budget. The tables included in this chapter are designed to help you choose what you need.

CLOTHES

Buying children's clothes is much more fun now than it used to be. Colors and styles are fresh and bright, and there is a broad range from which to choose. Babies grow very rapidly, so don't buy too many first size clothes. Budget to allow for some second size as well so that you will have something available as soon as the baby needs it. Babies born in winter or summer will obviously have different immediate requirements. In cold weather several layers of clothes are warmer than one thick layer.

Choose fabrics which are easily washable – preferably machine-washable – and can be tumble-dried. If you do not have a washing machine or tumble drier you may need one or two extra garments, especially in the winter when everything takes longer to dry. Woollens are more difficult to

FIRST CLOTHES

Undershirts	3-4 cotton. Overlapping necks (boatneck) are easier to pull over the baby's head than round necks. Wrap over undershirts tend to be fiddly. Some are like 'body-suits' which fasten over the diaper with snaps; these are snug in winter.	**Sleeping bag**	Usually made of quilted polyester. Similar in style to the sleepsuit, but warmer, a sleeping bag will keep your baby warm in the buggy or baby carrier, or when he or she is sitting up in the buggy. Smaller babies may feel warmer in a buggy with blankets and a quilt than with a sleeping bag.
Shawl	Useful as an extra wrap for night feeds, but if lacy, avoid wrapping the baby in it in bed in case fingers are trapped. A lightweight blanket does better.	**Stretchsuits**	6 at least. These are comfortable, warm and practical. Those with poppers all down the front and inside the legs make diaper changes easier. Beware of stretchsuits with small unshaped feet, they may constrict your baby's feet as they grow, and cause damage. Most have shaped feet. If these appear to be getting too tight, you can always cut them off and dress your baby in socks and bootees instead. Fold-back mittens on the sleeves are useful in cold weather or if your baby is inclined to scratch himself. Stretchsuits with short sleeves and no legs are useful in hot weather. It is a good idea to have at least one second size stretchsuit – better slightly too large than slightly too small.
Nightdresses	4. Useful as they make night-time diaper changes easier. Some have a drawstring through the hem to stop them riding up.		
Sleepsuits	1-2 for cold weather. Usually made of synthetic fleecy fabric. Some are like a sleeping bag with arms and a hood and have a zip opening which makes it easy to lift the baby in and out. Others have legs, less easy to put on but still snug. Useful for night feeding or for keeping warm in the buggy.		
Sweaters	2 wool or acrylic. These are not essential unless you find it difficult to keep your home warm. Those which button all down the front are warmer than those with one button at the yoke or neck. Be careful of the fastenings and avoid any styles with drawstring tie fastenings at the neck as these can be dangerous. Close-knit ones are better than loose lacy ones in which little fingers can get trapped.	**Hats, mittens, bootees**	Wool or acrylic. 1 hat and pair of mittens in winter. A cotton hat is essential in summer to protect your baby's head and face from the sun. If the weather is very cool even in summer you may need a warm hat and mittens. Scratch mittens made of soft cotton are sometimes recommended; keeping the nails trimmed is even better. Bootees over a stretch suit keep a baby's feet extra warm. Beware of loose threads which may constrict fingers or toes.

wash than cotton or synthetic fabrics. Avoid clothes which need ironing, as you will have difficulty finding time for this. Clothes should be easy to get on and off, bearing in mind that diaper changes and soiling will be frequent.

BATHS AND DIAPERS

A baby bath is not an essential item; babies can be bathed in a large basin or an ordinary bath. However, it is practical, safe and the easiest place to bath your baby during the first few months. When you do start to use the full-size bath, use a mat if it doesn't have a non-slip surface.

There are several different designs of baby bath made out of rigid plastic. Some have plugs, which makes them easier to empty. You may need a separate bath stand if you do not have a good surface on which to put the bath – check that this fits properly and is stable. Some baths are designed to fit over the big bath; these can be easily filled and emptied without having to be carried.

Baths made out of soft plastics are also available, which have their own stand. This type of bath is very useful if you are short of space, as it can be folded away, and it does not need to stand in the bathroom. It can be filled from a bucket and emptied back into the bucket through an outlet tube. Some designs have an attached changing mat which fits on top, and a shelf for toiletries.

The big decision is whether to buy cloth diapers or disposable diapers – or both. Cloth diapers can be cheaper in the long run. They are more absorbent and softer than disposables, and they will fit babies of all shapes and sizes. Their main disadvantage is that they have to be washed and dried. If you do not have a washing machine this is a very laborious process, and even with a machine more work is involved than with disposables. Cloth diapers must be completely dried and properly aired, so you need plenty of space, or a tumble drier. Diapers come out softer from a drier than if they are air dried. For cloth diapers you will also require extra equipment such as buckets, sanitizing powder or liquid, washing powder, pins and elastic pants. Diaper service provides a supply of clean cloth diapers delivered to your home. The cost is usually comparable to disposable diapers in the long run.

Disposable diapers are quicker to put on – they do not have to be folded. However they do take up a lot of room, they are bulky to buy and store and they create large volumes of rubbish. They do not always fit very well and they can leak or cause chafing. They are also expensive, and with approximately 2000 diaper changes to look forward to in the first year this may be a major disadvantage.

Most parents find that a combination suits them best. The cloth diapers are fine for home use while the disposables are useful for outings, when convenience is the top priority.

CHANGING DIAPERS

Although changing diapers is usually regarded as one of the most unpleasant aspects of parentcraft, it does provide a wonderful opportunity for you and your baby to be close. Once your baby is comfortable in a clean diaper you can both enjoy spending a little time together playing and talking, getting to know one another. Parents often find that they notice their baby's first smiles while changing diapers.

The decision whether to use cloth diapers or disposables is discussed above, but the basic procedure for changing a diaper is the same, whichever type you decide to use. Although disposables are quicker to put on, it takes the same amount of time to cleanse, and, if necessary, to dress your baby in clean clothes whichever type of diaper you use.

WHEN TO CHANGE A DIAPER

In general, a baby's diaper should be changed when it is very wet, and as soon as it is soiled, in order to avoid diaper rash. Of course, you do not need to wake your baby at night just for a diaper change, but it is worth checking the diaper if he wakes for any reason. Sleeping through the night in a wet diaper does not matter as long as the baby is not cold or uncomfortable.

You will probably need to change your baby's diaper at every feeding and at other times to start with – as many as twelve times a day in the early weeks. Some babies move their bowels before a feeding, others during or after a feeding. There is little point in changing the diaper before a feeding if your baby is likely to produce a stool by the end of it. Your baby may prefer to be dry and comfortable before a feeding, or may be too hungry to wait despite having a full diaper. You will soon learn which pattern suits your baby best.

After a few weeks your baby will enjoy spending a period of time during the day kicking around on a towel or mat in a warm room without a diaper on. This is a particularly good idea if he or she has sensitive skin or a rash.

NORMAL STOOLS AND URINE

Most babies pass urine around the time of birth and about three to four times a day during the first few days. By ten days of age they will be passing urine about ten to twelve times per day. The color of the urine depends on how much the baby drinks; the less fluid he drinks, the more concentrated and darker ('stronger') will be the urine. If the urine always appears dark and is passed less frequently, the baby probably needs more to drink.

The frequency and consistency of babies' stools varies greatly. The stools of breastfed babies are soft and yellow, with the consistency of scrambled egg. Sometimes they are green and very loose and contain mucus. Most breastfed babies pass several stools a day, though it is not unusual for several days or a week to go by without a stool being passed. This is because breast milk is designed to fit your baby's requirements and there is very little waste matter left over.

The stools of bottle fed babies tend to be harder than those of breastfed babies. These babies do not usually go for more than one day without a bowel movement (see p. 109). The stools are browner in color and their consistency is more like clay. They can sometimes also be green. Very hard stools may indicate that the baby is not being given enough water to drink.

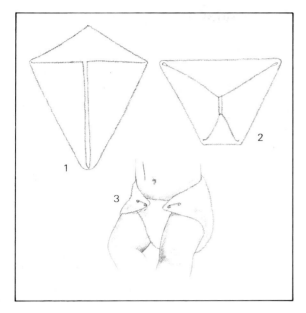

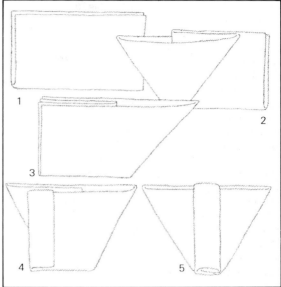

Folding cloth diapers

Kite method: 1 Lay the diaper in a diamond shape and fold corners inward 2 Fold points in neatly 3 Pin on each side, as shown.

Origami method: 1 Fold diaper in two with free edges uppermost 2 Pull left-hand corners across 3 Turn folded diaper over 4 Fold the two middle layers in and over twice. Pin as for the kite method.

HOW TO CHANGE A DIAPER

Assemble all the equipment you will need: changing mat, diaper, and diaper liner, pins and plastic pants (if required), clothes, if necessary, baby lotion or warm water, and baby wipes, diaper cream, diaper bucket filled with diaper sanitizing solution and garbage can. It is easier at home to set aside an area for changing so everything is close by.

If you are going to use a cloth diaper, fold it and put a diaper liner in place before you remove your baby's clothes and soiled diaper. Then remove the wet or soiled diaper and any of the baby's clothes which may also be soiled or wet. Clean the baby's bottom with a disposable baby wipe or baby lotion. (If soiled, clean the baby's bottom with a tissue first.) If the baby has diaper rash it is a good idea to wash him gently with warm water and pat dry. Girls must always be wiped from front to back to prevent germs from entering the vagina or bladder from the anus.

Dry the area thoroughly but gently, then lift the baby's legs and slide the diaper underneath. Apply a diaper cream if the baby's bottom is sore or chafed. Some parents prefer to use some form of barrier whether their baby has a rash or not – vaseline or petroleum jelly are soft and spread evenly without clogging and so are more suitable for use at every diaper change. Zinc oxide cream or other medicated

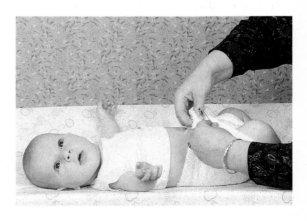

When pinning a cloth diaper, always make sure that you place your fingers behind the diaper, between the point of the pin and your baby's skin, so that there is no danger of pricking your baby even if he wriggles.

creams are thicker in consistency but are much more effective in forming a waterproof barrier if your baby has a rash (see p. 192). Try to avoid using too thick a layer of cream as it can clog the one-way action of diaper liners. Which cream you use is really a matter of personal preference – a really bad rash should anyway be referred to a doctor who may want to prescribe an antibiotic cream to assist the

CHANGING EQUIPMENT

Cloth diapers	You will need at least two dozen. Buy the best you can afford as the cheaper ones wear thin very quickly. Cloth diapers are traditionally square; you can also buy shaped diapers but they are more expensive and less efficient. You will need diaper pins with safety heads.	**Baby oil**	This is useful if your baby's skin is very dry. Baby lotion can also be used for this purpose. Talcum powder is not necessary after a bath. It can cause irritation, especially if applied to wet skin, and it must not be sprinkled too near the nose or throat as it can be inhaled.
Disposable diapers	All-in-one disposable diapers are plastic-backed and therefore do not need plastic pants. There are also disposable pads which fit inside plastic pants. These pads also provide useful extra protection at night for the older baby, worn inside cloth diapers or disposables. Disposables should *not* be put down the toilet but placed in plastic bags, sealed and disposed of in the garbage.	**Soap**	Pure soap or special bath-care liquid. This can also be used as shampoo for the first few months, but is not always necessary at first.
		Cotton wool	This is for cleaning your baby's face and behind. After a few months you can use a small sponge or face cloth for the face, keeping a second one for the rest of the body.
Diaper liners	Disposable one-way liners are worn inside cloth diapers. They help to keep the baby's behind dry and also protect the diaper from soiling. They can be flushed down the toilet. You can also use them inside disposable diapers.	**Bowls**	Any small container can be used to hold water for your baby's face and eyes. Sponge-bathing bowls can be bought, with two separate compartments for water and cotton wool.
Plastic pants	The choice is between snap fastening, elasticized and tie fastening pants. The snap type are easy to put on and are most efficient, but tend to chafe. The tie fastening type are easily adaptable to different sizes and shapes.	**Baby lotion and baby wipes**	These are for cleaning the baby's behind. Baby wipes are easy and convenient when you are out, but may sting if your baby has a diaper rash. Baby lotion or warm water on a piece of cotton wool is sufficient at home.
Diaper pail and diaper sanitizing solution	One or two pails with lids are needed for soaking cloth diapers, one for wet, one for soiled diapers (see opposite). Also useful for soaking white clothes or bedlinen (the solution tends to bleach coloreds).	**Baby bath**	With stand if necessary.
		Towels	Cotton towels are best. Some have a hood at one corner to keep the baby's head warm. One or two smaller towels are useful in addition to pat the baby dry.
Diaper cream	To form a protective barrier between your baby's skin and the wet diaper which prevents soreness, and protects your baby's behind if it develops a rash (see p. 193).	**Plastic changing mat**	A changing mat at home saves soiling towels or other surfaces when changing. A holdall which opens out to make a mat is useful. One variety has the mat attached to but separate from the bag.
		Storage	You will need to store the toiletries near the diaper changing area, on shelves, in a box or basket or in a set of pockets hung on the wall. A box or basket is useful as you can carry it around; you may like to keep it near the crib at night

healing process. Since some powders may promote the growth of yeast, it can be helpful to avoid their use if your baby is prone to yeast diaper rash.

Bring the diaper up between the baby's legs and fasten securely. When pinning a diaper always make sure you have one hand behind the pin, between the diaper and your baby's body, to avoid an accidental prick. Tuck in the edges of the disposable so that urine is less likely to leak out. Most disposables have resealable tabs so that if your baby wriggles or you think you have not secured the diaper firmly enough you can refasten it without having to use a new diaper.

Put plastic pants on over a cloth diaper, then dress your baby again. Diaper liners can be flushed down the toilet. When your baby is older and is producing firmer feces you will be able to flush the worst of this down the toilet whether using disposables or cloth. Disposable diapers should be thrown away into a closed diaper pail lined with a plastic bag, which should be emptied regularly. Cloth diapers should be put immediately in a bucket of sanitizing solution to soak. When you have finished handling a soiled diaper, always wash your hands before picking up your baby again.

WASHING DIAPERS

It is a good idea to have one bucket with a lid for wet diapers and a second one for soiled diapers. After soaking for at least twelve hours (or overnight), wet diapers should be thoroughly rinsed and dried; the 'rinse-only' cycle on a washing machine is ideal for this. Soiled diapers after similar soaking should be washed in very hot water using a soap powder. Thorough rinsing is essential as residual ammonia from the urine can cause a rash (see p. 192). Detergents and fabric softeners are also liable to cause an irritant rash. Boiling is not necessary; the soak solution should be changed every day. Cloth diapers are softer if dried in a tumble-drier, and should be well aired before use to ensure that they are completely dry.

WASHING AND BATHING

Bathing your baby is not essential in the first few weeks, but bathtime can be an immensely enjoyable occasion for all of you. Bathtime is playtime, and your baby will learn to enjoy kicking and splashing in the water, and later playing with bath toys and beakers. A cuddle and a chat when snugly wrapped up in a soft warm towel is part of the pleasure.

Tiny babies do not always enjoy being bathed at first; you may also lack confidence initially. If your baby was born in hospital you will have been shown how to bath your baby. When you return home the visiting nurse will help you to gain confidence. In the meantime there are other ways of keeping your baby clean. You can wash his face, neck and bottom (sponge bathing) once or twice daily, and every two or three days you can wash him all over (see below).

WHEN TO BATHE YOUR BABY

Most babies over a week old are bathed about every other day, and 'sponge bathed' once a day in addition. As the weeks pass and your baby's pleasure develops, bathing can take place every day. It does not matter what time of day you choose, or whether you bathe your baby before or after a feeding. Some babies may not tolerate bathing before a feeding if they are too hungry. Others may feel too sleepy after a feeding and will be uncomfortable or sick if they are bathed too soon. You will soon find out which time suits you and your baby best. This will vary with age as patterns of eating and sleeping change. You may like to bathe the baby mid-morning when he or she is neither too hungry nor too sleepy, or if the baby's father is out during the day, in the evening when you can share the enjoyment or he can take over completely and give you a welcome rest.

WHERE TO BATHE

Any warm room is suitable, as long as there is space or a good surface on which to put the bath and somewhere for you to sit. The bathroom is obviously convenient for filling and emptying the bath, especially if you do not have a baby bath with a removable plug.

Once your baby is about three or four months, you can start to use the big bath, especially if he or she likes splashing about. However you may find that holding the baby in the water is a strain on your back, and so put off using the big bath until your baby can sit up. Always use a safety mat in the bath to stop your baby slipping over. You might both enjoy sharing your bath with your baby, keeping him well supported between your legs.

SAFETY AND HYGIENE

High standards of cleanliness and hygiene are always important, but particularly so during the first few months, when your baby's immune system is not fully developed. This includes the care of all equipment and clothes with which your baby will come into contact, as well as all feeding utensils. Washing your hands thoroughly before tending to

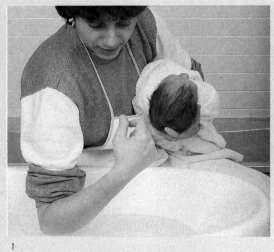

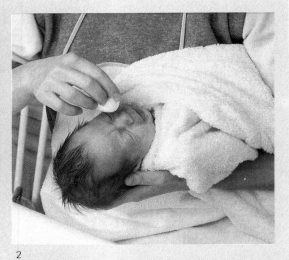

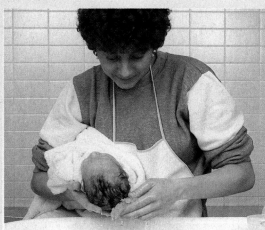

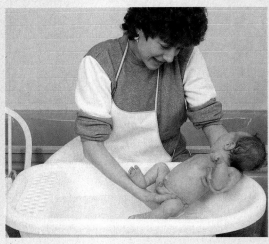

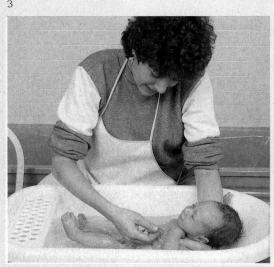

Bathing your baby

1 *Fill the bath. Undress your baby and wrap him in a towel. Test the water temperature with your elbow or wrist, not your fingers.*

2 *Wash your baby's face with cooled water. Wipe his eyes with separate pieces of cotton wool, from the inside corner outwards.*

3 *Holding your baby over the bath, wash his hair gently using water from the bath containing a baby bath preparation, soap or baby shampoo.*

4 *Carefully lift your baby into the bath with both hands as shown, supporting his head and shoulders with one hand and his bottom and thighs with the other.*

5 *Let him lie in the water for a few minutes, then lift him out in the same way and dry him carefully so that he does not become cold.*

your baby's needs sounds obvious but may be forgotten. Once your baby starts to put anything and everything into his mouth, the need for obsessive cleanliness diminishes, except when preparing food and changing diapers.

When preparing a bath, always pour the cold water in first, adding the hot water afterwards. Pouring hot water in first carries the risk of scalding if you put your baby into the bath too soon (see p. 274). It is best to turn down the thermostat on your hot water heater to below 120°F while babies or young children are in the house. Wrap a cloth tightly around the hot faucet to prevent an older child who can reach it from being scalded. Once your baby is sitting unaided in the bath, never, under any circumstances, leave him even for the briefest moment. Forget the telephone or doorbell, or wrap your baby in a towel and take him with you.

SPONGE BATHING

As with diaper changing, it is a good idea to assemble everything you are going to need for sponge bathing before you start. You will need a bowl of warm water, another containing cool water, cotton wool, a sponge or soft face cloth, towels, clean diaper and clothes. In a warm room, undress your baby except for his undershirt and lay him on a towel on your lap or a changing mat.

Wash your baby's face and neck creases gently with warm water and cotton wool (do not use soap). Use a separate piece of cotton wool dampened with boiled water for each eye, wiping gently from the inside outwards. Gently wipe away any dried secretions around the nostrils with more damp cotton wool. Do not poke up the nostrils with Q-tips as this can damage the delicate lining of the nose. Babies clear their own nostrils by sneezing.

Ear wax moves naturally to the opening of the ear canal and can be cleared away with cotton wool when it reaches the opening. Do not poke Q-tips down the ear; this is dangerous and only pushes the wax back inside. (As grandmother will tell you, 'Never put anything smaller than your elbow into the ear'!) Pat the face dry with a soft towel. You do not need to clean inside your baby's mouth until teeth appear (see p. 217). After about eight weeks you can start to use a soft sponge or wash cloth for washing the face. Keep this separate and do not use it for cleaning the baby's bottom. Change your baby's diaper and put on clean clothes.

TOWEL BATHING

Collect together the same equipment as for sponge bathing. Undress your baby and wrap him or her in a warm towel on your lap. Wash the face and neck as for sponge bathing, then lay the baby on the towel on your lap and wash the body, arms and legs with warm water and soap or baby bath, using your hands or a soft sponge. Turn your baby over on your lap to wash back and bottom, and in between the buttocks. Do not wash inside a baby girl's vulva, but gently wash the genital area from front to back to prevent germs reaching the vagina or bladder from the anus. Do not attempt to pull a baby boy's foreskin back as this may damage it (see p. 172).

Sponge off the soap and pat the baby dry, taking care to dry inside all the folds and creases. Put on a clean diaper and dress the baby. Be careful not to allow your baby to chill during a towel bath – keep the time between washing, rinsing and drying as short as possible.

BATHING YOUR BABY

Assemble all the same equipment as for sponge bathing in a warm, draft-free room. Fill the bath with cold water followed by hot, aiming for a temperature of 85°F. This temperature should feel comfortably warm to your elbow, but use a thermometer if in doubt. Put a safety mat into the bath if it has not been made with a non-slip surface.

Undress your baby and clean the diaper area. Wrap your baby in a large towel and lay him on the changing mat while you wash your hands. Wash his face and eyes as described above. To wash his hair, hold your baby on his back and tuck his legs and body under your arm, supporting his neck and head with your thumb and first two fingers. Lower his head as near to the bath as possible and gently wet his scalp with water from your hand. Then apply soap, or use bath water containing a baby bath preparation. If your baby has cradle cap (see p. 192) you may want to massage the scalp quite thoroughly. Do not be afraid of touching the fontanel ('soft spot') gently, as the brain is protected by a tough membrane. Rinse off the soap or water with clean bath water, holding him in the same way. Be careful not to splash any water in his eyes. Gently dry the head with a corner of the towel.

If you are using soap, unwrap your baby and wash his body while he is on your lap, as for a towel bath. Then lift him into the bath to rinse him. To do this, put your left arm under his neck, if you are right-handed, holding him with your thumb around the top of his left arm and your fingers in his armpit. Hold his feet or thighs with the other hand and lower him into the water.

Supporting his head and neck with your left arm, release his legs to let him kick, and swirl the water round him with your free hand. Two or three

Once your baby is about three months old, there is no reason why he should not share the bath with one of his parents, so long as he is well-supported.

minutes in the water is enough for a tiny baby.

Lift him back on to your lap and wrap him in the towel, covering his scalp so that he doesn't become cold. Pat him dry, taking care to dry inside all the creases. Lay him on a dry towel and put on his undershirt before putting on his diaper (see p. 167) and other clothes in the usual way.

THE NAILS

A very young baby's nails are soft and often flake off by themselves, or you can rub them off if they are too long. This may be safer than using scissors to start off with as it is easy to catch the skin. Once nails start growing more strongly, trim them straight across with round-ended nail scissors when they have grown well clear of the finger tip. It may be better to cut them when your baby is quiet rather than at bath time when he is active. Two people make the job easier; one holds, the other cuts.

THE UMBILICUS

Your nurse will show you how to clean your baby's umbilicus. Before the umbilicus is com-

pletely healed you should clean the area thoroughly with alcohol swabs. These will be supplied to you by the hospital. Don't be afraid to clean behind the stump; it is important to prevent infection. There is no harm in bathing your baby before the stump has dropped off or the umbilicus has completely healed (that is, in the first week or two) as long as it is properly dried afterwards. If there is redness or pus you should tell your doctor at once (see p. 193).

THE FORESKIN

At birth, the foreskin is attached to the tip of the penis and cannot be pulled back. It separates gradually over the next few years, and will usually be completely separated by the age of three or four. Before this age you must not try to force the foreskin back as this may tear the skin, causing bleeding and later scarring. There is no danger of dirt collecting under the foreskin in small babies; on the contrary, the foreskin protects the tip of the penis from infection and from the irritation of wet diapers.

CIRCUMCISION

Circumcision is the removal of the foreskin from the penis. Nowadays it is usually only performed for reasons of family preference, or for ritual religious reasons; there is no medical reason for routine

SLEEPING

Once again, your choice of equipment will depend on your lifestyle. You will definitely need a crib for your baby to sleep in until about two years of age. For the first months, however, you may prefer your baby to sleep in a cradle or a portacrib. These are more easily made draft-proof and are more snug and secure for newborn babies, although if they are not rigid they are not safe for use in the back of a car.

Bedding	Cribs and cradles are usually sold complete with a mattress, which must fit properly otherwise your baby could become wedged in a gap or trap his hands or feet at the side. Non-allergenic foam is the best filling. Some are partially covered with a waterproof plastic covering. A pillow is not necessary for the first year and suffocation. A pillow is not necessary for the first year and can be dangerous for a small baby. Small sheets and blankets can be made from full size bedding, or can be bought. Fitted stretch bottom sheets usually made in terry cloth or flannelette, are more expensive but are easier to put on and more comfortable for your baby. Sheepskins have become popular for babies to lie on. They are comfortable, expensive, but certainly not necessary. Top sheets in flannelette are warm and cosy and need less ironing than standard cotton sheets. A newborn baby will be swaddled in a shawl, light blanket or sheet for the first few weeks, and will need tucking in with a light blanket. The best blankets are made of cellular cotton, wool or acrylic; wool is warmer for winter, acrylic is cheaper and easier to wash. A satin or polyester edge prevents irritation.
Crib	Once your baby grows out of the cradle or portacrib he or she will sleep in a crib. This must conform to American safety standards. It must be well made with sides high enough to stop the baby climbing out. The bars must be close enough together to stop a little head getting stuck between them. If painted, the paint must be non-toxic. It is important to check this on a secondhand crib. Cribs with a wooden mattress rest are very good; some have adjustable bases so that a small baby can sleep higher up and be more easily lifted out and put down. Drop sides make it easier to put your baby in the crib, but check that the catch is not too easy to operate.
Cradle	A wicker or wooden cradle can be very attractive, though it is not an essential item. Cradles should be lined to make them draft-proof. Some have stands, others swing, which is useful for soothing a crying baby. These can be fixed so that they cannot swing when the baby is alone. Cradles are not really portable.
Portacrib	(see also p. 272) If you often travel in the car, a portacrib is essential. Many designs and sizes are available. One of the most useful comes with an adaptor frame which can be neatly folded or converted to a buggy. This type is usually quite small, light and easy to carry. Your baby will grow out of the portacrib by about nine months of age, although the buggy should last for about two years. Portacribs are versatile; they serve as a bed for the baby at home, they can be put in the back of the car (see below), or they can be used as a buggy.
Travel crib	If you often stay with friends or relatives you might consider buying a travel crib. These are light and quite compact when folded. They have a firm base and strong fabric sides. Sometimes these are available for rent locally, and most hotels or motels use them.
Baby alarms and intercom systems	If you are worried because you may not hear your baby crying, you might consider installing an intercom system. Most models do not require any wiring and can be plugged into a socket. An intercom should be sensitive enough to pick up soft crying or the sounds of a restless baby turning over. You can plug your receiver in wherever you are and feel reassured that you will hear your baby as soon as he wakes.

173

circumcision of the newborn. Moreover, there is no relationship between the incidence of cervical cancer in women with uncircumcised partners, so this cannot be considered as a reason for circumcision of an infant. However, some recent research suggests fewer urinary tract infections in circumcised infants. The medical reason for circumcision is usually a condition known as phimosis, which is severe scarring of the foreskin caused by forcible pulling back or repeated infection. Phimosis does not usually appear until well into childhood or later.

SLEEP

Babies vary in their sleep requirements just as adults do, depending on their personality. Newborn babies spend at least two-thirds of a 24-hour day asleep. At first they have little notion of night and day, and their pattern of sleep is quite random. Gradually they settle into a regular pattern of wakefulness and sleep. After a few weeks they become more aware that night differs from day and will sleep for longer periods at night, with more wakeful periods during the day. At about three months most babies will have three or four periods of sleep during 24 hours.

Some babies are active and wakeful, needing very little sleep. Hunger is not the only reason for being awake; the surroundings are fascinating and there is company and entertainment at hand – too much to see and hear to be asleep. Babies with a more placid personality sleep much more, and at four to five months of age may still be sleeping through much of the day time. Both patterns are normal; there is no set length of time a baby should spend sleeping each day. It is pointless to try to impose longer sleeping times on an active baby who does not need more sleep.

As your baby gets older you can try to adjust his or her pattern of sleep. For example, if he sleeps for long periods during the day but is wakeful at night, you could shorten his day time naps or space them so that he is more sleepy by nightfall. But do not worry about the total amount of time your baby sleeps, as long as he is contented.

A wakeful irritable baby who cries a lot may be uncomfortable or unwell. If you cannot find a reason for his irritability don't be afraid to seek the advice of your doctor. Similarly, if his sleep pattern has changed, ask your doctor to check that all is well.

WHERE TO SLEEP

For the first month or two when he or she is still needing night feeds, you will probably prefer your baby to sleep in your bedroom. The room should be warm – about 70°F for a tiny baby – and should be free of drafts. By two or three months of age the temperature can be lowered gradually to not less than 60°F. The room should not cool down too much at night, so the window will need to be kept closed in winter.

In a warm room, a baby wearing a stretchsuit or nightie should only require one or two light blankets or a light comforter to keep him warm in a crib or portacrib. Babies who are too hot will probably wake and cry; those who are too cold may not. Overheating and overcooling can both be dangerous. Small babies are less well able to regulate their body temperature, and can become very cold very rapidly, being unable to shiver or move about to keep themselves warm. Check your baby's temperature by feeling his abdomen; it will feel cold if he is too cold, and warm and sticky if he is too hot. When you lift your baby out at night for a feeding or diaper change, you may need to wrap him in a shawl or blanket to keep warm.

With the crib near your bed, you can easily take your baby into your own bed for a feeding, if you wish. Don't worry if you fall asleep during or after feeding; your baby will not suffocate and you will not roll over on top of him. A baby will naturally move his face out of the way if his breathing is obstructed. Parents filmed asleep at night with their baby between them have been shown to roll away from the baby each time the baby touches them. However, you may find that your baby gets too hot in your bed and is happier back in the crib after the feeding. A note of warning: do not let your baby sleep in bed with you if you have taken alcohol or any kind of sedative drug, as your reflexes will be dulled. Babies wearing a splint (for example for a dislocated hip) should not sleep with you either because they are unable to roll over.

You may prefer your baby to sleep in a separate room from yours from the beginning. Babies snuffle quite a lot when they are asleep and parents can find this very disturbing. If there is no separate bedroom, there is no reason why he or she should not sleep in the living room or even in the hallway, as long as it is warm and free of drafts and you can hear when the baby cries. You could let the baby sleep in your room until you go to bed, then move him to another room, though this obviously becomes more difficult as the baby gets older and you will eventually need to find an alternative solution.

SLEEPING POSITIONS

Generally, babies prefer to have their limbs free to move. They should not be swaddled, or put on their

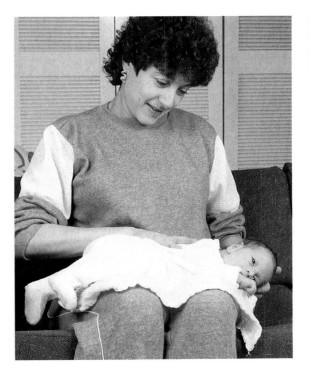

A fretful baby can be worrying for parents, but there are ways you may soothe him. Try laying him across your knee and stroking his back gently (above), or putting him against your shoulder and walking about or gently rocking in a chair (below).

side as this position is unstable, but should lie on their stomach. The safest position is lying on the stomach with the head to one side. Any regurgitated milk will dribble out of the mouth, so there is less risk of choking. A pillow should not be used for the first year, as there is a risk of suffocation during the first few months.

If your baby wakes and is unable to roll over on to his back to look around, he may get bored and will cry until someone comes to the rescue. Toys or a small mirror where he can see them may help provide distraction for a while.

DISTURBED NIGHTS

After a few weeks, settling your baby to sleep may be easier if you establish a familiar routine. This may be different for daytime and night time sleeps. For example, your baby may feel sleepy in the evening after a bath and a cuddle, so you can establish this as a bedtime routine.

Babies who are overtired find it difficult to get off to sleep and may cry for a long time before they finally settle. Rocking your baby in your arms for a while often helps. However, your baby may fall asleep happily in your arms, only to wake and cry as soon as you put him down again. If this happens, you could try cuddling him in the crib without picking him up, laying him down gently when he is asleep. Sometimes your baby just needs to get his crying done before he can go to sleep.

Babies who wake frequently at night are exhausting for their parents, but this is inevitable during the first few weeks. If you are bottle feeding you can take it in turns with night feedings. If you are breastfeeding but exhausted, it is helpful to let your partner give the baby a bottle at night once breastfeeding is established (see p. 158). If one or both partners is working while night feedings are still a regular feature, it might be worth discussing sleeping in separate rooms occasionally. During the day it is important for you to have a rest in the afternoon when your baby is sleeping; try not to use it as an opportunity for fitting in additional chores.

When your baby wakes in the night it is best to deal with his needs immediately – but as briefly as possible. Prolonged playing or cuddling sessions will encourage your baby to believe that waking you in the night carries a special reward. Once he learns that he will be fed or comforted as needed but is unlikely to get extra bonuses, he will begin to modify his behavior.

When your baby is fast asleep, nothing is likely to disturb him. It is better not to aim for a silent household whenever your baby sleeps, or he will later wake at the slightest sound. He will not be

TRAVELING

The amount of driving, traveling by public transport or walking you do and the time of year your baby is born will affect your choice of equipment. Babies born in winter will be warmer in a portacrib or buggy than in a stroller. For those born in summer the newer designs of stroller suitable for tiny babies are excellent.

Front carrier A front carrier is a wonderful way of carrying your baby about, indoors or outdoors. In a carrier he can snuggle up against your chest leaving your arms free. For very small babies a front carrier must provide good head and back support; some styles have a detachable headrest, others enclose the baby almost completely – these are usually very good. Check that those with a headrest do in fact provide adequate support. Choose a front carrier with wide, comfortable shoulder straps which are adjustable, and with an easy fastener at the back – don't be afraid to try on the different types in the store.

Back pack Once your baby has good head control he or she will enjoy going for walks in a back pack carrier. This is very light, has a tubular aluminum frame and can be used until two to three years old, depending on the weight of the child and the strength of the parent! Some have adjustable seats for the smaller baby, and others have a stand so that the baby can be propped up on the ground without having to be lifted out of the back pack (a useful feature).

Buggy If you intend to do a lot of walking with your baby, and you have a large area at home in which to park a buggy and not too many steps to reach it, you will probably find a buggy very useful. A buggy is larger than a portacrib and will therefore last longer. Buggies with a well-sprung chassis and large wheels are extremely comfortable for your baby, and less bumpy than the smaller-wheeled strollers. This type of buggy is usually higher than the average portacrib and stroller so is more comfortable to push if you are tall. When old enough the baby can sit up and look around, and will be high above ground level where the view is more interesting and he is at your level. When he is tired you can simply lie him down to go to sleep. In the summer your baby can sleep out in the buggy, as it is more stable than a portacrib on wheels. You will need an insect net. Another advantage of a carriage-built buggy is that it can hold a toddler seat, useful if you have two children quite close together. When choosing a buggy, check that it is balanced and stable, has fittings for a safety harness and efficient brakes. Check that it is easy to maneuver, and whether a shopping bag can be fitted.

disturbed by background noises, but will find them reassuring. Your routine of daytime noises and night-time silence will help him to adjust to a similar routine, especially if you do not seem to be interested in playing with him at night.

CRYING

A crying baby exerts a profound emotional effect on his parents. A placid baby who cries infrequently and is easily soothed, sleeping most of the time between feedings, makes his parents feel relaxed and gives them time to rest and catch up. A baby who cries for long periods during the day and night may induce enormous anxiety in his parents, especially the mother. She feels inadequate in dealing with his needs; nothing seems to settle him. She becomes more and more exhausted and irritable and her baby senses this and cries even more. A mother feels very much to blame when her baby cries frequently – other people's babies seem to be so much 'better behaved'. Society's expectations of the perfect mother and housewife, always organized, fully rested and never flustered, smiling

Stroller	Ordinary non-adjustable strollers are unsuitable for newborn babies, who are unable to sit up. Several newer designs adjust to a reclining position so that a tiny baby can lie down flat. These can usually be adjusted so the baby can either face you or face forward. This type of stroller is small, and your baby will have grown out of it by six to nine months of age. As soon as he can sit up for a reasonable length of time he can use an ordinary stroller. Some of these do recline to some extent, and this is an advantage since babies prefer to sleep lying down. Strollers are much easier to take shopping as they are narrow enough to push through a supermarket checkout. Collapsible strollers are light, easy to fold and compact to store in the trunk of the car or at home. If you are likely to go for long walks along roads and pavements, you might prefer to buy a traditional reclining buggy with a high back and large sprung wheels. These are heavier and less compact but are very comfortable for your baby.	**Infant car seat**	Several designs of infant car seat have recently come on the market which are suitable even for tiny babies. These are secured in the front passenger seat with an ordinary seat belt. They can be adjusted to a lying down position and can face backwards or forwards, so that you and your baby can look at each other. This type of seat will last until your baby is about six to nine months of age.
		Car safety seat	Standard car safety seats are designed for babies from six to nine months of age until two to three years. These fit in the back of the car and are fixed either by the car's rear seat belt or by a special anchorage system which is usually bought separately.
Stroller accessories	Strollers are unstable when heavy shopping is hung on the handles, but some models have a firm shopping tray underneath. A waterproof cover is worth having for rainy days, and you will need a hood if it does not already have one. A hood will also protect the baby from strong sunshine, or you can buy an umbrella which fits on the handle. An umbrella is cooler than a hood in hot weather. In cold weather a warm quilted bag for the baby's legs is useful.		

at her invariably calm and happy baby, are unlikely to be fulfilled, especially during the first few months.

The fact is that some babies simply do cry more than others. Studies have shown that some babies aged two weeks cry for about two hours a day; those aged six weeks may cry for almost three hours a day. By about three months crying time has fallen to about one hour a day. A few babies cry excessively throughout their first year, which can be very trying for their parents. Crying is most frequent in the late afternoon and evening (see 'Colic' on page 190).

WHY DO BABIES CRY?

Babies cry for a variety of different reasons. These include hunger, thirst, discomfort from a wet or soiled diaper, boredom or frustration, loneliness, fear, feeling too hot, or feeling unwell or in pain. Parents can usually distinguish different types of cry in their own baby. The hunger cry differs from the cry of temper or tiredness. It often begins as a weak but restless whimper, gradually developing into an insistent, angry wail. The cry of a distressed or uncomfortable baby is different again. Parents hearing this cry know they have to see to their baby immediately; with the hunger cry they know they can afford to wait a few minutes. You will soon learn to recognize what the different cries mean.

If hunger is not the cause of your baby's crying, check whether he or she is uncomfortable in a wet diaper, or feeling too hot or too cold. If you fed him recently, he may be thirsty rather than hungry. Pick him up and talk to him and cuddle him for a few minutes; if he stops crying and looks happier, he may have been feeling bored or lonely, want to change position or simply feel the security of being close to you. Pain is very difficult to assess (see pp. 255 and 256). A shrieking baby should first be comforted, reassured if frightened, and then stripped naked and *carefully* searched for a cause of pain, such as a bite, sting, pin prick or tightly-wound hair or thread around a finger or toe. Check the temperature rectally for fever.

Sometimes you will be unable to discover any reason at all for your baby's crying, and will feel frustrated because you do not know how to soothe him. Indeed there may not be any specific reason, other than perhaps a need for him to release tension and energy before going to sleep. Babies will usually settle down before long if they are not unwell. If your baby cries persistently for a long time, don't be afraid to telephone your doctor for advice, especially if he refuses to feed or seems otherwise unwell (see p. 255).

HOW TO COPE WITH A CRYING BABY

Although you cannot avoid feeling distressed if your baby cries a lot, you must try to accept that it is not your fault. Your baby is struggling to adapt to his surroundings, and it will take you a while to learn all the reasons for his cries. Don't try to keep your anxiety to yourself; share it with your partner and perhaps with your own mother, a friend with small children, or your doctor. This will help you to keep things in perspective. It helps too, if both parents can share the daily routine, and if grandparents or relatives are able to take over if the situation becomes tense.

FEEDING TIMES

Feeding times will not be rigid during the first few weeks (see p. 153). Some babies require more frequent feeding than others, and you will find it very difficult to keep your crying baby waiting for an hour just because he had a feeding only two hours before. Just as adults' appetites vary, so do babies', and the time they take to feel hungry again between feedings. Nor does giving a larger feeding necessar-

There is evidence that the close proximity to a parent which babies derive from being carried in a front carrier actually increases their sense of security and makes them less clingy when older.

ily mean a longer sleep before the next one. Feeding and sleeping are independent activities to some extent, and your baby's rhythms depend more on his personality than how much milk he has taken.

'SPOILING'

There is absolutely no danger of 'spoiling' a tiny baby by picking him up or feeding him when he cries. On the contrary, this is essential, in order that he develops a sense of security and a feeling that he is loved. Babies who feel insecure are likely to be much more demanding; they soon learn how to get their parents' attention, while a secure baby is much more willing to accept discipline later on. Most young babies respond very well to the security of being carried in a front carrier, which has the added advantage of leaving your hands free to do other things.

After the first two to three months you may become aware that your baby is crying not because he is hungry but because he knows he will be picked up or put on the breast. He will rapidly learn how to manipulate you in this way if you let him. However if he feels secure in the knowledge that you will respond to his needs but not necessarily to his every whim, you will have more peaceful nights.

ROCKING

Motion is often helpful in soothing a crying baby. Rocking your baby in your arms, over your shoulder or on your lap is traditional and effective. Babies who cry frequently may enjoy being carried around in a front carrier or sitting in a bouncing chair. Many babies are soothed by an outing in the stroller or in the automobile.

PACIFIERS

Pacifiers can be useful if your baby wants the comfort of sucking rather than a feed. With twins they are particularly useful when one twin has to wait while the other is fed.

Pacifiers are not harmful unless they are sweetened by dipping into honey, syrup or any other sugar-based substance, since this can damage the teeth even before they have appeared. They will not cause teeth deformity if they are discarded at a fairly early age. The disadvantage is that when a pacifier falls out of the baby's mouth, someone has to find it and put it back again, and a pacifier should be rinsed clean at least for the first three or four months. The practice of attaching a pacifier to string to make it easier for the baby to find is dangerous, as a mobile baby could be strangled.

The picture of a baby or a toddler with a pacifier constantly in his mouth is not a very attractive sight, and may even be impeding the normal desire of a child to talk. Tempting though it may be to plug in a pacifier every time your baby starts to cry, this may not satisfy all his needs for stimulation and company, and he may be inclined to seek more attention as a result. It is better to spend a little time trying to find out why your baby is crying than merely trying to stop the noise.

THUMBS AND FINGERS

Many babies enjoy sucking their own fingers and thumbs from birth and even before, if they happen to reach the mouth, and later, once they learn how to bring their hands to their mouths. This is normal and safe, and certainly more attractive than sucking a pacifier. The only disadvantage of a thumb is that it cannot be taken away (unlike a pacifier) when you think your child is too old to suck it. Intensive thumb-sucking in older children can cause dental malformations: pacifiers are thought to cause less pressure against the teeth. Neither is likely to cause any problems at all in infancy.

LEAVING YOUR BABY TO CRY

Your small baby has been fed and changed, cuddled and comforted, and still will not stop crying. Should you leave him to cry? If you are feeling exhausted and angry, your baby will probably sense this, and you are unlikely to be able to soothe him. In these circumstances it is better to leave him for a short while, returning every five to ten minutes to check that he is coming to no harm. Small babies should not be left for longer than this.

Better still, let your partner or a friend deal with the problem once in a while. An occasional evening out leaving your baby with a reliable babysitter may result in a calm baby as well as calm parents. (See page 196 for advice about this.) Leave the telephone number where you can be contacted with the sitter, as well as your doctor's telephone number, and brief the sitter carefully on what to do if problems arise or if the baby does not settle down. If the crying persists, it may be because your baby is unwell and you should check for fever and telephone your doctor for advice.

GROWTH AND DEVELOPMENT

From birth to two years, babies grow and develop very rapidly, especially during the first six months. It is exciting to watch your baby developing new skills almost every week, and growing into a toddler with a unique personality. Babyhood is short-lived, and all the joyful moments when new achievements are reached are easily forgotten. Photographs and a regularly kept diary will provide you with a fascinating record of these milestones. You will also be able to compare the progress of a sister or brother, and see how very differently each child develops.

Regular assessment of growth and development is important because any delay can be detected early and a cause found, thus avoiding or minimizing any permanent problems and helping your

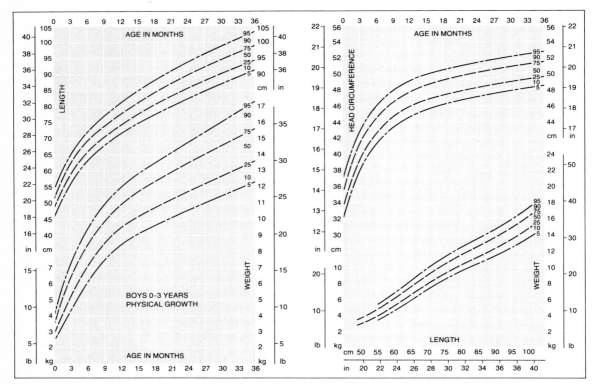

child to reach his or her full potential. Growth and development influence and affect each other.

GROWTH

Growth is one of the most sensitive indicators of well-being in childhood, although your doctor would never take it in isolation, always taking your child's physical and mental development into account as well. It is easier to measure than development, and is done by measuring weight, height and head size.

The size of a baby at birth depends mostly on the function of the placenta, through which the fetus is nourished. This in turn, depends on the health and environment of the mother during pregnancy. For example, pre-eclampsia (see p. 70) reduces the efficiency of the placenta, and babies born of mothers with this condition may be smaller at birth. Babies born of mothers who smoke also tend to be smaller (see p. 72). Babies whose mothers are diabetic are usually large (see p. 74). A mother who is small in build is likely to produce a smaller baby. This is simply because her small size limits her baby's growth in the uterus.

After birth growth is extremely rapid in the first two years. During this time the prenatal factors which help to determine birth weight gradually wear off, giving way to inherited growth patterns. Taller than average parents will usually have taller than average children, but this effect may not be seen until after the age of two.

GROWTH CHARTS

Your baby's growth will be plotted by the pediatrician (see p. 187) on special 'centile' charts, derived from the measurement of hundreds of babies. There are separate charts for girls and boys; for each sex there is a standard chart for weight, height (or length lying down for babies under three) and head size. There is a chart from birth to three years, and one from about three to eighteen years, since the rate of growth varies throughout childhood.

The charts show that there is a very large range of normal weights and heights at any given age. The 50th centile can be regarded as the average, since 50 out of every 100 children will have a weight or height less than that level, and 50 will have a weight or height greater than that level. A child whose weight is on the 5th centile is still normal; 5 out of every 100 children will weigh less than him or her, while 95 will weigh more.

Children growing normally will grow along a line parallel to one of the centile lines; it is the rate of growth which is important, not any single measurement at a particular age. Several measurements

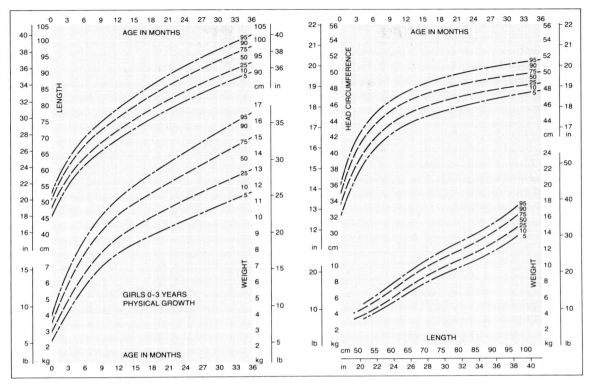

Examples of centile charts for growth, for boys (left) and for girls (right). The measurements of weight and length at birth and during the first three to five years are plotted on a chart similar to these. Each line represents a different centile. Although the range of normal is extremely wide, most babies and children will follow roughly the same centile during this period, although they may dip below or rise above it at different times, since growth rates vary. Any significant dip or imbalance between weight and length or height will be examined more closely by your doctor.

need to be taken over a period of time before the rate of growth can be seen. A child who is growing rapidly will have a steep growth curve, crossing centiles upwards. A child who is growing slowly will have a flatter curve, crossing the centile curves downwards.

Centiles may also be crossed during the first few months of life, when a baby may be 'catching up' on slow growth in the uterus and adjusting to his inherited growth rate. This is quite normal, as long as weight, length and head size all increase at the same rapid rate.

Allowance has to be made for premature babies, whose actual birth weight should be plotted before the age of '0' on the chart. For example, the weight of the baby of four weeks old born four weeks early would be entered at age '0' on the chart. Parental size also has to be taken into account when interpreting charts. Children who appear to be abnormally large may be well within the normal range when the size of both parents is considered.

If a child's growth curve crosses centile lines (apart from during the first few months) he or she should be investigated by the doctor. Investigations should also be done if there is a big difference in the growth curves for weight, height and head size. For example, if a child's curve for head size is along the 95th centile, this is normal if the curves for weight and height follow a similar centile. However, if the

weight and height curves follow a much lower centile, close observation may be needed, unless one or both parents clearly had a similar pattern of growth in infancy.

MEASUREMENT OF WEIGHT

Your baby's weight is a useful guide to his well-being, but should not be overrated as an indicator that all is well. Too frequent weighing is likely to cause anxiety, especially since a baby's weight varies considerably from day to day, and at different times of the day. A baby weighs more immediately after a feeding, and less after he has moved his bowels or passed urine. Babies should always be weighed naked; wet diapers are quite heavy!

Weighing scales are often relatively inaccurate, too.

Newborn babies nearly always lose weight during the first week (see p. 108), but are usually back to birth weight by the tenth day. During the next six months they gain on average 5-6 ounces per week. An average-sized baby will be approximately double the birth weight in the first four to six months, and treble it by one year, though this may not be true of babies who are smaller or larger than average at birth.

Although you may find it reassuring to take your baby to be weighed every week, it is not really necessary to do it more often than once every three to four weeks. A contented energetic baby is a better indicator of good health and satisfactory progress than weight gain.

MEASUREMENT OF LENGTH

Under the age of two, babies prefer to lie curled up, which makes it more difficult to measure their length. In the clinic they are usually measured on a special table or mat with a headboard at one end. One person holds the baby's head straight, touching the headboard. A second person gently straightens out his legs so that they lie flat on the table, then brings up a moveable footboard against the heels. It is quite difficult to get an accurate measurement of length with a moving, crying baby – and almost impossible with only one person.

Measurement of length is not always done routinely at the clinic, so don't be surprised if your baby is not measured in this way. Over the age of three children can be measured standing up.

MEASUREMENT OF HEAD SIZE

This is simply done by measuring the circumference of the head at its widest point with a tape measure. The head grows at a very rapid rate during the first twelve to eighteen months, reflecting the growth of the brain. A baby's head is very large relative to the rest of the body, being about a quarter the size of the trunk at birth, becoming about one eighth in adulthood. The skull bones do not join together until the rapid phase of brain growth is over, and the 'soft spot' (anterior fontanel) on the top of the baby's head does not usually disappear before about twelve months. The smaller posterior fontanel closes by about three months.

INFLUENCES ON GROWTH

Weight loss is likely to accompany even minor illnesses such as colds or diarrhea. More prolonged and serious illness or malnutrition will affect length as well as weight. Unless it is very prolonged (exactly how prolonged is not known), this slowing of growth will not be permanent, and will be followed by a period of rapid 'catch-up' growth when the child recovers. Slow growth in the absence of obvious illness may be due to a hormone deficiency or a failure to absorb food, for example due to an allergy to cow's milk (see p. 146).

Failure to gain weight may be simply due to insufficient food, and your doctor will be able to advise you if this is the case, or if there may be other problems which need invesigation. However, overfeeding will lead to obesity and this is not healthy. Very obese babies may grow into fat adults; again, your doctor will be able to discuss your child's growth charts with you and advise you about feeding.

Disturbances in the rate of growth of the head are rare but it is important to detect them early, in order to arrange treatment to avoid brain damage.

DEVELOPMENT

Development is more difficult to assess than growth. There is no standard rate or age at which milestones are reached, and the range of ages over which babies and children achieve various skills is very wide indeed. It is common for your baby to be ahead in one area of development and behind in another. Even within the same family two children will probably have very different patterns of development. Keeping a simple baby book or diary for each child is an interesting source of comparison.

Development in one area depends on development in other areas; vision, hearing, language, movement, intellectual, emotional and social development are all interconnected. For example, if a child does not hear well, his or her language and communication will be affected, which in turn will affect social development. This is why healthy children are regularly assessed to see if there is any developmental delay. The earlier any such delay is detected, the earlier it can be treated.

As parents, you are in the best position to observe your children's development. You can tell if your child is not seeing or hearing properly much earlier than anyone else, and your comments and anxieties should always be taken seriously. When reviewing your baby's progress, your doctor only sees the baby for short periods of time, and babies and children do not always present themselves at their best if they are tired, hungry or irritable, or simply frightened of strangers. The table of simple questions and observations given on page 188 will help you to assess your own baby's progress particularly in the areas of hearing and vision during the first year of life. They are meant for reassurance – if you are at all doubtful contact your own doctor or the clinic doctor who will check your baby in more detail. Development checks can easily be arranged in addition to those done routinely at the child health clinic.

If your child seems to be walking or talking later than you expect, the chances are that he will be advanced in other ways. Children are constantly learning and developing new concepts, and sometimes their understanding is far ahead of, say, their manipulative skills or their ability to move around. Development usually follows a certain sequence – for example sitting, crawling, pulling to stand and then walking. However, some children find that they can get around quite well on their bottoms, instead of crawling. These 'bottom scooters' often start walking later than usual (see p. 208) simply because they have found a very efficient way of getting around without needing to stand up.

INFLUENCES ON DEVELOPMENT

Your baby's development depends not only on his or her inherited characteristics, but also on the opportunities he or she has to learn and practice new skills. A baby will not be able to sit up before his nervous system has reached a sufficient stage of maturity, no matter how hard you try to teach him and encourage him. Moreover, he or she will sit up sooner or later without any encouragement at all. However, a lack of stimulation is discouraging and slows down progress.

Instead of trying to influence your baby's development in a particular area, it is much better to provide a generally stimulating and loving environment in which to encourage development. Don't try to push too hard to achieve a new skill. Learning should always be fun, and should give you and your baby great pleasure. Your delight in day-to-day achievements will be a further incentive to learn. Play is an essential part of learning – indeed, play *is* learning and vice versa.

Prematurity influences development only in that allowances have to be made for the age at which milestones are reached. Actually the development of premature babies tends to be speeded up, so that a baby born six weeks early, who might be expected to smile at the age of twelve weeks, may smile at around ten weeks.

Development may be delayed for a period of time by illness. Sometimes a child may even revert to an earlier stage of development after an illness or an emotional upset. For example, a child may start bedwetting again following the arrival of a new baby (see p. 240). This usually expresses a need for love and attention when the child is feeling insecure. Normal behavior is resumed when a feeling of security returns.

The more time you can both spend with your small baby, playing with him, talking to him and loving him, the more independent he or she will become later. Within a strong and secure relationship, your baby will be able to reach his or her full potential.

DEVELOPMENT FROM BIRTH TO SIX WEEKS

At birth, babies can focus on objects which are about 9 inches away, which also is the approxi-

As early as three weeks a baby's eyes are sufficiently focused to enable him to stare fixedly at his own reflection in a mirror.

PLAYING

From birth onwards your baby will enjoy watching moving colors and shapes, and will be fascinated by a mobile strung across the crib or buggy, or hung from above especially if it makes a pleasant sound as it moves. Equipment which helps to stimulate your baby's normal development is good value.

Bouncing cradle

From about one month he will have developed enough head control to be able to sit comfortably in a bouncing cradle from where to watch you and see what is going on. These chairs are light enough for you to carry your baby around the house in the chair, but never place it on a worktop or table, however tempting. Some are made of rigid plastic and can be adjusted to a reclining position. The cheaper varieties do not adjust but they are equally comfortable, and are made of cotton or soft plastic. Make sure the fabric is washable and easy to remove from the frame.

Baby walker

This is by no means an essential item but some babies do enjoy being able to move around in an upright position. However, a baby walker is not likely to cause a baby to learn to walk any earlier. Do not use a walker for a baby under nine months, and do not leave your baby in a walker for long periods, or unsupervised; stairs are a particular hazard. Furniture is also likely to suffer. Baby walkers do take up a lot of space, though some models are foldable.

Playpen

A playpen is not a substitute for a childproof room but it comes in useful for short periods of time, from about six months of age until your child is walking. Babies should not be left for long periods in a playpen, as they can feel confined and restricted. The square wooden playpen with bars and a built-in floor is sturdy. You can fix toys or an activity centre on to the bars, but check that the bars are close enough together to prevent the baby's head getting trapped in between. Some playpens are foldable, but those without a built-in floor are very easy for a child to drag around the room. A circular or oval 'lobster-pot' design is available which is very light and has fine mesh sides and a padded plastic top rail. This is foldable and may be useful for travelling but is very small. Since it is difficult to tell if paint is non-toxic, it may be safer only to buy a natural wood playpen if you are getting one secondhand. Check that there are no sharp fittings.

Baby bouncer

Many babies enjoy baby bouncers as they can swing and jump and twist and turn, or just dangle and bounce. A bouncer has no effect on walking abilities, although your baby will learn the feel of the floor under his feet. Baby bouncers are only suitable for babies over the age of four months, when they can fully support their heads. Never leave a baby in a bouncer for more than fifteen to twenty minutes, even if he still seems to be enjoying himself.

Toys and storage

You may prefer to plan in advance where and how you will store your baby's toys and clothes. Shelves are useful for baby equipment, later for toys and books. Nursery furniture is often expensive and doesn't last too long because it is small. Wire drawers, plastic stacking boxes and drawers on rollers are all practical and reasonably cheap, or you can build your own simple shelves.

mate distance between the baby's and mother's faces in the standard feeding position. Mothers automatically bend this close to their babies when talking to them. A favorite time is while changing the diaper – this is when many parents see their baby's first smile. During the next few weeks babies become able to focus on more distant objects. Watch your baby closely when he is alert and wakeful but not crying – you will be astonished at how interested he is in his surroundings and particularly in your face.

A new baby responds to loud noises by being startled and screwing up his eyes as if to withdraw. If you repeat the loud noise several times he will no longer be startled; he has learned that he will not be harmed by the noise and ignores it. Babies only several days old will turn their head in response to a rattle or to their mother's voice; however, they are easily distracted by what they can see. If your baby hears your voice and sees your face at the same time, his interest is likely to be held and he will follow you.

Young babies seem to respond more easily to high-pitched noises than to low-pitched noises; to their mother's voice rather than their father's. The reason is uncertain, but it may be partly due to the fact that they have become accustomed to hearing their mother's voice while still in the uterus.

During the first few weeks babies lie curled up with their arms and legs close to their body. A newborn baby lying on his stomach is just able to lift his head and turn it aside to avoid being suffocated by the mattress.

By six weeks however, most babies can focus on objects 18 inches away, and will follow a brightly colored ball. There is more eye-to-eye contact, and your baby will often watch you intently during feedings. Most babies will smile back in response to a smile by now, though you may have noticed your baby smiling long before six weeks. Ninety per cent

At birth a normal baby is usually curled up when lying on his front. Although he can move his head from side to side, he does not have the strength to lift it from the mattress.

At six weeks a baby will have begun to extend his legs and move his arms around. Although his head is still floppy, he can usually lift it up from the mattress when lying on his front.

By three months a baby can lift his head and shoulders up to look around when lying on his front supporting himself on his arms. (By four months he will be doing push-ups – pushing himself right up on his hands.)

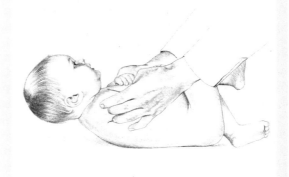

At three months, a baby's neck and back muscles are also strong enough to begin to stop his head from falling back when pulled to sitting. By four months he will be able to keep his head in line with his back – a first stage towards sitting.

By six weeks, and often earlier, many babies smile freely when they can focus their attention on a familiar face, especially one of their parents.

of babies will be smiling by seven weeks. At this age you will be able to sense his pleasure at being handled and bathed, and the enjoyment he shows in faces. Even a very tiny baby will look intently at his own image in a mirror; a mirror fixed inside the crib will give interest and delight for several months.

By this age you will probably have noticed your baby attending to a sound, and turning his head towards its source. He will be starting to show his pleasure by making 'cooing' noises, as well as communicating his discomfort or displeasure by crying. Six-week-old babies are generally alert and interested in their surroundings.

Head control is beginning to develop, alongside the ability to see more clearly. When lying on his stomach, your baby will briefly lift his head and turn his face to one side. When pulled to a sitting position from lying down on his back, he will lift his head for a moment before it lags. You should not do this often, however, as his head is still very unstable. A certain amount of head roll is inevitable, for instance when passing the baby from one person to another, but you should try to support it when you pick your baby up or when holding him since a sudden jerk could be damaging.

A six-week-old baby has sufficient head control to be able to enjoy sitting in a bouncing cradle, although these do give enough support for babies from about three weeks. A row of brightly colored toys strung across the chair will amuse him, and he will be able to see what is going on around him. A mobile hung over the crib will give him pleasure from birth, and some of these are musical. You can make your own mobile by tying pieces of brightly colored cloth or paper cut into spirals or squares on to a wire coat hanger with string. Items of jewelry or even kitchen foil make good mobiles at least while the baby cannot reach them. With this sort of stimulation your baby may be happy for a while when awake but by himself.

When asleep on his stomach, a six-week-old baby adopts the same posture as a newborn baby – curled up with the pelvis high. When awake, he will lie flatter, with his legs outstretched and his pelvis lower.

The primitive reflexes (see p. 112) are beginning to disappear by this age. The stepping reflex disappears by six to eight weeks, the grasp reflex and Moro reflex by about three months.

DEVELOPMENT AT THREE MONTHS

By now your baby will have become more sociable, smiling spontaneously when spoken to, and will be just as ready to smile at a stranger as at his mother or father. He will also communicate his pleasure by squeals and the beginnings of repetitive babble using consonants. He sleeps less during the day and may sleep through without waking for a feed in the early hours of the morning. He will have begun to look at his hands, and will bring them together in front of his face, playing with his fingers, studying them with fascination. He is learning that his hands are a part of himself. He will pull at his clothes.

His vision is now very well developed and he will turn his head to see where people are going. He is also learning to coordinate his eyes with his hands. Soon he will be reaching out for things suspended above the crib – this starts by three to four months. Already by three months most babies will hold on to a rattle for a few moments when it is placed in one hand. The hands of a three-month-old baby are open – ready for grasping – unlike those of a newborn baby, which are closed most of the time.

Head control is much firmer, and there is very little head lag when you pull him up to a sitting position from lying down. When lying on his stomach he will stretch his legs out behind him and lift his head and shoulders off the bed, propping himself up on his forearms. It is a good idea at this stage to let him spend some time lying on a rug on the floor in this position rather than always leaving him on his back or propped in a chair, since it helps to strengthen his back and arm muscles.

Rattles and toys which can be grasped or squeezed will help him from this stage onwards, as well as things to look at and listen to. Your baby needs to spend some of his time playing alone and

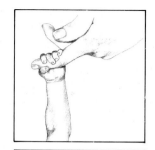

A newborn baby's hands are usually tightly clenched; the grasp reflex means that a baby will involuntarily grip a finger placed in his palm strongly enough to be lifted up.

At six weeks of age the grasp reflex has usually disappeared and the baby's hands are generally more relaxed. However he cannot hold anything or make very purposeful movements.

By three months a baby can open his palm and may start to reach for a toy. But he still has little control over whether his hand is open or clenched.

some of it playing with his mother and father. The time you spend with him is an essential part of his learning and development, for he needs the security and the encouragement as well as the stimulation.

VISITS TO THE PEDIATRICIAN

You and your baby will be visiting the pediatrician quite frequently in the first year of life. A series of visits is recommended by the American Academy of Pediatrics in order to allow your doctor to assess your baby's growth and development, respond to the many concerns and questions you will have, and also to provide immunizations against common childhood diseases. Most states mandate a series of childhood immunizations and local school systems require proof of these, before entry into kindergarten. In addition, certain screening tests, for anemia, lead poisoning and urinary abnormalities, as well as additional immunizations are suggested (immunization against H. influenza infection – HIB or ProHIBit).

The usual schedule for immunizations appears on page 252. These are accomplished by seeing your pediatrician at a series of office visits; the first –

HOW WELL CAN YOUR BABY HEAR?

A parents' check-list

In the newborn baby:	Your baby should be startled by a sudden loud noise such as a hand clap or a door slamming and should blink or open his eyes widely to such sounds.
At four to five weeks:	Your baby should be beginning to notice sudden prolonged sounds like the noise of a vacuum cleaner and he should pause and listen to them when they begin.
At four months:	He should quieten or smile to the sound of your voice even when he cannot see you. He may also turn his head or eyes toward you if you come up from behind and speak to him from the side.
At seven months:	He should turn immediately to your voice across the room or to very quiet noises made on each side if he is not too occupied with other things.
At nine months:	He should listen attentively to familiar everyday sounds and search for very quiet sounds made out of sight. He should also show pleasure in babbling loudly and tunefully.
At twelve months:	He should show some response to his own name and to other familiar words. He may also respond when you say 'no' and 'bye bye' even when he cannot see any accompanying gesture.

HOW WELL CAN YOUR BABY SEE?

A parents' check-list

In the newborn baby:	The center of the eye (pupil) should be clear. If you think that it looks white or red, then report this as soon as possible. The baby should look at your face when he is feeding and the eyes should be steady.
At six weeks:	He should look at you and also follow your face as you move from side to side. The eyes should be steady when looking at something and should move together. If the eyes are not working together, then there will be a squint. This should be reported.
At six months:	He should take great interest in looking at everything around him. He should reach out and grab small toys, for example small bricks. Any squint, however slight, must now be investigated.
At nine months:	Very small objects, the size of raisins, will be looked at and raked up. (Watch that he doesn't choke on small objects.)
At twelve months:	Neat 'pincer' grasp of raisin-sized objects. Points to things across the room.

Problems with hearing and vision often run in families, so if parents or brothers and sisters have eyesight or hearing problems, then there is a higher risk of this being found in your baby. If you are worried about your baby, get advice from your doctor.

typically between two weeks and one month – will be scheduled before you leave the newborn nursery. After this first visit, you will be returning at two, four, six, nine months and one year for routine check-ups. Obviously, if your child becomes ill or you are concerned, you will have additional visits to take care of any worrisome problems.

Almost all babies are in more often than this schedule indicates during the first year of life because ear infections, stomach flu, feeding difficulty or developmental concerns are so widespread that you can virtually count upon something happening along these lines. Obviously, many problems can be handled by a telephone call to your

doctor. Most physicians maintain a morning 'call hour' when they make themselves available for advice calls. This is a good time to discuss problems with breastfeeding, behavioral concerns and so on when your doctor is not distracted by the busy pace of the office.

However, you can usually get through during the day for a quick consultation, or you will receive a late afternoon call back if you leave a message. This is the best way to get answers to the many questions you will have, and find advice for difficulties you are having, such as with feeding, bathing or any other aspects of your baby's behavioral patterns – sleeping, crying, or emotional distress. Do not be afraid to contact your doctor freely for any worry you may have, even if you feel it is trivial. Certainly you should call if there is any concern about illness. It helps to know what the baby's temperature is before you call and you should go over in your own mind what the problem and symptoms actually are.

The value of your pediatrician goes well beyond his or her ability to provide check-ups. Your doctor provides you with a link to someone experienced in baby care whom you will get to know and trust over the next few years. It is very reassuring to know that your baby is progressing normally. If you do not feel up to going in to the doctor – perhaps because you are feeling depressed or very tired – be sure to call. The doctor may be able to arrange a home visit from the Visiting Nurse Association staff.

Another benefit of going to the doctor's is the opportunity to meet other parents. Many mothers feel especially isolated at home during this period of early infancy and such contact with other adults is vital. You will also notice information about various groups and facilities on the bulletin board hanging in the office.

CHILD HEALTH RECORDS

Your community, or state, is likely to provide you with a small booklet in which to record your baby's immunizations, growth and any special items of interest. Typically, this will be given to you at your first two week appointment with the pediatrician. Keep this record as it allows you to monitor your child's growth very simply, and is also valuable at the time you register your child for school when the school system will require proof of immunization. Usually, there is space in the book to record significant developmental milestones and any other pertinent medical information.

THE TWO-WEEK CHECK

At about two weeks, your pediatrician will want to see you and the baby. While there is little medical necessity for this visit (your doctor usually discharged the baby from the nursery and did a complete exam at that time), you will have a long list of concerns and questions at about this time. It will be reassuring to have your doctor tell you that all is going well physically and developmentally. Additionally, you and your partner can get all those worries off your chest that have been so troubling. Typically, parents are convinced by this time that a number of abnormalities have developed in their baby (seizures, limb deformities, for example) or are coming to grips with how much their life has changed since the addition of the new baby, and

need guidance on how to manage.

Sometimes it is wonderfully helpful to learn from the doctor that everyone has moments of exasperation (including the pediatrician with his or her own children) and we all need a break in order to avoid throwing the baby out the window. Talk about feeding, development, advice from grandmother, fears about safety, or a sensible approach to taking baby outside. Doctors may vary with their advice, but at least they have seen thousands of babies and thousands of concerned parents. While you may receive nothing more than reassurance for your concerns, this alone is well worth the visit.

THE ONE- OR TWO-MONTH CHECK

The one- or two-month developmental check may be done by your pediatrician or clinic doctor. If your baby had problems at birth, the check will probably be carried out by the pediatrician in the hospital. The check is an opportunity for reassurance that your baby is healthy and to air any difficulties you may be having.

To begin with, the nurse will see you and your baby, who will be weighed and measured. She can advise you about feeding and any other problems you wish to discuss. She will also remind you about

You will be provided with a small booklet for your child's health records – the immunization page will look something like this.

CERTIFICATION OF IMMUNIZATIONS							
Name					Date of Birth		
Vaccine					Date	Signature of Physician	Date of next immunization
DTP/DT/Td	DTP	DT	Td	1			
(Check				2			
appropriate				3			
box)				4			
				5			
POLIO				1			
				2			
				3			
				4			
MMR							
Hib							
Other							

the date of your baby's first immunization at two months.

The doctor will be interested to know how you have been feeling and what sort of difficulties you have encountered. He or she will ask how your baby has been responding – whether he has smiled, whether he seems to respond to your voice or to other sounds, whether he watches you or follows objects. The doctor will check the growth charts and enquire about feeding.

You will be asked to undress your baby (bring along a spare disposable diaper or two) and the doctor will look at his posture lying on the exam table. At the same time the skin can be inspected for any marks or rashes. The doctor will pull the baby to a sitting position to observe the degree of head lag, then will hold him under his abdomen, face downwards to see how well he holds his head up.

The doctor will check the baby's reflexes (see p. 112), and will examine the baby's vision by getting him to follow a brightly colored ball or block from side to side. The doctor will look into the baby's eyes with an ophthalmoscope (eye examination light), looking for evidence of a squint or other abnormalities such as a cataract.

The doctor will feel the fontanels (soft spots) to make sure they are neither too tense nor sunken, and will feel inside the baby's mouth to check the sucking reflex.

The baby's heart and chest will be listened to, and the pulses of the arteries felt in the arms and the groins to ensure that the circulatory system is normal. The umbilicus will be checked to see that it is properly healed, and the abdomen felt to make sure that the internal organs are not enlarged. The doctor will look for hernias in the groin, and, in a boy, will check that both testes have descended into the scrotum.

Examination of the hips for dislocation is very important. Although this is checked by the pediatrician in the hospital or by your doctor after the birth (see p. 112), occasional babies slip through and babies are rechecked at one month. Clicking hips are not uncommon in babies of this age; they are usually due to loose ligaments and will disappear with a few weeks. If your baby's hips do click, your doctor will want to recheck them later. If there is any suspicion of a dislocated hip, the doctor will need to arrange an x-ray and an appointment with an orthopedic specialist. The doctor will also look at your baby's feet, to exclude a club foot or any other deformity.

PROBLEMS WITH YOUNG BABIES

All parents have worries about their new babies.

The problem may seem trivial, but nonetheless if it is causing anxiety it makes parenting that much more stressful. Many of the conditions listed here are common – most babies suffer from them some of the time. Many are normal, but if you are at all worried that your baby is unwell or if the suggested remedies aren't effective don't hesitate to contact your doctor.

COLIC

Quite a number of babies have regular long crying sessions, usually in the evenings. They often draw up their knees and appear to be in pain, and are said to have colic, because it is assumed that gas in the bowel causes the pain. Although there is no good evidence of this, no-one has yet come up with a better explanation. Babies draw up their knees whenever they cry, so it is impossible to assess whether or not they actually do have pain in the abdomen.

Whatever the cause, it is undoubtedly true that a baby with what is known as colic is extremely trying for his or her parents. Evening crying is particularly wearing if you are a single parent or if one or both partners has a job, since this is usually the only time during the working week that they can be together. The parent who has been at home with the baby all day is likely to be very tired, while his or her partner will also be wanting to relax after a day at work. If both are faced with a baby that cries for two, three or even four hours with little respite, the situation can become very tense, and that tension can be transmitted to the baby, who may become even more upset.

Rocking, singing a comforting lullaby, walking about with the baby, laying him or her over your knee and rubbing the back, are all methods to soothe your baby at least temporarily. Some mothers who breastfed have found that cutting milk and milk products out of their own diet has helped.

Try to get out of the house and away from the problem once in a while – this is a very good way of getting the situation back into perspective (see p. 194). It is much easier for a friend or relation who understands babies to deal with a crying baby who is not his or her own. Friends who have already suffered from a colicky baby are often very sympathetic. The important thing to remember is that babies grow out of this condition and colic almost always disappears by about three or four months. But if you are worried about prolonged bouts of crying, check with your doctor (see p. 255). He may prescribe either an anti-spasmodic or, more commonly, an antiflatulant, or, most commonly, no remedy at all.

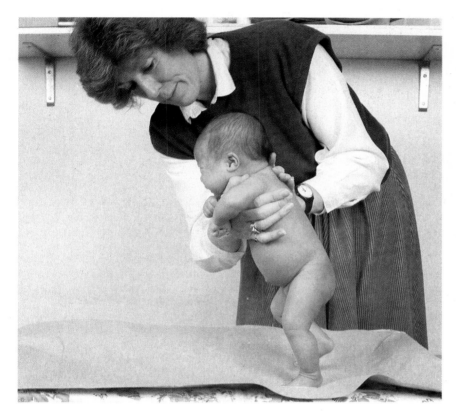

At the one-month check, your baby's newborn reflexes may be tested to see if they are still present, such as the walking reflex shown here.

REGURGITATION

Regurgitation of a small amount of milk after a feeding is perfectly normal. Spitting, when a small amount of milk is brought up with a burp is also normal. Most babies will occasionally vomit an entire feed, and this is not a cause for alarm. However, repeated vomiting is a sign of illness and you should seek medical advice as soon as possible, especially if the vomit is projected forcefully in one go (see p. 262).

CONSTIPATION

The frequency of passing a stool varies from baby to baby and between breast and bottle fed babies (see p. 109). Breastfed babies pass loose stools but may do so infrequently – even once a week or less. Bottlefed babies pass harder stools more frequently. If your baby's stools are very hard as well as infrequent, he or she may be constipated. Passing a hard stool may be painful and sometimes causes a small crack to occur at the anus (anal fissure), which can bleed.

Constipation is often due to lack of fluid, and sometimes due to lack of food or to vomiting. Occasionally there are other causes. Giving more to drink may be all that is required. Some people suggest adding a little corn syrup to the formula or giving fruit juice to drink, but this is rarely necessary; constipation should not be a cause for worry.

DIARRHEA

Loose, green, explosive stools may be perfectly normal in a breastfed baby. Copious diarrhea which is more frequent than normal may be due to infection (see p. 261). If your baby is not drinking very much or is vomiting, dehydration can occur very rapidly and you should call your doctor as soon as possible. Mild diarrhea in a breastfed baby may be due to the mother taking a laxative, or may be related to her diet. Diarrhea is treated by giving the baby clear fluids only to drink – no milk. You can give your baby boiled, cooled water in a bottle, but your doctor may prescribe an electrolyte solution which replaces the glucose and salts lost during dehydration. There are various types – the most usual come in a prepared bottle. Milk can be restarted when the diarrhea has settled.

ACNE AND RASHES

Up to about eight weeks, babies often have small

rashes. This may be due to the change of environment from liquid to air which occurs at birth, or to hormonal changes. Although they can be rather unsightly especially on fair-skinned babies, these rashes are harmless and they disappear in time. They have nothing to do with milk. Heat rashes may appear on the face and neck, shoulders and chest when a baby is too hot and sweats a lot.

If your baby has a very dry skin, a little baby oil added to the bath water applied after a bath will help. If you add oil to bath water be careful when lifting your baby out as it makes the skin more slippery. Excessively dry or flaky skin requires a medical opinion. Infantile eczema does not usually appear before two to three months of age (see p. 270).

Pustules are important to recognize as they are caused by bacteria and may require treatment with an antibiotic. They usually have a white central part with a red inflamed area. If you have any doubt about any spots or rashes, it is best to ask the doctor to have a look.

CRADLE CAP

Babies whose skins tend to produce a lot of grease are likely to develop cradle cap, or seborrheic dermatitis of the scalp. Brownish scales or crusts develop on the scalp, occasionally with very mild inflammation. The condition is harmless, and usually disappears on its own during the first few months.

Recently formed crusts can usually be washed off with a solution of one teaspoon of sodium bicarbonate to 1 pint of water. You can use one of several medicated shampoos which are available. Persistent crusts can be removed by softening them overnight with olive oil, then lifting them off gently with a comb or toothbrush. Once the crusts have been removed, regular shampooing keeps the condition under control.

DIAPER RASHES

Since it is not always possible to change a diaper as soon as it becomes wet or soiled, babies inevitably spend some time each day in a wet diaper. Not surprisingly, from time to time they will develop a sore bottom, and this can happen very early in life, if your baby has a particularly sensitive skin.

Ammonia dermatitis is the commonest form of rash. It is caused by the ammonia released when urine reacts with feces. The longer your baby lies in a wet and soiled diaper, the more chance there is of ammonia forming. Breastfed babies produce an acid stool which discourages this chemical break-down; babies fed on cows' milk produce an alkaline stool, so they are more likely to suffer from this type of rash.

Cloth diapers should be washed and rinsed very thoroughly to remove all traces of ammonia (see p. 169). Use soap powders; detergents can themselves cause irritation if any trace is left. A final rinse in diluted vinegar (acetic acid) in the proportion 1 fluid ounce to 1 gallon will help to prevent ammonia forming. If your baby's bottom looks sore, wash and clean it very gently, be sure to dry thoroughly and apply a thick diaper cream. Avoid plastic pants as they prevent air from circulating around the skin and they make the diaper soggier. Use a one-way liner inside the diaper. If possible, let your baby spend a few hours each day without a diaper on, perhaps lying on a diaper or a towel on the floor, as exposure to the air helps the rash to heal. Otherwise change the diaper as frequently as possible and as soon as you are aware that it is wet or soiled.

Seborrheic dermatitis is an occasional cause of diaper rash, and may be extended to the armpits and the groin as well as the genitals and buttocks. Cradle cap will most probably be present as well. Treatment of the cradle cap and management of the diaper area as described above usually leads to clearance of any other areas affected.

THRUSH

Thrush (Candida albicans) is a kind of yeast which thrives in warm, moist areas. It is commonly found in the mouth as well as in the diaper area. In the diaper area, the appearance of the rash is often difficult to distinguish from ammonia dermatitis (above).

If a thrush rash in the diaper area does not respond to the measures described for ammonia dermatitis, or if you are concerned, ask your doctor to have a look. Thrush is easy to treat using an antibiotic cream which your doctor will be able to prescribe.

It is common for infants and young children to have yeast diaper rash recur until they are out of diapers completely. Also if mothers and babies bathe together, this may transfer yeast back and forth occasionally, if mother has vaginal yeast herself.

Thrush in the mouth appears as little white patches inside the cheeks or on the palate and the tongue. These cannot be easily scraped off, unlike milk curds, and they make the baby's mouth sore, so that feeding becomes uncomfortable.

Mouth thrush is common in babies because they have not yet developed resistance to infection.

Thrush is treated using an anti-yeast preparation in liquid form, which is dropped on to the tongue after feedings.

THE UMBILICUS

A moist umbilical stump can be encouraged to heal by cleaning with alcohol swabs (see p. 109). If there is any sign of inflammation your doctor should have a look. Very occasionally a bright red fleshy 'polyp' forms on the stump. This can be treated by your doctor, who will touch it with a silver nitrate applicator which will make it heal.

An umbilical hernia is common in babies. It is caused by a delay in the closure of the muscles around the umbilical cord. No treatment is required and most umbilical hernias will disappear within a year or two. Unlike inguinal hernias (see p. 261) there is no danger of the bowel getting stuck inside the hernia, so an operation is not needed. Although umbilical hernias can be quite large and protrude even further when the baby cries, they are no longer strapped up as they used to be, as this treatment makes no difference and may even delay the disappearance of the hernia.

COUGHING AND SNEEZING

Sneezing is the normal means by which a baby clears his nose, and it does not indicate that he or she is unwell. Many babies become mucousy from time to time. This is not a problem as long as it does not interfere with feeding. A home humidifier may help the problem in winter.

Babies sometimes cough a little during or after a feeding, but more persistent coughing usually indicates an infection (see p. 265).

STICKY EYES

A yellowish discharge from the eyes occurs very commonly during the first few days after birth. Later this may recur and is sometimes due to a bacterial infection (conjunctivitis). This usually clears after a day or two of cleaning the eye gently with clean water or cotton wool, wiping from inside outwards. If it does not, or if the discharge is profuse and the eye red, see your doctor (see p. 261).

A few babies have a blockage of the tear ducts, which drain tears from the eyes to the nose. This causes watering of the eyes and frequent mild attacks of conjunctivitis. Antibiotic drops or ointment may be sufficient to clear the blockage. The ducts normally reopen spontaneously within about nine months; if they do not, they can be opened by gentle probing under a general anesthetic.

SQUINT

Many babies have squints or 'lazy eye' during the first few weeks, until the muscles which move the eyes become sufficiently developed and co-ordinated to move the eyes in parallel. By three months they should have disappeared.

Squints may be divergent, when the eye looks outwards, or convergent, when it looks inwards. One or both eyes may squint. Babies whose noses have a broad flat ridge often appear to squint because the whites at the inner side of the eyeballs cannot fully be seen. Chinese babies always have this appearance. Your doctor will be able to distinguish this from any true squint. If you think your baby has a squint, all or part of the time, you should ask your doctor to see him (see p. 261).

THE EXASPERATING BABY

No babies are easy all the time, and some babies are particularly difficult most of the time. Nearly all parents, at some time, become quite desperate and feel capable of shaking or hurting their child. When you reach this stage you know that the only thing to do is to put your baby in another room for a while and make yourself a cup of tea. Parents who do batter their children react abnormally and cannot control their feelings at this dangerous stage.

If you are worried that your feelings for your baby are not normal, either because you very frequently have the feeling that you could hurt him, or because you feel you cannot love him or you dislike him intensely, do try to talk this over with your doctor. Loving your baby does not happen immediately or automatically. There is no doubt that some babies make it easier for their parents to love them, by responding to attention and by being easily contented. Difficult babies evoke mixed feelings in parents, which in turn give rise to guilt.

You may need help to get your feelings into perspective, and to learn to understand your child's development and cope with the difficulties. There may be underlying psychological or emotional problems which need to be explored, and feelings which need to be released. A friend at the end of the telephone may be an invaluable help at a crucial moment. Many communities maintain 'Child Abuse Hotlines' for obtaining counseling when feeling overwhelmed. Even if you feel no more than a vague uneasiness, it is better to share this with someone than to keep it to yourself.

LEAVING YOUR BABY

The first time you go out without your baby you will

probably have very mixed feelings. On the one hand you probably need a change, may be tired, tense and generally lacking in confidence. On the other hand you feel guilty at leaving him in someone else's care when he is so tiny.

There is no good reason why a very small baby should not be left with someone else for a few hours, as long as it is someone you can trust. It is better for you to take a break from your baby than to remain constantly with him when you are too tense to enjoy him. A babysitter only has to cope for a few hours; you are with your baby 24 hours a day. You should not feel guilty about leaving your baby; the adjustment you have had to make in your life is, after all, enormous. It would be very surprising if you didn't need to take an occasional 'breather', and afterwards you will probably be better able to cope with your baby's demands once more.

MAKING CONTACTS

Many parents, especially mothers, begin to feel trapped and isolated when they realize how time-consuming looking after a baby and a home is. There seems to be no time to see friends and no free time in the day. But it is important to maintain contacts and to establish new links with mothers in a similar situation. You will feel very reassured to know that you are not alone in finding life with a new baby tough going. Your pediatrician can aim you at local mothers' groups, or you may see notices in the library or child health clinic in your area. You may already have heard about such groups through your prenatal classes.

GOING TO WORK

There is no right or wrong time to return to work; this is a very individual decision. Some women feel the need to return to work – either full-time or part-time – soon after their baby is born, while others feel unwilling or unable to do so for a long time. You may also be obliged to go back to work for financial or other reasons.

The decision to return to work is often a very hard one, and again you will probably feel ambivalent about it. If you had a fulfilling career before your baby was born, you are likely to miss the stimulation and may feel bored at home. On the other hand, some women feel pressurized to return to work but suffer guilt at leaving their baby.

You must decide what is right for you and your family. A bored, unhappy mother at home all day with her baby but not enjoying him is worse than a happy, relaxed mother who is away from home for part of the day but has the energy to enjoy and care

for her baby when she returns home. Don't feel guilty about needing stimulation outside the home. Neither should you feel guilty, if you feel wholly satisfied in your role as a mother. As jobs go this is one of the most demanding and the most rewarding.

When you do return to work, you may have the possibility of taking your baby with you if there is a daycare center. Otherwise, you will have to decide carefully who will look after your baby while you are away, unless in your family it is the father who is the primary caretaker.

THE FATHER AS PRIMARY CARETAKER

Women in our society are no longer limited to the roles of mother and housewife. A woman's career is just as important as a man's, and society is slowly changing to accommodate this. The father who adopts the role of primary caretaker at home with the child, while his partner is out at work, has gained greater acceptability. Although still uncommon, this organization of the family may well happen more often in the future.

As a father, you may have some difficulty in adjusting to this new role, just as a woman does. As a woman out at work, you need to support your partner in his role and understand his difficulties; don't underestimate just how demanding a job it is. Share the difficult times as well as the rewards.

Parenting does not come automatically for men or for women; there is no right or wrong about who should be at home with the baby. What is important is that it should feel right for both of you. If this is so, the atmosphere at home will be relaxed and loving, and your child will grow up feeling secure.

CHOOSING THE RIGHT KIND OF HELP

There are a number of options available, and it is worth considering very carefully what kind of help would suit you best, depending on your lifestyle as well as on your financial situation. Young babies are best looked after in their own home where the surroundings are familiar. This is not always possible, however, especially if your job is not well paid.

It may seem early days to be thinking about the right kind of help in the first three months of your baby's life, unless the demands of your career mean you are going back to work very early. But most women taking maternity leave will be returning to work within three to nine months of the birth, and it sometimes takes a month or two to find the right kind of help, especially if you are employing a nanny who may have to give a month's notice from her previous job. It is always worth pointing out that around six months of age babies start to cling to their mothers and be wary of strangers, so you may have difficulty if you start to leave your baby just at this time (see p. 214).

Try to introduce a new helper a little earlier than this age if you can, and spend time together so that your baby will learn to feel safe with the new person before you have to leave.

GRANDPARENTS

If you or your partner have parents of your own who are able and willing to help, you are indeed lucky. Grandparents can be a tremendous help. Your own mother may have been brought up in a different generation, but her experience and support will be invaluable.

Be careful not to take grandparents for granted, however. They will find their grandchildren very tiring after a while. They may be delighted to babysit for you quite often but might understandably resent being expected to do so on a regular basis. It would be unfair to expect a grandparent to look after your baby when you go back to work; they do still have their own lives to lead!

A sensitive grandparent can often be helpful with a difficult child. When you are caught up in a vicious cycle of tension and tiredness, they remain relatively detached emotionally, and will be able to

More and more fathers are taking on and enjoying the main responsibility for their children's care, and in running the household generally.

take over for a couple of hours to provide you with welcome relief.

Difficulties can arise at times, however, especially if there is disagreement about methods. Sentences beginning 'In my day . . .' are apt to be irritating. Implied or outspoken criticism can be undermining at a time when you feel the need for emotional support. Do listen, though, before you reject advice. Parentcraft hasn't changed all that much over the years, and experience still counts for a great deal. Perhaps the best approach is to talk to your doctor, and decide for yourself what is best. Point out that there are several equally good methods of coping with a problem, and that you are choosing the one you think is best.

Having your own baby may bring you much closer to your mother. So many aspects of your upbringing and your mother's feelings become clear for the first time. Of course the difficult areas may also be reopened, but often the whole family will experience a renewed warmth and harmony.

BABYSITTERS

Babysitters can be useful from the moment you come home from hospital. Clearly, the younger your baby, the more carefully you must choose and brief a babysitter. A babysitter needs above all to be responsible and trustworthy. He or she should also have some experience of handling babies, though most have no special training. Relatives are often good and willing babysitters, but again you must be careful not to take them for granted. Agencies generally provide reliable sitters but you may find them expensive. Local groups of parents who have set up their own babysitting circles are often the best answer. Your local child health clinic will probably have information on these. It is probably best not to employ young people under sixteen to babysit for a baby under two.

If you leave your baby with a sitter when he is only a few weeks old, make sure the sitter feels comfortable with handling an unpredictable, crying, hungry baby and knows how to feed him, and change a nappy. If you are breastfeeding you can leave milk which you have expressed in a bottle. The older baby will have developed a routine; let the sitter know exactly what this is, including any rituals, for example before going to sleep.

Always leave telephone numbers, yours where you will be, and your doctor's, so that the sitter can contact you if there is any problem.

FULL-TIME CARE

Presently in the United States, the need for full-time child care outstrips the available supply. There is a nationwide shortage of programs providing reliable care for infants and children during ordinary working hours. This forces many people to compete for available resources, making the cost of day care a tremendous expense, and also making many people resort to jury rigged arrangements in order to allow both parents to work. Short of a national and comprehensive program for child care, there can be no solution. Private industry increasingly makes child care available as a benefit. Local governments have begun to organize for the provision of child care services also, but still, too little is available. In the end, working parents will have to figure out the best solution for them and this may require an unusual amount of resourcefulness. Do not hesitate to discuss the problem with neighbors and friends whose children are a little older; they are likely to have worked out something which may help to guide your own decisions.

NANNIES

Nannies (properly licensed or certified) are marvelous if you can find them, if you can afford them, and if you have room in your home. Presently, there is little tradition of using nannies in the United States and they are mostly young women from England or the Continent. While programs for training nannies are just beginning in the United States, it will be years before the numbers available match the need. Nannies from England will have acquired a specific qualifiation, which is the result of an intensive two-year course covering all aspects of baby and child care, child development, and pediatric nursing. This credential is very highly regarded in all parts of the world and allows such a trained nanny to command the highest salary.

If your nanny is coming from overseas, she must be legally able to work in the United States (green card) and you must make arrangements for income tax, social security and health insurance. It is likely she is looking for comfortable living quarters in a separate part of your home, with a fair degree of privacy when she is 'off duty'. The legal and financial barriers to acquiring a foreign nanny are substantial and should not be underestimated.

Nannies are not expected to do any domestic work. They are 'mother-substitutes' in that they take over the job of caring for your child which is valuable if you are out at work all day. With two or more children they are a tremendous asset. While you may worry that your child may become overly attached to the nanny and may be confused by having two mother figures, this rarely turns out to be a major problem. A good nanny will be careful not to interfere with the child's relationship with his parents and children rarely have any confusion as to who is really their mother.

When choosing a nanny make sure she is someone you like as a person, in addition to having proper qualifications. Discuss her ideas on upbringing so that you are certain they conform to your own notions. Even more important, satisfy yourself that she is a flexible and adaptable person, not unduly set in her ways. Do not forget that she must adjust to a new country, your household with all its quirks, and to a new child.

MOTHER'S HELPERS AND AU PAIR GIRLS

Mother's helpers and au pair girls are not professionally trained. However they are more adaptable and will help you with housework as well as with your child. They tend to be more temporary than nannies. This may be disruptive for you and your child, but it lessens the problems of deep dependence which arise with a more permanent mother-substitute. They are probably less help when your baby is small than when he is older. They may be ideal if you are only out for a few hours each day.

Au pair girls come from abroad to learn English. They generally work for a few hours a day, attend language classes and live as part of the family. They are entitled to board and lodging and pocket money and they will probably want to spend a little time every day trying out their English with you! Mother's helpers are paid a wage and work full time. Some live in, some live out.

As with a nanny, it is worth interviewing an au pair or mother's helper very carefully, especially if your child will be spending a lot of time in her care. Most are young girls who enjoy children and are very good with them, even if their knowledge of English is limited. A few may only be interested in social life and aim to do a minimum amount of work.

DAY CARE AND BABYSITTERS

Employing a nanny, mother's helper or au pair is only possible if your income and/or your accommodation is large enough. For most people, the alternatives are care outside the home in the form of day care and babysitters. In many large cities, both agencies and private organizations provide day care. Most must conform to local or state regulations which mandate a license for all operators of day care programs. The younger the child, the fewer places are available for day care. For children age three to five, there are a fair number of programs to accommodate your needs. Once your child is in

school, there is often an after school program which runs until 5:00 or 6:00 pm, readily facilitating the schedule of two working parents.

To help find a local day care agency, you might discuss this with your pediatrician, other parents of young children, or call up a local children's advocacy group such as the Office For Children or similar agency. The local newspaper may organize a section of advertising for child care, and local government might find an office or individual who helps identify available local resources.

Because of the great need for child care, it pays to start arrangements early on, well before you anticipate enrolling your child. Furthermore, it makes good sense to visit the place and interview the care providers. Talk to other parents whose children are enrolled in the day care center and ask for references. If your state has a licensing board, you might check with them to see if any complaints have been filed or if there have been any irregularities warranting investigaiton. While the overwhelming majority of such day care providers offer an excellent and reputable service, there are occasional cases of suboptimal care for children, often with tragic consequences for the children and their families.

If you are thinking of bringing your child to someone for home day care, interview the person and ask for references. It is unlikely that an individual will have a license, as these arrangements are usually informal. However, it is worth satisfying yourself that the conditions in the home look pleasant and cheerful and that the person is the sort of individual you would like to have caring for your child. Obviously, if there are three other children under age two in the home, it is unlikely that your infant will receive the full attention he or she needs.

Some of the best day care available is that offered through the work place. If your job has a program set up where you work, this is a marvelous benefit. Hopefully, this type of offering will spread more widely in the American work place and will help to alleviate the worries and frustrations of finding appropriate, safe, reliable day care for infants and children.

Finally, if you have any concerns about your day care arrangement, or observe or hear things that seem peculiar to you, do not hesitate to discuss them with your doctor, other parents, and the administrative or staff people involved. Few things are as frightening for parents as rumor and innuendo when it comes to the care of their children. It is best to move promptly to clarify any such questionable circumstance so that both parents and children can carry on with their lives.

CHAPTER THIRTEEN

THE GROWING BABY

Advice on the major milestones in your baby's growth
and development, from three to fifteen months

From three to fifteen months, a baby makes astonishing and rapid progress in understanding, mobility, communication, play and self-help. From being a helpless infant, he develops into a small child with a defined personality. Keeping up with his changing needs and abilities can be great fun for both you and your baby as you discover new skills, but it can also be tiring at times.

Each baby is different and it is the parents who are the experts on their individual child, rather than the professionals whose job it is to advise them and to share their knowledge of child care and development. While there are general principles, there are few hard and fast rules in baby care. However, the belief that there are rules – which are constantly being broken – is a cause of anxiety to some parents. But it is extremely difficult to do harm to something as well made as a healthy baby. Parents and other caring adults bring to the baby growing understanding of the world around him and also build trust and an understanding that this is a good place to be.

FEEDING IN THE FIRST YEAR

The young baby's life centers round food. Feeding is a pleasurable experience in its own right, as well as being a time when the baby has the full attention of the person who is feeding him. As the baby grows and becomes more curious, food becomes a fascinating plaything to experiment with, and mealtimes are an excellent opportunity to exercise new skills, such as self-feeding or dropping things on the floor. The trouble is that what your baby thinks is interesting and fun may not always coincide with your thoughts on the matter. When your baby rejects some lovingly prepared meal you may feel hurt and upset; when he smears it over his high chair in a determined effort to feed himself you may feel disgusted or angry. Food and feeding can take on a disproportionate importance in the minds of some parents; like all aspects of baby care it's as well to keep things in perspective.

Parents often worry whether their child is getting enough food or not. Babies themselves are by and large able to regulate their own intakes far better than we can judge it for them. Where parents and baby disagree on this, mealtimes, far from being an enjoyable experience for both, can rapidly become a battleground in which no one is the winner. Remembering that it is difficult to do harm by giving your baby food, and that he will generally take as much as he needs, can avoid most of these problems. To a baby and parents, giving food and giving love are often much the same thing. When problems arise, both can feel hurt and rejected. In contrast, mealtimes can also bring pleasure for everyone and should be a time in which company and attention are shared.

VARIATIONS IN INTAKE

Although there are recommended intakes of food for babies these are only guidelines. The variation within the range of normal babies may mean that one baby may be taking double, or half, what another is taking, depending on which way one looks at it. Both babies can be growing normally. Rather like the automobile, some of which do fifteen miles to the gallon and others do 30, babies may also need quite widely differing amounts of food.

MILK FEEDING

Until the age of six months the only suitable milks for babies are either breast milk or infant formula. From this age, although of course breast milk and formula can still be used, whole pasteurized cow's milk can be introduced instead (see p. 158). Pasteurized milk does not have to be boiled at this age. Skimmed milk or semi-skimmed milk should not be offered to babies in the first year of life since the low fat content means they do not have enough calories (energy). From twelve months, whole pasteurized cow's milk is the most suitable one to offer to most babies.

Your growing baby is a constant source of delight as he responds more and more to the people he knows and loves best – his parents.

HYGIENE

Bottles and nipples should still be very thoroughly washed and rinsed in hot water. Of course, general aspects of hygiene are important throughout life, both for yourself and your baby. It is important from an early age to get into the habit of washing his hands before eating and letting him see you do the same, so that when he is old enough to do it himself it will happen as a matter of course. Remember that hands are the main source of food-borne infections which can be dangerous for babies and children.

INTRODUCING SOLID FOOD

Milk is the only food that babies need until the age of three to four months. Some babies are happy to continue with milk feeding until six months, but after that milk is not enough to provide all your baby's nutritional needs. If you don't introduce solid food until six months, you may also find that you are feeding more frequently in order to keep your baby satisfied.

Introducing solids can take quite a while. Babies often need time to get used to the spoon, and to the texture and taste of solid food, even though the consistency of these first meals will be similar to thin cream or soup. Baby cereal is probably the best food to start with. Prepare it exactly according to the manufacturer's instructions on the pack and do not add sugar.

GIVING THE FEEDING

Choose a time when you know your baby is usually contented and amenable – perhaps the morning feeding, or in the middle of the day. Don't bother if you know your baby is tired and likely to fall asleep right away. Trying to offer solids under these circumstances will only lead to frustration and tears.

At first simply offer a tiny amount on the tip of the

When feeding solids to your baby for the first time, sit him on your lap, holding him firmly with one hand, while you gently introduce the spoon into his mouth with the other. To start with, just stroke his upper lip and gum with the end of the spoon and let him suck the food off (it should be the consistency of thin cream). Later he will learn to open his mouth in anticipation and may try to grab your hand or the spoon, so be prepared for mess.

EQUIPMENT FOR FEEDING			
Bottle feeding equipment	Bottles and nipples are covered in Chapter 11.	**Plates, cups and bibs**	Feeding cups, plates and cutlery are to be found in abundance. Plastic bibs with a 'drip tray' are easier to keep clean than fabric or terry cloth.
High chair	A high chair is essential and will be used for at least two years. Choose carefully, for practicality and safety as well as for looks. The chair must be stable and have fixing points for a safety harness. Look for a chair with an easy-to-wipe surface. A lip on the tray helps to avoid spills. Some high chairs can be adapted to a low chair with a table. Wooden chairs are not always as practical as some of the simpler metal and plastic chairs – nor as cheap. One model adapts from a low reclining chair to a swing or a high chair.	**Portable chairs**	Table-mounted chairs are a simpler, less expensive alternative. Two types are available: one kind balances on the table with rubber bumpers above and below the surface, the other kind has to be clamped to the table. These chairs are reasonably stable provided that the table is too. Even simpler for traveling is a fabric support which is designed to be hung over an ordinary chair. Booster seats which strap on to an ordinary chair are useful for an older child but give insufficient support to a young baby.

teaspoon after the feeding. Alternatively try offering it during a 'natural break' or rest period in the middle of the feeding, when the baby's initial urgent hunger has been satisfied, but he is still interested in the idea of food.

You can either sit at a table with the baby on your lap, firmly held in the crook of your arm, or you can sit the baby in a baby chair or bouncing cradle in front of you. This latter method probably involves the least mess, but it is wise to protect your own clothes with an apron, and your baby's with a plastic-backed bib.

Don't try to force your baby's mouth open, but just stroke his upper lip with the tip of the spoon and let him suck the baby cereal off the end. The first few attempts may not be very successful – the baby may spit the food out, or let it dribble out of the corners of his mouth simply because he doesn't know what to do with it. But with patience, good humor and the acceptance of a certain amount of mess on your part, your baby will soon learn how to get the cereal into his mouth and keep it there.

New tastes should be introduced one at a time with intervals of several days in between. In this way, if something disagrees with the baby, it is easy to identify what it is. You can always try it again at a later date.

Always remember to let the food cool down to a suitably moderate temperature before offering it to the baby. Rejection might mean that the food is too hot rather than that the taste isn't acceptable or your baby not hungry.

FOOD FOR YOUR BABY

Commercial baby foods are nourishing and convenient, but you can also try making your own. Use boiled rice, lentils and beans, root and green vegetables and some fruits (avoid soft and citrus fruits to start with). Cook the food first then sieve or blend it to the right consistency, adding boiled water or a little infant formula.

The main rules are to use fresh ingredients and to ensure that everything you use to prepare them is clean, especially your own hands. Never add salt – a young baby's kidneys cannot get rid of salt, so it could build up to dangerous levels in the blood, particularly when the baby is ill with diarrhea or vomiting. Do not add sugar to baby foods either (see p. 217). Your freezer is a very convenient place to store ready prepared baby meals. When the baby is small and taking only one or two spoonfuls at a time, freezing your home-made food in ice-cube containers allows you to prepare it in suitable quantities.

Left-over food from the baby's plate is best thrown away. Open jars or other containers from which some food has been removed should be covered and stored in the refrigerator for not more than 24 hours. If a microwave oven is used for re-heating food, remember that the inside can be very hot while the outside is still cold. Always test the temperature of food heated by this method to avoid burning his mouth. Microwaves do not sterilize food unless it is cooked for a very long time.

Once your baby can hold an object firmly, at seven or eight months, he will be ready to try finger foods such as pieces of carrot, toast or apple. However, never leave him alone with food as he may choke.

Once solid food has been established on a regular basis, try to aim for balance in your baby's diet. Include fruit, vegetables, cereals and dairy products such as eggs and cheese, plus meat and fish if you want. If you can introduce a wide variety of foods at this stage, you may find your child is less fussy later, although this is unfortunately not always the case.

Children, unlike automobiles, can thrive on a wide variety of fuels. Much is written about some foods being good for babies and children, and others being bad, but a course of moderation is probably the best one to steer between the various pressures which can and do cause a lot of anxiety to many parents. Food is meant to be enjoyed by everyone rather than just being a vehicle to provide for the nutritional needs of the child.

TRANSITION TO FAMILY FOOD

From six to seven months, when the baby begins to chew, you can introduce food which is more substantial, such as grated cheese, flaked fish, more coarsely mashed fruit (such as bananas), boiled eggs or yoghurt. A baby doesn't have to have teeth to be able to chew – watch your baby put a toy into his mouth to prove this – and enjoys food which can be held, such as toasted crusts, pieces of raw carrot or apple and even celery. This is often a good way to persuade a baby to eat a type of food he might otherwise reject in cooked form. However, never leave your baby alone with any food, as he may choke (see p. 274).

From now on, more and more of the family's normal diet can be introduced. Babies do differ in their ability to cope with lumps, but hopefully by the beginning of the second year, they should be sharing many of the same foods as their parents, except perhaps highly spiced food or food with lots of small bones. Avoid also giving lumps or chunks of beef (such as cut up steak) as babies readily choke on them. Always grind the meat first. There is really nothing magical about baby food apart from its consistency and the fact that it should not contain salt or sugar.

DRINKS

Ordinary tap water is perfectly suitable for babies – and it is obviously cheap. Bottled mineral waters are not always suitable for babies; many contain high levels of sodium (salt). Too much salt can make a baby more thirsty, which will make him want to drink more, thereby setting up a vicious circle. As it is sometimes difficult to discover how much salt is contained in these waters they are best avoided altogether, unless there is no other source of safe water.

Softened water is also high in salt. If you have a water softener installed, make sure the kitchen faucet is not in the system and take all water for the baby from this source only.

Of course, babies can have many other types of drink, particularly fruit juices. Avoid juices with added sugar, and also bear in mind that some 'pure fruit juices' naturally contain very high amounts of sugar, so could be just as bad for teeth as those with sugar added (see p. 217). Fruit juices can be quite strong and may result in loose stools, so it is as well to dilute them at least half and half with water.

Fruit squashes are best avoided as these are often very sugary (or contain artificial sweeteners and coloring (see below).

VITAMINS

A balanced diet including milk as already outlined should provide your baby with all the essential vitamins. Infant formula milks have the correct vitamins added and breast milk should supply sufficient vitamins if the mother's diet is adequate (see p. 151). In addition, nearly all commercial baby foods contain added vitamins. For this reason, vitamin supplements are not necessary for all children. Some diets may be lacking in vitamins and for these babies suitable vitamin drops are available from your doctor. If you are worried whether your child is receiving enough vitamins there is no harm in giving them – you cannot overdose your baby by giving him the recommended daily amount. Sweet syrups containing vitamins should not be used, however, as the sugar in them will damage developing teeth (see p. 217). Where fluoridation of the water supply is not practiced ask your doctor about supplement fluoride drops.

CANDY AND CHOCOLATE

Candy and chocolate are not appropriate to offer at this age. They encourage the habit of high sugar content which leads to early tooth decay and obesity. Young babies can also easily choke on small candies. Never give babies and children under two years of age peanuts to eat (see p. 274).

ADDITIVES

Foods manufactured specially for babies are usually free from artificial additives such as colorings, preservatives and flavorings. By and large, however, babies moving over to the usual family diet do not seem to suffer ill effects from these substances when they come across them. In a few children, however, additives may possibly cause problems in behavior or allergic reactions (see p. 270).

SELF-HELP WITH FEEDING

As soon as your baby learns to grasp objects he will be transferring them to his mouth. It is not surprising therefore that babies will want to grab the spoon that you are using for feeding and will also want to feed themselves with their fingers. Some babies become very frustrated because they want to feed themselves, but are unable to do it. Having a spoon each may help, and with practice the baby's skills will gradually improve.

Sometimes parents discourage self-help as a baby's first attempts are so messy. It is however best to persist so that by nine months he should be skilled at finger feeding and beginning to be able to handle a feeding cup or a bottle by himself. Given the opportunity, by the age of twelve months, your baby should be able to handle a cup and spoon-feed himself with only occasional adult help.

Food can be good to play with as well as eat, but adults might not share the child's delight in fingering, smearing and playing with food. To avoid the problems of playing with food it is best to remove the plate once your baby has had enough to eat. If your baby goes through a stage of throwing food about, put newspaper or plastic sheeting under his high chair to minimize the mess.

Once your baby is able to feed himself, then mealtimes at which everyone eats together become a more practical proposition. But remember that babies are not very good at waiting for their food,

When your baby wants to feed herself, the first few tries may not be very successful, so stand by with another spoon to fill in the gaps.

especially when they are hungry, and are poor respecters of other people's (usually adults') wishes to eat in peace and quiet!

DIFFICULT FEEDERS

Some babies and young children are particularly difficult at mealtimes and it is very easy for their parents to become angry and irritable. Unfortunately this type of response only conditions the baby to be even more difficult when he is being fed. Letting him feed himself, however messy, may get round some of the battles. Force feeding is never recommended as it achieves the opposite of what is intended and the baby can easily end up by eating less. There is no doubt that hungry babies *will* eat if

offered food, so your baby's appetite might not be as big as you think it is. A patient, relaxed attitude will succeed in the end.

If you are worried about your baby's behavior at mealtimes, it is best to get help before difficult feeding patterns are established. Advice on feeding is often easier to give than to put into practice, but regular support from friends or family can be very valuable.

VOMITING AND DIARRHEA

Vomiting (or 'spitting up') after feeds, which is fairly common in young babies, usually improves dramatically when solid food is introduced. If it does not, it is useful to discuss this with your pediatrician so that he or she can check the baby is growing normally. However, it should be said that some babies, especially if they have been bottle fed, continue to vomit after meals for some time. It occurs effortlessly, and the baby is not upset, and in this type of vomiting the whole feeding is never regurgitated. It usually subsides at eight or nine months when the baby can sit up properly. You may find it helps to add a little cereal to the milk to thicken it slightly, though not so much that it does not flow properly from the bottle (see p. 158).

Some babies who are growing perfectly normally develop persistent diarrhea starting between the ages of six and 24 months. The stools contain undigested food such as peas and carrots. The problem ceases as the child gets older and is not due to any serious disease. However, it is wise to see the doctor to check that the baby is growing normally and that there is no other cause for the diarrhea. If the doctor reassures you that it is not due to illness, you might be able to reduce the problem by cutting down the fiber (roughage) in your baby's diet – don't give him such things as peas or corn for a while, and mash vegetables such as carrots and potatoes. Avoid soft fruits as well until the diarrhea subsides.

GROWTH

Growth is a good means of checking on the baby's overall health, as has been described already in Chapter 12, but for a healthy baby who is lively and active and eating and sleeping well, frequent measurements are not needed and can be combined with the visits for immunization and hearing testing (see p. 212). The variation in size at all ages is wide and comparisons with other babies can be misleading and cause unecessary worry. For instance the size of baby clothes is often recorded in months. This is a very crude guide and many babies need the size bigger or the size smaller.

Big babies are not necessarily fat or unhealthy. Some are generally big in every dimension and this reflects the body build of their parents. Others are significantly above the average weight for their length and age. It used to be believed that these would grow up to be overweight adults, but the majority will not. One of the best signs of whether a child is likely to be overweight in adult life is if the parents themselves have weight problems; where this is so, a little early caution in controlling the intake of fattening foods might be helpful.

Most small babies are also healthy. They usually take after their parents. A small lively baby is most unlikely to have any serious illness. However, a child who is growing slowly and has signs of ill health such as recurrent loose stools, vomiting, difficulty breathing and who seems lethargic or unduly irritable should be carefully examined by your doctor.

CHECKING ON DEVELOPMENT

At the doctor's office and at home, both you and your doctor will want to check the baby's development. His speed and pattern of development will depend very much upon characteristics that he inherits from you, the experiences that he has in his everyday life and his general state of health.

Looking at babies' development in the clinic is not quite like having an automobile checked over. Although some babies might not necessarily accomplish all the tests that we might expect from their age level, this does not mean that there is something seriously wrong. In fact, eight out of ten babies whose development gives concern early in life will have no problems whatever when reviewed at an older age. What seems to be important is not looking at the baby on a single occasion but development observed over a period of time and looking at its rate. The rate may obviously vary over time, being sometimes slow, sometimes very rapid.

When you go to the office to have your baby's development checked, a few observations of what your baby can do combined with the doctor's own tests form a reliable guide that he is progressing well. If there are problems, for example in the areas of hearing or seeing, parents are usually the first to recognize them (see p. 188). So go to the office prepared to share the knowledge of how your child is getting on, together with any concerns you may have.

Although development over this age band from three to fifteen months is quite remarkable, it is easy sometimes to over-estimate babies' understanding and ascribe to them motives and reasoning which they could not possibly have. Although your baby may seem difficult at times and you may be frustrated by his behavior, at this age he is not doing it deliberately to irritate you – though he may well be trying to gain your attention. This is a sign of his close attachment to and need for you, so try to respond positively.

The next section summarizes development over this period, looking at ways that you can help and indicating how you can also help to pinpoint some problems early on.

PROGRESS TOWARD WALKING

The progress from a small baby only capable of lying where he is placed by his parents to an inquisitive and mobile toddler is one of the most exciting elements of development in the first fifteen months or so. As has already been mentioned (see p. 182), this usually follows a set pattern (though *not* a set timetable).

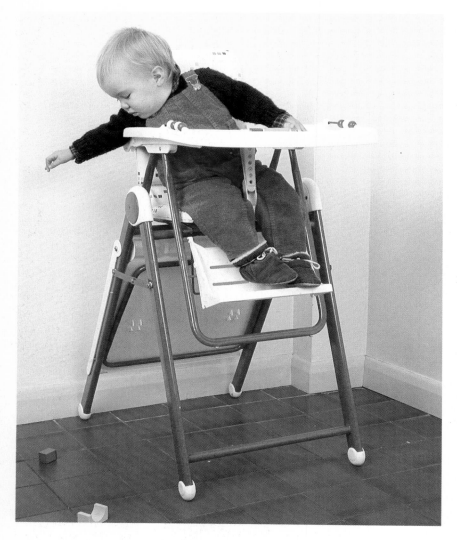

The high chair is a favorite place to practice dropping things on purpose, a game that twelve-month-olds love, but which adults find exasperating.

'PRESS-UPS'

By the age of three months, most babies have developed strong arms and good control over the position of their head. This means that when lying on their fronts they can lift their head and upper part of the chest clear and maintain this position, both to their own delight and that of their parents.

ROLLING OVER

In learning to roll over the baby has learned to co-ordinate not only the right and left sides of the body, but also the movements of head, arms, trunk and legs. Some babies become very alarmed at the sudden changes of posture that they can now bring about, and all are now at risk of falling off surfaces on which they were previously safe.

SITTING UP

Most babies will learn to sit on their own between the ages of five and eight months. To do this the baby requires not only physical strength in the back but, just as important, the ability to balance. At first the baby needs to use his arms to secure his position on the floor and needs to make lots of rather clumsy adjustments in order to maintain this posture. Eventually he will topple over, or will not remain stable while sitting if at the same time he is using his hands to grasp a toy. By twelve months, however, the baby can sit for an indefinite period of time and does not topple when he is reaching out for objects or using his hands to play with toys. He is also easily able to get himself into the sitting position, and his view of the world for most of the day is now the same way up as it is for adults.

The development of mobility begins at five or six months with the ability to roll over (above) – a movement which often takes babies by surprise at first. The next step is to sit up unaided (left); for the first time a baby sees the world from the same angle as an adult, only usually much lower down.

Standing up and getting her balance has to precede walking; at nine to twelve months most babies will have learned to pull themselves up in the crib or playpen, on items of furniture, or even your legs!

With crawling and standing comes the ability to climb. Stairs become a particular hazard, as babies take much longer to learn how to walk downstairs, so it is sensible to fit a safety gate.

CRAWLING AND STANDING

A baby must learn to sit before learning to stand. Standing requires strength, balance and courage in view of the inevitable association with falling. Crawling provides a good intermediate step between sitting and standing. It also provides a rapid and convenient method of getting about before walking is established. However, not all babies crawl and those who do not, take longer to be able to stand and walk. The most common variation of crawling is scooting on the bottom, in which the child bounces along on the seat of his pants. These babies also learn to stand and walk later as they are doing things the hard way. It does not indicate that anything is wrong.

At first the baby can only stand while holding onto something. Most babies will be doing this by ten months, and can pull themselves up, so that you often find your baby standing in his crib waiting to be lifted out after a sleep. It may take a further three or more months before they can stand on their own.

WALKING

Most babies go through the sequence of crawling, standing and walking. Some, as have already been described, scoot along on their bottoms, a few haul themselves along using their arms alone and a few creep along on their hands and feet. Some miss out all these alternatives and go straight from sitting to walking. At first a baby needs to hold onto objects when walking ('cruising') and cannot get across gaps where there is nothing to hold onto without going down on all fours again. Between twelve and fifteen months most children are walking on their own, though others, particularly bottom scooters, might not walk until after the age of eighteen months. At first, walking on his own is an uncertain process consisting of wide based and unsteady movements prompted by frequent falls.

It helps to allow your baby to walk with bare feet to start off with as he will find it easier to balance, though this may not be possible if the weather is very cold. Soft shoes with non-slip soles are suitable

Walking is the big milestone between infancy and childhood, and is looked forward to by parents, even though it brings its own problems of safety and so on. The first steps are often very uncertain, and may be interspersed with bouts of crawling before walking is fully established. Babies learn quickest in bare feet – shoes are not necessary for the first few weeks except out of doors.

at this age. Do not let your baby walk around only in socks since he may slip on polished floors, and socks come off very easily. It is not usually necessary to buy specially fitted shoes until your baby has been walking steadily for at least four weeks. When buying shoes look for cheap sneakers rather than expensive brand name baby shoes.

CLIMBING

Crawling on the horizontal soon leads to the ability to crawl upstairs and to get on and off furniture. However, children learn to climb up before they learn to climb down. Thus, like the kitten in the story, they can be 'trapped' on the object onto which they have climbed or are likely to fall when trying to get down. They, of course, are unaware of this potential hazard, so it becomes vital to keep your baby in sight at all times.

THE EFFECTS OF MOBILITY

Learning to move about increases the child's ability to explore. It also vastly increases the possibilities for mischief and for danger. Try to anticipate these hazards and provide restraints in the home, the street and the automobile. These may take the form of gates to restrict access, particularly on stairs, guards to keep young hands away from the stove top and seat belts in chairs and automobiles (see p. 272).

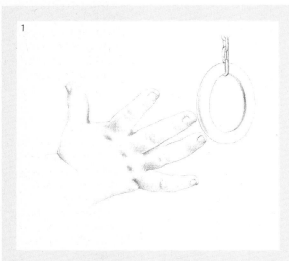

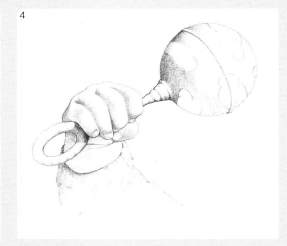

Developing manual dexterity

Your baby will develop increasing hand control during the first year or so of life, combined with visual development.

1 *At three months, your baby will make efforts to grab for toys he thinks are within reach.*

2 *At four to five months he can grab an object and hold it, soon learning to bring it up to his mouth for further exploration.*

3 *From six months, he will be transferring objects from one hand to the other.*

4 *From about nine months, the more efficient way he grasps an object (see opposite) enables him to shake a rattle, responding to and experimenting with the noise.*

5 *Being able to co-ordinate two hands at once to do different things means that around twelve months your baby may be banging one object against another.*

USING THE HANDS

Learning to use the hands does not depend upon the hands alone, but the correct use of vision in locating objects and watching and directing what the hands are doing. At first this co-ordination of hand and eye requires intense concentration.

EARLY STAGES

At first the baby stares and stares at his own hands watching carefully the movements that occur, perhaps trying to work out what they do and how the movements can be controlled. This watching occurs around the age of three months, when the child will also be able to reach out and grab at nearby objects such as a row of beads across the buggy. When the baby first reaches out and grasps an object he may, rather like a learner driver, 'over-steer' to both sides before grasping the required object very crudely in the palm of the hand. The baby soon lets go of the object involuntarily, and it is then forgotten.

From six months, as the baby gets better at holding onto things, these are soon transferred to the mouth for further exploration. His own feet are also objects which can be grasped and explored in the mouth. Once the grasp is secure, the next stage is to learn to transfer the object from one hand to the other.

From the age of nine months a much more useful grasp is developed using the thumb and index finger rather than the palm. This enables the baby to manipulate smaller objects and to be more precise in his movements. The repertoire of movements increases, including shaking, banging and pulling, and toys such as an activity center, cups and rattles provide good practice in all these movements.

At about one year the child is able to pick up small objects such as crumbs and dirt on the floor, much to his parents' disgust. Throwing things off the highchair or out of the buggy or stroller and seeing how they drop, is a favorite game. Objects can be grasped in both hands at the same time and banged together.

At fifteen months most children will be quite good at using both hands together. They may be able to build a tower of two bricks and the index finger can be used for pointing to desired objects.

NEW SKILLS, NEW HAZARDS

Developing skills in hand control and in mobility means that children can get to and reach objects that previously were not a hazard for them. They can pull electric wires, open cupboards and gain access

Developing hand control
At about six months a baby grasps an object crudely with his whole palm and all five fingers, like a scoop.

Later on, at about nine months, he can begin to use his fingers and thumb together to grasp an object between them (human thumbs are said to be 'opposable' in this context).

By twelve months, most babies can use the index finger and thumb together in a fine pincer movement, to pick up quite small objects such as a raisin.

to household chemicals such as bleaches, plumbing supplies, medicines and other dangerous substances. The baby's natural desire is to explore and this is only moderated by a rudimentary sense of danger. It is therefore necessary to imagine things through a child's eyes and remove or lock away dangerous things before your baby develops the skills which would help him to gain access to them.

HEARING

Babies need perfect hearing in order to develop and understand speech. Sound also gives them lots of clues as to what is going on around them, such as hearing footsteps coming, the sound of dinner being prepared, the sound of traffic. Parents are the best people to detect hearing problems and are nearly always right (see the check-list on p. 188), but if you have doubts about your baby's hearing at any age you should contact your doctor. Most children's hearing problems get better on their own and are often related to congestion from a cold (see p. 266). However, all babies with suspected hearing problems must be carefully assessed, which may mean going to a special audiology unit either in a clinic or in a hospital, on referral by a doctor.

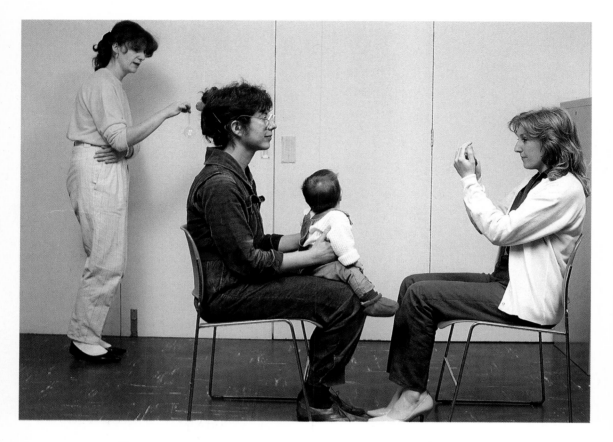

HEARING TESTS

The hearing of babies is tested by the doctor between the ages of seven and nine months. The test used is called a distraction test, and it needs two people as well as yourself to carry it out.

The baby sits on your lap and his attention is focused on a toy held by the person sitting in front of him. When the baby is alert and his attention fully focused on the toy, this is removed from his sight and the second person makes a very soft sound about one yard from the baby's ear and outside his line of vision. The baby should turn toward the test sound. The baby's hearing is tested, using this technique, for both low pitched and high pitched sounds.

Babies who do not respond appropriately are usually re-tested after a short period of time. Test failures can be due to the baby being tired or irritable, having temporary hearing problems associated with a cold, or sometimes because he is too immature to localize the sound properly yet. However, if a baby fails the test twice, then referral for specialist examination is necessary. Later re-assessment may also be recommended if it is thought your baby's speech development is delayed.

VISION

Just as in the case of hearing, parents are also usually the best people to detect whether their baby has any eyesight problems (see p. 188), and again this can be verified using a simple test.

Your baby's sight will be assessed by the doctor at around the same time as his hearing. This is usually done by observation, by seeing how alert the baby is to his surroundings and his ability to reach out for and handle fairly small objects, which indicates how well the baby can co-ordinate the movement of his arm and hand with what he can see.

The doctor may also look closely at the baby's eyes. In young children only major problems that seriously interfere with eyesight need to be detected. Such problems would include anything which prevents light getting into the eye, examples being a cataract in the lens or clouding of the pupil. Parents usually notice this and with early treatment normal development of the child's vision can be ensured. It is also important to detect squints or 'cross eyes'. A squint will produce a different image in each eye and the baby can only cope with this by ignoring one image. This will eventually lead to a 'lazy eye' (see p. 261).

The doctor will test your baby's sight at seven or eight months (left) by observing his general alertness and his ability to follow a moving object such as a ball. She may also shine a special light (ophthalmoscope) into the pupil to look at the retina.

A baby's hearing is tested at seven to eight months by using the so-called distraction test (far left). Once the baby's attention is distracted by an assistant with a toy, the doctor will make a number of different, very soft noises about a yard away and out of the baby's sight. Hearing is tested by seeing if the baby turns to the sounds.

THE DEVELOPMENT OF LANGUAGE

Language is the most complex and highly developed of human skills. It is needed to transfer thoughts and feelings, and is also used internally when we are thinking. The unfolding of child development is in itself a miracle, but the ability to acquire speech is the most amazing part. It involves skills of listening and discriminating the individual sounds in what the child hears, being able to repeat those sounds and to recognize meanings to which those patterns of sounds are attached. The child also picks up important laws of grammar in an easy and painless way, in contrast to an older child or adult's difficulty in learning other languages at a later age.

Babies begin to vocalize by making indiscriminate babbling noises at four to five months, which gradually coalesce into more recognizable consonants like 'ba', 'na' and 'ma', usually repeated. At first they learn to make and copy sounds, and then to understand that some of these sounds have a specific meaning. Your baby may be imitating words like 'mamma' and 'dadda' at nine months or so – eventually realizing that you respond to these words in a specially rewarding way. By about twelve

months your baby will probably have found at least one word that signifies 'mother' or 'father' – possibly one that is interchangeable!

Babies learn speech by hearing you speak to them. Therefore, in everyday life, talking through all the daily activities will help your baby to begin to learn the meaning of words. For instance, tell your baby about his spoon, cup and plate at mealtimes, about his clothes while you are dressing him, and parts of the body whilst you are bathing. Nursery rhymes are enjoyed from a very early age and certainly do help the development of speech. Most importantly, they are fun for you and the baby. Very simple stories from simple picture books can be introduced from the end of the first year, when your baby will show genuine recognition of objects illustrated on the page.

It is a long journey from the first babble, to gaining understanding of simple words such as 'Mommy', 'Dad', and 'no', through the copying of whole words without meaning, to the production of the first proper words used correctly, at about the age of one. It is often difficult to appreciate how few words a baby or young child actually understands. The child of one year will understand 'no' but not an explanation about 'no'. A young child will pay

Even as early as twelve months a baby will be able to recognize a simple object in a book, and to point and try to name it, even if she hasn't started speaking properly yet. Words with strong consonants, like 'cup', 'duck', and 'cat', which are also familiar everyday objects, may be the first words she says after some version of 'mommy' or 'daddy'.

attention to sound because it sounds nice, and because it is combined with loving attention from his parents. Understanding the full message comes a lot later on.

THE IMPORTANCE OF MEMORY

Memory is one of the most important developments in the first year of life. With it the child can build upon previous experience. A young baby lives very much in the immediate world and that which is not immediately visible is forgotten; a young baby forgets a toy once dropped, whereas a full-term baby of seven months will look for it. Memory develops with regard to people, events, strategies for solving problems, games and rules. For example, from about seven months of age, babies recognize which people are familiar and which people are unfamiliar and become wary of strangers, which can make babysitting difficult (see p. 196).

GROWTH OF CONFIDENCE AND TRUST

Between the ages of three and about fifteen months your baby should gain confidence in himself and trust in the world about him. He is helped in this by having his needs for both care and love met and by there being a consistency in his daily life. He will gain confidence by being successful in things he is trying to do, and by other people's appreciation of that success. Where parents' expectations are too high, putting success out of reach of the child and giving rise to what in the parents' eyes is failure, then the child may well grow up to be unsure of himself.

DIFFICULTIES WITH SLEEP

Many babies do not reliably sleep through the night until they are eighteen months old and some even older. They come to no harm through this, but clearly their parents do. The baby has very little control consciously over when he is awake and when he is asleep and only an anesthetist can alter this situation with any degree of certainty. As the child gets older he may no longer disturb his parents at night, though he is likely to be equally wakeful but without their knowledge.

GETTING THE BABY TO SLEEP

It is unrealistic to expect that a wide-awake, active baby, or for that matter an adult, will go to sleep simply by the action of being put to bed. The first rule is not to start under these conditions. A bedtime routine is the single most important technique to establish for getting a child to sleep. This may consist of a meal, followed by putting toys away, a bath and finishing off with a bedtime story or lullaby depending upon the baby's age and preference. It is important to make sure that the baby does realize that the night is different from the day by making the room dark, though obviously not so dark that the child cannot see. A room of his own is often very helpful if this can be arranged. If a baby wakes up and immediately sees his parents, he will obviously demand attention. In the case of a breastfed baby, the smell of mother's milk may act to stimulate his appetite.

IF YOUR BABY WAKES

Don't rush in immediately your baby wakes at night, unless the cry is obviously an unusual one. Waiting five to ten minutes and then being comforting is much more effective than responding straight away but being irritable. Because breastfed babies may have their appetite stimulated by the smell of mother's milk, it may be easier for the father or someone else to go to an older baby at night. It is often useful to leave a night light on and some safe toys in the crib for the baby to play with if he awakes. These simple maneuvers will help with quite a lot of children. However, for some, only patience and the child growing older will solve the problem.

Where regular night waking is becoming an exhausting problem, seek advice from your doctor, who may suggest some strategies to cope.

DAYTIME NAPS

The amount of sleep the older baby needs over 24 hours is incredibly variable. Some parents find that their baby may get up at eight in the morning after twelve or fourteen hours' sleep, have breakfast and be ready to sleep again almost immediately for another two hours! Another baby may be wakeful most of the day, perhaps 'catnapping' for half an hour or so. Both these examples are normal – though the latter may be more inconvenient.

You will soon recognize the signs which let you know that your baby is tired during the day. At this age, babies will always sleep if they are tired, although it is not surprising that a lively baby will cry when you leave him, as you are the best source of interest to him. It is reasonable to expect that your baby will want a nap in the morning and afternoon, but for how long varies enormously. If your baby is alert and happy while awake there is no need to worry about the length of time actually spent asleep.

CRYING

Babies cry for many reasons. They may be hungry, they may be uncomfortable, they may need changing, they may also be bored or unwell or sense you are not at ease or are worried. Prolonged crying causes stress in the adult and the reaction to this, far from relieving the baby's distress, may actually serve to enhance it. Parents can become extremely tired due to the amount of attention the baby needs and as a response to the constant loud noise. You may also become emotionally strained due to the frustration at being unable to soothe your baby, or from a sense of failure. The response may also be anger, which all parents feel at some time because of the baby's incessant demands and their own apparent inability to fulfill them.

When the baby is crying, look for a physical cause, such as hunger, discomfort or fatigue. If you feel that the baby is unwell or not his normal self, check his temperature and call your doctor. Your baby may be bored, or frustrated by being unable to do something either because he is too small or because you have prevented him. In this case you might find a break from routine, such as a walk outside, or changing to a new activity may well benefit both you and the baby. Unfortunately at this age babies cannot wait to have their demands fulfilled however much we would like them to.

At times it is very easy to feel that everything is getting on top of you. It is essential at these times to share the load by getting help from your partner, from relatives or from neighbors. You need a break to sort yourself out. Looking after a young baby is the only job that lasts 24 hours, seven days a week, with no holidays. It is therefore not surprising that parents as well as their children can often feel angry and frustrated. You should see your doctor if you feel that things are getting on top of you and that you are losing your temper too easily.

AIDS TO GETTING THROUGH THE DAY

As your baby gets older and sleeps less during the daytime, your daily activities need to be planned to ensure that both your needs and his are met. A little advance planning can resolve a lot of troubles. If he is hungry he cannot wait, so planning meals in terms of timing and preparation is very important. Planning of activities both indoors and out will give a variety of experience and stimulation, relieves boredom and keeps the baby happy and contented.

Along with the baby's needs, of course, your own needs must also be met. It is hitting the right balance that is important to ensure that you are both contented. Where life seems frustrating and difficult

Babies often enjoy swimming from quite an early age, although it is advisable not to take them before nine months. They revel in a freedom of movement which they may not have attained on dry land!

it is often useful to write down your day's activities to see how your own and your baby's needs are being met. There can also be conflicts between time given to your baby and time given to your partner. The best solution is for you to share the load as far as possible between you and try to get some time together on your own regularly (see p. 193).

TEETH AND TEETHING

The ages at which teeth first appear are very variable. Some babies are born with teeth, though this is rare, and others do not cut their first teeth until they are twelve months old. However, on average, the bottom two teeth in the middle, known

as incisors, appear at around the age of six months. These are soon followed by the appearance of the two upper teeth. By ten to fourteen months the four top and bottom incisors have come through and usually the first of the molar teeth are also seen.

The appearance of teeth is said to give rise to lots of other complaints. There is no doubt that it can be painful, is associated with excessive salivation (enough to soak many bibs) and the baby indicates the site of his discomfort with his fingers. Babies who are teething often appear to have a cough. This is usually due to pools of saliva, which, instead of dripping out of the front of the mouth, accumulate at the back. The baby may then cough, though this is not usually due to infection. It is possible that when babies are teething, they might be more susceptible to other problems such as rashes, diarrhea and colds. It is dangerous to dismiss such symptoms as simply 'due to teething' and it is wiser to consult the doctor. Remember that teething does

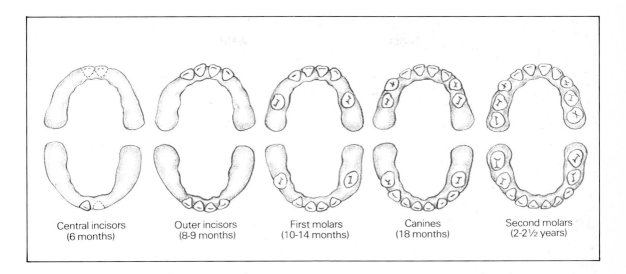

| Central incisors (6 months) | Outer incisors (8-9 months) | First molars (10-14 months) | Canines (18 months) | Second molars (2-2½ years) |

A baby's first teeth usually start to appear between four and twelve months in the order given above.

not cause a fever; call your doctor if one develops.

DENTAL HYGIENE

Once teeth come through, to start with clean them gently with a small piece of gauze or a Q-tip. Introduce a tiny toothbrush and fluoride toothpaste at twelve to fifteen months or when your baby has at least six teeth. The importance of avoiding sugar (see p. 201) cannot be over-emphasized – sugary foods and drinks can damage the teeth even before they erupt through the gum. Sugar is broken down by bacteria in the mouth, forming acid which attacks teeth, causing them to decay. Cleaning the teeth properly should remove the acid, but avoiding sugar and introducing fluoride (see below) help to avoid the problem in the first place. Especially harmful to young teeth is the practice of giving a baby a bedtime bottle in the crib. The milk sugar sits on the teeth all night and causes terrible decay.

THE USE OF FLUORIDE

The addition of fluoride to water supplies in most areas has dramatically reduced the amount of dental decay seen in children living in these areas. Your doctor should know if the water contains an adequate amount of fluoride or not. You should also be able to obtain this information from the water authority. Fluoride drops are available for babies living in areas with low levels in the supply; your dentist should be able to tell you the right dose for your area. The drops can conveniently be added to your baby's bottle or drinking cup.

KEEPING YOUR BABY CLEAN

As your child gets more mobile, day-to-day tasks of washing and diaper changing might become more difficult, and the opportunities for getting dirty become infinitely greater. The most important parts to keep clean are of course the hands and face as stomach upsets, especially diarrhea, can be caused by the introduction of germs into the mouth. A little dirt elsewhere is not such a big problem. Babies generally enjoy a bath, which can be a time for play as well as for washing, as long as an adult is always with them. Babies often enjoy swimming too, as long as you are close at hand, although it is wise not to take a baby under nine months.

Some babies dislike having their hair washed, probably because of the sensation of water going into their eyes. If your baby wriggles and gets soap in his eyes, it may also make him apprehensive in the future. Lying the baby down, well-supported, on his back in the bath can avoid this, or you could use a special cap which prevents water running down over the face. However this is not always successful and it is probably best then to wash the hair no more than once a week and get it over with as quickly as possible.

An active wriggling baby who has learnt to roll over may be extremely difficult when diapers need changing, and cloth diapers and pins may present hazards under these conditions. A switch to disposable diapers may ease the situation considerably. Children are not usually ready for toilet training until at least the age of two years, so don't try to introduce it as a way to get round the difficulties associated with diaper changing. It will only serve to increase tension between you since your baby is being asked to do something which he is not yet able to carry out.

CHAPTER FOURTEEN
EXPLORING THE WORLD

How to cope with the joys and frustrations of the toddler
years, from fifteen months to two and a half

From the age of fifteen months, your child will become more and more mobile and the clinginess and separation anxiety of the one-year-old will decrease. With intellectual and language development allowing a better understanding of the world, there is an increasing need to explore. Exploration takes place from a safe base, usually with frequent retreats to a parent to check that all is well. A child of fifteen months will be climbing stairs, climbing onto low stools and chairs, and showing great delight in her new abilities. To start with she will not be able to get back down, and you may have to show her how to turn round and climb down backwards. She'll be falling over a lot too, so she needs to be watched closely at most times. There is an urge for new discoveries, and cupboards will be turned out, baskets emptied, and possibly even the contents of the refrigerator pulled onto the floor, given the opportunity!

FROM BABY TO CHILD

Although children of this age may play with something that interests them for as long as 20 minutes, mostly they have a constant urge to go from one thing to something else. An active toddler has a short concentration span, toys get rapidly thrown to one side, and a great deal of imagination is needed to keep her occupied. On the other hand, when something does interest her she will examine it minutely and will try to see how it works. For instance, instead of examining things with hands and mouth, she will use her fingers with more precision: a toy automobile will be turned over and the wheels pushed round with one finger.

However tiring, this period can be rewarding since you can share the excitement as she acquires new skills literally every day. As young children often enjoy activities which involve imitating their parents, your child may happily push a toy vacuum cleaner around, make attempts at sweeping with a dustpan and brush, bang with a toy hammer or splash in washing-up water with a cloth and plastic dishes while you get on with the chores yourself. She may even enjoy actively helping, with varying degrees of success!

SAFETY FIRST

Because of the child's natural curiosity and interest in discovering what is inside and on top of things, this is the period when you have to give your home a hard look to make sure that it is child-proof – a little forethought about safety and about the whereabouts of your own treasured belongings will save battles and breakages later. For instance, make sure equipment like the telephone and the stereo are placed well out of reach – and bear in mind that a piece of furniture will often be used by a curious eighteen-month-old to push up against a wall or chest, in order to climb up and get to something which looks interesting. Don't let wires trail where inquisitive hands might try to pull them, either.

If you don't want books pulled out of the bottom shelf of the bookcase, empty it for the time being or put books or other objects there which don't matter. Fix safety catches to kitchen cupboards where breakables or dangerous household cleaning substances are kept. You could keep one cupboard accessible with pots, pans, wooden spoons and other interesting items in it so that she can explore there without causing damage to herself or anything else. Keep medicines locked away and use child-resistant containers – her new manual skills mean that she will try her best to open a tempting looking pill bottle and she may still want to put the contents in her mouth. Eighteen months to two and a half is a peak period for accidents in the home involving the swallowing of things like pills, bleach, drain opener or weedkiller, and can be avoided by taking a few simple precautions (see also p. 272).

PHYSICAL GROWTH

Growth during this time begins to slow down, the rate of weight gain becoming very much slower than in the first year. The proportions of the body gradually change so that the head is less large in

Small children are extremely imitative and enjoy being allowed to join in with household chores and other tasks which older children – and many adults – find boring!

Negotiating stairs can be hazardous, even when your child is walking steadily, and at first she should be encouraged to turn round and climb down backwards. But by 20 to 24 months she may have gained the confidence to come down forwards, a step at a time, and usually with the help of a steadying hand on the wall or balustrade.

relation to the rest of the child's body. A glance at the growth charts on page 180 and 181 will show you that in the second half of the second year (from eighteen months to two years) average weight gain is around 6½ ounces per month, with average weight at two years being 28 lbs and average height 34 inches. Of course, this varies a lot from child to child and depends on such factors as birth weight, how active the child is, the sort of family the child comes from, the child's diet, illness and stress, race and social class. For instance, a Chinese baby is, on average, smaller than a middle class white baby coming from a Northern European background with similar living standards.

A child's activity level will influence body weight at this age, as at any other, with the active toddler who is never still for a moment likely to be lighter than a more placid, less mobile child who does not burn up as many calories in spontaneous exercise. Hence there is no 'correct' weight for a child of, say,

eighteen months, but plotting weight and height on the chart should indicate that all is going well. A falling off of weight across centiles can indicate that a child is not eating enough, or can sometimes be an indication of illness (see p. 261). If there is any concern about your child's weight or height, it is sensible to consult your doctor.

LEARNING TO SPEAK

At fifteen months, your child will have already started to say one or two words (see p. 213). The first words are usually naming words, most often 'Mommy' or 'Daddy' or some equivalent. Quite often, the recognizable name of a sibling or grandparent may be used at the same time, or another familiar person such as a babysitter, or even a family pet. People are of most importance in the child's world, so naming them usually comes a month or two before naming objects.

The first objects to be named are familiar everyday items which are talked about often, such as 'shoe', 'drink', 'ball', 'teddy', 'cat', and by eighteen months the average vocabulary is six to 20 words, as well as a lot of unrecognizable chatter. Sometimes quite difficult words are acquired by a child early on if they are important in that child's world. For instance, apart from 'Mommy' and 'Daddy', the first word a little boy who lived on a farm could say was 'tractor'. Other early words which are commonly used are those which produce an effect when used, such as 'up' when wanting to be picked up or placed on a chair, or 'more' for more milk, and so on.

Words expressing feelings and descriptive words come soon after and by the age of two, words such as 'no' and 'bad girl', are often used, and it is remarkable how early a small child can perceive the feelings of others and put them into words, often accompanied by gesture. Well before developing a vocabulary, the child has learned a lot about the meanings of tone of voice and inflections, and will use speech sounds in a musical way to ask questions, or make disapproving or demanding noises. Taking turns in speech, as when you hold a conversation with someone, is also an early part of language development, which is established long before words are used with meaning. Vocabulary rapidly increases during the second half of the second year and thereafter, and by two-and-a-half most children will have a vocabulary of around 200 to 300 words.

USING SENTENCES

While vocabulary increases rapidly, developing the use of sentences is a much slower process. This starts by the child putting two words together to make a short phrase, such as 'Daddy gone', 'more drink', 'baby cry'; by two years most children are using these sort of two-word utterances. By three years, sentences of three and four words are being

As children's language develops during the third year, they often use imaginary conversations, perhaps on a toy telephone or to their toys and pets, to experiment with this new skill.

used, although the grammar is often incorrect. It is interesting that children do not imitate the 'correct' sentences that they hear adults using, but first develop their own sort of 'telegraphic' speech.

Alongside the use of words to communicate, the child is learning to understand the meaning of other people's speech, and an understanding of speech develops before the child can use the same words herself. So a child of eighteen months, when asked to go and close the door, will understand and do so, although she cannot yet say the words 'door' and 'close'. She will also, by two, be able to understand a more complicated request such as 'can you get your shoes, which are on my bed?', again long before being able to say this herself. Also, she will know the names of parts of her body and be able to point to eyes, nose, mouth, belly and so on when asked, particularly if you play such naming games regularly when dressing and at bath time.

TALKING TO YOUR CHILD

There is quite wide variation in the ages at which children start to speak, and on the whole, girls are somewhat ahead of boys, just as they are in some other aspects of early development, such as gaining bladder control. Many factors can interfere with the process of language development, but the most important influence is the amount that the child is spoken to. So, talking a lot to a child right from the early weeks is important, and even children as young as one year will enjoy looking at picture books and magazines with their parents and pointing out well-known objects. Playing games like pat-a-cake and other rhyming games, singing songs and nursery rhymes are very much a part of childhood experience in almost all societies; they are fun for parents and children, and there is no doubt that they encourage language development. Reading stories, too, encourages speech and, later, reading skills; it is sad, but probably true, that parents read to their children less since the introduction of television sets into most homes. While taped stories and music or nursery rhymes are no substitute for mother, they are also much enjoyed, encourage listening, and are useful on automobile trips and for times when one is busy, or perhaps occasionally at bed time, if it is difficult for you or your partner to read a story yourselves.

DELAYS IN SPEECH DEVELOPMENT

Apart from the amount of stimulation in the child's home as outlined above, there are other factors which affect the rate of speech development. Children mature at different rates, and just as some

children walk a lot later than others, so some will begin to talk later. Many children who appear to have slow speech development are simply 'late talkers' with no other problems. Others may be generally a little slower in all aspects of their development. A doctor who is asked to see a child where there is concern about slow speech will want to find out how much the child can understand, how her overall development is progressing, and of crucial importance, whether her hearing is normal.

Hearing loss will obviously affect speech development, and one type of hearing loss ('glue ear', which is due to fluid in the middle ear, behind the ear drum) can appear gradually. It can also vary, depending on whether or not the child has a cold, so may not be detected by parents. It is not always accompanied by ear ache, but can be detected by careful testing of a child's hearing and examination of the ears (see p. 266).

OUT OF DIAPERS

In the early months, babies pass urine fairly frequently with dry periods, but are certainly not in control of either bladder or bowels. It used to be thought that babies could be 'trained' to open their bowels when a few months old, and if put on a potty after a feeding some babies will 'perform'. However, this is due to a reflex opening of the bowels, not due to the baby controlling the situation and responding to a cue. Toilet training is not normally started until well into the third year of life, when children are really able to understand what is happening, rather than having it forced onto them. In reality, we do not 'toilet train' children, rather we facilitate their own efforts to train themselves.

At around the age of sixteen months, some (but not all) children may be aware of being wet, and may cry to have their diaper changed. At some point after this (around eighteen months to two years) they may indicate that they are passing urine, and may even acquire a word for it, such as 'pee-pee'. At this stage, they do not have control over their bladders, but recognition of passing urine is a first stage. Soon after this they may recognize the feeling of having a full bladder and may tell someone before passing urine. When this stage is reached it is a good time to start toilet training; trying before this will probably result in frustration. Bowel control is a similar process, but is usually acquired a little earlier than bladder control. The urge to move the bowels is a more recognizable feeling and is usually slower to build up, so less urgent. However some young children seem to prefer to continue using a diaper for this purpose even though they may be dry in other respects, perhaps only moving their bowels

While your child is learning to use the potty, it is a good idea to keep it near where she is playing, so you can respond immediately when she asks for it.

once the diaper is put on at night. This is inconvenient, but you should try not to make an issue of it. The two skills match up in the end.

By about two-and-a-half, most children are able to tell their parents (by gesture if not words) that they need to pass urine, and some may be completely dry during the day at this age. However, many children are not reliably dry during the day until around three years, and even then are likely to have accidents.

TAKING YOUR TIME

Different children gain bladder and bowel control at different ages, and like speech, this depends on a process of maturation. Girls tend to develop control earlier than boys. There will always be somebody down the road whose child is dry several months before your own! What is important about toilet training, whenever you decide to start, is to be relaxed about it. Tension and anxiety over toilet training is usually counter-productive, with a child becoming resistant, and it is an area where conflict should be avoided.

The approach that seems to work best is plenty of praise and encouragement for dry pants and using a potty or toilet appropriately, with no fuss when accidents occur. It helps to let your child go around without diapers, underpants or pants some of the time, so that it is easy to use a potty. If you want your child to use a toilet, it helps to have a child's toilet seat (sitting on a large toilet can be scary!) and a low stool to stand on, unless the toilet is low. Because behavior at this age is often imitative, seeing other

	Vitamins and Nutrition	
Vitamins	**Food Source**	**Function in Diet**
A & Carotene	Carrots, squash or any green vegetable. Fruits, liver, butter and fortified margarine, fortified bread, fat fish such as herrings, sardines and tuna fish	Normal vision, growth, healthy skin and nails
B1 (Thiamin)	Pork, nuts, potatoes, whole grains, peas, beans, lentils	Helps the body to utilize carbohydrates
B2 (Riboflavin)	Liver, meat, eggs, milk, green vegetables	Helps the body to utilize carbohydrates, protein, fat
Niacin	Liver, poultry, meat, fish, whole grains, peas, beans, lentils	Helps the body to utilize carbohydrates, protein, fat
Pantothenic Acid	Liver, poultry, meat, fish, whole grains, peas, beans, lentils	Helps the body to utilize carbohydrates, protein, fat
Pyridoxine	Liver, poultry, meat, fish, whole grains, peas, beans, lentils, bananas	Helps the body to utilize amino acids. Assists in blood formation
Folic Acid	Green leafy vegetables, eggs, liver	Assists in blood formation and growth. Gives resistance to infection
B12	Meat, especially liver. Dairy products. (Absent from plants)	Formation of new red blood cells
Biotin	Peanuts, mushrooms	Helps body use fats
C (Ascorbic acid)	Citrus fruits, cabbage, parsley, sprouts, tomatoes	Helps to keep the body cells healthy; gives resistance to infection
D	Fish liver oils, egg yolk, butter, margarine, liver and commercially available milk, which is fortified. (Sunlight is another important source.)	Healthy bones and teeth. Regulates calcium and phosphorus usage in the body, particularly the bones

children, as well as their parents, using a toilet or potty encourages a small child to want to do the same. Children will soon want to be independent over wiping their own behinds – so teaching a child to do this for herself is a good idea. (And even if they prefer a parent to do it, they will need to be able to manage by themselves by the time they start preschool.) Little girls' behinds should be wiped from front to back, to avoid spreading germs from feces into the vagina and urinary tract. Children don't usually wipe themselves completely clean to start with, but this is not important, and dirty marks on underwear are to be expected until a child is quite a bit older. It is a good idea to encourage and teach children to wash their hands after using the toilet to reduce the risk of infection.

Becoming dry at night

For some children, bladder control at night happens at around the same age that they become reliably dry during the day. More usually, however, night time dryness takes longer; the child has to maintain control for ten to twelve hours, and during a period of deep sleep. This requires a considerable degree of maturation, and like any other aspect of development some children get there earlier than others. Although the majority of children are dry at night by three-and-a-half to four years, around one in ten will still wet the bed most nights at five years. This may be inconvenient for the parents and unpleasant for the child, but it is not necessarily abnormal.

When your child shows signs of being able to be dry all night, perhaps by having a dry diaper in the morning, or only wetting it when she wakes, you can try leaving the diaper off. Expect to have some wet beds at first, but reward the dry nights with praise and don't fuss over the wet ones. If she is wetting the bed every time it is obvious she is not capable of staying dry all night. Return to diapers for a while. Don't try to get your child out of diapers too soon or you will both be disappointed.

FOOD AND NUTRITION

At this age children will usually be eating more or less the same as the rest of the family, although without added salt. A healthy diet is a balanced diet, with a variety of food providing all the nutritional requirements. If left to select from a variety of foods, on the whole, children will end up eating a reasonably balanced diet with all the vitamins, protein and minerals they need, and nutritional deficiencies are uncommon. It does help to understand about the sources of essential nutrients, and your doctor's office is a good source of information and leaflets on diet for toddlers.

Vegetarian diets are perfectly healthy for growing children, with protein requirements being provided by milk, yoghurt, cheese, legumes (beans, peas and lentils) and nuts, instead of meat and fish. With

If your child's timetable can be fitted in with yours, mealtimes can be more interesting for everyone if she is able to join the family at the table, rather than being isolated elsewhere.

increasing evidence that excess animal fat is a cause of raised cholesterol (linked to later serious heart disease) more people are cutting down the amount of meat they eat, as well as limiting high fat foods like butter and cream, and the same principles are recommended for children. Since milk and cheese are the main sources of vitamin D, which is essential, together with calcium, for healthy teeth and bones, it is important not to omit them altogether from a child's diet. Most nutritionists and doctors now also recommend a diet which is high in fiber. Fresh fruit and vegetables, wholemeal bread, legumes, brown rice, familia, dried fruits, are all high in fiber and also contain vitamins and other nutrients. (See the table, opposite.) A diet which is high in fiber will prevent constipation, and is also thought to prevent some of the bowel disorders which can occur in adulthood. Added vitamins are not normally necessary at this age, although some Asian diets are low in vitamin D and vitamin supplements are then recommended. Talk to your pediatrician about whether vitamin supplements are necessary.

MAKING MEALTIMES INTERESTING

If they have been encouraged to do so, children are usually feeding themselves with a spoon by the age of eighteen months. In fact, they are often extremely reluctant to let anyone else feed them and inventive games may be needed to help the lunch down if there is limited time!

Mealtimes are often messy occasions, for food is interesting to explore with the fingers, as well as to taste, and some small people always seem to end up with mashed potato in their hair and peas all over the floor. If this becomes irritating, remember it is only a stage, and placing newspaper or a plastic sheet on the floor under the high chair can make cleaning up a bit easier. Learning to feed by oneself is part of learning independence, and exploring the texture of foods is a necessary stage of development which does not persist for many months. Gentle correction in holding a spoon and fork can help, but don't make an issue of it.

THE PICKY EATER

The child who is picky about certain foods is sometimes more of a problem, but it is very rare for a child to develop unhealthy preferences. Preferences tend to go in phases too so that after a month or two of eating what seems like only hot dogs and peas, the favorite food will probably change, and your child will surprise you by finishing every mouthful of something she has been refusing for weeks. Even a little bit of variety helps, and small pieces of fruit or raw vegetables are often eaten, even if the more usual vegetables are consistently refused. It helps to be a little inventive, and to present food in an interesting way; also remember that fish fingers and baked beans do make quite a good diet. Sometimes, eating with other children is helpful – a child will sometimes try something that she sees other children eating.

It is important to avoid giving snacks and drinks between meals to picky children, or children who refuse to eat much at mealtimes. It is often tempting to give a child who has refused breakfast a few cookies and a glass of milk to 'keep her going' until lunchtime, but this only increases the likelihood that lunch, too, will be refused. Snacks are also often sugary, and sugar is best avoided for two reasons: first, it is bad for children's health and increases the risk of tooth decay, and secondly, it is habit forming. Children who are brought up not having sugar on cereal and avoiding sweet puddings, do not miss it, do not need sugar, and are less likely to spend their allowance on candy when they are older!

PROBLEMS WITH EATING

Children who refuse to eat, or eat very little, usually make their parents very anxious. Part of everyone's idea of good parenting is providing nutritious meals to build your child into a healthy young person, and it is very frustrating if your child blocks your best attempts to do this. When carefully prepared and cooked delicacies are spat out, thrown on the floor, or ignored, this provokes even the calmest of parents to anger. If this is happening, it is tempting to try and force your child to eat – but this should be avoided at all costs! The battle is inevitably won by the child, but in any case, mealtimes should never become battle grounds. The child will begin to associate cooking and mealtimes with negative feelings, whereas meals should be a time for relaxing, talking, and enjoyment.

If your child refuses to eat what is on her plate, at the end of the meal simply take it away. Try not then to give chocolate pudding, or she will think this always happens if she refuses a meal! Sometimes, putting very small amounts on the plate helps, sometimes things which can be eaten with fingers are preferred to those needing a spoon, and sometimes distractions, or games, can help over a difficult period. Remember that if your child is looking healthy and is active and gaining weight then there is no real cause for worry. It is often helpful to discuss these sort of problems with your pediatrician, and checking your child's weight periodically (but not every week) can be reassuring. If you continue to be worried, talk again to your doctor – also talk to lots of other parents and you will probably find that other people have gone through similar experiences.

THE FAT CHILD

Some children go the other way; they have large appetites, eat everything put in front of them and always seem to want more, as well as drinks and snacks between meals. Such children can become overweight, and there are a number of reasons for this. Mostly, they are just eating more calories than they need for normal healthy growth. Some children are less active and burn up less calories than others, so tend to put on weight easily. This tendency often runs in the family, but eating habits also run in families, and overweight children are quite likely to have overweight parents. As any overweight parent knows, dieting is difficult – so it is worth keeping an eye on the weight of a small child who seems to eat a lot. It is much easier to alter and cut down on a two-year-old's diet than a six-year-old's. Again, ask

Bedtime need not be a problem if you try to establish a simple routine for your child, such as a bath, teeth cleaning and a bedtime story, which you can stick to night after night.

your doctor for advice, and get your child's weight plotted on a growth chart if you think there is cause for concern.

SLEEPING PATTERNS AND PROBLEMS

Parents of young children have to cope with all sorts of problems and worries in the first few years, of which sleep problems are one of the most common and certainly the most exhausting. Children do not always need as much sleep as their parents do, although many people think that all children need twelve hours' sleep each night. In fact, the amount of sleep needed by each child is very variable – one child may regularly sleep eleven or twelve hours each night while another needs only nine hours' sleep. There are some children, usually the very active, alert sort of child, who need much less sleep than this, which can put enormous strain on their parents.

The most common sleep problems in the age group one to two-and-a-half years are difficulties in settling down to sleep at night, and waking during the night. Many children who have difficulty getting off to sleep, and go to sleep late, will then sleep soundly until morning. Others will be difficult to settle down *and* wake up again in the night. Parents need time to relax and at the end of a busy day it is good to get children to bed and then sit down for some peaceful moments. It is understandable then that having a two year old underfoot and wanting to play until eleven o'clock causes irritation and frayed tempers.

SETTLING DOWN TO SLEEP

It helps to establish a bedtime routine from early on – perhaps supper, bathtime, then story – always allowing time to quieten down and unwind after the day's activities. Many children need special routines to help them settle down to sleep– some will only sleep if a parent stays with them, others fall asleep on a sofa, others need the same song or story every night. These routines are hard to alter, so it is good, if possible, to find one which suits you as well as your child. A dim light, a musical box or cassette, favorite toys in bed, all help to make bedtime comforting and falling asleep easier. It helps to make your child's crib or bed a special place with favorite pictures and toys around, and perhaps a familiar mobile hung overhead. Although the house does not need to be quiet, it is more difficult for a child to stay in bed if there is a lot of noise and activity going on that she feels she is missing out on. Perhaps the most difficult situation is where there is only one room for living and sleeping, and it is clearly hard to settle a child down to sleep in a corner with the light on and activities continuing.

NIGHT WAKING

Night waking, either every night or most nights, occurs very commonly in children under two, with about one in every four children waking frequently. It tends to occur less often as the child gets older, but for one in ten children it is still a problem at the age of four years. It is also often a persistent problem: about half the eighteen month olds who regularly wake at night will still be doing so six months later. It helps to know that children themselves very rarely suffer from lack of sleep, but their parents certainly can! It is perhaps our expectation that a child should sleep through the night that is wrong, for in cultures where children sleep in the same room or bed as their parents it does not seem to be a problem.

Sometimes, waking at night can be triggered off by an illness (such as an ear infection, or whooping cough), sometimes by a major change, such as moving house, or going into hospital. Other children may show night waking, or difficulty settling down to sleep, as a symptom of anxiety, such as a separation anxiety. It is often difficult for a child to express the cause of her anxiety, but time spent trying to understand it is helpful. You may then be able to reassure the child that all is well, and helping her express her fears and anxieties can help the sleep problem. Where family arguments or tensions are contributing, clearly these need attention before tackling the sleep problem. Ways of coping with sleep problems vary from family to family, and no one solution will suit everyone. If you are happy with your own way of coping, then do not listen to someone else's advice to try a different strategy. Perhaps the most important thing is to be consistent; if you leave your child alone to cry one night, then take her into your bed the next night, you are giving conflicting messages which will confuse her and the problem will continue. Where there are two parents, it is sensible to discuss the issue and agree between you how to manage it. If the father wants to do one thing and the mother the opposite, again the child will get conflicting messages. Sometimes, simple maneuvers will help, such as cutting down on daytime sleep, and giving warm milky drinks at bedtime.

It is worth stopping to think about what happens, and how you react, when your child wakes up. If she is picked up, cuddled, talked to and given a bottle, this is all rather nice and will probably encourage her to wake again as it reinforces the habit. Of course, you will do this if your child is ill or distressed about something, but on the whole the less you interact with a child that wakes up, the sooner she will learn that it is not worth waking you. Try keeping talking to a minimum, and don't pick her up or play, but gently and firmly tuck the child in and settle her back to sleep. You need to make it clear that night time is for sleeping and not for games and company. If your child has been used to being picked up, you may need to withdraw gradually – say by sitting beside the crib for a night or two holding hands or stroking her, then moving further away for a few nights until, finally, you do not need to stay with your child until she is asleep.

Some parents prefer to take their child into bed with them, but others cannot sleep and find this very irritating, in which case it is not the solution. However, if everyone manages to sleep well it is one of the simplest solutions. It can become a habit which is hard to break, but you can sometimes move your child back into her own bed or crib once she is asleep. If you do this, it is a good idea to have a warm bed to put the child in, as cold sheets may wake a sleeping child. One problem about having your child in your own bed is that it is bound to interfere with your sex life, so it can become a cause for resentment if it goes on for long. Sometimes one partner minds this more than the other, so it is best to discuss this, although resolution of this difference is not always easy.

HELP AND ADVICE

Other people do understand the strain and exhaustion of having a child who has sleeping problems, so if it is getting you down it is worth discussing with your doctor, and also with other parents. Drugs are not the answer – they usually only provide short term relief, can be habit forming, and may have side effects. Rarely, they may be prescribed by your doctor for very specific situations. Time off from a persistently waking child is important when you are exhausted – sometimes sending her for a night or two with a grandparent or friend is helpful. If your child sleeps through the night at a grandparent's house, you may well feel guilty and wonder if it is your fault the child is waking – the answer is no, parents are *not* responsible for children waking, but a child may not cry out if she knows her parents are not there to come to her!

FROM CRIB TO BED

At around the age of eighteen months some children will get fed up with their cribs, resenting the restriction of the bars, and will increasingly demand to be lifted out, or may even learn to climb out. If this is happening, a low bed or mattress on the floor will be safer, and usually results in a better night's sleep for everyone. By around two to two-and-a-half, most children will prefer to be moved from a crib to a bed, and as with a crib, it helps to make the bed a special place with favorite things around.

FEARS AND HABITS

One of the earliest fears is of strange people, and is shown as 'separation anxiety' – the nine month old who gets very upset and anxious on being taken away from her mother. This is a developmental stage, which all infants go through, starting around seven months (see p. 214), peaking around fifteen to eighteen months, then gradually getting less. Many two year olds are still upset and distressed when separating from their parents, but by three years very few are. This sort of anxiety is to be expected, and reflects the personality of the child and her previous experience, as well as her developmental age. A few children are very clingy and will not let you out of their sight – even to go to the toilet. They are often children who also demand a lot of attention and can leave you feeling drained and exhausted with no space to yourself. However, lots of support and reassurance for these children during this stage is important and will help them to be independent later. You cannot force independ-ence on children, and they have to be the ones who decide when they can cope without you. It may help to find a small playgroup where you can be in the same room as your child, while they play, meet other children, and learn to socialize in the safe knowledge that you are there if needed.

Other common fears in the second year are fears of noises, of falling and of strange objects. Fears about animals may start around two years, but fear of the dark usually only occurs later in the third or fourth years. Mostly, these sort of early childhood fears are not too distressing, and with reassurance and kind handling they do not persist long. Some people feel that children must be made to confront fears by deliberate exposure, but this is a misguided punitive approach and will make matters worse. Some fears are learned from other people – so if you yourself are terrified of spiders, or large dogs, it can easily be transmitted to your child. Although it is not always easy to avoid sharing your fears with your children, if possible you should avoid letting them know about them until they are older when they are less likely to be influenced by them. If your child shows fears that are very distressing, or longlasting, or you are worried about how to handle these, it is usually helpful to talk to your pediatrician or a playgroup leader about your worries.

PACIFIERS AND COMFORTERS

During the first year, many babies have bottles and often a pacifier as a comforter, and if not weaned off these at the end of the first year they can become a habit. A lot of children need some comfort object to help them fall asleep and when they are upset, and some children use their thumbs or a corner of a blanket, while others like the nipple of a pacifier or bottle. There is nothing wrong with this, and no point in distressing a child by removing the favorite object. Using a pacifier constantly during the day tends to discourage the child from speaking and, if possible, the use of pacifier or bottle should be reserved for bedtimes and perhaps when the child is upset. The main worry is tooth decay – sweet drinks in a bottle or honey on a pacifier should be avoided. If you are anxious because you think your child is *never* going to give up that bedtime bottle, just remember that one never sees ten year olds going to bed with bottles!

OTHER HABITS

Apart from pacifiers or comforters, young children sometimes develop other habits, such as hair twiddling, or stroking, or perhaps finger sucking. Nail biting is uncommon at this age. Most of these

Many children form a special attachment to a particular object, such as a blanket or a soft toy, which forms part of the ritual of bedtimes and rests.

habits are similar to using comforters, and will diminish over a period of time. Getting angry about these does not usually work, but distraction to other things sometimes does. If it becomes a serious problem, such as hair being pulled out, see your doctor, who may refer you to a child psychologist who will suggest ways of helping to break the habit.

Head banging or rocking may occur in babies, often when tired, and sometimes appears to be a soothing mechanism for getting off to sleep. Head banging can be quite alarming, especially in a hard crib, and although babies do not injure themselves they can sometimes get bruises. It is wise to pad the crib with foam or rubber pads covered in cotton. Too much attention paid to the banging or rocking may increase the problem; it tends to diminish in the second year without anyone interfering. Very occasionally, a child who persists with rocking or banging may have an underlying emotional problem; it is more commonly seen in children, for instance, who have been separated from their parents. Habits of this sort are a little more common among children with developmental problems, and

in such children habits like head banging may persist for quite long periods. If you are at all worried about your child's habits, then do talk to your doctor for reassurance.

CHILDREN'S SEXUALITY

From a very early age, children learn that it is pleasurable to touch their genitals, and one study of one-year-olds found that genital play occurred in over a third of children. Baby boys get erections even earlier than this – this is not due to anything sexual, but is a reflex associated at first with a full bladder or bowels. Masturbation is common at all ages, but much more common in boys than girls. It need not be discouraged, but should be accepted as a normal part of children's sexual development. As children grow they should be advised that masturbation is a private activity and not to be done publicly. Very occasionally a child masturbates frequently and compulsively, although this is pretty unusual below the age of three. This may be due to anxiety or an escape from some stress in the child's world, and if you are concerned you should discuss this with your doctor.

Interest in the opposite sex usually occurs when children discover that there are physical differences between boys and girls. Often this occurs after starting at playgroup or nursery, and exploratory games out of curiosity are then common; adult over-reaction should be avoided.

TEMPER TANTRUMS

When temper tantrums start, often around the age of eighteen months, many parents are unprepared and begin to think they have done something wrong. However, tantrums are so common that they can be considered a normal part of development (indeed they too often persist into adulthood). Small children do not have the same control over their emotions as older children and adults, and do not understand their own feelings of frustration. If they are upset and angry, or unable to do something at

Temper tantrums can be so overwhelming that they can frighten the child, so parents need to combine firmness with comfort.

the stage before they can express their feelings in words they will react with a tantrum. Two is the peak age for tantrums, and at that age around one in four children have tantrums at least once a day: some have three or four a day. The frequency of tantrums tends to decrease with age, although a few still have them by school age.

Tantrums are more likely to occur when children are tired, hungry or unwell, and if tantrums are regularly occurring just before lunch or dinner, it often helps to bring mealtimes forward.

The world of a two-year-old is full of intense feelings about what is happening *now*, with very little understanding of time. If a child of that age wants something, she wants it now and not when Mommy comes home, or after lunch, as she cannot think that far ahead. Also she is becoming increasingly independent and wants to control the world around her (which she sometimes seems to be able to do!). When things go wrong, or she does not get what she wants, then anger can explode as a

temper tantrum. This is often provoked by something very simple, like being unable to reach a toy or book from a shelf; often, too, by being refused something such as a tantalizing candy bar at the supermarket check-out. However, most tantrums at this age arise because of some conflict between child and parent, usually because the child has been prevented from doing something. Because your child's anger seems to be directed against you, it can often make you feel angry too. But responding with anger by smacking or shouting back only makes things worse and tends to prolong the outburst. If you feel angry with your child try to walk away, and calm down, and understand that your child really cannot control all those powerful feelings inside her.

Because you know your own child best, you are likely to know what will trigger a tantrum, and can handle each tantrum sensitively. Sometimes you can distract a child and stop one happening, which needs imagination and humor. If you can pull a funny face or find something else interesting for the child to do, or spot something outside the window, you may be able to prevent a full-blown tantrum.

HANDLING A TANTRUM

If a tantrum has been caused by your refusal to give your child something, or let her have her own way, then don't give in – if you do, she will learn that by having a tantrum she gets what she wants, so you would, in fact, be encouraging her to have more in future. Probably the best way to deal with a tantrum is to keep cool and try to ignore it. Either walk away and get on with something else until it all subsides, or take the child quietly to another room for a brief 'time out'. If the child appears very deeply upset you may prefer just to hold her gently and talk quietly – but it is no good holding a child if you feel really tense and upset yourself. It sometimes helps later on to have a quiet talk and a hug to show you are not angry, and perhaps to discuss what caused the upset.

When a tantrum occurs in a public place, such as a supermarket, it can be extremely embarrassing. Everyone around will be staring, and making judgmental remarks. In these circumstances, it is often best just to pick up the child and carry her out firmly, even if kicking and screaming, and let it blow over away from public view.

Tantrums occur much more commonly in children who are late to talk, and tend to lessen as communication with words becomes easier. Tantrums are more likely too if you are forever saying 'no' to your child. If everything is forbidden and every exploration results in a restriction, or a 'don't

do that', it is bound to cause frustration. Some children are endlessly on the go and into everything and will be helped by going to larger spaces, like playgrounds or parks as much as possible, where they are less restricted. Perhaps one of the biggest problems of bringing up young children in cities is the lack of safe play space nearby. You may have to travel some distance to a park or playground, but the opportunity for your child to let off energy makes the trip invaluable.

WHEN TO SAY NO

Sometimes days may go by when you seem to be saying 'no' and 'don't do that' all the time. If this happens, stop and think about what is really important. It is not worth having battles over every little thing; your child will win many of the battles and you will feel exhausted and demoralized. It is easier for everyone to have fewer rules and fewer arguments, and only say 'no' about the more important things, particularly those that involve safety: for instance, playing with electric plugs or the stove burners.

It may be easier sometimes to let your child choose what clothes to wear, and when you are not in a hurry, which way to go to the stores. Children need to feel that some of the time they do have a choice – remembering that you will be making the decisions 90 per cent of the time. It helps to avoid fuss and pressure if you give your child a few minutes' warning before you need to do something. Tell her 'it's time to start clearing up, because we're going out in a few minutes', rather than 'stop that now and put your coat on, because we're going out now'. Remember to encourage and praise your child for trying, even if she hasn't quite managed or finished something. If it has been a difficult day and you have been tired and upset, it's good to sit down for a cuddle and to say sorry – it is a way of teaching her to be able to apologize to you.

Try not to have unrealistic expectations of your child, and not to be unduly upset when she is unco-operative or does just what you have asked her not to do. Children are at times overcome by their own curiosity and desire to do something, which may be a stronger urge than needing to please you. It helps if you are firm and reasonable (even when your child isn't!), but stay calm; shouting at your child is only effective if you don't shout often.

Again, an occasional smack on the hand or behind does no harm, but repeated smacking is not only unhelpful but can get out of hand. The use of physical punishment such as smacking will often result in the child becoming aggressive, as children learn from the behavior of adults. Many parents

*Toddlers don't always need to play with
conventional toys: household objects like pots,
pans and wooden spoons provide plenty of interest.*

decide they will never smack their child, but then
will do so in a tense moment, and feel very guilty
about it afterwards. Most parents have done this at
some point and it certainly does no long term
damage. But if you feel yourself getting tense and
angry, it is sensible to try to walk away from the
situation – breathe deeply and count to twenty, or
go next door and make a cup of tea – just to give
yourself time to calm down before going back to
talk to your child.

LEARNING AND LIMITS

Sometimes life can seem one long battle with an
active two-year-old – not for nothing is this period of

life sometimes referred to as the 'terrible twos'. This
is a time for exploration; the child is learning what
she is capable of doing and trying out new skills, as
well as learning what the limits are, and what is
acceptable behavior to the adults who care for her.
It can be a confusing world for the child, and it may
help to think about what children of this age need, to
plan ahead and anticipate some of the difficulties.

As well as having their physical needs met,
children need love and security, and praise and
encouragement for their achievements. Without this
they cannot develop self-confidence and a positive
view of themselves. They need stability in their
relationships with adults, and consistency in the
way their behavior is dealt with, so they can
recognize the adult 'rules' of their world. If one day a
child is allowed to pull out the contents of her
mother's handbag and play with them, and the next
day is told off for doing so, she cannot learn what is

expected of her. If she is allowed to fall asleep on the sofa in the living room for a few nights, then the next night put in her own bed to fall asleep, she will be confused about the rules of bedtime and will, understandably, protest.

THE NEED FOR PLAY

Children also need to play – a lot of learning in the pre-school years happens through play – and this does not mean expensive toys. With imagination, and a little thought, many things around the home are good play material. Cardboard boxes and an old sheet can make a play-house, plastic bowls and wooden spoons are good for cooking meals for dolls, and dried food, such as pasta, beans or lentils, makes 'real' food. You cannot spend all your day involved in playing with your child, but setting up an activity for her just takes a little thought and time and may even mean you can get on with something else.

Try to give your child, whichever sex, a range of playthings. Dolls are not just for girls. Girls, too, enjoy playing with automobiles and garages and tool kits. It is wiser to offer a choice, so that children will not have their innate gender stereotyping exaggerated by upbringing. They will, of course, imitate the behavior of the parent they most closely identify with, so girls often want to use their mother's lipstick, or put on scarves and beads. But given the chance, both girls and boys love to play football, and to cook and wash up.

WIDENING THE HORIZON

Every child is different, with different needs and different personality. You will know your own child best and will learn that some children need much more structured boundaries than others. While some children are content and enjoy playing at home for long periods, others are more restless and active and need to be watched every minute. Activities outside the home can provide fun and stimulation and be more relaxing for you. As well as parks and playgrounds, in many areas there are places that welcome parents and young children. Libraries have a children's section, and many recreational centers and swimming pools now cater for toddlers.

Mother and toddler groups pave the way for nursery school or playgroup later, so ask what is available in your neighborhood. Many communities produce a booklet on facilities and services for under fives and this is normally obtainable from public libraries, schools, or a local doctor's office. As well as providing facilities which can be difficult

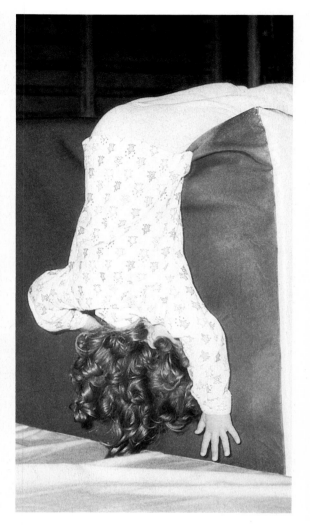

to organize at home – such as sand and water play – these activities will help your child to socialize with other children, and are good places to meet other parents of young children. It can be extremely lonely and isolating to be with a small child, or children, at home all day, and although going out can seem a big effort it usually makes everyone feel better. You, too, need people to talk to and meeting other parents can be a real tonic. You may feel able to invite them to your home, too, providing a new interest for you and your child, and probably leading to further invitations out in return.

LEARNING TO SHARE

Although children from eighteen months to two and a half years enjoy being with other children, they are not ready yet really to play with another child. They will play alongside, but have not yet learned about

Physical development is just as important as intellectual growth for the pre-school child, and there are now a range of activities available for this age group, such as toddlers' gym clubs, or inflatable 'bouncing' apparatus which vary the routine of park or playground.

taking turns in games, and so on, and can find sharing very difficult. Hence, there is often some aggression – fighting over toys, pushing another child off the tricycle, which will need gentle handling and an explanation about taking turns from an adult. With time, children learn all these things, but it may seem a slow process.

TRAVELING WITH CHILDREN

Planning ahead is essential if you are traveling with small children. Think about exercise, games and entertainment, and food and drink. Children cannot be expected to sit still for long periods, so it is best to plan a few short stops, unless, of course, you are traveling by air. Ask your travel agent what facilities are available for young children on your airline – package tour charters are usually rather basic, but some airlines can be helpful on scheduled flights.

If you are in an automobile, stop and let them run around for five or ten minutes every hour or so. In a train, take them for walks down the corridor and to look out of a different window for a bit. Taped music and stories on cassettes are useful in automobiles, but might annoy other passengers in a bus or train. Games and drawing materials do not take up much space and will help pass the time. Children who are occupied are much less likely to experience travel sickness. A supply of fruit and crackers (less harmful than candy!) and small drinks is useful – somehow children are always hungry or thirsty the moment they are settled in a car and off on the trip. A box of tissues, and a damp face cloth in a plastic bag, or a box of disposable wipes, are always useful for sticky fingers, or emergencies. If your child is hooked on using her own potty, take it with you – it could save a scene over using an unfamiliar toilet, or peeing on the grass.

TOWARD SCHOOL

**The transition from toddler to school child through
your child's developing independence**

The years from two until school age are a time of increasing independence and socialization, and for most children this period passes smoothly. In America the majority of children experience some form of pre-school program before starting compulsory education at the age of five years, and over half of children (in 1987) will have attended either nursery schools or nursery classes in primary schools before starting 'real' school, in addition to those who have attended playgroups, etc. A child's main security and support remains her home, with the love and affection given there ensuring the confidence to enter the wider world and explore relationships with other adults and children. For many children, going to some sort of pre-school program at around the age of three may be their first experience of relating to other children, or having a significant relationship with an adult other than their parents. It is an important time for a child, both for intellectual development, and for learning to inter-relate with other people.

DEVELOPING INDEPENDENCE

In these years many new skills are mastered, children's conversation becomes more interesting as their vocabulary and experience widens, and questions are increasingly asked from the age of three. This is the age when you will forever be answering the question 'Why?', and you will probably find that you are asked the same question several times in one day. It can sometimes be exasperating, but it is evidence of your child's natural curiosity, which is the basis of learning. If you get fed up explaining why the bus is yellow for the seventh time, try to distract your child's attention with another topic or by singing a song. It won't be long before the next 'Why?' comes along, but it will give you a little respite!

Your child's increasingly complex language development involves recognition of rules of grammar now, and the way she can use speech to communicate a wide range of ideas reflects both her growing understanding of the world and her own intellectual development. This is the age when adults are being constantly surprised and delighted by a child's original view of the way things work both physically and socially, and listening to two three-and-a-half or four-year-olds playing a game of make believe can be hilarious.

Children at this age master skills which increase their independence, such as going to the toilet on their own and making pretty good attempts at dressing and undressing. This often goes along with strong views on what to wear and what not to wear! This can lead to the occasional tantrum in the particularly obstinate child, but on the whole temper tantrums tend to occur much less frequently. Most of the earlier feeding problems resolve themselves, too, although again a minority of children may still be picky about certain things and can articulate their dislike more forcefully now.

Difficulties over settling down to sleep and waking up in the night are much less common over the age of three, although this is cold comfort to those whose children are still waking up. However, older children who do wake up at night will often not need their parents to get up to them as they are more likely to be prepared to play on their own by finding a favorite book or toy before falling back to sleep again.

The imaginative child may still have worries and fears especially at night which need reassurance, but children at this age are capable of listening to reason and accepting explanations which younger children could not. As with younger children, however, praise and encouragement and simple rewards will reinforce good behavior. However, there are still likely to be occasional conflicts, and many parents still find their children difficult to manage between the ages of two-and-a-half and three-and-a-half. The advice given in the previous chapter will still be relevant for this period.

BEDWETTING

Children from families where one parent wet the bed after the age of five, or children who have perhaps been a little delayed in some other aspect of their development, often take longer to be reliably

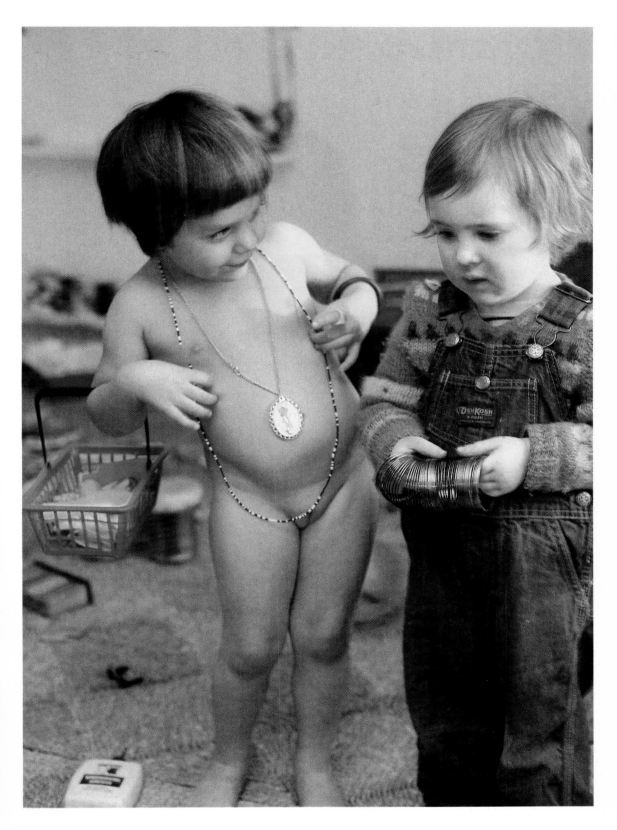

Pre-school developmental checks use simple but effective techniques in an informal atmosphere to test a wide range of skills.

dry at night (see p. 224). Any child may wet the bed in response to stress or during an episode of illness, and children who have an unhappy experience during the time when they would normally become dry (such as separation of their parents, starting school or a stay in hospital), may go on bedwetting longer than others.

Bedwetting is not a deliberate act, and some children become extremely upset when it happens. Try to avoid scolding your child or punishing her if she wets the bed – it makes matters worse as the child then becomes anxious. Lots of praise and encouragement for dry nights and a gentle 'never mind' approach to wet beds is best. You can avoid the problem to some extent by taking your child to the bathroom at the time you go to bed yourself. Most children will urinate in this situation without really waking or protesting. However, if you find this wakes your child and she has difficulty in going back to sleep, or if it upsets her at all, it is probably best not to pursue it as it could again be counter-productive and actually delay the slow but steady transition to dry nights.

DEVELOPMENTAL CHECKS

Every visit to your pediatrician offers an opportunity for you and the doctor to reaffirm that development is proceeding normally. While there may be a number of important items to complete during the regular health visit, the doctor will always spend time on assessing your child's progress. Early on this will be geared mainly to behavioral and motoric skills. However, as your child moves past the first two years, increasingly there is attention shifted toward cognitive development and the acquisition of more sophisticated language skills. Always voice any concerns you feel; no matter how trivial or outlandish are your feelings 'in the light of day', get them off your chest while you have the experience of the doctor and his expertise available.

Most school districts in America offer developmental checks to children before the time they enter kindergarten. You will probably be offered an appointment at a screening clinic, or you will be asked to have your child see your own pediatrician; perhaps both will be requested if the school system has a more elaborate 'kindergarten readiness' assessment that they perform. The aim of such examinations is to check that each child is developing to his or her full potential and to spot any

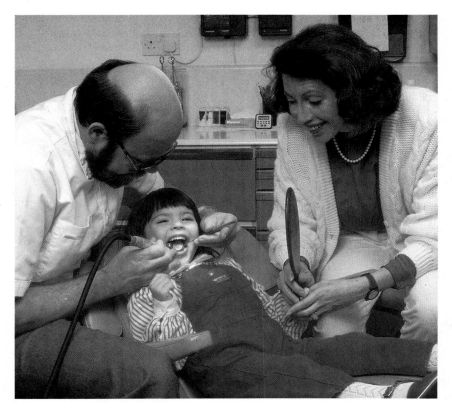

Dental check-ups can be fun for your child with a dentist who has a special interest in caring for children's teeth. Start six-monthly visits at the age of about two-and-a-half, and if these are combined with the prevention of tooth decay by regular brushing and avoiding too much sugar, your child need never be frightened of going to the dentist.

problems at an early date. In addition to simple items like checking height and weight, there will be an assessment of the child's overall development, hearing and vision. There will probably be a physical examination also, arranged either through your own doctor or through the school system's physician.

THE THREE-YEAR CHECK

A check at three years old is particularly important, since a child's speech and understanding should normally be such that a quite detailed examination of such things as sight and hearing can be done reasonably accurately. It includes looking at the way your child uses her hands (fine motor abilities), by such activities as brick building, drawing and bead threading; and the use of her body and limbs (gross motor abilities), such as running, jumping and kicking or throwing a ball. Her language development will be assessed as well. Hearing is tested, and the eyes examined for a squint ('cross eyes'), which would be obvious by now and should be treated without delay. At three-and-a-half to four sight can usually be successfully tested by matching the shape of letters on a card, even if your child isn't able to name them yet.

Use the check-up to spend time talking to the doctor about your child's development and behavior, and discuss any worries or problems that may be brought to light. Quite a number of children may refuse to co-operate or do things in an office that they are quite capable of doing at home, although if you don't make too much of the check-up to your child beforehand and let her think of it simply as a special series of games with the doctor, you will probably avoid trouble. However, as parents are the people who see most of their children and usually know exactly what their capabilities are, don't be afraid to tell the doctor of any skills which your child is unwilling to display to order!

If there is even a slight doubt about some aspect of your child's development, the doctor may refer you to a specialist. For instance, if it is felt that your child's speech development is slow, she may be referred to a speech therapist. Sometimes the doctor will just want to keep an eye on your child, after discussion with you.

Although the check-up is one particular opportunity for you to discuss your child, you do not have to wait for an appointment if you have any worries. Your doctor is available at any time to discuss your anxieties, just as when your child was a baby, and often by raising things early on you can stop minor worries from becoming major ones.

CARE OF THE TEETH

Encouraging brushing of teeth after meals and particularly before bed is good practice, and sensible from around the age of eighteen months. Regular visits to the dentist should be encouraged from two and a half years onwards, as initially the idea is to get the child used to opening her mouth and having her teeth examined. Not all dentists are skilled at communicating with young children, but many health centers and clinics offer a dental service which is particularly aimed at children. If a child does require dental treatment, such as a filling, at any age, it is clearly an easier experience if the child is already used to the dentist and to being examined. Most dentists recommend check-ups at approximately six monthly intervals.

A NEW BABY

The decision when to have another baby is a very personal one, which varies with individual families. The decision may well depend on such factors as housing and income, as well as the age of the mother, and of course even the most careful plans don't always work out as expected. Babies are not always conceived when you hope for them, and miscarriages can occur. While some families choose a small gap between children of two years or less, others prefer to wait until the first child is three or older. The advantage of having two small children close together is that the years of diaper changing and broken nights are over consecutively, and with luck the two children will get on well without fighting constantly. On the other hand, a three year hiatus allows you to 'get over' infancy and recover a bit before the next onslaught.

Many people feel that two is an age of extreme jealousies, but this depends more on the child's personality than her age, something that may be difficult to predict when you are contemplating whether to try for another baby. An older child is able to understand and communicate more about a new baby's arrival, and will participate actively in the baby's care if given a chance.

THE EFFECT ON THE OLDER CHILD

The birth of a younger sibling can be both an exciting and a worrying time in a young child's life. Inevitably, there will be anxiety about being displaced from the parents' love and affection, as well as some jealousy of a new baby. It helps to give a lot

of thought to preparing your child for the arrival of a new baby, and to encourage her to participate both during the pregnancy and after the baby is born. Talk to your child about the baby, how it grows inside and moves around, and answer any questions as honestly as you can.

Try to involve your child in practical preparations, like choosing baby clothes and toys, and try to make her feel it is her baby too (not just yours). Stories and picture books about babies are helpful to read to your child, and if you are not having a home birth, she will need to know that her mother will go into hospital for a few days, but that she can visit. Reassurance about little things is important – and the maintenance of the usual routine even while you are in hospital. The more both parents are involved in the care of the child the easier it all is – there is some evidence that children who are close to their fathers and used to being looked after by them are less adversely affected by the birth of a new baby. Lastly, bring home a small gift from the hospital for the other child as a token of extra attention.

NORMAL REACTIONS

You can expect jealous and angry reactions, which are quite normal, and commonly some regression to an earlier stage of development. Some children may start wetting the bed again, having been previously dry; others may want to go back to having a bottle or pacifier 'like the baby'. There is no need to discourage this – the child needs to be able to work through jealousies of this sort before becoming more mature. Some children react the opposite way and decide, now they are the older brother or sister, they will behave in a very 'grown up' way – perhaps by giving up an earlier habit, or starting to do something for themselves which you previously had to be involved in.

Jealous and angry reactions to a new baby brother or sister are by no means inevitable, and even when they do occur there will also be very positive reactions. Children, even as young as two, can be clearly upset when a baby cries, and will often try to comfort the baby; they will also enjoy making the baby laugh and chuckle, showing that even at this young age they are sensitive to a younger child's expression of feelings.

GIVING YOUR CHILD ATTENTION

How a child reacts to a new baby depends as much on their own individual personality as on how the situation is handled by the parents. Inevitably, the new baby will need a lot of attention, and time to

Learning to work together as a group is one of the most important aspects of nursery education. Children particularly enjoy singing and counting games which also help speech and co-ordination.

spend alone with an older child will be difficult to find. It does help if you can organize some time alone with the older child, even if briefly. But grandparents and friends can help too – by giving special attention to the older one and going out for walks and expeditions so that she does receive the undivided attention of one adult for a time. Interestingly, children who seem to show no jealous feelings about their own baby sibling are quite capable of showing marked anger and resentment when one of their parents cuddles someone else's baby. It is almost as if they understand the obligation to love and care for the baby in their own family, but an outsider's baby may be the last straw!

The time of arrival of a sibling is not the appropriate time to start a child at nursery or other form of pre-school program. The child may then feel she is being pushed out of the way so that you can be alone with the baby. Plan it so that a child is already happily settled in before the baby arrives – or wait three or four months until she has adjusted to the reality of life in a larger family before planning to start at a nursery.

PRE-SCHOOL PROGRAMS

There is a range of programs in this country for pre-school children, although there is enormous variation from area to area in the amount and type available. Handbooks which list the local facilities and services for under fives are produced in many areas. They can be obtained by asking at your local library, city hall, community services agency or health clinic. Nursery schools and classes may be run by the local school department, and have a specifically stated educational purpose. The ratio of staff to children is quite high compared to primary school, and the staff will have professional teaching qualifications. In most areas nursery schools will

Experimenting with the color and texture of paint is just one of a number of 'messy' activities which a nursery school or playgroup can offer.

admit children as young as three, so long as they are toilet trained. There is often considerable demand for places, and, whether privately or local authority run, many nursery schools have quite long waiting lists, with priority given to brothers and sisters and families living close to the school. Nursery schools are also run by many independent bodies (such as Montessori nurseries) and private individuals.

Playgroups exist in many parts of the country, but more particularly in towns and cities. They are usually run by the parents themselves, and a key feature is that parents are expected to be involved in helping in these 'co-op' organizations. Many playgroup leaders have taken courses or have degrees in this field. They usually cater for children over the age of two and a half and are often run in a local church hall or similar facility. If there is no playgroup in your area, it might be worth getting together with other parents to start one up – help can be obtained from either city hall or a state agency.

Nursery schools and playgroups are not really designed as childcare facilities for working parents; most operate on a part-time basis with quite short

morning or afternoon sessions, although a few will take priority children for two sessions with lunch. Even then, the afternoon session generally finishes at or before 3.30 pm, and nurseries will have normal school holidays. If you want or need to go back to work once your child reaches this age, you may be able to get a day nursery place; otherwise you will need to look at the childcare options already discussed on page 196.

PLAYGROUPS AND NURSERY SCHOOLS

Places at playgroups or nursery schools are usually available either on a daily or half-daily basis, for a limited number of days a week, or a five day week. Clearly, your own needs in terms of hours must be considered when making your choice, and practical factors, such as the distance from your home and travel arrangements, will need to be taken into account. A playgroup or nursery close to your home makes it easier for your child to have local friends, and is a good way to meet other parents who can often become quite a supportive network both to you and your child.

The aim of playgroups and nurseries is implicitly educational – not just in the field of encouraging the child's intellectual development but also enlarging the child's social skills in relating to other children

Matching shapes and colors in a simple game supervised by an adult helps pre-school children to begin to think mathematically.

and adults, and encouraging independence. Children at play need time to run around and let off steam, as well as time for constructive play, and a good nursery or playgroup will offer a healthy balance between free and structured times of the day. It is important to have some structured activity in each play session, as this encourages concentration and task-solving, hence encouraging intellectual development. Typical activities of this sort which children enjoy are all types of art work (you will be presented with armfuls of drawings, paintings and collages every week!), color matching games, construction materials, puzzles and make-believe sessions, such as dressing up, doll's houses, hospital corners, and so on.

Three-year-olds and onward particularly enjoy periods of make-believe and will develop complex imaginative games and conversations, particularly if left alone without adults to inhibit their imagination. In these imaginary games at this age children often play best in pairs, and most often seem to choose friends of their own sex. By three, children are well aware of whether they are boys or girls, and may already be developing stereotyped ideas of how

each sex should behave in response to adult and environmental conditioning. One hopes to find nurseries which employ staff of both sexes, and where children are encouraged to play within a wide range of activities, such as woodwork, cooking, and so on in a way which does not encourage sex stereotyping.

Although at times liking to play with one special friend, for much of the time children also enjoy playing in groups, particularly for singing and dancing games, and stories. Being with other children encourages learning to co-operate with others, to respect other children, and to listen to and help others. All this increases a child's self-confidence as well as helping their social development, and helps to make the transition from home to school an easier process.

CHOOSING A PLAYGROUP OR NURSERY

Selecting any form of pre-school program may seem rather daunting, particularly if you are lucky enough in your own area to have considerable choice. It is very much an individual decision, based on your own needs and what you feel is most appropriate for your own child. Do not be too influenced by other people's opinions, but go and see for yourself and trust your own intuitive feelings.

POINTS TO LOOK FOR WHEN SELECTING A
PRE-SCHOOL PROGRAM

☐ Is there a warm, welcoming atmosphere?

☐ Is there parental involvement?

☐ What variety of activities are available?

☐ What is the staff/child ratio?

☐ How do the staff interact with the children – are there plenty of hugs and humor, or are attitudes authoritarian and judgmental?

☐ Do the adults talk to the children, or to each other?

☐ Is the group (including staff) multi-cultural, and what are attitudes towards sexism and racism?

☐ Are children adequately supervised, and what safety precautions are taken?

☐ How is a distressed or angry child handled and how is aggression coped with?

☐ How are new children helped in their adjustment?

☐ Do relationships between the staff seem good?

☐ What is the level of communication between playleaders and parents?

☐ Do kitchen areas and toilets appear clean?

It is important to find somewhere that seems truly to like and value children, and that is warm and welcoming to both parents and children. Beware of the too-tidy nursery, and be sure to ask about the aims and philosophies of the place in order to find out if your ideas are similar to theirs. This is particularly important in respect of discipline, competitiveness, attitudes to toileting and meal-times. Don't be afraid to ask questions about aspects you find worrying, and look for open, frank answers. Good nursery teachers and playgroup leaders will welcome parental interest and constructive criticism, and will be happy for parents to become involved in nursery activities.

Some nursery schools stress the educational nature of the activities offered to children and may even encourage early reading. Although some children will enjoy these, those who aren't ready for reading (the majority of four-year-olds) will be put off or discouraged by these activities, especially if they are forced to join in. There is no evidence to suggest that it is helpful for children to learn to read before starting school at five, and for many children it is an unnecessary pressure which can undermine self-confidence. Education is far broader than learn-ing to read and write, and all the 'play' activities in pre-school groups are in themselves educational (see above).

ADJUSTMENT

When considering any change of environment for your pre-school child, try and plan it carefully. Small children do not respond well to sudden changes although there can obviously be circumstances that cannot be planned for, such as a parent becoming ill and having to go to hospital. But with most arrangements for childcare there is time to think about it well in advance and to plan for adjustment in a way which will least upset your child. Some children are sociable and extrovert and will cheer-fully wave goodbye on their first day at a new nursery; others are perhaps more apprehensive and anxious about separation from a parent and will need a few weeks of settling down.

Many children's centers suggest that a parent plan for a two-week adjustment time, during which they will be around as much as necessary – this is because they recognize that a considerable number of children do find the transition from home to another environment quite difficult. It depends not only on your child's temperament but her age, and also her previous experiences. At three and older it is very much easier for a child to cope with new adults and children and playthings than at two – a two-year-old may well be a bit bewildered, but a three-year-old has had more experience and is better able to understand that if you go away you are coming back again later.

Children who are used to playing in other people's homes, have extensive networks of family or friends and are used to relating to other adults, have no difficulty in adjusting on the whole. For children who have previously always been at home alone with their parents the period of adjustment will almost certainly be longer. Talk to the nursery or playgroup staff about what they expect, try to visit a few times with your child before it is time to start, and be a bit wary if the staff try to tell you that you need not stay on the first day! Any pre-school center that understands parents and children will know that you both need to come to start with. It is reassuring for you as well as your child to meet the other children and experience the morning routine and see perhaps how another child who is upset is handled by the staff.

If your child finds it hard to leave you she will need one special adult to relate to and make a friend of – so that if necessary you can physically hand your child to that person when you have to leave.

Depending on your child, you should plan to spend several sessions at the center, not always directly with your child but just being around for reassurance, before going away for short periods. Be prepared to be flexible – but don't try to go away for hours until you and the staff feel your child is reasonably happy and secure. Even after a long period, some children will always cry on saying goodbye – but usually they are cheerfully playing ten minutes later. A phone call to check can be reassuring for you. A favorite toy or something of yours, like a scarf, can be reassuring for a child to have with her until it is time to go home again. If you have a child who is clearly unhappy after three or four months, then it is important to discuss this with someone, as you may need to re-think and have your child back at home until she is a bit older.

PROBLEMS WITH BEHAVIOR

It is not unusual for a child to show some change in behavior after starting at a playgroup or nursery. Some children become a bit quiet and withdrawn until they have made friends and become confident in their new setting; others may be quite boisterous and bossy with other children. Sometimes the behavior can be distressing for you and other parents, if your child starts to be aggressive towards other children, or is at the receiving end of this sort of behavior.

Biting, kicking or hair pulling are not uncommon, and may simply be a reaction to a new environment and learning to share with other children. Sometimes biting happens in response to aggression in a different form – perhaps being pushed by another child – or if a child is angry and upset about something she finds hard to talk about. With careful handling by the staff and parents this behavior usually stops fairly soon. It must be made clear that the biting is unacceptable, but punishment by smacking or biting back should be avoided as this will make matters worse. If such behavior persists, do discuss it with the staff and your doctor – other parents are understandably protective of their own children and may not be too tolerant.

STARTING SCHOOL

The transition to school is a big step, which on the whole is easier for children who have experienced some sort of pre-school program. Even so, the school environment is very different, there are perhaps different expectations of behavior, a lot more children, and certainly far fewer adults around to give individual attention. Most five-year-olds cope well after the first few days, and it will be easier for

them if they have visited the school beforehand. Some schools arrange for a 'staggered' intake at the beginning of term, so children can be settled in a few at a time with plenty of attention on the first day.

Generally, children enjoy the stimulation of school, but are likely to be very tired after school and may be irritable for the first few weeks. It is after all an effort to cope with all those other children and another new environment. For the majority it all quickly settles down, but around one in ten will still have some difficulties with coping after the first semester. It is important to discuss with the child's teacher how she is coping in class – sometimes a child who appears upset and clingy and demanding at home will be fine at school, and just needs extra reassurance from you. But any anxiety should be discussed with your child's teacher, and parents are always welcome in the classroom.

Your child needs you to take an interest in the work (and play) she is involved in at school, and as at playgroup, you should expect to come home with armfuls of paintings from time to time.

ANXIETIES ABOUT SCHOOL

Common dislikes and complaints in the first year or so are often about intimidation in the playground, teasing by other children, school meals, changes in friendship, and so on. Toilets, too, can be a cause of anxiety. Sometimes the cause of a worry is obvious – such as not being able to put boots on alone – and a note to the teacher about a little extra help will cure the problem! However, some children find it hard to tell their parents what is worrying them and subtle questioning may be needed.

If you continue to be anxious about your child after discussion with the teacher there are other sources of help – the principal, your doctor, and the school's psychology staff can be contacted to help sort out your child's difficulties.

SCHOOL PHOBIA

Occasionally anxiety over some aspect of school will cause a child to refuse to go to school (school phobia) – she may even develop the symptoms of an illness. This is fairly uncommon in the first years at primary school but can occur at any age. It is important to find out what is the cause of the problem, which will usually mean a visit to the school. Your child will need a lot of reassurance but you need to be quite firm about the fact that she does have to go to school. Visiting the classroom with your child and encouraging her to tell you all about her day at school will usually identify the source of the problem.

Sometimes school phobia is not due to a problem at school at all, but may occur if a child is worried about leaving home for any reason. This can happen if one parent is ill or has perhaps been in hospital, a situation which can make a child very anxious and reluctant to be separated again. Discussion and reassurance will again be needed; if you can anticipate a possible time of difficulty, such as a time when one parent has to go into hospital, tell your child's teacher so that he or she can keep a special eye on the child during this period.

SLOW LEARNERS

There are two or three children in every class who are not really ready for formal schooling at the age of five and may experience considerable difficulty

The age at which a pre-school child can produce even a crude human face varies enormously, as can be seen from the drawings reproduced below, by a two-and-a-half-year-old (below) and a four-year-old (bottom).

with mastering early reading and writing skills. Children develop and mature at different rates and need to be allowed to go at their own pace without being made to feel they are failing to keep up with others. In many countries formal schooling does not start until the age of six, since it is recognized that many children are too immature at five to cope with some of the classroom demands. Some American schools mix five- and six-year-olds in groups, which benefits both slow learners and early developers.

If your child seems slow to learn, don't apply pressure but encourage by reading stories and looking at books together. Find out what reading scheme is used in the class, and talk to the teacher about how you can help. Trying to force the pace is counter-productive, and pressure can put a child off attempting to tackle any new task for fear of failing. If both you and the teacher continue to be concerned about slow progress then the school may feel it is appropriate to consult the school psychology staff, and you can initiate a 'core evaluation' to help identify any learning problem.

THE SCHOOL MEDICAL EXAMINATION

Almost all school systems have a policy of offering a pre-school screening check-up at about age four-and-a-half to five. Usually, this takes place the summer before your child enrolls in kindergarten, or soon after beginning school. While varying in scope and comprehensiveness, the aim of such an examination is to ensure that each child is going to get the most from their schooling, and to identify any medical or developmental problems that might interfere with the child's education. None of these examinations involves tests which will be 'passed' or 'failed', nor do they involve producing a score or IQ for each child. It is recognized that different children develop and mature at different rates.

Children differ in the things they enjoy doing and in the things they are good at. Special skills may exist in one area, perhaps drawing and creative skills, while the same child might lag behind others of the same age in another area. The aim of any assessment of a child is to offer help if it is needed in any particular area, and to discuss with parents and teachers the best way to ensure a child's optimal development. Some children may need help with concentration, and be better in small groups for teaching, while those who are very active may not be able to cope with too structured a day and will need time to let off steam. Some may need extra help with copying and writing skills; children who perhaps have had some hearing loss in the past may need help to develop listening skills.

A school medical examination should not take

Drawing helps children to express themselves while learning the control of a pen or pencil eventually needed for writing.

place without the parents, as it is an opportunity for discussion with those who know the child best. A check of both eyesight and hearing will be done, as clearly any defect in either of these areas (which may be unsuspected by parents) can interfere with optimal learning.

Sometimes stress at home, such as illness in a family member, or separation of the parents, can helpfully be discussed – teachers too need to know of such events. If a child is anxious or worried about something going on at home he may be quite unable to relax and concentrate at school, and in some instances family stress can be a cause of learning difficulties.

PRIVATE SCHOOLS

Some private and parochial schools do not have a school doctor or nurse, and parents are expected to consult their own doctor over any medical or developmental problem. There will not be any routine checks of your child's eyesight or hearing, so subtle defects can go unnoticed, possibly leading teachers to think your child is lazy or slow. If you have any cause for concern, and particularly if your child's learning seems to be suffering, make sure you seek your doctor's advice and arrange for your child to have hearing and vision checks to be done in the office or elsewhere.

THE SICK CHILD

Understanding the pattern of your child's health, and preventing or coping with illness or accident

Children in our society enjoy a very high standard of health. Medical advice, at varying levels of expertise, is widely available in the media and books, and everyone has access to health care providers who aim to look after members of the whole family, including children. However, the breadth of advice may be bewildering and is often conflicting. Furthermore, many parents are interested in caring for their children and making their own decisions about coping with childhood illnesses.

Unfortunately there is an assumption by many patients and doctors, that illness, even relatively trivial, requires medication. This is not always necessary, particularly for children. It is essential therefore that parents should be familiar with the common illnesses of childhood to understand, not only when formal medical advice is needed, but also when they should be able to manage the problem themselves, particularly when there is no specific treatment and general supportive measures alone are appropriate.

Understanding the patterns of illness and treatment will allow both parent and doctor to discuss the management of each problem and appreciate each other's viewpoint. In the past doctors were accustomed to dictating to patients, and their advice was usually followed without discussion. Fortunately this situation has changed so that parents, and indeed children themselves, are now readily involved in the process of health care.

THE SICK CHILD AND YOUR DOCTOR

Your pediatrician (or family doctor) is a vital source of information and advice about illness. His knowledge of disease as it relates to individuals within a family, particularly when he is familiar with the family, will enable him to work out the most appropriate treatment of a condition. He also can coordinate other expertise, both medical (such as hospital-based specialists) and para-medical (such as physiotherapists or visiting nurses), for diagnosis and treatment of serious illness, and provide guidance for more minor difficulties.

Although Emergency Departments in a hospital may seem more accessible, especially during the night and at weekends, the value of your own doctor's knowledge of your family should not be underestimated. It is more appropriate to use the hospital only in case of genuine accidents or emergencies, or when the pediatrician requests that you go there.

CHOOSING YOUR DOCTOR

It is important that the family and pediatrician have established a relationship before illness arises. Trust and confidence will improve the value of future consultations, particularly as some problems may require only telephone advice.

It is therefore worth choosing your child's doctor carefully. Ask friends in your neighborhood and interview the doctors themselves about their facilities, attitude to children's health, availability, and coverage arrangements for when they are unavailable. Generally, it pays to set up a series of interviews with local pediatricians so that you can meet the doctor first hand. Many pediatricians set aside time at the end of the work day to sit down and meet new parents. Some offices even set a time aside to meet the entire group so you can have a sense of all the people who will be caring for your child. Considering what a vital decision this may prove to be in the future, the time spent investigating your child's doctor is well worth it. Find out what the receptionist is like, how accessible the doctor will be, whether a nurse practitioner works in the office, and what is the philosophy towards managing the illness and using medications.

If your child has a particular condition which may need specialized attention, you should discuss referral arrangements with the pediatrician at the outset. Obviously, extremely complex problems, or long-term handicaps mean that many specialists will be involved in the care of your child and it is crucial that you select a pediatrician who has the ability to orchestrate the varying sources of care and advice you will receive. One person really does have to look after the whole child while all the specialists are attending to their individual areas of concern.

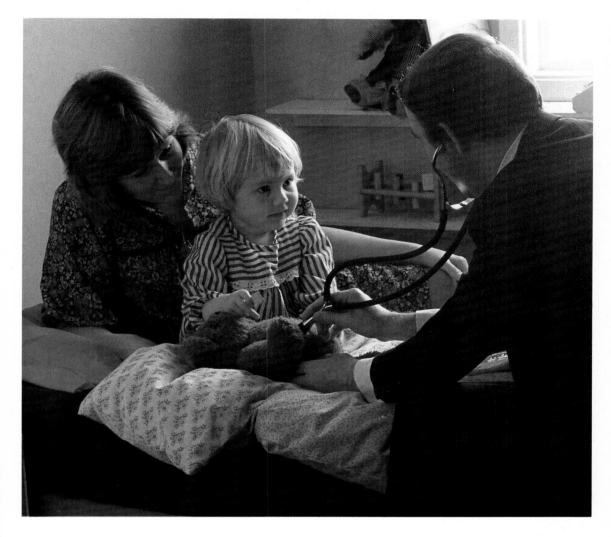

The relationship between you and your family doctor is a partnership based on the shared desire to care for your child's health.

CALLING THE DOCTOR

Doctors who make home visits to see sick children are a vanishing species. In urban and suburban America, most problems are handled with a telephone call to the doctor and a visit to the office if necessary. Since virtually all practicing doctors carry beepers and have some arrangement for an answering service, a tremendous amount of 'care' for your child is rendered by telephone. The system works remarkably well and with a little experience, the doctor is able to sort out the urgent, the sick and the well over the 'phone. Some common childhood problems always occasion serious concern by your doctor – such as severe belly ache or croup. You are unlikely to receive a quick reassurance on these matters. However, the colds and coughs and upset stomachs that plague young children can often be very successfully managed at home with ongoing telephone guidance from your doctor.

Many doctors have established morning 'call hour' before their normal office hours begin. This is an excellent opportunity to report in on your child's condition or to notify the doctor that you will need an appointment urgently because the baby seems sick. Before calling spend a moment trying to assess how sick your child is. What is the temperature? What is his behavior and feeding? Is anybody else in the family ill (including baby-sitters or child care providers)? Have you just returned from a recent trip which could contribute to the illness? Since the doctor is almost certain to recommend acetaminophen for any high fever, it makes good sense to treat your child (except during the first six

249

months of life), before calling the doctor. We all get flustered when trying to take care of our sick children. They often appear so helpless and so terribly ill, that we begin to panic, especially when they are very young and it is the first time around with a sick child. Rest assured that your parenting instincts will see you through, with a little help from the doctor. Also, you are almost certain to recognize a serious problem instinctively, and you can trust your judgment pretty much as to whether a true emergency exists.

Some emergencies might be better managed by taking the child directly to hospital, although this may depend on whether your home is near a hospital, or in the country, where family doctors are often happy to cope with a wide variety of problems. Accidents such as deep cuts or fractures, or head injuries, should be taken to hospital. Any situation where there is very severe pain or some change in the level of consciousness, may require calling an ambulance directly. It is useful to inform your doctor first as he may be able to warn the hospital that a sick child is about to arrive.

AT THE DOCTOR'S OFFICE

If possible children are best seen early in the day, or at least early in the afternoon. Children get irritable when waiting and distress themselves and their parents, so the time spent waiting should be short. Well equipped offices will have toys and books, and one advantage of a large health center is the provision of a play area. Parents should be prepared for some wait, however, both for their pediatrician and for hospital clinics, and should bring favorite toys, a bottle of milk or fruit juice, and, if appropriate, an extra diaper and changing equipment.

It is also useful for parents to come prepared with one or two points about their child's illness which they have already noticed; for instance, the period of the illness, the appearance of specific symptoms and any particular concerns that they may have.

The success of a doctor's appointment depends very much on the cooperation of the child. This requires both a gentle and unhurried approach by the doctor, and also the preparedness of the child. If he is old enough to understand, the child should have the purpose of the visit explained to him, and the possible use of any equipment, such as a stethoscope or an otoscope for examining the ears. False reassurance isn't helpful, but you can reinforce the idea of the doctor's good nature. It is in everyone's interest that the child be relaxed and as unthreatened as possible.

When your child's ears are examined, hold her gently but firmly on your lap and rest the side of her head against you (right), holding it steady with a hand on her forehead if necessary. You may find it easier to grip a wriggling baby's legs between your thighs.

To have your child's eyes or throat examined, position her on your lap as for examination of the ear, but hold her head forward (left). A young baby may be wrapped in a towel or blanket to control the arms and hands.

The possibility of any painful procedures should be explained but this is perhaps best left until very soon before the event. However, children who are forewarned about these procedures very often tolerate them well. Doctors, dentists, hospitals and 'unpleasant' medical events should never be used as threats, as this ultimately undermines the confidence of the child in the doctor as someone who cares and helps. Never promise your child that the doctor 'won't give you any shots'. If blood tests or extra immunizations prove necessary, the child will have lost confidence in both you and the doctor.

Parents should make themselves familiar with the standard procedure for holding a child being examined. This is not only useful to comfort the child and reassure him, but also allows the doctor to examine the child safely and without causing undue force. Although inevitably some procedures, such as examining the throat, do cause some slight distress, most doctors are expert in obtaining information as quickly as possible.

IMMUNIZATION

The elimination or limitation of several fatal infectious diseases during the twentieth century has been a major contribution to the improvement of health care. Poliomyelitis and diphtheria now occur very rarely in the developed world, smallpox has been eradicated, and many other conditions such as tetanus, typhoid fever, yellow fever and hepatitis can now be controlled by immunization. Unfortunately there is a tendency to forget that there is still the potential for these dangerous conditions to return, and it is essential that routine immunization of everyone in the community continues, to maintain a high level of general immunity, so it is important to ensure your child has the full schedule of immunizations.

HOW IMMUNIZATION WORKS

The body's immune system responds to a foreign organism (or germ) by producing antibodies to neutralize or kill that germ. The immune system can 'remember', for a varying period of months or years, how to produce more specific antibodies if someone again comes into contact with the same organism. Immunization is an artificial challenge to the immune system performed in two ways.

Killed organisms, or a portion of killed organisms, may be injected on several occasions over a period of months. This is the basis for immunization against pertussis (whooping cough) and typhoid fever. The 'memory' against these infections usually only lasts a few years. Periodically a reminder or booster injection is required. One alternative form of providing immunity is to inject a harmless live organism, similar to that causing the disease, but altered to avoid producing symptoms. Vaccines against measles, rubella, yellow fever, smallpox, tuberculosis and poliomyelitis use this principle. Another technique is to inject an artificial copy of a portion of the germ. This is quite harmless and works well for a type of meningitis – H. flu ('HIB' or ProHIBit).

Some infections need to be protected against for life (TB, smallpox, poliomyelitis), but others, such as whooping cough and measles, have their most serious effects on children, and so protection is needed only during this period of life.

MINIMIZING SIDE EFFECTS

Most immunizations produce some side effects, but in the vast majority of children these symptoms are mild such as slight fever, minor irritability, redness and a lump (which may persist for several weeks) at the site of the infection, and in older patients a general feeling of being off color. However, the inconvenience of these symptoms is far outweighed by the advantages of immunity.

Nevertheless many parents will be concerned about possible adverse effects and it is sensible to minimize the likelihood of their occurring. Injections should be given only when the baby or child is well, without fever or severe illness, but should not be postponed just for a runny nose or mild cold. Acetaminophen in syrup or pill form is useful for fever if this occurs after the injection.

Most injections are given into a muscle or under the skin. The usual sites are the upper arm, buttock or front of the thigh. Oral vaccine is taken by mouth; a few drops of liquid are placed on the tongue and the baby or child will swallow this without difficulty although it does taste bitter and is therefore usually mixed with flavoring.

TIMING OF IMMUNIZATION

The timing of the immunization is important. Babies are protected from many infections by the mother's own antibodies transferred across the placenta before birth. These antibodies last for about six months; after this time young infants are particularly at risk from the common infectious diseases. It is for this reason that the program of routine immunization starts at two months. Immunization against tuberculosis (BCG) is often given to newborn babies from families where there is an increased risk of

IMMUNIZATION SCHEDULE	
AGE	**VACCINE**
2 months	Diphtheria, pertussis, tetanus (known collectively as DPT or Triple Vaccine) and poliomyelitis
4 months	DPT; polio
6 months	DPT; polio
15 months	MMR (combined measles, mumps and rubella)
18 months	DPT; polio; H. flu
School entry	DPT; poliomyelitis
15 years	Tetanus, diphtheria, poliomyelitis (and every 10 years thereafter)

contracting tuberculosis (such as a recent family history of TB or in immigrant families who have come from countries where the disease is still widespread), although the practice does vary.

Routine immunization includes protection against poliomyelitis, measles, mumps, tetanus, diphtheria, rubella and H. flu meningitis. The table above gives a common immunization schedule.

If a course of vaccination is interrupted for any length of time, there seems to be no need to start again and the course should simply be completed. Babies born prematurely should be immunized at the same age as other babies – in this case no allowances are made for their prematurity.

These vaccines do not guarantee total immunity against these infections, but the illness, if it does occur, is usually mild. It is very useful for parents to keep a record of those immunizations given and to note when the next dose of vaccine is required.

PERTUSSIS (WHOOPING COUGH)

Considerable controversy has arisen about the use of this vaccine because of the possible link between vaccination and neurological (brain) damage. Unfortunately this has led to a decrease in the number of children being vaccinated. Although it does not eliminate the possibility of contracting whooping cough completely, vaccination does lessen the severity of the disease if it does occur. The lower percentage of children immunized has led to a very large increase in the number of reported cases during epidemics in subsequent years.

It is difficult to answer the question 'Does vaccine

cause brain damage?'. The apparent effects of vaccine are extremely rare and in 1981 a national study suggested one in about 300,000 injections was *associated* with, but did not necessarily directly cause, long-term neurological damage. To put these statistics in perspective, your child has the same risk of suffering brain damage from pertussis vaccine as from taking an automobile journey of 500 miles or more. On the other hand, neurological damage occurs with the disease whooping cough itself, and there is evidence that serious side-effects such as severe effects on breathing and seizures are probably more common than previously recognized. So it is important to maintain a high rate of vaccination because a high level of immunity within the population tends to protect those who have not or cannot be immunized by preventing epidemics.

Immunity against pertussis is not transferred from mother to baby in the uterus and the baby is theoretically at risk of contracting it from birth. Immunization, however, needs to be delayed until two months of age, as the baby's immune system is not able to respond appropriately to immunization until that time. Minor side effects are common, as mentioned previously, but severe reactions such as prolonged, inconsolable crying or a very high temperature are very rare. When these very serious reactions occur, further vaccination against pertussis should not be carried out but diphtheria, tetanus and polio should still be given.

Some groups of children require special consideration: if parents or siblings have epilepsy, or the child has a continuing disease of the nervous system, the risk from immunization may be slightly higher. But the benefits of vaccination may still outweigh this increased risk, and the doctor may still advise immunization. If there is doubt about the advisability of immunization, the issue should be discussed with your pediatrician. Newer vaccines are being developed which may provoke even fewer reactions.

It is commonly believed that children with asthma, eczema or allergy should not be immunized. This is not so, and in fact such children need the protection of vaccination. If immunization has been missed or parents have reconsidered an earlier decision, it can be given until six years.

DIPHTHERIA

This serious and usually lethal illness is now very rare, largely as a result of the effect of the vaccine. But it is important that diphtheria immunization should be given to everyone, for there is the risk that the disease could return if a high level of immunity in the community is not maintained. Serious reactions to the vaccine are very rare, and there are no medical conditions which should prevent immunization.

TETANUS

The germs for this dangerous illness are present in the earth and dust. Both children and adults are susceptible and repeated immunization is important throughout life. Following the initial course, booster injections should be given every five years. Generally, if an open injury occurs and immunization is known to be up to date, an additional injection is not required. In non-immunized children, however, a booster should be given at the time of injury and possibly an injection of anti-tetanus immunoglobulin to provide immediate protection.

POLIOMYELITIS

The widespread use of a very effective live vaccine against poliomyelitis has led to the virtual disappearance of this disease in the US, but it is still common in some parts of the world. The vaccine is given by mouth and a minimum of three doses are required to provide full immunity. It should not be given during an acute illness, particularly gastroenteritis. Parents who are not themselves immunized should also receive a course of vaccine. Side effects are mild and very rare.

MEASLES

Measles is commonly thought not to be a serious illness, but it can frequently cause considerable distress to the child and may lead to pneumonia, encephalitis (inflammation of the brain) and ear and throat infections. One injection at about fifteen months provides immunity, although a mild attack of measles may still occur in those immunized. A slight fever and rash may occur about a week following the injection, and very rarely a febrile convulsion may occur. However, the incidence of this is far less than a convulsion occurring with measles itself. If the child has had convulsions previously, or parents or brothers or sisters have had convulsions, an injection of immunoglobulin should be given at the same time. The triple vaccine MMR protects against measles, mumps, and rubella or German measles (see below).

RUBELLA (GERMAN MEASLES)

This mild illness causes few problems to a child or adult. It may however produce very serious congenital abnormalities in an unborn baby if the mother becomes infected during pregnancy (see p. 13), so vaccination is mandatory. One injection produces immunity for many years, although older women may need reimmunization.

It is essential that women given vaccine should *not* become pregnant for three months and women contemplating pregnancy should, if they are unsure about their own immunity, discuss their plans with their obstetrician. A blood test can confirm if a woman is already immune to rubella. A mild fever might occur after immunization. Boys are immunized routinely against rubella to increase the immunity of the general population and therefore prevent further transmission of the disease.

MUMPS

While not a terribly serious illness, mumps can be an unpleasant childhood experience. The illness produces a typical swelling at the angle of the jaw, which may occur on both sides of the face. These represent the swollen salivary glands inside the mouth which are just in front of the ears. As no treatment is available, immunization is important. The major concern with mumps is the acquisition of the illness in puberty or early adulthood which, occasionally, can lead to sterility because of inflammation of the testicles in boys. Use of MMR vaccine at age fifteen months confers a high degree of immunity to the virus.

TUBERCULOSIS

Cases of tuberculosis are again on the rise in the United States. Recent immigration and the increasing spread of AIDS account for most of this rise. People coming to the country from the Caribbean, South East Asia, and some parts of Africa are at high risk for having contracted tuberculosis back home. Poverty, poor housing, and crowded living conditions increase the spread of tuberculosis, including to children. Routine skin testing for tuberculosis is carried out at nine to twelve months using a Tine test (skin-prick) or PPD (subcutaneous needle). The small injection is given on the forearm and the reaction noted two days later. If no reaction occurs, the infant has not been exposed to tuberculosis. However, if the injection produces swelling and redness, this indicates 'conversion' to a positive skin test to tuberculosis. Children need to be evaluated further by the local TB clinic or your doctor.

H.FLU B

This unfamiliar name is short for Hemophilus influenza B, a germ (not to be confused with influenza, a chest illness caused by a virus), giving rise to serious infections in young children. Particularly concerning is meningitis, but equally serious is epiglottitis which mimics croup but is far more devastating and always life threatening. HIB (or ProHIBit) vaccine is given at eighteen months.

OTHER VACCINATIONS

Immunization against other common illnesses is available, but is usually reserved for those patients with other medical problems or who are at special risk. Immunization is possible against hepatitis B, influenza, pneumococcal disease and meningococcus. Usually, you will find out about any such risk from your doctor, but if you are worried you can consult your local US Public Health Service office.

TRAVEL VACCINATION

Many illnesses, such as poliomyelitis and diphtheria, which have almost ceased to exist in the US, are still prevalent in many countries and it is essential that parents should check that their children are up to date with all the routine immunization. In some countries, immunization against other infections is compulsory, although for others, immunization is advisable but not a prerequisite for entry. Immunization against yellow fever, cholera, typhoid fever are commonly given, and immunogloblin for hepatitis A, while not giving complete immunity, may help prevent infection. Smallpox vaccination is no longer required anywhere.

The recommendations vary widely and parents should check the requirements for each individual country. Consult your local US Public Health Service office for further information and for guidelines on health care for travelers. You may also, of course, need to consider immunization for yourself.

SCREENING TESTS

In addition to immunizations, pediatricians commonly perform blood tests to screen for lead poisoning and for anemia. Typically, a drop of blood is obtained by a prick of the finger at either nine or twelve months of age and annually thereafter. Many doctors now screen urine annually starting at about one year of age, checking for the presence of blood or protein in the urine, diabetes (sugar in the urine) or for a urinary tract infection which may not manifest itself with symptoms. These tests are both simple and cheap and can avoid untold trouble by early detections of these conditions.

SYMPTOMS AND SIGNS OF ILLNESS

All children will become ill a number of times during childhood and the vast majority of these episodes will be because of common minor infections, most of which do not require specific medication or medical advice. However, parents may worry that a symptom may be a signal that something more serious is going on with their child, so it is important to gain some familiarity with the various signs and symptoms of illness in children. Inevitably some of these will be the same for both simple and more serious infection or illness. As a general rule, a symptom which becomes gradually worse or which goes on over a long period of time, perhaps more than a day or two, often points to something serious occurring. Parents who are coping with their first child will find the decision between a minor or serious problem more difficult to make since, as with all things medical, experience counts considerably in making the right decision. When in any doubt, call the doctor!

SYMPTOMS NEEDING MEDICAL ADVICE

There are several common signs and symptoms which may guide parents in their decision. These are often non-specific and may be related to a number of different disorders. Where there is a clear connection between a specific symptom and a disease the decision is easy; if not, medical advice may be required. Certainly if you are at all anxious or undecided a phone call or visit to the doctor may be very valuable.

APPEARANCE

Most parents are able to judge when their child looks ill, and there is usually an obvious difference between the child who feels just 'off-color', and one who is seriously ill. Particular signs to look for are dry mouth and sunken eyes, which are a sign of dehydration; pale, mottled or bluish coloration of the skin, which may indicate a serious infection; most rashes are usually obvious. Many rashes start behind the ears or on the face, but in some serious infections, the rash may start elsewhere on the body and not be obvious in the early stages.

The child who is unwell will often be apathetic and uninterested in what is going on around him and may not be comforted in the usual way by his parents. In particular, an ill baby may pass rapidly through a phase of crying frequently to one where even this is too much effort. It is worthwhile noting unusual smells from a child. Drug ingestion such as alcohol will often leave a characteristic smell. An ill child who has not been eating well will also produce substances called ketones which can be smelled on the breath. These smell like acetone (nail polish remover!).

BREATHING DIFFICULTIES

Different respiratory problems may produce a different sign or change in the breathing (see also Emergencies, p. 258). A particular sound produced during abnormal breathing often indicates the physical site of the problem. A blocked nose or pharynx (back of the throat) from mucus produced during a cold will produce a characteristic nasal voice and obviously stuffy nose. In particular, a baby may not be able to feed normally as he relies particularly on nose breathing during the feeding process. Babies or young children may also find it difficult to sleep if their noses are blocked.

An inflammation or swelling of the throat around the vocal chords will produce a characteristic croupy cough which is harsh, barking, dry and rather brassy. Breathing will be obviously noisy, often sounding worse when the child breathes in. Croup is usually caused by a virus infection of the throat, often during the winter months. If it occurs very suddenly, particularly during the day, it may be due to an inhaled foreign object such as a peanut or a bead. The noisy breathing may also be associated with choking and a cough.

Inflammation or blockage of the airways in the lungs themselves, will produce a characteristic wheeze such as that produced during an asthma attack. In this case the noise is more marked where the child breathes out. If the breathing problem is marked, young babies may be seen to breathe very fast. This usually means a rate of over fifty breaths per minute. They may make a grunting sound with each expiration. Older children who are having breathing difficulties may prefer to sit up and lean forward, supporting themselves on their extended arms. Sometimes leaning over a pillow or a cushion during an asthma attack may be helpful. If the child has a bluish color medical help needs to be sought immediately, because this means he is not getting enough oxygen.

CRYING

All children cry (although the amount varies considerably from one child to the next) and parents soon become used to the nature of the different types of their children's crying, which varies depending on the problem. Most babies and young children cry because of simple needs, for example hunger, need for affection, or because of discomfort (see p. 166). However prolonged crying may indicate pain or distress. If there is obvious illness the cause of the cry will be quite clear. However, if the child starts crying unusually, once the basic needs have been attended to, a possible illness should be looked for. It is often difficult to assess the cause of the cry, so medical advice may be useful.

Many children and babies may readily be comforted if the illness is not serious. However, if a young baby or infant screams or cries continuously and is not readily consoled, the underlying problem may well be serious. Older children can frequently indicate, even in simple terms, where they have their discomfort. Note that very ill babies or children may be too ill to cry at all and may lie apathetically, despite being in pain or discomfort. As a first step, strip off all clothing, check carefully for any pin sticking in or hair wrapped round a toe or finger. Then check for fever.

FEVER

Children very frequently develop a raised temperature, but it is quite frequently an indicator of only a minor illness. Most common virus infections such as colds or 'flu, ear infections or tonsillitis, may produce a raised temperature. Furthermore, many serious illnesses may occur without a fever. If the cause for fever is straightforward, such as a cold, then medical advice need not necessarily be sought, even if the fever persists for several days. Provided that the fever is controllable and the child is not deteriorating, then simple measures at home are usually sufficient. However, if the temperature rises rapidly and remains very high (above 103°F) medical advice may be useful.

LOSS OF APPETITE

This is often the first symptom of a child being unwell and is particularly so in a very young baby. Parents know the eating habits of their children very well and are frequently aware that a change in the feeding pattern is the first sign that all is not well. In association with a change of appetite, diarrhea or vomiting may occur, and it is important to remember that these symptoms do not necessarily indicate a disturbance of the stomach or bowel; these symptoms frequently occur with other infections such as tonsillitis, ear infection, urinary infection or other general illness.

Over a longer period of time a child who fails to gain weight, or in fact loses weight quickly, will also need further advice and perhaps investigation unless there is a clear reason for the weight loss. Even straightforward common ailments may stop the child from eating normally for long enough, perhaps only a few days, for some weight loss to occur, but provided the appetite returns at the end of the illness this should not cause concern.

PAIN

Pain may be very difficult to assess, particularly in the young baby. Although crying can be a symptom of pain, it may be a more general indicator of a general feeling of being unwell. A doctor, however, may be able to find the cause of the pain during a physical examination. Younger children have difficulty in localizing pain and frequently a sore throat or painful ear may produce apparent pain in the abdomen or neck.

Pain originating in the abdomen may seem always to be near the navel in a child, when in fact it is occurring elsewhere in the abdomen. Here again a doctor may gain valuable information from examination of the abdomen. Older children may readily localize pain in the appropriate part of the body, as well as giving more sophisticated information such as time of onset, frequency and possible factors which produce the pain or relieve it.

POSTURE AND MOVEMENT

Further information about the site of pain or discomfort may be gained from observing the child's movements. For example, if a limb is damaged or affected by a disease then the child will be reluctant to use it or will find it distressing to have it moved or touched. It is important to take seriously a symptom of limping or non-use of a limb. Once again, however, children have some difficulty in localizing pain, and very often a pain in the hip in a young child may be described as a painful knee.

As in adults, a certain posture may be taken up by a child which gives him greatest relief. Abdominal pain is sometimes relieved by drawing the knees up to the abdomen and the child will be very reluctant to straighten out. Similarly, pain in the back of the neck, which is sometimes a symptom of meningitis, may be made worse by moving the legs. From a general point of view a very ill child or baby may remain unusually still and appear floppy. They may seem indifferent to their surroundings or people who are with them. Such stillness or lack of movement should be treated seriously and medical advice sought urgently.

CARING FOR THE SICK CHILD AT HOME

Parents vary in their attitude to illness and while

some would prefer to look after their children at home, others would have them cared for in hospital. Most common illnesses do not need hospital admission and it is certainly preferable that convalescence from a more serious illness, which has required admission, be done at home. Although children's hospital wards are now much more welcoming and pleasant, most children would prefer to remain at home with their toys, family and familiar surroundings. Admission to hospital involves considerable disruption of the family routine, and parents often feel that the care of their child is taken out of their own hands, although nowadays parents are positively encouraged to be involved in the needs of their child while on the ward.

The early stages of an illness may be very worrying for parents, particularly when the nature of the problem is unclear. It is important to observe the child closely and note any changes, as an illness may progress quite rapidly. Advice from a doctor, and perhaps an office visit can be very reassuring, and may well be adequate to keep the child out of hospital. Infection, particularly respiratory and bowel, and the common childhood ailments (such as chicken pox) are the most common cause of illness in children. Although the specific medical treatment for these problems may vary, there are practical considerations common to them all.

STAYING IN BED

The child will probably choose himself whether he wants to be in bed. There is usually no need to go to bed if the child feels well enough to be up, and the temperature has come down. During the day he may prefer to lie on the sofa in the living room rather than feeling isolated in the bedroom. He can still feel part of the family and watch them working and playing. There are also other distractions such as the television. But a child who is particularly miserable may want the peace and quiet of his own bed, where he may well sleep for long periods.

While it is wise to have familiar toys and possessions in the room, the bed itself should be uncluttered. Early in the illness children will often prefer books or quiet toys, but as they feel better they will want to be more active. A child confined to bed for a time will enjoy the novelty of something new each day, even if it is a cheap book or puzzle, and they will also love to have their parents spend some extra time talking, playing or reading to them.

TREATING FEVER

Fever is a very common accompaniment to illness, particularly in childen. They often produce surpris-

ingly high temperatures, which do not necessarily reflect the severity of the illness. Infection by both bacteria (which may require antibiotics) and viruses (which do not) may produce the same degree of fever, but attempts need not be made to reduce it completely to normal. On the other hand it is important not to encourage a high temperature by wrapping up the child. The myth of 'keeping warm' should be re-read as 'keeping comfortable'. Often light bedclothes are enough, and if the temperature is very high, specific measures should be used to reduce it. As a response to the high temperature, the body may sweat naturally which helps the loss of heat by evaporation. Shivering may be a sign of a very high temperature and is often seen as 'rigors'.

A thermometer at home is a useful guide to when to treat a fever, but it is important not to concentrate on actual temperature without taking into account the appearance and degree of discomfort of the child. Nowadays, normal temperature is usually given as 100°F rectally, and 98.6°F from the mouth (under the tongue) in the older child. For most home situations, a rectal temperature is most accurate and causes only minor discomfort to the young child. Commercially available temperature strips which are placed on the forehead are wildly inaccurate.

There are several procedures which help to bring the temperature down. Provided the bedroom itself is not cold the upper clothing may be removed and the child's trunk sponged with lukewarm water and allowed to dry in the air. This may be repeated several times. Do not use cold water or place the child in a cold bath, as this may in fact make the temperature worse by reducing the flow of blood through the skin, so that heat cannot escape. Acetaminophen either in liquid or pill form is a useful medication for reducing the temperature and can be given four to six times during the day in a dose suggested on the packet. Aspirin is now not recommended for children or adolescents because of the possible risk of a very rare illness, Reye's syndrome, which can occur in children after taking aspirin. If the temperature remains very high or the child develops unusual behavior such as confusion or delirium, then medical advice should be sought promptly.

FOOD AND DRINK

Many children will not feel like eating solid food when they are unwell. However it is very important that they be allowed to drink plenty of fluids, particularly if a fever is also present or the weather is warm. Fluids are also very important if the child has diarrhea or vomiting. When vomiting and diarrhea are the major symptoms of the illness, it is best to stop all solid food and milk and give just clear fluids. In childen under three or four this fluid is best given in the form of commercially available rehydration solutions, which are available at the drugstore. Older children may manage on diluted ginger ale, apple juice or flat lemonade. Do not try to make up a rehydration solution at home.

Clear fluids should be continued for a day or two and then a normal diet gradually re-introduced over the next few days. For younger children this should include gradually increasing the strength of milk over two days, and for the older child a bland diet may be introduced after a day or so. Do not worry if the child has not taken solid food for several days. Most children can tolerate many days without food, provided they are drinking adequately. In the convalescent phase some children will remain rather difficult about eating. If this occurs some attempt should be made to choose particularly appetizing or interesting food, provided it is appropriate and sensible.

MEDICINES

Apart from acetaminophen, your doctor may pre-scribe a specific medication such as an antibiotic. Most of these medicines are available in a form appropriate for children, either in a flavored syrup or in small pills. Fortunately there are now a number of sugar-free preparations available which are more appropriate. Generally it does not matter whether the child takes pill or syrup; it will depend on the child's preference and ability to swallow. Many children dislike taking medication, and it may be necessary either to disguise a crushed pill, or perhaps to make a game of the procedure, such as 'Some for dolly and some for you'.

ISOLATION

In theory childen with an infectious illness should be kept out of the way of other children so as to prevent them passing it on. In practice, this is difficult to do, and often an illness is at its most infectious before anybody realizes that it is more than just a simple cold or flu. Many infections, such as chicken pox, are very readily caught in a family; this is often inevitable, and should be anticipated. However, if there are very young children in a household it is sensible to keep them out of the way of a child who is obviously unwell until it is clear that the child is improving.

A child should probably not be taken outside until the infection is improving and the child feels better. It is difficult to give advice about the timing of return to school, but in general since most infections are spread by droplets from the nose or throat, it seems sensible to ensure that the child no longer has a productive cough or runny nose, that he feels better and the fever has subsided, and that any previous rash has faded or completely dis-appeared. After two days on antibiotics, children with minor bacterial illness may return to school.

GOING TO HOSPITAL

The number of children with conditions or diseases which require hospital treatment are, relatively, few – but most parents will at some time find them-selves facing an emergency.

Not all emergencies will need hospital admission but it is important to call the doctor straightaway, or if the emergency seems very serious, call an ambulance or the police.

Another main reason for going to hospital is for testing and evaluation. Some investigations require admission to hospital for a day or two or a prolonged stay during the day in one of the hospital wards. Testing may need to be performed over a period of time, and it is often done for a number of reasons, such as severe weight loss, prolonged

EMERGENCIES	
Take your child to hospital or phone for an ambulance in any of the following situations.	
Looks very ill	Very weak or floppy, or even semi-conscious; unresponsive. Very pale or bluish (cyanosis)
Convulsion	May be obvious with shaking limbs, or may be just stiffening of the body. May not need admission, but if a new event for that child, should be examined by a doctor
Severe pain	Sometimes difficult to be sure if pain is the problem. If in doubt, ask for advice.
Persistent diarrhea and vomiting	Signs of dehydration such as a dry mouth, fast heart beat, poor urine output, lethargy
Persistent bleeding from injury	See first aid section, p. 276
Accidents	eg: burns, scalds, head injuries (see first aid section) or ingestion of poisons, tablets or solid objects
Breathing difficulties	eg: choking, obvious breathlessness, asthma or croup

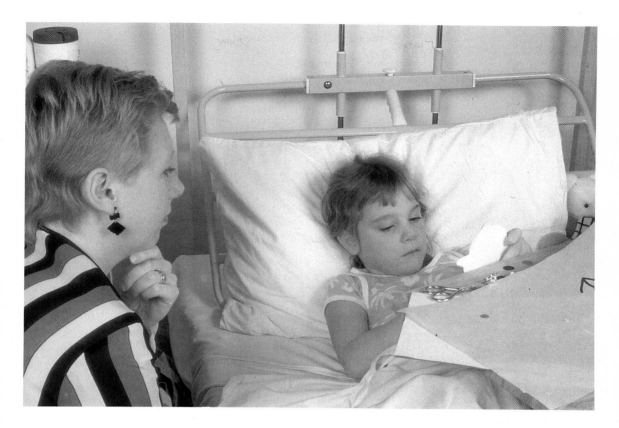

Even though your child may be bedridden in hospital, there are still interesting things to do, such as cutting out and gluing.

diarrhea, investigation of growth disorders, or evaluation of breathing problems. The reasons for these investigations should be explained to you by your doctor or the hospital staff.

Finally, your child may have to go to hospital for an operation. These can either be 'acute', such as appendicitis, requiring immediate treatment, or 'routine', such as repairing a hernia, a tonsillectomy, adenoidectomy, or insertion of tubes in the ears to treat serous otitis media (see p. 266).

PREPARING FOR HOSPITAL

It is very important to take some time to explain to a child why he is going to hospital either for a short stay, for evaluation, or for an operation, or because he is unwell. Even if the admission is unexpected, spend a few moments explaining simply to the child what is going to happen and why. Children are able to understand a great deal, and it is important not to talk to others in front of them without explaining what is going on. Their fantasies, worries and misconceptions are often far worse than the reality and they are usually reassured by a factual explanation. This may need to be repeated but it is important to be clear and tell them that hospitals are to help them get well. They should be reassured that it is not a form of punishment (they are prone to irrational feelings of guilt), and that they will soon be well and coming home again.

IN THE WARD

It is important to take some favorite toys, games and books along to the hospital, as children get considerable reassurance by having familiar objects around them. Childen's wards should provide sleeping facilities for at least one parent. It is often possible to put a bed next to the child's own bed on the ward. You should always ask for accommodation and expect to stay with your child (particularly if he is under five) for the whole of his hospital visit.

During the early stages of the hospital stay, it is important for parents to explain again what is going on and to point out the various activities going on around them, which may be unusual to the child. It is important to maintain a sense of normality, and it is nice for parents to wear their usual day clothing, bring photos and other familiar objects, and perhaps bring other relatives to visit.

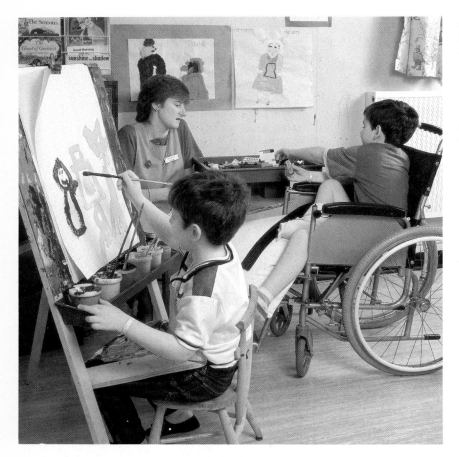

Many pediatric wards now have separate supervised playrooms, where mobile children can play with a variety of toys and join in activities such as painting and modeling.

OPERATIONS

It is very nice if you can accompany your child to the operating room, so it is worth asking if this is possible. Hospitals vary in their policy here. While in principal it is desirable for parents always to go with their child to the anesthetic, there are sometimes practical difficulties with this. It is useful for parents to discuss the policy in their local hospital before the child is admitted.

A simple explanation of what will happen in the operation is important for the child. Children have many fantasies about which parts of their anatomy they may lose while they are asleep and it is often very important to reassure them that they will not lose anything essential. Operations on the genitalia in boys (such as circumcision) often provoke such anxiety, and they will need to be reassured that their penis will remain in place! It is useful to describe the 'special sleep' of the anesthetic, so that the child understands he will not feel anything during the procedure. It is also important that the parents are there to comfort the child when he wakes from the operation.

PLAY AND EDUCATION

Most pediatric wards are now equipped with play areas, teachers and various equipment. This means that most children enjoy their hospital experience. Play workers have special training so that they can find the most enjoyable activities for children to do, in spite of any possible restrictions due to the child's condition. Every child of school age in hospital needs continuing education, and it is the duty of the local school department to provide this. Hospital teachers are specially trained in the problems of handling children's education while on a hospital ward.

GOING HOME

Parents should remember that the child may be difficult when he returns home. He is often demanding, irritable and clinging, and may often regress to a more babyish stage. For instance, it is very common for children to start wetting the bed again. How long this stage lasts varies, but it makes it easier to cope with if you expect it.

Common ailments in young babies

It is always distressing when a young baby is ill, but fortunately, with careful treatment, the common ailments of infancy can pass fairly rapidly with no long-lasting effects. However if you are at all worried about your baby's condition, telephone your doctor for advice.

Acne neonatorum
This is a very common rash which occurs usually in newborn babies. There are small red spots with a white or yellowy raised center to them. They appear on the face or trunk and may be few in number, or rarely quite extensive. They usually fade over a few weeks and are entirely harmless.

Diarrhea
The frequency of bowel movements in babies varies a great deal (see p. 109), but diarrhea is usually very watery, almost like urine, and is usually foul smelling and very frequent – much more frequent than your baby's normal pattern. Watery diarrhea is very serious in babies under twelve months, especially if accompanied by vomiting, so consult your doctor immediately.

If accompanied by vomiting, the most common cause of diarrhea is gastroenteritis, or infection of the bowel. If the baby is not unwell and vomiting and diarrhea is not serious, then stopping the normal milk feedings in a bottle fed baby for a day or so, is usually enough. Substitute one of the commercially available rehydration mixtures. Breastfed babies may usually continue their normal feeding pattern.

Eye problems
The commonest problem in a young baby is conjunctivitis (pink or sticky eye, see p. 193). This usually responds to frequent cleaning with sterile water, and sometimes the use of antibiotic drops or ointment obtained from the doctor. A rare cause of persistent conjunctivitis is due to a blocked tear duct which may need further medical attention.

A squint sometimes causes parents concern. This is a problem of development of the muscles of the eye and may eventually require treatment. However many babies do not align their eyes and may appear to squint for the first few months of life; in most cases this will have corrected by the age of six months. However, if parents are still concerned at this stage then medical opinion is essential because sometimes an operation is necessary. Some babies do appear to have a squint because of an extra thickness of skin at the corner of their eye, but the eyes themselves are normal.

Failure to gain weight or weight loss
There are many causes of a baby failing to gain weight appropriately, although it is uncommon. The usual cause is difficulty in establishing a normal feeding pattern, and you can get very good advice from your doctor. However, if the problem persists or there are other symptoms of illness, there may well be other medical problems causing the weight loss, and these may require investigation in hospital. Serious problems may be associated with a change in well-being and slowing of development.

Hernias
Organs inside the abdomen, such as the bowel, sometimes bulge through a weakness in the abdominal wall. This is called a hernia. In babies, a hernia usually occurs in one of two places. The commonest is at the navel (umbilical), and the other is in the groin (inguinal). An umbilical hernia appears a week or two after birth, and in some parts of the world, such as Africa, it occurs in almost every baby. The swelling is more noticeable when the baby cries, but it is quite soft and can be flattened completely with a little pressure. It usually enlarges over the first few months, then gradually disappears.

No treatment is needed as it cures itself. The small hole in the abdominal wall, which allows the gut to escape under the skin, gets smaller with age and eventually closes. Strapping the hernia does not make it disappear earlier; in fact there is some evidence that it slows things down. An occasional child needs an operation at six years or later if the hernia has not gone.

Inguinal hernias produce a swelling in the groin which often extends down into the scrotum around the testicle. The swelling comes and goes with crying. These hernias occur more often in premature babies; in them the hernia may disappear spontaneously, but in all other circumstances an operation is needed.

A worrying complication of an inguinal hernia is strangulation, when a piece of bowel may become trapped. The hernia then becomes hard and tender, and there is often vomiting. If this happens, you must contact a doctor urgently.

Common ailments in young babies

Infantile eczema

This is a common skin disease which occurs in children of all ages although usually it begins about three to six months after birth. It is commoner in families who have a history of allergy (see p. 270). The skin, usually in the elbows, behind the knees, the diaper area, and sometimes over the face and behind the ears, is red and sometimes weeping but may also become dry and cracked. The site of the eczematous skin may become infected. Eczema is usually managed by simple moisturizing creams but may require treatment by a gentle steroid cream or anti-infectious cream, which should be prescribed by the doctor.

Infections

Early signs of infection in a young baby are often vague. They include loss of appetite, vomiting, fever and irritability or lethargy. The commonest problems in this age group include respiratory infection, gastroenteritis, an infectious rash and occasionally a urine infection. Most infections are caused by viruses and are not helped by antibiotics. However if the infection is bacterial, your doctor will choose an appropriate antibiotic to clear it.

If the cause of the baby's illness is unclear, your doctor's advice is necessary, particularly for the diagnosis of a urine infection. However if the cause is obviously an upper respiratory infection, then the baby can be looked after quite easily at home. This infection is, of course, a simple cold. But the problem for young babies particularly is difficulty with breathing and feeding because of a blocked nose. Coughing or sneezing may develop during this infection, which is the normal response for clearing the airway of mucus. Decongestants and nose drops may help but should not be used for more than a few days.

Bronchiolitis is a relatively common viral infection of babies under twelve months of age. The symptoms may start with a mild cold, but the baby rapidly goes on to have marked breathing difficulty, poor feeding and a cough. If there are feeding difficulties and the baby is having difficulty in breathing, admission to hospital may be necessary.

Pustules or boils

These infective boils occur from time to time in young babies. They usually require antibiotics given by mouth to clear them up. However on occasion, if severe, they may mean the baby has to be admitted to hospital.

Thrush (Yeast)

Thrush may occur in the mouth as a white coating to the tongue, and in the diaper area as a red, weeping rash which is sometimes confused with simple diaper rash (see p. 192). If normal treatment for diaper rash does not help and it gets worse, then thrush may well be responsible. Both mouth thrush and thrush in the diaper area require treatment from your doctor, who will prescribe a special antibiotic called nystatin, as drops or a cream, which eliminates the yeast causing the problem.

Vomiting

Vomiting has many causes in young babies and many are harmless if the vomiting is not prolonged (see p. 191). There are, however, other more serious causes of vomiting. The vomiting is usually obvious – large amounts of milk will come back, often projected several feet in front of the baby. Serious causes of vomiting include obstruction to the bowel or infection such as gastroenteritis; always consult a doctor.

Another cause may be the relatively common problem of pyloric stenosis, which usually affects babies between two and four months. This is an abnormality of the muscle which controls the exit of milk from the stomach into the intestines. Over a period of weeks the muscle becomes thickened and blocks the outlet of the stomach. Vomiting occurs during feeding or just afterwards, is often profuse and, rarely, will have a small amount of blood mixed with it. The baby is often well, although hungry and may lose weight. It is important that a doctor is consulted as this condition requires admission to hospital and probably an operation. Any cause of vomiting which is unexplained and worrying should of course be discussed with your doctor.

Common ailments in children

Older children are in a way easier to deal with when ill – they can explain reasonably accurately how they feel or where they may have a pain, and it is also easier for them to understand the necessity for treatment, even if it is only to take a regular dose of medicine. If children feel ill, they generally go to bed when they need to; the most taxing time for parents is usually the recovery period when boredom is the worst symptom!

It is sometimes rather more difficult to get the co-operation of a toddler, who may not have the intellectual development to understand what is happening to him, and may also be very resistant to treatment. Young children especially may be wary or even frightened of medical personnel, and most doctors and others who regularly care for children will dispense with their white coats and will have developed strategies to put children at their ease. It is undoubtedly true however that children's fears have to be taken seriously and it can involve a great deal of patience and tact on the part of both parents and doctors.

If your child develops one of the common infectious diseases of childhood, such as chicken pox, you should always contact your pediatrician to confirm the diagnosis, even if he doesn't need to prescribe any medicine or suggest any specific treatment. This is because all doctors have a general obligation to notify some of these infectious diseases to the public health authorities, in order to provide them with a record of their frequency in the community.

Appendicitis

This relatively common serious abdominal problem usually occurs over the age of five. A child often complains of feeling generally unwell and slowly abdominal pain develops around the navel. Over a period of hours the pain gradually seems to move to the right lower side of the abdomen. The child may vomit, have a fever, and may also have constipation although diarrhea can also be present.

These symptoms may also be found in other conditions such as mesenteric adenitis (see under sore throats and tonsillitis). If you suspect appendicitis, and your doctor agrees, your child will usually be referred to hospital for an opinion by a surgeon. Treatment is, of course, by surgical removal of the appendix.

Other conditions which may be confused with appendicitis include urinary tract infection, recurrent abdominal pain (see p. 268), and gynecological problems in older girls.

Bone and joint disorders

There are a great many minor variations of anatomy which occur in children. Most of these are self-correcting as the child gets older and include bow legs, knock knees, flat feet, in-toeing and bent toes. A pediatrician or school doctor will advise on these minor abnormalities if the parents are concerned. More serious is a bent spine (scoliosis) which will need hospital advice. Other conditions which require treatment in hospital include arthritis, broken bones, and rare diseases which cause bending of the bones.

Breath-holding attacks

These are also common in young children. They are frightening to parents but in general are completely harmless. A child who has a tantrum or cries or becomes upset, often when being scolded or thwarted in some activity, will suddenly stop breathing and go blue or red in the face. He may become briefly unconscious but usually wakes up without any effects. Breath-holding attacks are sometimes used manipulatively by children, and parents should do their best to keep calm during one. You will need to comfort your child afterwards as it is frightening for the child as well. However, try also not to allow your child to get his own way unreasonably. The advice on handling tantrums on page 231 may be helpful here.

Common ailments in children

Chest infections

Three types of chest infection are common in children. Bronchitis and pneumonia are caused usually by a bacterial infection of the airways or lungs. The child is usually breathless, sometimes with a wheeze and chest discomfort. The cough is marked and may be productive of thick sputum, although most children swallow their sputum rather than coughing it out. Antibiotics are usually required. Sometimes the infection may be severe, in which case admission to hospital for a few days of antibiotic therapy and chest physiotherapy may be necessary to loosen the accumulation of fluid in the lungs.

Chicken pox

This very common infection of children is particularly contagious and often spreads through the family. Before the rash appears, there is a period of fever, headache and sore throat. The rash is characteristic: there is a red raised spot with a clear vesicle (small blister) on the top. The rash is very itchy. Several batches of these spots will appear over a period of a few days – perhaps three or four batches.

The vesicles will usually heal to scabs and disappear by themselves, although unfortunately they often become infected because of scratching. The child may feel happier in bed, and the itchiness can be relieved at least temporarily by calamine lotion. Acetaminophen is useful for the temperature. If infection does occur on the rash and the child remains unwell, ask a doctor's advice.

Constipation

Constipation may occasionally be part of another illness. However, generally it is due to difficulty with toilet training or a diet deficient in high fiber. Occasionally it may be associated with a small tear (anal fissure) at the outlet of the bowel (anus). This causes pain at the moment of opening the bowels, so the child may resist doing this in order to avoid the pain.

It is worth trying to resolve the constipation at home by increasing roughage in the diet by introducing high-fiber cereals, wholewheat bread, plenty of fresh fruit and vegetables, and avoiding highly refined convenience foods. A gentle laxative, such as 6 fl oz of pure juice, may be tried but this should not go on for longer than a few days. If this fails and the child continues to have symptoms, ask your doctor's advice.

Convulsions (fits, seizures)

For parents to see their own child having a convulsion is very disturbing, particularly if they have never seen one before. However, seizures are fairly common under the age of five years, especially in association with a high fever. Most of these so-called febrile convulsions are usually harmless and very rarely cause any damage.

Often the child will have been feverish with a cold or other illness just prior to the fit and will frequently have seemed quite well otherwise. Suddenly he may go rigid, stop breathing, perhaps go blue or red in the face and sometimes pass urine or have his bowels open. After this rigid phase the child may then shake one or all of his limbs for a few minutes. It is rare for a febrile convulsion to last more than ten minutes.

While the seizure is in progress the parents should try to keep calm, turn the child on to his side to the recovery position (see p. 279), in order to prevent inhaling vomit, and perhaps loosen the clothing. It is probably unnecessary to try and open the mouth or attempt to stop the child biting on his tongue. If the fit continues beyond ten minutes then call an ambulance.

Once the fit has stopped then the temperature should be lowered as mentioned on page 257. If this is the first convulsion the child should be taken to hospital so that the cause of the infection can be determined. Sometimes a convulsion may be due to a serious infection such as meningitis or encephalitis and these conditions will need treatment in hospital.

About one third to one half of children who have one febrile convulsion will go on to have further fits in association with fever during the first five years of life. Occasionally it is recommended that such children are given anti-convulsant drugs on a regular basis to prevent these attacks from happening. However, this treatment should be discussed with a pediatrician or your family practitioner.

An even smaller proportion of such children will go on to have true epileptic attacks during childhood and adult life. Children who are epileptic can lead very normal lives provided they are given regular anti-convulsant medication. The side effects of these medications are generally minor and often the medication need only be continued until puberty. A discussion of these medications again should be undertaken with your family practitioner or the pediatrician.

Common ailments in children

Coughs and colds

Colds are common and most children will expect to have several in a year, particularly during the first two winters of life. The severity of illness in children is often made worse by living in a smoky city, or in families where the parents smoke.

The vast majority of these respiratory infections are caused by viruses, so antibiotics are not indicated, at least in the initial stages. Some colds which persist or seem to get worse may be due to a new infection by a bacterium, and in this situation antibiotics prescribed by your doctor may be necessary.

Coughing and sneezing are normal responses to blockages of the airway. It is important therefore, that during the early stages of the cold, when sputum and mucus are present, that the normal cough is *not* prevented by cough medicines. Most colds will resolve themselves in a week or so, going through the normal sequence of events: sore throat, runny nose, fever, and productive cough which may last for several days, followed by a gradual drying up of the runny nose, and eventually a dry non-productive cough which may last for a week or so, especially annoying at night.

In the early stages, the blocked nose may be treated by simple saline nose drops, which are useful particularly in young children. Decongestants such as ephedrine or triprolitine plus ephidrine (and many others), can be helpful temporarily when a baby's nose is very blocked. They should not be used for more than a day or two as they can make the obstruction worse. A cool mist vaporizer in the bedroom, perhaps with the addition of menthol and eucalyptus, may be helpful for a blocked nose and accompanying painful ears. Soothing drinks and cough drops containing lemon or glycerine may be helpful, particularly in the stages of a dry cough. Sometimes a cough suppressant should be used, but only on the advice of your doctor.

A child who coughs persistently, particularly at night, without other signs or symptoms of a cold, may in fact have underlying asthma, or perhaps have mucus in the back of the throat from enlarged adenoids. A doctor's opinion may be useful in this case.

Croup

This condition is caused by an infection of the upper throat causing swelling and narrowing of the airway. It produces a characteristic harsh cough (like a seal barking), and some difficulty with breathing, usually on the intake of breath. It may occur more than once in the same child.

Croup can be worrying to parents the first time they experience it in a child, but parents who have seen it before know that placing the child in a humid room, such as running the hot water in the shower to make steam, or in the kitchen with the kettle boiling, produces some relief. If this does not help, and the child seems to deteriorate, it is important that a doctor sees the child quickly. Call your pediatrician, or if symptoms develop suddenly, it may be necessary to take the child directly to hospital.

There is no specific treatment other than humidity apart from managing the temperature and discomfort. A child admitted to hospital will usually spend a day or two there, in a mist tent.

Diarrhea and vomiting

There are a great many causes of diarrhea and vomiting in children. Often the symptoms are a reaction to a more generalized illness, and are not necessarily related to infection or other upset of the bowel itself. But gastroenteritis, caused by either a viral or a bacterial infection, could occur in any home, although family hygiene does play a part in its spread. Vomiting usually precedes the diarrhea by a day or so and is often settling down when the diarrhea is at its worst. The diarrhea may be just like water and can be green, yellow or clear. Occasionally there is blood or mucus also present.

The treatment, as mentioned in the section on young babies, involves stopping solid food and taking clear fluids only for a day or so, gradually re-introducing a normal diet. If abdominal pain is present, or blood, then it is important to consult your doctor. Only on rare occasions are antibiotics or other antidiarrheal medicines prescribed.

Food poisoning, which usually means eating food contaminated by bacteria, may produce similar symptoms as for gastroenteritis. These may come on quite rapidly after the ingestion of the food. The vomiting, diarrhea and abdominal pain can be quite severe. The treatment is the same as for gastroenteritis.

Common ailments in children

Ear infections

Infections of the middle ear (otitis media) are common in children. They produce ear pain, temperature and irritability in younger children. Ear infections often follow a previous upper respiratory infection such as a cold. It is important that the child is seen soon by a doctor who will examine the ear and usually prescribe an antibiotic. It is important that the ear is rechecked by the doctor a week or so later and the hearing reassessed, as persisting fluid in the middle ear may interfere with hearing over a long period of time. 'Glue ear', or serous otitis media, is the name given to this situation. If you feel that your child's hearing is affected after a respiratory infection, or over a longer period of time, it is important to have it checked formally. Occasionally an operation to insert small drainage tubes (grommets) in the eardrum will be necessary.

Infection of the outer ear (otitis externa) may also produce pain. It is common in children who swim regularly, play with their ears, or insert foreign objects into the external ear, although it may occur spontaneously. The ear will require antibiotic drops for correct treatment.

Ear infections are sometimes aggravated by large adenoids which prevent drainage of fluid from the internal ear. If the child is having frequent ear infections or has poor hearing then removal of the adenoids may be necessary.

Eye problems

The eyes may become inflamed as part of general illness, for example, in measles or as part of hay fever. However infection of the eye itself is also common. Conjunctivitis may be due to bacteria or viruses. In general it is usually assumed that a bacterium is responsible and antibiotics are prescribed either as drops or as an ointment. If the inflammation does not settle down after a few days the doctor may suggest a change of antibiotic. Conjunctivitis can be highly contagious, so meticulous handwashing plus the use of paper towels will provide the best home defense against spread.

Infection of the base of the eyelashes (a stye) is common in children. Local treatment such as a warm compress may be helpful to ease the discomfort, but antibiotic ointment is also usually necessary. Sometimes styes occur in several crops, and it is important that the child be encouraged to wash his hands thoroughly and not touch the infected eye.

Hepatitis

There are two varieties of hepatitis. The commonest is infectious hepatitis (hepatitis A), caused by eating food contaminated with infected feces. Although thought to be more common in other countries, it is nevertheless present throughout the US. Symptoms include a long period of general aches and pains, headache, nausea and vomiting, and aching limbs. After this period a yellow color or jaundice is noted in the eyes and skin. The urine may appear very dark, and occasionally the feces may be lighter than usual. The illness is often prolonged and treatment includes temperature control, providing an appetizing diet, preferably high in carbohydrate and low in fat, and during the vomiting period, plenty of fluids are important. Admission to hospital may be necessary for young children or severe cases.

The other form of hepatitis, known as hepatitis B, is carried in the bloodstream. Pregnant women who may be at risk of carrying the disease can have their blood tested to see if they are 'surface antigen positive' (HBsAg). There is a vaccine available which can be given to any baby at risk of infection from the mother at birth.

Infestations

Infestations with parasites are also common, and are not just associated with poor hygiene in the home. They are usually easy to treat and include scabies, headlice and fleas. A school nurse or doctor may provide useful information or you can ask your own general practitioner. Headlice (nits), which occur frequently in school-age children, are eradicated by washing the hair with special shampoo.

There are many worm infections which occur throughout the world, but the commonest in the US are pinworms (Enterobius). These are harmless, although they produce symptoms such as anal irritation and itching and may keep the child awake at night. The diagnosis is made by examining the child's anus, underwear or feces, when the worms will be seen as small, white, wriggling threads. A doctor may prove the diagnosis by obtaining some eggs from the anal area and examining them under a microscope. They are easily treated with oral medication.

Common ailments in children

Influenza

Several virus infections may be responsible for the symptoms of influenza. These are similar to those in adults, including fever, aching joints and limbs, headache, nausea and a variable degree of misery. There are no specific diagnostic tests; the symptoms usually provide the diagnosis. Treatment includes temperature control, fluids and whatever the child wants to eat. As for an adult, the child may prefer to remain in bed for a day or two although the illness is not as prolonged as in adults. Although influenza vaccinations are available in the Fall, they are usually only given to patients who have other serious diseases.

Measles

There ought to be no reason for your child to have this illness, except perhaps in a very mild form, as there is an effective vaccine (see p. 253). However, when it is contracted, it starts with an obvious upper respiratory infection like severe bronchitis, and then is followed by a red rash which starts on the face or behind the ears and rapidly spreads to the trunk. Spots, which are separate to begin with, often join together and the child may look completely covered. After a few days it gradually fades, and may change to a brownish color before it disappears. As the rash disappears the temperature, which may be quite high, will gradually improve and the child will feel better.

Sometimes measles is complicated by an infection of the throat, ears or chest, in which case antibiotics may be necessary. Other associated symptoms may include vomiting, diarrhea, arthritis, and, very rarely, inflammation of the brain. There is no specific treatment other than encouraging the consumption of fluids, managing the temperature with acetaminophen, and general support and care at home. A doctor's office visit is not essential, but may be helpful if the parents are anxious or if secondary complications occur.

Blood tests to confirm the diagnosis are, however, important for public health reporting.

Meningitis

Meningitis is an infection of the lining surrounding the brain and spinal cord. It is a very frightening illness because it sometimes leads to death or handicap. However, the type that is caused by viruses is often a mild illness, and that caused by bacteria can be completely cured if treated early with antibiotics. The commonest form of meningitis is caused by H. flu. A vaccine – HIB – given at eighteen to 24 months will protect against this.

The symptoms include fever, irritability, convulsions and drowsiness or unconsciousness. In a child over two years there is a characteristic stiffness of the neck, where the child is unable to move his chin down on to his chest. In babies, the signs of the disease are less obvious, but bulging of the fontanel is very characteristic.

One particular type of meningitis is caused by a bacterium known as meningococcus. This can be very dangerous and causes a rash with tiny bruises anywhere on the body. If your child has a fever and such a rash contact your doctor urgently.

Mouth problems

Mouth infections are common and may be produced by herpes virus, causing ulceration around the mouth or on the tongue and inside the mouth, and bacterial infections which often cause crusting ulcers on the lips themselves. This may be a form of impetigo, which will need antibiotic ointment from your doctor.

Some mouth ulcers are small and not painful and older children may manage with simple analgesia. However younger children often find it difficult to eat, and more particularly, to drink, in the presence of these ulcers. A child may need admitting to hospital for a day or two if he is completely unable to take fluids.

Mumps

This illness produces a characteristic swelling of one or both of the salivary glands which are just in front of the ears. There is a swelling of the face in this area, which is tender and the child generally feels unwell. Parents often worry about inflammation of the testicles in boys, but this is very unusual in children and very rarely causes sterility, even if it does occur. There is no specific treatment for mumps and care is similar for the other infectious diseases. Routine immunization with MMR has almost eliminated this illness.

Common ailments in children

Recurrent abdominal pain

Abdominal pain is very common in later childhood – it usually occurs around the area of the navel. Urinary tract infection has to be ruled out before further investigations are made. Some people think that this sort of pain may be a form of migraine, especially when it recurs. It is common in families where migraine headaches occur and there may be food sensitivity involved such as cheese, chocolate and some food additives. There may be episodes of diarrhea which occur with the pain, and the attacks are provoked by periods of stress.

Treatment involves attempting to remove any offending food-stuffs, looking into possible psychological factors, and occasionally specific medication is indicated. Simple analgesia such as acetaminophen is valuable.

Roseola infantum

This rather less common infection in children is characterized by a long period, usually five or six days, of high fever, without other symptoms. Parents and doctors are often worried during this period because of the absence of any other diagnostic sign. On the sixth day, a pale pink rash comes out over the whole trunk, and the temperature rapidly resolves.

The treatment involves control of the high temperature, but sometimes these children are seen by doctors or even admitted to hospital because of the difficulty in making early diagnosis. In young children a febrile convulsion (see p. 264) may occur during the fever period. There is no other physical treatment, and the illness has no serious after-effects.

Rubella (German measles)

This is a mild infection which may show itself only as a slight fever with a pale pink rash covering the face and trunk. There may be occasional large glands in the throat and a mild upper respiratory infection. Complications are rare. Again, treatment is supportive. It is important that the child does not come into contact with any women who may be in early pregnancy (see p. 13), and all children should be vaccinated at fifteen months via MMR.

Scarlet fever

This is due to a bacterial infection (strep), usually following a sore throat or tonsillitis. The child develops a fever and is rapidly covered with a continuous red rash which may last for a few days. It should be treated with antibiotics from your doctor.

Sinusitis

This is a relatively rare infection, usually seen in older children. The signs and symptoms are similar to adults: pain in the bone under the eyes or around the nose, with a high temperature and sometimes the production of thick mucus from the nose. Antibiotics are sometimes necessary, but more immediate relief may be given by steam inhalations, pain relief such as acetaminophen, and nasal decongestant.

Skin problems

These are very common in children and include sunburn, boils and warts. Many of these problems can be managed with a medication available over the counter at the drugstore, which usually will do no harm and occasionally some good.

It is important not to make the condition worse, however, as many of these will improve if left alone. Warts in particular are often over-treated. They are common in children and usually resolve themselves over a period of years, but a doctor's advice is essential if these conditions prove troublesome – plantar warts in the feet can, for instance, be extremely difficult to eradicate.

Ringworm, which is not a worm infection but a fungal infection, occurs anywhere on the body, scalp or feet (athlete's foot). All these conditions are usually readily treated by prescribed medication.

Sore throats and tonsillitis

Like ear infections, a sore throat may be due to a virus infection or infection from a bacterium. It is very difficult for a doctor to decide by appearance which organism is responsible and if a child is unwell with fever, most doctors would prescribe an antibiotic.

Most children have enlarged glands in the neck. Sometimes they become very enlarged and painful during an illness like tonsillitis, but they usually resolve spontaneously. Abdominal pain may be present with a sore throat, and is

Common ailments in children

probably due to abdominal glands being infected with the same virus. This condition, called mesenteric adenitis, is sometimes confused with acute appendicitis, where abdominal pain is the major feature. The condition usually resolves on its own without treatment.

Tonsillectomy is performed far less often than it used to be. The usual indications are extremely infected or enlarged tonsils, tonsils which obstruct the mouth or airway, and when a child is missing long periods from school because of recurrent infection.

Testicular pain

A boy's testicles may be damaged by external injury such as kicking or occasionally may become unexpectedly painful, swollen, and with a blue discoloration. Abdominal pain may also be present, however, and indeed may be the major symptom. It is important therefore that the testicles are examined if a boy has abdominal pain. If the testicle becomes severely painful, with or without injury, your child should be examined by a doctor at once, as sometimes the testis becomes twisted by itself (torsion), which may require an operation. If neglected, the testicle may be irreparably damaged.

Whooping cough

Unfortunately this condition still occurs. It is most serious in young babies and toddlers, although it may occur in children or even adults. The early stages are typical of a straightforward cold – runny nose and cough – but the cough gradually becomes worse, persistent and prolonged and eventually is followed by a characteristic 'whoop', or very noisy in-drawing of the breath. Babies and toddlers may become red in the face or even blue during the coughing episodes. The cough may be associated with severe and persistent vomiting immediately following an attack. An early serious complication is a coughing attack being followed by the baby stopping breathing.

Mild attacks may be managed at home, although it is as well to get your doctor's advice. Apart from that, control of the temperature and feeding the baby immediately after a vomiting attack are all that is needed. Cough medicines are rarely helpful. In more severe cases, the baby may need to be admitted to hospital for other therapy, including feeding by tube, inhaled medication and sometimes oxygen.

Long term effects are serious in a small number of cases, and include fits, brain damage and perhaps damage to the lungs. There is no specific treatment, which is why universal immunization is so important. Young babies are particularly susceptible to this illness and should not be in contact with other children who may have the illness. Antibiotics given early in the disease, if another affected child in the family is diagnosed before the others, may prevent a severe attack.

Urinary infections

Infections in the urinary tract occur more commonly in girls although boys too may be affected. A child may complain of abdominal pain, vomiting, diarrhea, or pain on passing urine, and may want to pass urine frequently. The urine may be rather smelly and occasionally have blood in it. Children who are normally dry both day and night may start wetting the bed again or become incontinent during the daytime. Infants may be unwell without any obvious cause for their illness.

It is important that your doctor is consulted early on in order that a urine test can be taken and appropriate antibiotic treatment started. As a general rule a child should have some x-ray investigations at the local hospital to rule out any anatomical abnormality of the bladder or kidneys. An abnormality may require either medical treatment or surgical correction.

If a child still has recurrent infections then there may be a place for regular antibiotic treatment over a long period of time. This should obviously be discussed with the doctor.

ALLERGIES

Allergy is an abnormal response to the body coming into contact with a substance foreign to it. The foreign substance may be swallowed, inhaled, or just in contact with the skin. An allergic person will react to this substance in a variety of ways which may be unpleasant or even harmful, and the symptoms produced may vary depending on which part of the body has come into contact with the foreign substance.

Allergy tends to occur in families, and most allergic patients are sensitive to more than one substance. Tests for allergy to specific substances are possible but in practice are not always useful. They often serve only to confirm the presence of general allergy, rather than providing a clue to precise identification. However in a small number of cases, where a patient is allergic to only one or two substances, it is useful to identify these so that contact with them may be avoided.

Desensitization, usually in a series of injections, may be undertaken in a few individuals where only one or two offending substances can be identified. Unfortunately, for the majority of people, this form of treatment is not useful.

ASTHMA

Asthma is a common condition probably more widespread than previously thought. It involves narrowing of the airways due to constriction of the small muscles in their walls and is made worse by the production of mucus. It is often provoked by an allergic reaction to a foreign substance, but it may also be provoked by changes in the weather, exercise, the effects of emotion, infection, or sometimes without any obvious cause. It is recognized as shortness of breath accompanied by a wheezing sound from the chest and also a cough. The particular difficulty is with breathing out, which produces the characteristic wheezing. Sometimes a cough alone, often during the night, is the only sign of the condition.

Although asthma can be serious, it is now very amenable to treatment by a number of medications available, and ordinary life should be interfered with as little as possible. Many children often tend to get less severe attacks as they grow older, and may in fact not have any further attacks beyond adolescence.

Treatment involves the use of medication prescribed by the pediatrician. Some of these drugs are used on a daily basis to prevent attacks from happening, and others are taken during an acute episode to control the symptoms. There are a number of drugs available and the combination of these will vary in each patient, so it is important to follow the doctor's advice in this regard. The commonest drugs are those that relax the small muscles in the walls of the airways during an attack, such as Albuterol, which is given by mouth or inhalation, often by a sort of spray. Other drugs are used to prevent asthma, by inhalation or orally. These may be Theophylline, cromolyn, or a very small amount of steroid.

It is useful to identify any trigger factors so that these may be avoided. Taking medication before any exercise or during a cold may prevent symptoms developing. Many patients are allergic to house dust and a tiny creature, the house dust mite, which feeds on this dust. Exposure to this mite may be avoided by frequent vacuuming of the carpet and cleaning of the bed clothes.

Many parents learn to manage their child's asthma very well but it is also important to remember what to do if home management fails. A child may deteriorate rapidly in this situation. If your doctor knows the child well his advice may be useful, or alternatively take the child to the Emergency Department at your local hospital. Sometimes admission to hospital may be required for a stay of several days in order to treat the attack effectively.

Most cities have an Asthma Society which provides useful information for parents, holds meetings and discussion groups, and provides valuable support. It is well worth joining your local branch of the Society if your child is an asthma sufferer.

ECZEMA

Eczema is common in both infants and older children. While it may be due to allergy to a specific substance it is often difficult to identify this. The eczema may occur in small areas often behind the knees or on the elbows, but may also be widespread, covering the trunk, face and limbs. It is important that the treatment of your child's eczema is discussed in full with the doctor who advises on the appropriate regime. Treatment varies from the use of moisturizing creams and emollients in the bath to tar preparations and steroid preparations. Parents are often worried about the use of steroids but in practice these drugs are safe and extremely valuable if they are used correctly. Steroid creams come in a variety of strengths and most doctors will start with the most gentle preparation, gradually changing to more potent strengths if the eczema does not respond.

Allergy to food may play a very small role in the development of eczema (see below).

HAY FEVER

Hay fever is an allergic response of the lining of the nose to inhaled substances. In addition to the mucous membrane lining, the eyelids may also become inflamed. The symptoms produced include a runny nose, nasal stuffiness, itching of the nose and eyes, and eye redness.

Antihistamines may be useful to prevent these symptoms during the hay fever season which occurs in spring and early summer, because of the various pollens which are in the air at that time. Some people produce similar symptoms when in contact with cats or other furry pets. If antihistamines do not control symptoms, then other medication such as cromolyn, usually applied directly to the eyes or the nose, may give some relief. Desensitization is only occasionally helpful.

URTICARIA

The response of the skin to an allergic substance, often swallowed, may be urticaria or hives. This fairly common reaction is shown as a sudden onset of itchy raised blotches or lumps on the skin. The commonest substances are fish, nuts, aspirin, some food colorings and fruit, and occasionally insect bites, particularly fleas. However, some specific allergies are difficult to identify. Very rarely, the mouth and throat may become swollen also, producing difficulty in swallowing and even breathing. In this situation a doctor's advice on referral to hospital is very important.

Where it is known that children are allergic to specific substances it is useful to keep an antihistamine at home to treat each episode when it occurs. However it is of course best to avoid contact with the substances altogether.

DRUG ALLERGIES

Many drugs may be responsible for producing allergy, and there is a wide variety of reaction which may occur. The commonest offender is penicillin but it is extremely important to be sure that true penicillin allergy has occurred. Penicillin-like drugs, such as ampicillin, may produce a rash which is not a true penicillin allergy. A true penicillin allergy usually shows itself as urticaria, sometimes associated with joint pains and a feeling of being unwell.

True penicillin allergy is unusual and unfortunately it is often overdiagnosed. Any other drugs which are known to provoke allergic reactions should of course be avoided. Parents and the child, when he is old enough, should know the names of these.

FOOD ALLERGY

Discussion of food allergy is widespread in the media. However our understanding of this allergy is still very limited. It is alleged to cause a wide variety of disorders in children, including eczema, hyperactivity, diarrhea, weight loss and many other symptoms. However, it is very difficult to prove such allergy in individual cases and true food allergy is distinctly unusual.

There are no specific tests for food allergy. The only way of establishing allergy is by an exclusion diet which means removing various food-stuffs from the diet and gradually reintroducing them so that symptoms which may at first disappear, then recur with the re-introduction of the offending food.

The substances which are thought to be allergy-provoking include egg yolks, milk, preservatives and artificial coloring. It is sensible to avoid preservatives and colorings in any case, for all children. But it is also very important to avoid becoming too obsessive and end up by excluding everything from the child's diet. This may provoke unnecessary misery and tension between you and your child. Food allergy, if it does occur, is usually a minor problem. If parents are convinced that food allergy is important in a child's disease, the problem should first be discussed with your pediatrician.

The commonest symptom which is acknowledged to be due to food allergy is diarrhea, probably due to cow's milk protein allergy. This is usually a condition which occurs in infancy, and which usually resolves by itself after the baby has been on a cow's milk free diet for six to twelve months. The management of this should be discussed with the doctor. It is greatly over-diagnosed.

SIDS (CRIB DEATH)

Sadly, about one in every three or four hundred babies is found dead, usually in the crib, at home by one of his or her parents.

Considerable research is at present going on looking into the cause for these unexpected deaths, known medically as 'sudden infant death syndrome' (SIDS). Despite examination at autopsy, the majority of these babies have no obvious cause for their death. There are several theories which may explain these occurrences, however, and in fact there are probably several different causes which may be responsible for the death of a baby in this way. The possible causes include a congenital abnormality of heart function, a sudden drop in blood pressure for an unknown reason, a sudden and overwhelming infection, an abnormality of the breathing mechanism or other rare abnormalities of the control of body chemistry. Accidental suffocation by a pillow or blanket is extremely rare.

The episodes tend to occur at weekends, and in the winter months, probably because of the increased likelihood of virus infections at that time of the year. The baby may occasionally have seemed slightly unwell in the day or two prior to the episode but frequently there is no evidence that the baby was at all unwell before the event.

Apart from the overwhelming grief which parents feel, they also have understandable feelings of guilt. They are often bewildered by what has happened, and their distress is compounded by questions from friends, neighbors, doctors and the police. However, all health workers who are likely to be involved with the parents are well aware of this reaction and are usually able to offer considerable support. Parents should feel that they are able to discuss the problem with their pediatrician, social worker or religious adviser.

If the baby has been taken to hospital, the parents will need to talk to doctors about the events which have occurred. Usually, an inquest is held, following a post-mortem examination. The findings of this should be discussed with the parents either by the coroner or by the hospital pediatrician. The doctor will prefer to have several discussions with the parents over a period of time.

It is important to reassure parents that they are in no way responsible for the sudden death of their baby and, in fact, they are not alone in their experience. An organization called the SIDS Foundation should be contacted and will get parents in touch with families who have had a similar tragedy. Support from others in this way is frequently a source of comfort and reassurance for recently bereaved parents.

THE RISK OF RECURRENCE

At a later stage many parents will want to discuss the risks of this happening again. At present the evidence from research studies is difficult to assess, but there is a small increase in risk of this episode happening to another baby. When a baby is born who is the sibling of a child who has died, the pediatric department at the hospital may offer to perform some investigations to assess the newborn baby's health.

Although there are alarm systems which detect when a baby stops breathing, they do not provide absolute protection. They are often troublesome and frequently sound without cause, but some parents are greatly reassured by their use in the first few months of their next baby's life.

The older siblings of a baby who has died will also need to talk about the death. Many children fantasize and may worry that a similar episode will occur to them. They should be reassured and encouraged to talk about their feelings freely (see p. 291).

PREVENTION OF ACCIDENTS

Children have a natural curiosity which often overcomes their own fears, and indeed their own previous experience of life may be inadequate to prevent their exploration from becoming inappropriate or even dangerous. Children will eventually develop a sense of self-preservation but each child will do this at a different stage. Some children seem particularly accident-prone from early childhood (usually boys), while others may rarely get involved in difficult situations.

It is important for parents to develop a balance between supervising adequately while avoiding over-protectiveness. If children have accidents, parents will of course feel guilty but it is probably worth realizing at the outset that children are bound to have accidents and indeed will probably injure themselves on numerous occasions, during the process of growing up.

It is however possible to limit the number of significant accidents occurring by making the house itself as accident-proof as possible. When a new baby arrives it is well worth while preparing the home for safety in anticipation of potential problems. (The tables of equipment in Chapters 12 and 13 will be helpful here.) In this way parents can, for the most part, keep one step ahead.

SAFETY OUT OF DOORS

It is essential to purchase strollers and buggies which are stable and not likely to collapse unexpectedly. Make sure that strapping is available to keep the child in place. Although it is tempting, do not overload the handles with shopping bags as the stability may be affected. Be careful about allowing younger children to wheel a stroller: their instinct for caring for the baby's safety may not be adequate.

IN THE AUTOMOBILE

A child or baby should *never* be carried on an adult's lap in the front seat as the forces in an accident can easily throw the child against the windshield. Children should always be carried in either specially designed safety seats for the front and rear or, if the child is older, in conventional seat belts. Portacribs should never be placed on the back seat as they offer inadequate protection.

Children should never stand in an automobile or lean out of the window while it is in motion. Never allow a child to remain alone in an automobile. Make sure that the automobile doors are fitted with appropriate childproof locks. Older children should be dissuaded from playing games which may catch the attention of a driver following in a car behind. It is too easy to distract someone else's attention and thereby cause an accident.

ROAD SAFETY

Children should be taught road sense as soon as possible. These rules should be repeated on frequent occasions and every opportunity taken to reinforce them. However, it is not recommended that children under eight should have to cross roads on their own, and children under school-age should *never* be allowed on the road unaccompanied.

Make sure that gates to the house or driveway are securely locked to prevent children from wandering out on to the road. Take extra care when driving your own automobile from the house, such as reversing out of a garage, particularly if it is near a play area.

THE SAFETY CODE

Teach your children this simple safety code.

☐ First find a safe place to cross, then stop.

☐ Stand on the pavement near the curb.

☐ Look all round for traffic and listen.

☐ If traffic is coming, let it pass. Look all round again.

☐ When there is no traffic near, walk straight across the road.

☐ Keep looking and listening for traffic while you cross.

POISONING

Despite frequent and widespread warnings, children are still admitted to hospital daily having taken dangerous drugs and medicines. It is essential that drugs are kept high up in a locked cabinet; even quite mild proprietary medicines can cause severe poisoning if taken in quantity by a small child. Children are extraordinarily versatile when it comes to gaining access to drugs. Don't keep drugs in the refrigerator – this is not safe. Make sure that all medicines are purchased in child-resistant bottles or preferably in blister packs.

Household and garden chemicals should similarly be kept well out of reach. *Never* put toxic substances in familiar bottles, such as soda bottles. If you live in an older house which may be covered with lead paint, remove paint in those areas which are accessible to the child. Make sure that toys are also lead free.

There are of course many poisonous plants some of which are particularly appealing to children, such as laburnum pods and trees with bright berries. Children should be warned frequently about the dangers of eating such berries.

ACCIDENTAL INJURIES

It is impossible to warn against the great many and varied injuries to children. Many precautions are commonsense such as purchasing safe toys, avoiding toys with small removable objects or which fall apart readily, and the need for keeping sharp objects such as knives, needles, pins and scissors well out of reach.

Children have a natural tendency to explore and a common danger is getting locked or trapped in a small enclosure such as a cupboard or wardrobe. Make sure the locks or latches do not only function on one side of a door, and make sure that your child cannot reach and open any door that leads into a street where traffic is passing.

Make sure children do not play near unsafe structures such as glass partition doors, removable screens or tall unstable objects. Place vases, pot plants, electrical equipment such as televisions and stereo on high and deep ledges, pushed well back out of reach. Warn children about running around with sharp objects in the mouth like lollipop sticks. Pencils and scissors are particularly dangerous and have often caused penetrating injuries to the face and inside of the mouth.

Supervise young children in playgrounds or by ladders or other high objects they might be tempted to climb. Many may not be able to get back down or may lose their balance and fall because they are not very aware of different heights.

FALLS

All equipment at home, including cribs, strollers, highchairs and harnesses, must be stable. Most equipment these days is well designed and appropriate, but it may be necessary to have a close look at secondhand items to make sure the legs are even, the springs of buggies are still firm and that the brakes work properly.

If a child is in a highchair or unstable stroller it is important not to leave him alone, even if he is harnessed. Furniture must be securely fixed to avoid it being pulled down on top of the child. Stair-gates, either at the top or at the bottom of the stairs, should be fitted, and accessible windows should be locked or vertical bars placed across them. It is essential that a baby is never left alone on a table or high surface. Babies seem to have a knack of rolling off if left alone!

Pillows are unnecessary under the age of one year. Most babies will sleep happily without one and they are potentially dangerous. Other sources of suffocation include large or small plastic bags, old refrigerators where the door may close on an inquisitive child, and if you have a swimming pool or ornamental pond, fence the pool and drain the pond until children can swim well. It is essential that the child is not allowed access to these areas without supervision. Drowning is unfortunately still a common accident, and it does not take much depth of water for a child to drown. Cats and dogs should not be allowed direct access to a small baby as they may inadvertently lie on top of the child.

BURNS AND SCALDS

It is worth making a rule always to buy clothing, curtains and other fabrics which are fireproof. Most material should be appropriately labeled – the usual phrase is 'flame retardant'. Fireguards should be fixed across electric and gas heaters, as well as open grates. Matches should always be kept out of reach. Other hot objects, including irons, stoves, fireworks, and handyman tools should similarly be kept safely. When the child is old enough to understand, the dangers of each potentially harmful object should be explained, several times over.

Never leave a child alone in the bathroom or indeed in the bath. When filling the bath add hot and cold water simultaneously, never hot water before the cold. Always test it yourself before putting the child in, and remember that a child's skin is much more delicate than an adult's.

Scalds very commonly occur in the kitchen from kettles or long-handled saucepans which are easily pulled off the stove. Always turn the handles inwards, or provide a safety rack around the stove itself. Beware of hot teapots which are unsafe on tablecloths or filled cups left on low tables in the living room. Learn to drink your tea or coffee with milk until the children pass through toddlerhood.

ELECTRIC SHOCKS

Make sure your home has safe wiring – you can ask the local building inspector to check it if you are not sure. Choose sockets which have integral guards or provide socket covers. It is worth remembering not to leave the electric kettle disconnected from the power if the cord is still plugged into its socket. It is too easy for the child to place the live end into his mouth.

CHOKING

A child's natural impulse to put something in the mouth frequently leads to choking. Small objects are easily inhaled and may lead to serious difficulty with breathing. Young children should never be given peanuts or other small hard food (peanuts can do particular damage if inhaled into the lungs), and be sure that toys do not have small removable parts.

Never leave a baby or small child alone while eating, and a baby should not be left lying or asleep with a bottle propped in the mouth. Apart from serious choking this often leads to small amounts of milk being inhaled eventually leading to lung damage. Furthermore, continuous sucking of sweet substances will certainly lead to damaged teeth.

THE ABC OF RESUSCITATION	
Check these points in an emergency, such as drowning, accident or electric shock.	
Airway	Is the child breathing? If not lay him on his back on a flat surface, gently open the mouth and look for foreign objects or vomit. Carefully remove obstruction with the finger.
Breathing	If the child still does not breathe, place your mouth over the child's mouth or mouth and nose, blow gently, observing the rise of the chest. Breathe at about 20 times per minute.
Circulation	Check for the pulse, feeling over the heart or the side of the neck. If you have been trained in resuscitation, start cardiac massage by pressing on the chest. If not, it is probably best at this point to call for help by ringing an ambulance or someone in the vicinity. It is important to keep trying to resuscitate the child until help arrives.

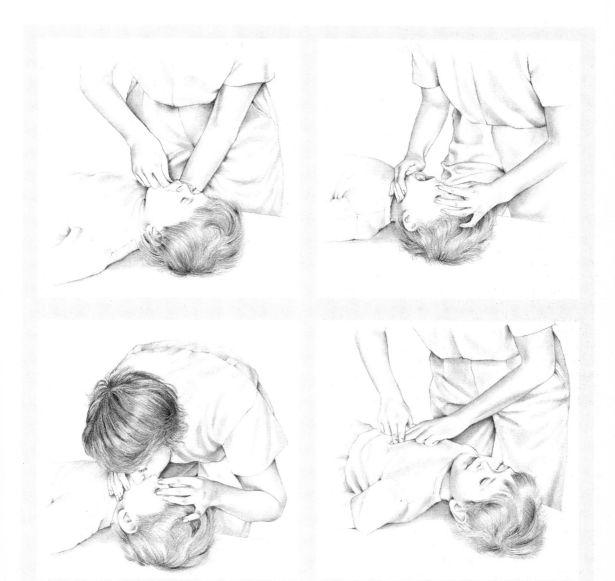

Artificial respiration

This guide is for emergencies only. It is always better to be taught in a recognized First Aid class run by a reputable organization such as the Red Cross.

1 *If a child has stopped breathing, lay him flat, loosen all clothing and tip the head right back so that the chin is pointing up. Clear the mouth of any obstruction with a finger.*

2 *Pinch the child's nose between the thumb and forefinger of one hand and open the child's mouth wide with the other, holding it open with your thumb.*

3 *Lean right over the child and cover his mouth completely with your own, keeping the chin pulled down and the nose pinched shut. Breathe in through your nose and out through your mouth into the child's mouth in several smooth, long breaths, watching to see if the lungs inflate.*

4 *Then place two fingers from each hand crossed over the soft base of the breast bone. (The full weight of your hands on a young child's chest may be too strong and rupture internal organs.) Make ten compressions, then return immediately to mouth-to-mouth breathing. Continue with this sequence until the child takes over his own breathing, or until professional help arrives.*

A-Z of First Aid

Everyone facing an acute emergency at home will feel frightened and sometimes guilty. It is important, however, to keep calm and be reassuring, and to handle the first few minutes by following the guidelines listed below. It is worth memorizing the principal points. It is also useful to make a list of the telephone numbers of your doctor, local hospital and other members of the family who may need to be contacted urgently. Make sure all adults who are involved in the family, including babysitters and nannies, know of this list, and also where to find the First Aid kit. Ideally, parents should take a course in First Aid.

THE FIRST AID BOX

☐ 10 individually wrapped adhesive dressings

☐ Triangular bandage

☐ Large sterile covering (eg for burns)

☐ Sterile eye pad

☐ Bandaids – various sizes

☐ Safety pins

☐ Cotton wool

☐ Antiseptic cleaner

☐ Antibiotic cream

☐ Calamine lotion

☐ Acetaminophen (pills or syrup)

☐ Scissors

☐ Tweezers

☐ Syrup of Ipecac

Artificial respiration	See the illustrations on the previous page.
Bites	Animal bites are common. If bleeding is slight then carefully wash out the bite with antiseptic solution and apply a dry dressing. If it is deep, it may need suturing (stitching) and perhaps a tetanus booster (see p. 253).
Bleeding	If a bite or wound is freely bleeding, pressure on top will stop it. You may use either a dressing, piece of clothing or even a hand if necessary. Pressure should be continued for about five or ten minutes until the blood flow stops. The dressing should be placed on the wound as soon as possible afterwards. If the wound continues to bleed, place a second dressing on the top and continue pressure. Medical advice at this point will be necessary.
Broken bones, dislocations and sprains	Broken bones will require x-ray and treatment in hospital. If the fracture is an arm and the child is well enough, the limb should be placed in a sling and the child taken to hospital. If the fracture is elsewhere, particularly in the leg, the child should be moved as little as possible, and an ambulance called immediately. Do not attempt to straighten or splint the broken limb, as this will be done when the ambulance arrives. An open wound at the site of a fracture should be covered with sterile dressing, if possible; otherwise a freshly laundered handkerchief or table napkin which has been ironed can be used. If you suspect a fractured skull or spine the child should be moved only if absolutely essential to avoid further danger as more injuries may result. Sprains and dislocations should be treated in much the same way, as it is difficult to tell the difference between sprains and fractures until an x-ray has been done. An arm or shoulder should be placed in a sling and an ankle should be left alone and the child taken to hospital immediately. If the parent or adult has trained First Aid experience then an ankle support bandage may be applied before going to hospital.
Burns and scalds	These should be treated immediately by holding the affected area under cold running water for at least five minutes, or covering the area with a bandage soaked in cold water, replacing the bandage regularly as it warms up, to keep the area cold. Do not break open blisters. Small burns can be kept covered with a dry dressing. Large burns should be lightly covered and the child taken to the Emergency department at your local hospital.

A-Z of First Aid

Choking

Choking is a common occurrence and usually implies that a piece of food or foreign body has become lodged in the airway. Most people will cough it out spontaneously, but if it is clear that the child is unable to breathe with development of blue or pale tinge to the lips and face and perhaps loss of consciousness, immediate treatment is essential. You may be able to reach in to the child's mouth and physically remove the object with your fingers, but if this is at all difficult don't pursue it as you may push it further down. A young child or baby may be held face downwards against your shoulder and several sharp slaps to the back are then given. The foreign body may then appear in the mouth where it can be removed by the fingers. If this does not help and further treatment does not dislodge the foreign body, call for help immediately, and attempt mouth to mouth resuscitation. An older child may be placed face down on the ground and slaps given to the back.

Convulsions (seizures)

(See also p. 264). Place the child in the recovery position (see p. 279), and loosen the clothing. Do not put anything in the child's mouth as it may cause damage. Do not try and restrict the abnormal movements which occur during a seizure: this may do the child harm. Most seizures are brief; try to keep a clear head, even though it is a frightening experience for you. If the seizure continues beyond ten minutes, then an ambulance should be called. If the child is known to be epileptic, and the seizure not prolonged, then the child may not need to go to hospital. If, however, the seizure is a new occurrence, then the child should be seen by a doctor.

Most children will sleep for a variable length of time, sometimes several hours, after a seizure. They may be rather drowsy and perhaps have a headache for some time after the event. Make sure that no other injuries have occurred during the seizure episode.

Cuts and grazes

These are common in childhood and usually only require simple cleaning with antiseptic solution, and a small bandaid or dry bandage placed on top. Check that tetanus immunization is up to date. If your child sustains a very deep cut or a cut on the head, then it is sensible to take him to the Emergency department of your local hospital. Your children frequently fall and bite their lips, which can bleed very profusely. However there is not usually any need for the wound to be looked at by a doctor as it usually heals very quickly, although the lip may be swollen for a day or two.

Electric shock

If the child has obviously sustained an electric shock, and is unconscious, attempt to turn off the current at the main switch. If this is impossible, first move the child with a non-metal pole or thick piece of clothing so that he is no longer in contact with the electric circuit. Then call for help and commence artificial respiration (see p. 275).

A-Z of First Aid

Eye injuries

Eye injuries are best treated immediately in hospital. If there is an obvious foreign object which can readily be removed, do so and then place a clean eye pad over the eye and take the child immediately to hospital. If a substance has entered the eye causing irritation then wash immediately with running water, (for example, from a shower), for ten to fifteen minutes. The eye should then be seen in a hospital.

Fainting

Fainting is generally harmless, and it is important not to interfere with the natural process of recovery. Most people will wake up very soon after fainting but recovery can be hastened by making sure that the child is lying flat, perhaps with the feet higher than the body. Loosen the clothing and place the child in the recovery position (see illustration). If the child does not wake up quickly then an ambulance should be called.

Foreign objects

If a foreign object, such as a splinter, is small and superficial, it may be readily removed. However deep foreign bodies are often best left in place for removal at hospital, as removal may cause injury, and its presence may also prevent more severe bleeding. A light dressing should be applied before the child is taken to the casualty department. Take care not to press down on the bandage or the object may be pushed further in.

A foreign object that has been pushed or inhaled into a nostril should not be tampered with as it may lodge further inside the nasal cavity. Take the child to the nearest Emergency department where the doctor will have the right instruments to remove it. This advice is also true for objects pushed into the ear canal, where further interference may damage the ear drum.

Head injuries

Most head injuries are minor and are not usually associated with loss of consciousness. Even a straightforward head injury will sometimes produce sleepiness in a younger child. If however there has been loss of consciousness or severe drowsiness following a head injury, the child should be seen in the Emergency department. If the child is unconscious from the moment of the injury, gently place him in the recovery position and call an ambulance.

Nose bleeds

Nose bleeds are common but can be frightening. There often seems to be far more blood than has in fact been lost. The child should be asked to sit slightly forward over a bowl and to spit out any blood which is present in the mouth. The bridge of the nose should be squeezed tightly for about ten minutes and the child must be asked not to swallow the blood, or to blow his nose for sometime afterwards. If you've got one, put a cork between your child's teeth to keep his mouth open. A cold compress held on the forehead can help reduce blood flow. If the bleeding continues or recurs then a doctor's advice is necessary.

A-Z of First Aid

Poisoning

If you suspect a child has swallowed some dangerous substance do not attempt to make the child vomit by putting the fingers down the throat or giving salt and water. Both procedures are potentially dangerous. Call Poison Control and follow their advice. Have Syrup of Ipecac available to induce vomiting. If very serious, take him to an Emergency department. Make careful note of the substance which you suspect has been swallowed; if you are unsure what it is, take a sample with you to the hospital. If the child is unconscious, then it is best to call an ambulance.

Stings

Bee and wasp stings are frightening and painful for the child but rarely cause serious illness, unless the sting has occurred in the mouth or throat. If the stinger has been left in place remove it by scraping it out of the skin through pressure applied as close to the point as possible. Do not squeeze the outside of a sting as this may cause more poison to enter. The wound should be washed with antiseptic and a light dressing applied. An analgesic such as acetaminophen may be necessary.

Shock

Shock is caused by a sudden drop in blood pressure after an accident or injury. The child will be pale, sometimes unconscious, with a fast heartbeat and shallow respiration. There may be associated injuries. Call an ambulance, loosen the clothing, and lightly cover the child. Reassurance is important both for the child and the parents. If the child is unconscious follow the instructions under 'Unconsciousness', opposite.

Unconsciousness

If the child is not breathing, follow the instructions for Artificial Respiration, p. 275. If the child is breathing normally but not responding, place him in the recovery position, below, and call for an ambulance. Continue to check that the pulse and breathing are regular, and make sure that no bleeding is occurring (see Bleeding, p. 276). Do not try to wake the child up by shaking or other stimulation. Do not give anything by mouth as this may cause choking.

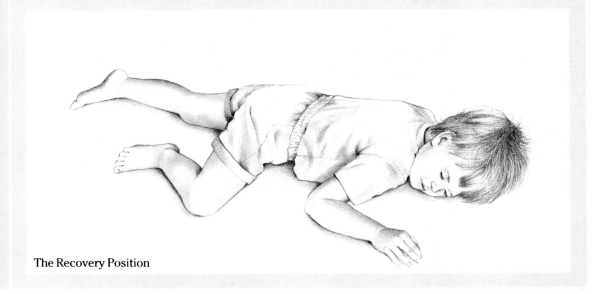

The Recovery Position

CHAPTER SEVENTEEN

CHILDREN WITH PROBLEMS

Advice and reassurance for parents whose children have special physical, mental or emotional needs

Sometimes it happens that a child is born with problems. Sometimes these problems develop or become apparent as the child grows older. Some children have to cope with a lot of changes in their home life, either as the result of divorce, remarriage of their parents, adoption or being fostered. Sadly families sometimes have to cope with the death of a child. A parent may be trying to manage alone.

All the children in these circumstances have special needs, and you as their parents need and deserve a lot of support, advice and help. This chapter is about these situations and the professionals, voluntary organizations and statutory benefits that will help you.

Most important of all, your child, whatever his special situation, still wants to be a child and to have the same opportunities and love as other children. It is the teamwork of you the parents, your child and the professionals trained to help and understand, that together can minimize the difficulties you face and achieve maximum happiness and wellbeing for all involved.

THE HANDICAPPED CHILD

What do you do if you find your child is learning to walk and talk more slowly than other children? What do you do if your toddler has uncontrollable outbursts of temper and cannot seem to concentrate on playing? Where do you turn when your doctor tells you that your newborn baby has Down syndrome?

Whether suddenly, or over a period of months or even years, a significant minority of parents have to come to terms with the fact that all is not well with their child – that their child has a handicap. Whenever it happens, it is a devastating blow which leaves parents wounded, confused and frightened. But there is help at hand; there are teams of people working in your health district whose job is to help you and your child. Although nobody would deny that having a handicapped child is difficult and distressing, with proper support families can learn to come to terms with it and to bring their child to his or her full potential.

A handicapped child is a child suffering from a continuing disability of body, intellect or personality, severe enough to interfere with his normal growth, or development, or capacity to learn. These can take many forms; some of the most common are described below.

PHYSICAL HANDICAPS

The most important cause of physical handicap is damage to the central nervous system (the brain or spinal cord) during fetal life, at birth or in the first few years of childhood. The central nervous system is developing very rapidly at this stage so any damage is likely to have a profound effect, often causing delay in the normal development of body movement and control, speech, vision, hearing, social; emotional and learning skills.

CEREBRAL PALSY

A child with cerebral palsy has suffered some form of brain damage involving the nerve pathways which control movement. The problem may be mild, affecting tasks involving fine movement only, such as use of the hands, or it may be severe enough to prevent the child from ever learning to walk.

The layman's term for a child with cerebral palsy is 'spastic', but this is only one form of cerebral palsy. Damage to different parts of the brain causes the different patterns of cerebral palsy: spasticity, ataxia and dyskinesia. Spasticity is characterized by increased tone and weakness of the muscles; ataxia, by incoordination of the limbs and sometimes hand tremor; and dyskinesia by involuntary movements of the limbs or sometimes the whole body.

The initial damage to the brain is non-progressive, which means it does not get worse, but

Many child development teams run toy libraries for handicapped children and their parents, where toys can be tried out and borrowed and problems discussed informally with the staff.

as the brain continues to mature during childhood, the symptoms of cerebral palsy may change, either because damage to some maturing part of the brain becomes more apparent, or because the brain develops and becomes better able to cope with the consequences of damage.

The child with cerebral palsy may also have damage to other parts of the brain, resulting in speech, hearing or visual problems, behavior disturbances, epilepsy or specific learning problems. Children with cerebral palsy may have normal intelligence, but many are also mentally handicapped and are slower to learn to look after themselves.

SPINA BIFIDA

The brain and the spinal cord develop from the neural tube within the first 28 days of pregnancy (see p. 40). The two folds of the neural tube occasionally fail to fuse, which can also be associated with defective closure of the spinal column, resulting in spina bifida. The reason why the neural tube develops incorrectly is unknown, but it is thought to be connected with both genetic and environmental factors. Some spina bifida lesions may be surgically treatable. Spina bifida may be diagnosed during pregnancy by the measurement of alpha feto protein levels in the mother's blood, plus ultrasound scanning and amniocentesis (see p. 27).

Spina bifida does not always result in complete disability. In fact, the very mild form known as spina bifida occulta, where the outer part of one or more vertebrae is not completely joined, is only indicated by a dimple or small hair growth on the back and most people have no symptoms. Children with spina bifida complete, however, have both the outer part of some of the vertebrae split and the meninges (lining of the spinal cord) pushed out through the opening to form a sac. If there is little involvement of the underlying spinal cord, the opening is termed a meningocele, and there will probably be only a few neurological signs in the body below the level of the opening. But if the spinal cord and nerve roots are also involved (a myelomeningocele), the consequences are much more serious. This usually means that movement and sensation in the lower part of the body are impaired or lost, often resulting in incontinence.

HYDROCEPHALUS

Maldevelopment of the neural tube can also be associated with defects at the base of the brain, interfering with the flow of cerebro-spinal fluid (CSF) through or around the base of the brain. This causes hydrocephalus, an accumulation of the cerebro-spinal fluid within the brain, shown by an abnormally fast growth rate of the head. Hydrocephalus may be apparent in utero (by ultrasound), at birth, or after the surgical closure of the spina bifida back lesion.

Many babies with hydrocephalus are helped by the insertion of a 'shunt' to reduce the raised pressure inside the skull. The shunt drains away the cerebro-spinal fluid into a vein in the neck or into the abdomen. Hydrocephalus, with or without a shunt, may cause no disability.

EPILEPSY

A previously normal child may develop epilepsy, but it can also be a complication of maldevelopment of the brain, brain damage or brain surgery. The degree to which the child is disabled by seizures (convulsions or fits) will depend on the form that they take, their frequency and the child's response to anti-convulsant drug treatment, which can be very successful.

OTHER PHYSICAL PROBLEMS

The baby may be born with abnormalities which interfere with seeing or hearing. This will require referral to a pediatric ophthalmologist or audiologist who will advise on treatment and special ways to help the clinical problem. There may be an abnormality of the heart which will limit normal activity and require surgery.

Cystic fibrosis is a serious inherited disorder affecting many tissues of the body, especially the lungs and the pancreas. There is no cure but a lot can be done through medication, nutrition and physical therapy to improve the health of the child and delay the progression of the disease.

There are several different types of muscular dystrophy and a large number of other neuromuscular diseases. Many diseases are hereditary in nature, so that genetic counseling to reduce the likelihood of recurrence in further children is important (see p. 14). Some of these muscle diseases cause the child to become physically more disabled as the years pass and these children, and their families, need special help in coming to terms with this.

THE CHILD WITH A MENTAL HANDICAP

Mental handicap is a permanent disability that can happen in any family. Over the years names have varied from mental defect, subnormality, mental retardation to mental handicap, but all these terms have essentially the same meaning: the child has been born with a brain which does not mature as fast, or function as well as that of a normal child, so that the full mental capacities of a normal adult will not be reached. 'Developmental delay' is an acceptable term only while the diagnosis is in doubt. Sometimes it is important to understand that mental handicap is not the same as mental illness.

Causes of mental handicap include chromosome abnormalities, such as Down syndrome; single gene defects, such as phenylketonuria; infection of the fetus during pregnancy by rubella, cytomegalovirus and other organisms (congenital infections) and damage to the baby's developing brain during pregnancy by alcohol or an underfunctioning thyroid gland. Babies starved of oxygen at birth, due to serious problems associated with the delivery, may develop cerebral palsy with or without mental handicap, but it is unusual for these children to develop mental handicap alone. Mentally handicapped children are often associated with a difficult pregnancy or birth, but it is likely that the obstetric problems are a consequence of the abnormally developing brain, rather than a cause of it. Sometimes the cause of a child's mental handicap cannot be discovered.

DOWN SYNDROME

Three-quarters of the children with a chromosomal abnormality have Down syndrome. They have an extra chromosome in the nucleus of every cell in their body (47 instead of 46) as a result of abnormal cell division at the time of conception, and which interferes with normal development. Sometimes the extra chromosome is joined to another one (known as translocation), or appears after the formation of the zygote (see p. 39), resulting in mosaicism. The risk of the mosaic form of Down syndrome increases with maternal age (see p. 27); if a parent is a translocation carrier, the risk of recurrence in subsequent pregnancies is high.

Down syndrome babies have abnormal features recognizable at birth but the condition is confirmed by chromosome analysis. The potential for the baby's development cannot be predicted with any reliability in early infancy, though generally children with translocation or mosaicism are less severely handicapped. Down children can be very loving and rewarding children, and many grow up to lead sheltered but independent lives. Some schools are beginning to introduce Down syndrome children into classrooms with normal children of their own age ('mainstreaming'). This has been beneficial for all concerned – children, parents and teachers – and is likely to become a more widespread practice as people's general acceptance and understanding grows.

CONGENITAL RUBELLA

There is a serious risk of damage to the fetus or of spontaneous abortion if a woman contracts rubella (German measles) during pregnancy (see p. 13). Although the incidence is falling due to immunization, rubella remains an important cause of handicap with damage occurring to the heart, eyes, ears or brain.

DIAGNOSING MENTAL HANDICAP

In many cases the diagnosis of mental handicap slowly emerges over the first few years of life, so that it may be only when a child starts school that the handicap becomes clearly apparent. Parents often accept the concept of developmental delay, but find it very hard to accept the not infrequent sequel of mental handicap.

Many parents in this situation may have read about autism or dyslexia and may believe, or have it suggested to them, that these terms could be more appropriate for their child than the label of mental handicap. Both autism and dyslexia seem to be socially more acceptable diagnoses, and where correctly applied, they require highly specialized teaching. Sadly, the use of these terms without professional verification may perpetuate the non-acceptance of the child's true problem, that of intellectual limitation.

THE HANDICAPPED CHILD'S PARENTS

Perhaps your child is handicapped. What do you feel? What support do you need? The effect on a family of a handicapped child can be profound and should never be under-estimated. Outwardly it may cause parents to seem aggressive and ungrateful for help and sympathy offered. Inwardly most parents experience guilt and worry as to who will care for their child when they are no longer able to do so; they are concerned for the effect of the handicapped child on normal brothers and sisters. Relationships between the two parents may become strained. All these feelings may occur even though you love your child and continue to try to give your best.

Where a handicap emerges slowly, parents have to cope with a long period of doubt about their child. They often withdraw from discussing their uncertainties with others and feel isolated. Sleepless nights and the child's antisocial behavior may add to the enormous burden of these years.

If your child is handicapped, you need to be told what is wrong with your child, its cause, how it can be treated and what the future holds. If the handicap is due to chromosomal abnormality or some here-

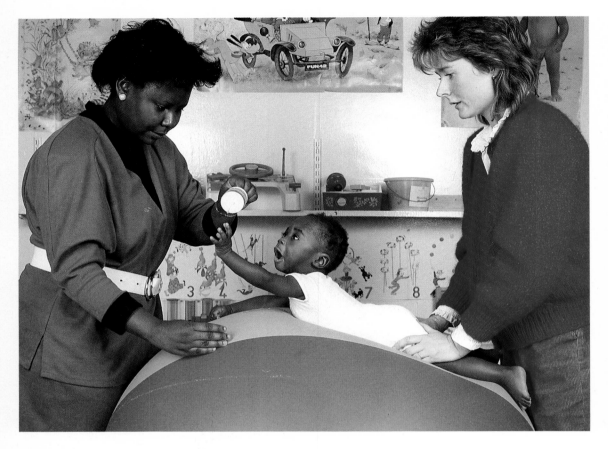

Even quite young babies can benefit from the help of a physiopherapist, who will always involve the parents in physical therapy sessions.

ditary defect, genetic counseling can help to alleviate the guilt by showing you that there was nothing you could have done to prevent what happened, and to assess the risk to future childen (see p. 14).

Many parents lack confidence in their ability to cope with the special problems likely to arise from their child's handicap. The support of a local Child Development Center (see below) will help you to gain confidence and learn the skills you need to become part-provider of your child's treatment, alongside the appropriate therapist. The pediatrician heading the team will guide you in possible courses of action, and will discuss your child's developmental progress. A social worker or contact person from the team will be assigned to you and you will be given his or her telephone number so that you will always have a quick and ready point of contact when problems arise. The social worker will probably be the therapist most closely involved in your child's treatment.

HELP FOR HANDICAPPED CHILDREN

In most cities and towns nowadays there are multidisciplinary Child Development Centers which are responsible for the clinical care and coordination of management for handicapped children. Usually, the team includes a pediatrician, social worker, psychologist, physical therapist, and occupational therapist. As needed, other consulting specialists are available such as child psychiatrist, child neurologist, speech therapist, etc. Typically, the local school system also will have a representative on the team – either a teacher, or a learning specialist – to help integrate the findings of the team with an educational plan for the future.

In fact, in some well developed services, you may be bewildered by the number of professionals who are all eager to help your child. Don't be afraid to ask exactly what each person does, and remember that the person assigned to look after your child's progress will be happy to explain anything that is confusing or frightening.

The Child Development Center may be located in a hospital allowing ready access to the specialist services necessary for each diagnosis, assessment

The speech therapist is encouraging this two-year-old Down syndrome child to recognize objects and match them to pictures. Speech therapy begins as early as possible with simple games to encourage listening and making sounds.

and treatment. Some provide a day nursery or play group for young handicapped children, through which part of the assessment of the child's needs can be carried out. Most centers also run 'Toy Libraries' which enable parents to borrow and use toys which particularly help to stimulate their child's development.

REFERRAL TO THE CDC

If your child's development shows signs of delay or impairment, your doctor will probably refer you to the Child Development Center. This is most likely to happen after one of the regular developmental checks but can happen at any time, especially if you have expressed anxiety through your own observations of your child's development. The child is seen first by the pediatrician who decides, through discussion with the team, which other members it is appropriate to involve in the assessment.

The children referred for assessment may have either mental, physical or behavioral handicaps, or a combination. They may be showing some delay in development or they may have certain learning problems which need investigation. The aim of the assessment by the different team members is to recognize and define the handicap so that a diagnosis can be made and a plan formulated to help the child develop his full potential. The CDC team liaises with the family doctor and the special schools over a child's need, and is able to give information to the parents. The therapists involved devise treatment plans which they discuss with the parents. Therapy sessions may be arranged. All therapists work closely together and their roles with children often overlap.

TYPES OF THERAPY

The physical therapist (or physiotherapist) aims to help the child towards independent normal movement, paying particular attention to posture, movement and balance. She will advise parents on how to handle their children to encourage this by showing them the best way to carry, position and play with their child. Occasionally if there is a particular handicap, specific exercises may be given.

The occupational therapist assesses the quality of movement in general, but in particular, concen-

One of the main aims of occupational therapy is to help children to gain independence in the ordinary tasks of daily life.

trates on the upper limbs, and the ease with which the child can use these in fine movement. She assesses difficulties the child may have with the activities of daily living such as feeding, dressing, bathing and going to the toilet. She advises on the best positions for all of these activities, as well as for play.

The occupational therapist gives advice on the equipment necessary for the child, such as tables and chairs of the correct height and giving adequate support, and any special devices that may be required. In addition the occupational therapist will suggest suitable toys to develop hand function and perceptual skills, needed for activities such as writing or dressing.

ASSESSING THE CHILD'S NEEDS

The child's problems and ways to help them are then discussed at a special meeting ('case conference') between the parents and the professionals involved. The child's teacher or pediatrician may have been asked to come to the meeting. A date for reviewing the progress of the child is planned. This review may take a similar form to the initial assessment and re-occurs at varying intervals depending on the need. Wherever possible continuing therapy is planned to take place in the child's home or school.

The Child Development Center is also an information base from which you can obtain advice about voluntary organizations that can help you and your child, financially, emotionally, through self-help groups, and about leisure activities.

THE HANDICAPPED CHILD AT SCHOOL

As the handicapped child reaches school entry age, the focus for medical services shifts from the Child Development Center to the school. This should not interrupt the continuity of care for your child's specific needs, for within the school health system is a similar team of health professionals as found in the Child Development Center. They continue to review and make provision for the needs of the child and his family.

SPECIAL SCHOOLING

The need for special schooling for a child may have been apparent from a very early stage, or its suggestion may be the first time parents have had to face the fact that all is not well with their child. Nowadays the emphasis is on abolishing the sharp distinction between a handicapped and non-handicapped child, concentrating instead on the concept of children with 'special educational needs'. Federal laws mandate the consideration of each child's individual needs and require that suitable educational provision be made to meet them, whether handicapped in the clinical sense of the word, or not.

The principle has been established that all children with special educational needs should be educated in ordinary schools if possible, but takes into account parents' views, whether the school can meet the child's needs, the efficient use of resources, and whether the education of other children is likely to be adversely affected. Your local school department will have full details of the procedure for assessing a child's special educational needs and how they can be provided for.

SUPPORT GROUPS AND FINANCIAL HELP

As parents of a handicapped child, you will find there are many services and organizations which can help you emotionally, financially and in other

Many of the exercises of occupational therapy for children are presented as games, such as throwing magnetized darts at a bull's-eye, which will help develop normal movement and coordination in a way which children find enjoyable.

practical ways. Many self-help groups have been formed by parents who have already experienced the same problems and have found comfort in the mutual support of families in similar circumstances. Information on some of these is given at the end of this book. Your local social security office, voluntary organization or the social worker at the Child Development Center will be able to advise you on the financial benefits that may be available to your child or to the family.

ADOPTION

Adoption is a way of providing a substitute family for children whose natural parents are unable or unwilling to look after them. It is first and foremost for the benefit of the child.

Most couples applying to adopt do so because they are unable to have a child themselves; coming to terms with infertility takes time and men and women cope with this differently. The problem still focuses on some of the most primeval forces in us

all. Facing up to infertility includes examining what sort of lifestyle a couple may want in the future. If there is mutual support and discussion between both partners, a united decision can eventually be made as to the best way to cope with childlessness. If you choose to try to adopt, then you are making a very positive step towards acknowledging that you truly want children.

Currently, adoption can entail a wait as long as five or more years for a healthy child who is white. Increasingly, prospective adoptive parents turn to private agencies either to arrange an adoption directly of an American child or to go overseas looking for an available foreign child. There is no national 'Adoption Bureau' which is run by the Government. Consequently, you must contact your local family agency as an initial step. Many people write hundreds of letters to lawyers, agencies, child care associations, and even friends in the hopes of speeding up a long delay encountered in the public sector. It is not the place of this chapter to direct you to private agencies. However, it is easy enough to discover this whole separate arena through friends, or even through your local community adoption agency.

Coincidental with the wish to adopt, comes the necessity for you to define your own limitations. It is important to be totally content with what you receive; if you want to impose restrictions – for instance, it must be a boy or a young baby – then it is better for you to be honest and face these limitations prior to a placement for the sake of the happiness and security of the children involved. Adoption is for ever.

Nowadays there are far more people who want babies than there are healthy babies available. If you are black, you may find it easier to adopt a baby, as black babies often have to wait longer than white babies before suitable parents can be found. But there are many older children, or groups of brothers and sisters, or handicapped children, who have missed out on family life and who need a substitute family to care for them.

RECEIVING AN ADOPTED CHILD

The act of receiving your child is wonderful yet strange. For months you will have kept your feelings strictly under control. It is likely that you will have had little of the intensive build up, as with a pregnancy. So your emotions and lifestyle are likely to change very rapidly when your child finally arrives. Beforehand you may wonder if the child will appeal, and what to do if he or she does not. But like most pinnacles in our lives, the point of reaching it arrives and is past almost before it is

realized, and at the time all that most of us do is to behave quite naturally.

Gratitude and happiness follow while you adjust to your changed circumstances. Older or handicapped children may present special problems which can tax the resolve of the strongest parents, who may need special support in coping. Happiness does not preclude parents from questioning their actions, and it is not unnatural to wonder in these early stages if bonding between you and your child will eventually feel complete. But you will find that emotions between all of you become consolidated with time.

Quite naturally, you will find yourselves trying to develop to the full the potential of your child, to recognize and try to help his limitations and to provide as effective and loving environment as is in your power to do.

BEING AN ADOPTIVE PARENT

It is a growing experience which will teach you a lot more about your partner through the crises which you will have had to face, and the support and understanding you give each other. It is a humbling experience because it puts to one side the arrogant desire of most of us to see our own selves reproduced in some form in front of us. It is a saddening experience to realize that the natural mother is missing many happy experiences. It is a huge responsibility to have the total care of some other parents' child, but it is a great privilege to be a part of it all.

Laws affecting access to birth records for adoptive children are changing state by state across the country. Once a child reaches the age of maturity (typically 18) many states now permit access to the original birth certificate. This change has brought about far reaching implications for natural parents as well as the child and his adoptive parents. It is an issue that warrants deep thought and consideration before arriving at a conclusion as to how best to proceed with regard to what information to disclose to an adopted child and when would be the right time to disclose it.

Of course, there are many hurdles special to the adoptive situation which the child and his new parents may meet over the course of time. Some find it particularly difficult to discuss the 'real' mother. Some children want to try to fill in gaps in their knowledge of their background. Children enmeshed in the discovery of their original biography need counseling services for themselves and for their parents to adjust to their newly discovered situation. Specialists in this field are available and their services can be invaluable.

CHILD ABUSE

No one enjoys dealing with the problems of physical or sexual abuse of children – not parents, doctors, agencies, lawyers and judges, and especially not the victims. However, the problem is pervasive, terrifying and aggravating, and unlikely to be 'cured' in the near future. Unlike conventional medical problems, child abuse does not lend itself to simplification or straightforward solutions and cannot be dealt with in one paragraph of discussion. Signs of physical abuse include bruises (other than on the lower leg, which most children have from the daily trauma of ordinary play), burns such as those inflicted by cigarettes, skin injuries whose pattern suggests choking around the neck or the mark of a belt buckle or other instrument used to strike the child, multiple fractures in the toddler or unusual fractures, such as ribs or skull in the infant. This is not an exhaustive list, just a catalog of the common findings. Depression, withdrawal, and disturbances in eating and sleeping patterns are all well known to accompany child abuse. If you have *any* reason to suspect that your child (or, indeed, any other child you know well) is being victimized, it is essential that you obtain consultation with your pediatrician immediately.

SEXUAL ABUSE

Sexual abuse of children is even tougher to deal with. Physical findings are rarely apparent to parents, because most of us do not examine the genital area of our children. Also, the findings can be quite subtle, such as enlargement of the hymenal opening in a young girl or abrasions around the anus in boys or girls. Sadly, sexual abuse often goes on for a long time before detection, and probably

Adoption brings many extra worries and responsibilities, but it can also be a source of great happiness for both you and your children.

most cases are never discovered. Young children exhibit behavioral manifestations of their sexual abuse, rather than displaying physical signs. For example, bed wetting, sleep disturbance, unusual fears, depression and withdrawal, unnatural sexual curiosity, nightmares, altered behavior in relation to parents and siblings, and secretiveness, can all occur in cases of sexual abuse. Of course, any one of these symptoms on their own does not necessarily mean that you should be concerned. Rather when a pattern of these symptoms descends upon a child you should start to think about the possibility that sexual abuse is taking place.

Generally, the best way to sort out the situation is to seek evaluation through a team of experts, typically located at a larger hospital or pediatric center. Occasionally, sexual abuse becomes apparent through the discovery of an unusual infection in the genital area which suggests sexual transmission as a likely cause.

When it comes to physical abuse or sexual abuse of your child, it is always better to be safe than sorry. Despite the trauma of the investigation, the child is better off once it has been clarified whether abuse is going on or not and, if so, once the identity of the perpetrator has been established.

BEREAVEMENT AND THE DYING CHILD

We talk a lot about birth, but death is still a little discussed subject. Consequently many of us are unsure of how we will cope with it or how best to support others who lose a parent, friend or relative. Our reactions to losing a child depend on the circumstances and age of the child. The tragedy of stillbirth or newborn death has already been discussed (see p. 100); losing a baby or child that one has got to know and to love presents parallel but different problems.

SOURCES OF HELP AND INFORMATION

With sudden death at home, parents have a greater need to discuss the events leading up to the tragedy and its possible causes, than for pre-existing medical situations. Your pediatrician can help to answer your questions. So also can the SIDS Foundation and you can contact them yourselves. Parents often find great benefit in sharing their feelings and distress with others who have experienced the same tragedy and therefore possess similar understanding and seeing that they do gradually recover.

SUDDEN DEATH

When a baby dies suddenly for no apparent reason, a 'crib death' (or SIDS – see page 271), there is no warning or time to prepare. Parents often feel they must in some way be to blame and go over and over in their minds what they did or did not do that could have influenced the situation. Unexpected death is always devastating but sometimes eased and better understood if there has been an obvious cause, such as an automobile accident.

One of the main causes of death in the older child is accident – by drugs, in a fire, in an automobile accident, from overdoses or ingestion of poisons. Inevitably the sense of guilt is great for the parents, as well as the feeling of loss. Sometimes action can be taken to prevent it happening to a future brother or sister.

FACING UP TO DEATH

While there is still hope of a cure for a child who is seriously ill, intense medical activity persists, but if a time comes when you realize that the illness is incurable, and is not responding to treatment, the aim of care changes to one of adequate relief of symptoms, and support for the child and his parents. Some final illnesses come suddenly at the end of many years of acceptance of a chronic disease. Thoughts of sudden deterioration have been far away.

Whatever the circumstances, all parents told of their child's possible death will find the implications hard to grasp. You will need, and must be given, plenty of time to talk through your anxieties. Facing up to death, or bereavement, involves several stages of feeling which are remarkably similar. The immediate reaction is of disbelief which may allow parents to seem calm and detached. There follows a phase of anger and trying to deny that the death is imminent or has occurred, a stage of being unable to accept the concept of loss. Bargaining for time may follow, and then despair and desperation pervades. But with the passage of time, it becomes easier to remember, without feeling pain and sadness. Then it is possible, and right, to become more involved in new and old interests. Parents sometimes feel guilty and disloyal to the person who has died in doing this, but this should not be so. The past will always be a part of you.

Parents are helped in their grief if they can look back on their child's last illness as one in which the child felt strengthened by their support. Frank discussion about the illness and their child before death, and arrangements for it finally to happen at home are positive memories. But the duration of the illness, the effect it has had on the family in that time, the emotional repercussions with each phase of hopes raised and then crushed, leave their particular toll. The grief of some family members may be out of step with others; some find it easier to talk of the event and their feelings than others. Family members may need help to understand each other's response.

THE DYING CHILD

Dying children need help too. Their degree of understanding will vary with age; younger children tend to accept events from day to day without too much looking into the future, while older children are comforted if they feel you are responding seriously to their anxieties. They will want to have their questions answered honestly and you will need to be frank in your replies. Children seldom talk about dying but may ask about death itself. You may wish to talk with your child about where this should happen. Normal events – friends visiting, new clothes, perpetuation of usual play by siblings within the home, should continue. At all times drugs will be adjusted by your doctor to ensure your child's comfort, yet allowing as much activity as possible.

THE REACTION OF BROTHERS AND SISTERS

Brothers and sisters of a dying child need the situation explained so that they have something to explain to others. Their reaction to the death will depend on how close they were to their brother or sister. Children under two years have little awareness beyond events directly concerning themselves. Between two and about six years they will interpret events at face value. This means that previous sibling rivalry may now leave them irrationally blaming themselves for the loss of their brother or sister. They may react in a similar way to the loss of a parent.

From seven or eight years old, the child more easily believes what he is told, even though deeper understanding of the event comes more slowly. But he is now more aware of the reactions of those around him and he will feel less excluded from your grief if you can show your feelings in front of him. He may need to talk through his own worries of whether a similar illness could happen to him. It is a valuable idea to give a photograph of the dead child to each of his brothers and sisters, and then to continue to talk about him whenever appropriate. The process of recovery is a long one. It is just as important for children to grieve as it is for parents. Ultimately the other children in your family will be grateful to have been fully involved and to have worked through their grief with their parents.

DIVORCE

Year by year, the divorce rate is rising. Currently, the divorce rate in the United States approaches 50 per cent. While disturbing, the rise has slowed recently, and may have started to trend downward. It is inevitable that your marital difficulties will eventually have an effect on your children's feelings and perhaps behavior. Your divorce will, however temporarily, result in a one-parent family situation. Between two-thirds and three-quarters of divorced parents marry again, perhaps to a partner with children, but this also means that yet another new family environment may arise for a child to adjust to. You may find yourself with step-children. It is a confusing, sometimes painful, time for children who lack the level of insight of an adult.

Prior to parental separation, your child may witness considerable verbal or physical abuse, and may react with minor but real physical symptoms; school performance may fall and bed-wetting return. Even if the separation is not accompanied by particularly dramatic or emotional scenes, or if the parents conceal them from their children, the children are bound to be affected. Children often have a greater awareness of what is happening than their parents realize.

Separation causes conflicting loyalties and is hazardous for any child. Too ready access to the parent who goes away may be damaging for the very young child, while those older may wish to reject their absent parent, at the same time as feeling rejected.

Divorce courts hold the welfare of the child as paramount, and even have the power to place the child in the care of the local authority if they consider neither parent suitable for the continuing care; this rarely occurs. During the Hearing, the custody and care are discussed and formalized, and financial maintenance agreed. Access arrangements for the estranged parents are also discussed. A new family concept begins for the child which ironically may bring greater social, economic and emotional strains than the one which he had learned to tolerate. Loss of a parent can cause a child to become insecure, lack confidence, and be emotionally disturbed with reduced school performance.

Completion of divorce proceedings does however bring some positive consequences. There begins the opportunity for you all to return to a routine, and for peace and calm to prevail. It will take time for you and your children to forget the emotional bruising but with the greater stability you will all begin to feel more secure and your children will start to grow again mentally and physically within the new structure to your lives.

Many women are now in the position of bringing up children on their own, some even by choice. Although it can be hard work and sometimes lonely, there is the reward of a special closeness with the child.

ONE-PARENT FAMILIES

There has been a steady increase in the number of one-parent families over the last decade and now over 1,000,000 children are being brought up in this way. The largest rises have been in families headed by a divorced or single mother. Widowed parents or lone fathers form the remainder of the group. Most parents who find themselves in this situation don't do it from choice; however a significant minority of women choose to become mothers on their own.

If you are a one-parent family it is likely that you will already have discovered that one of the most acute problems is a shortage of money. Many two-parent families find it hard enough to manage, but statistics show that one-parent families have to manage on less than half the income of two-parent families. Sadly this can result in children of one-parent families suffering materially – they may be less well dressed, lack material possessions that they see other children with, and even be unable to participate in extra activities. In the United States AFDC (Aid For Dependent Children) is available for all children below a certain income level and a single parent can claim an extra allowance on this basis. Welfare and Medicaid payments also provide benefits directed at single parent families.

You may have found, as a single parent wanting to work rather than depend on state benefits, that this is difficult because of a lack of day nursery provision and good childminders. However, day nurseries often give priority to children from one-parent families, and the development of daycare facilities at some places of work is easing this problem a little. A very real difficulty for single parents can be a lack of friends or family to babysit and yet a lack of money to pay other people to do this. Adequate housing is another costly need.

ADVICE AND SUPPORT

Single parents often do not know where to go or

where to start to sort out the many, varied and inter-related problems. A good resource is your local pediatrician or the social service and pediatric departments at your community hospital. While the support resources may be slim, at least they can help you get started in identifying which local groups are particularly geared toward helping out parents going it alone. You may also find that there is a local self-help group which you can contact.

Some situations cannot be changed and yet may not be ideal – you may feel that you and your children come into such a group. This is the time to look on the positive side of your circumstances. Your single parent state will mean that you will see more of your children which means the relationship between you all may be stronger than if you shared your time with a partner.

STEP-PARENTING

Step-parenting is an increasingly common situation. As divorce statistics rise, it is inevitable that more and more people contemplating marriage will be gaining a ready-made family as well as a partner, and the children will have been used to a different family pattern. Children can show a lot of love but they can also demonstrate their views without tact or tolerance. Even a baby gets used to distinguishing his carers, objecting if he wishes.

Step-parenting may succeed from the outset, but for some it may bring unanticipated stresses and problems. It takes time for a loving relationship to develop between step-parent and child, and in that time, when you are trying to reach out to your child, it can be very hurtful to be rebuffed, or to get little return of affection. If that is coupled with frank opposition, selfishness and difficult behavior, enormous strains are put on the new marriage. On the other hand, the child may be offering affection, but the step-parent may be rejecting him.

PREPARING THE GROUND

Some problems of step-parenting may be avoided by careful thought and discussion beforehand. Couples need to agree on the standards they will expect in bringing up the children. All of you need to discuss what the children will call you, and they may have to be weaned gently off wayward ways which have developed in the period between their parent's two marriages.

Time spent getting to know the children before the re-formation of the family will help establish the new parent-child relationship. It is very important not to be so caught up as a new husband and wife that the childrens' feelings go unnoticed. Talk

through where it is most appropriate to live with regard to the children's needs. Realize that a new baby may precipitate jealousy from the other children, particularly if favouritism is at all evident, and that it is not necessarily the answer to 'welding the two sides of the family together'.

There will have been pain for all parties through the broken marriage and that needs understanding. Children have feelings for the absent parent but may have difficulty talking about them. Few children are adult enough to cope with these divided feelings of loyalty. But if you can recognize them, it may explain behavior in many situations and you will understand better. Access agreements need to be carefully worked through. Be prepared for being viewed with caution by grandparents, other relatives and neighbors that you are also taking on. Of course you have to clamp down on interference but equally grandparents should be able to contribute, so make them feel wanted.

HELP AND ADVICE

Patience, communication and enjoyment of each other will eventually lead toward family unity, for some more easily than others. The time will arrive when the pleasures and tribulations are very akin to those felt by the 'normal' family. The process of feeling just like any other parent may take years to reach, but is worth striving for.

However, if you are encountering difficulties and feel you need extra help, you should get in touch with a marriage counselor or a therapist. Usually, through your local mental health agency, you can obtain a referral to a therapist particularly experienced in your sort of problems, and you can go and talk to them with your partner or on your own. A mental health agency may also identify local self-help groups and can put step-parents in touch with one another. There will be hard work ahead, and it may involve each parent, and then the two of them together, and even other children at times. However, the family counseling can be crucial to a successful outcome when trying to merge the family into a single cohesive unit. Do not lose sight of the fact that 'biological' nuclear families endure many of the same stresses, need the same kind of advice and help, and must work out many of the same problems. It can be terribly hard to keep the goal in front of you and remain steadfastly committed to building a family together. Despite the difficulties of the process, the outcome can be one of life's most rewarding experiences. And, one learns tremendously from the process which is so central to being an adult, and to remaining immersed in an adult relationship.

APPENDIX

INTRODUCTION

Parenting takes a great deal of work. One of the more persistent myths in our society is that parenting comes naturally to everyone as soon as a baby is born. While experience helps immeasurably, the skills of parenting must necessarily be acquired on a learn-as-you-go basis. With the disappearance of the extended family a vital information flow from one generation to the next, which used to take place on a daily basis (for better or for worse, wanted or unwanted), has been completely cut off. So, at least with a first child, help is needed. There are several ways to gain both the expertise and experience that make parenting more rewarding, satisfying, and fun. Networking (which used to be called 'talking to people') remains the tried and true source of information, but there is also an extensive literature discussing every aspect of parenting from theoretical and philosophical to concrete and practical, and everyone should select what fits their needs best from this array. In the past, survival was paramount and took so much energy that child rearing seemed less complicated. Now there are more options, and more leisure time to explore them, as we consciously try to do what we think is best for our children.

No one book, nor even a substantial home library, can begin to collect all the information helpful to rearing children. The situation, of course, is much better than it was 30 years ago when most of what was known resided in grandmother's head. Then, there were a few helpful books, occasional government publications, and academic articles in arcane journals. Now a visit to any large bookstore will quickly convince you that the thirty or forty feet of bookshelves devoted to children in all their aspects must contain a helpful sharing of the experiences and expertise of others. In addition to the plentiful information helpful to the ordinary rearing of children, all sorts of specialty books also abound. They cover every kind of physical and psychological problem that may occur, as well as dealing with problems of divorce, adoption, death, and so on.

Included in this chapter are books, videos, government organizations and private agencies recommended for understanding every child, as well as help for those with specific kinds of issues to solve. The information compiled ranges all over the lot with respect to degree of difficulty, practicality, and usefulness. Some parents appreciate an in-depth understanding of the psychodynamic unfolding that occurs through childhood, while others are seeking relief from a very vexing difficulty like a child who won't sleep at night. To accommodate a broad audience, the listing includes books and resources that seem to offer accessible information for a wide range of parents and children.

Finally, you may find 'classic' texts missing from the list of recommended reading in the Child Development section. While often quoted, authors like Freud, Piaget, Ilg, Gesell are tough going and, in any case, the important ideas from these pioneers have been incorporated into the more popular book titles you will find listed on the following pages.

USEFUL ADDRESSES AND BIBLIOGRAPHY

GENERAL RESOURCES FOR PARENTS

Books:

Bettelheim, Bruno *A Good Enough Parent: A Book on Child Rearing.* New York: Knopf, 1987. A very reassuring book for parents by one of the foremost authorities in the field of child psychiatry.

Expectant Mother's Guide to (Philadelphia, Boston, Washington, etc.). Pittsburgh, PA, Spindle Publishing Company, 1988. These guides are available in many cities, and include short articles and information about products and services.

Faber, Adele and Mazlish, Elaine. *Siblings Without Rivalry.* New York: Avon Books, 1987. These authors try to hold down the rivalry which usually ensues at some point.

Lovejoy Fred, and Estridge, David, (eds.) *The New Child Health Encyclopedia.* New York: Delacorte Press, 1987. A very complete (encyclopedic) text on child health issues. Not for the faint of heart; probably contains more than the average family would ever need to know, but certainly would be helpful in a situation involving major health concerns.

Shiff, Eileen *Experts Advise Parents: A Guide to Raising Loving, Responsible Children.* New York: Delacorte Press, 1987. Well-known experts in child development have written short articles on areas of concern to parents. Perhaps even more useful are the reading lists and other sources listed, including many children's books that may be helpful with such problems as death, sexual abuse, and alcoholism. More common problems, such as working parents, day care, and sibling rivalry are also well covered, as are problems in dealing with retarded or handicapped children.

Turiecki, Stanley and Tonner, Leslie *The Difficult Child: A Guide for Parents.* New York: Bantam, 1985. Though written with the "hyperactive" child in mind, every parent can benefit from this book.

Videos:

KIDVIDZ, Tucker/Murphy Associates, 618 Centre St., Newton, MA. Offers several titles of videocassettes for family viewing. The two presently available are *"Hey, What About Me?" (A Video Guide For Brothers and Sisters of New Babies),* and *Kids Get Cooking.*

Baby Basics, Vida Health Communications, P.O. Box 365, Wayne, NJ 07470. One hundred ten minutes of video, very well produced, chock full of valuable information on the first few months, presented simply and clearly.

Other:

There are many local newsletters for parents, such as *Baltimore's Child*, *The Boston Parent's Paper*, *Carolina Parent*, and *Seattle's Child*; these are usually distributed through retail outlets, secondhand clothing stores, and other businesses that cater to children's needs. They are frequently good sources of information on products, events, and services. Check in your area.

Many companies that make products for infants and children, such as diaper and formula companies, produce newsletters for parents that contain useful information regarding child development, nutrition, child care, and other topics. Contact the companies directly for more information.

ADOPTION

Adoptive Parents Education Program, P.O. Box 32114, Phoenix, AZ 85064. Information and referrals, videos, tapes.

Adoptive Services Information Agency, 7720 Alaska Ave. NW, Washington, DC 20012. (202) 726 7193. Information and referrals.

Gilan, Lois *The Adoption Resource Book: A Comprehensive Guide to All the Things You Need to Know and Ought to Know About Creating an Adoptive Family.* New York: Harper & Row, 1984. As it says.

Krementz, Jill *How It Feels to Be Adopted.* New York: Knopf, 1983. First-person stories by several children, accompanied by the author's always-engaging photographs.

Stein, Sara *The Adopted One: An Open Family Book for Parents and Children Together.* New York: Walker, 1979. A children's story with additional information for adults included.

American Association for Marriage and Family Therapy, 1717 K Street NW, Suite 407, Washington DC 20006. (202) 429 1825.

National Commission for Adoption, 419 7th St. NW, Suite 402, Washington DC 20004. (202) 638 0466.

CHILD DEVELOPMENT

Brazelton, T. Berry *Infants and Mothers.* New York: Dell Publishing, 1969. Different infants have different temperaments. By following them from birth, Brazelton helps understand what makes infants tick and what to do about it.

Brazelton, T. Berry *Toddlers and Parents.* New York: Dell Publishing, 1974. Similar to above for older children.

Erikson, Erik. *Childhood and Society.* Modern theory which draws on psychoanalytic insights but develops a unique and compelling understanding of both moral and cognitive development.

Esman, Aaron *The Psychology of Adolescence: Essential Readings.* New York: International Universities Press, 1975. Adolescents are incomprehensible; this book helps to understand them.

Fraiberg, Selma *The Magic Years.* New York: Scribners, 1959. Real insights into the psychological world of the toddler; somewhat psychoanalytic viewpoint.

Furman, Erna *What Nursery School Teachers Ask Us About.* New York: International Universities Press, 1986. Through consultations on toddlers, we learn a great deal about their behavior, both normal and difficult.

Gilligan, Carol *In a Different Voice: Psychological Theory and Women's Development.* Camb.: Harvard University Press, 1982. A landmark book. Gilligan proposes that moral development for women (and girls) comes about differently and contributes a crucial idea – "the self in relation to others" as a scheme for women's development. Should be read in contrast to Kohlberg's ideas on development.

Kagan, Jerome *The Nature of the Child.* New York: Basic Books, 1984. A very readable contemporary compilation on development of children. He includes and integrates a tremendous amount of information and makes it very understandable.

Kohlberg, Lawrence *The Psychology of Moral Development.* New York: Harper & Row, 1983. A theory of moral development and its stages as arrived at by Kohlberg's research into the problem. For a countervailing view of how women differ from this scheme, see Carol Gilligan's book.

Stern, Daniel *Interpersonal World of the Infant.* New York: Basic Books, 1985. A psychoanalytic look into the world of the infant; quite readable and fascinating.

DAY CARE AND CHILD CARE

Clarke-Stewart, Allison *Daycare*. Cambridge, MA: Harvard University Press, 1982.

Furman, Erna *What Nursery School Teachers Ask Us About*. New York: International University Press, 1986. A psychiatrist shares "consultations" on young children, in the school context.

Health in Day Care: A Manual for Health Professionals. A manual available from The American Academy of Pediatrics, Publications Department, P.O. Box 927, Elk Grove, IL 60009, or (800) 433-9016 (or (800) 421-0589 in Illinois). Includes answers to many of the most commonly-asked questions about day care.

Mitchell, Grace *The Day Care Book: A Guide for Working Parents – Find the Best Day Care for Your Children*. New York: Fawcett Columbine, 1980. A subject near and dear to the hearts of working or single parents.

Shiff, Eileen (ed.) *Experts Advise Parents: A Guide to Raising Loving, Responsible Children*. New York: Delacorte Press, 1987. Discusses day care, along with many other topics. Includes references.

The Consumer Guide to Choosing Day Care for Children. Office of Public Information. Phoenix, AZ: Arizona Department of Health Services, 1985.

DEATH

Grollman, Earl *Talking About Death: A Dialogue Between Parent and Child*. Boston: Beacon Press, 1970. A ground-breaking work that helps parents help children.

Krementz, Jill *How It Feels When a Parent Dies*. New York: Knopf, 1983. Another in Jill Krementz's series of books with first-person accounts by children. Very helpful in giving children the perspective that it *has* happened to other children.

Kubler-Ross, Elisabeth *Elisabeth Kubler-Ross on Children and Death*. New York: Macmillan, 1983. Dr. Kubler-Ross's work started with her observations of dying children, and her insight into both dying and bereaved children is very helpful.

Kushner, Harold *When Bad Things Happen to Good People*. New York: Schocken Books, 1981. Written by a rabbi when his son was born with an incurable disease, this book has found an enormous audience by helping people accept the unacceptable.

LeShan, Edna *Learning to Say Goodbye: When a Parent Dies*. New York: Macmillan, 1976. An excellent, realistic account that speaks to the bereaved child.

Rofes, Eric (ed.) The Fayerweather Street Project *The Kid's Book about Death and Dying*, Boston: Little Brown, 1985.

DIVORCE

Atlas, Stephen *The Parents Without Partners Sourcebook*. Philadelphia: Running Press, 1984.

Grollman, Earl *Talking About Divorce and Separation – A Dialogue Between Parents and Children*. Boston: Beacon Press, 1982. One in a series of books by an award-winning author of books facilitating communication between parent and child.

Krementz, Jill *How It Feels When Parents Divorce*. New York: Knopf, 1984. First-person accounts by some very articulate children.

Rofes, Eric (ed.). The Fayerweather Street School: *The Kid's Book of Divorce*. Lexington, MA: Stephen Greene Press, 1981. An excellent description by and about children of divorced parents.

Teyber, Edward *Helping Your Child with Divorce: A Compassionate Guide for Parents*. New York: Pocket Books, 1985.

FAMILY AND LEISURE TIME

Hadley, Leila *Traveling with Children in the U.S.A.: A Guide to Pleasure, Adventure, Discovery*. New York: Morrow, 1977. A good source of ideas on how to plan travel time, complete with tips for traveling with children of different ages.

Matheson-Ferry, Juanita *One Hundred One Inexpensive Ways to Entertain Children*. Harbor City (CA.): AFCOM, 1987. As it says.

Music for Little People, Box 1460, Redway, CA 95560, publishes a wonderful catalog of cassettes, videos, and musical instruments for children and families. It includes many of the most popular offerings as well as some much more unusual and hard-to-find items.

There are books such as *In and Out of BOSTON With (or Without) Children* (Chester b. Chester, CT: Globe Pequot Press, several editions). Check your local bookstores for a book on your area.

Trelease, Jim *The Read-Aloud Handbook*. New York: Penguin Books, 1985. An excellent book with lots of practical advice on how to incorporate reading into family and classroom time, with suggestions on titles, times, and ways of inspiring kids to acquire the reading habit themselves. An extremely illuminating discussion on how to turn off the television permanently (!) is included.

Wilford, Jane and Tice, Janet *What to Do with the Kids This Year: One Hundred Family Vacation Places with Time Off for You*, Boston: Globe Pequot, 1986.

FAMILY STRESSES

There are many storybooks written for children of all ages that deal with disturbing events in a child's life. These include divorcing parents, death, illness, alcoholism, physical and sexual abuse, as well as the more common themes of new siblings, new

step-parents, etc. Most bookstores and libraries probably have at least several listings on most of these topics. *Experts Advise Parents: A Guide to Raising Loving, Responsible Children*. (Shiff, Eileen, New York: Delacorte Press, 1987) contains good topic-specific bibliographies. It is probably most useful to choose the book carefully to fit the circumstances and the child.

FAMILY VIOLENCE

Childhelp U.S.A., 6463 Independence Ave., Woodland Hills, CA 91367. (800) 4-A-CHILD. 24-hr. hotline for victims of abuse, abusers, or those wishing to report child abuse.

Parents Anonymous. 6733 South Sepulveda Blvd., Suite 270, Los Angeles, CA 90045. (213) 410 9732. Help for parents who have abused their children or are afraid they might do so. Many cities have local chapters; check your local phone book.

National Committee for Prevention of Child Abuse. 332 South Michigan Ave., Suite 950, Chicago, IL 60604. Information about parenting and child abuse.

HANDICAPPED AND SPECIAL NEEDS CHILDREN

Hewett, Dheila *The Family and the Handicapped Child*. Chicago: Aldine-Atherton, 1970.

Michaelis, Carol *Handicapped Infants and Children: A Handbook for Parents and Professionals*. Baltimore: University Park Press, 1983.

Thompson, Charlotte *Raising a Handicapped Child*. New York: Ballantine Books, 1986. A good guide to many aspects of raising a handicapped child, including much practical information about clothing, access to services, etc. It also contains an extensive bibliography.

The following agencies may be helpful:

Association for Retarded Citizens of the United States, P.O. Box 6109, Arlington, TX 76000. (817) 640-0204.

National Information Center for Handicapped Children and Youth. 7926 Jones Ranch Drive, Suite 1100, McLean, VA 22102. (703) 893-6061. Information concerning educational rights to parents of children with physical, emotional, or mental handicaps.

National Down's Syndrome Congress, 1800 Dempster St., Park Ridge, IL 60068. (312) 823-7550 or (800) 232-6372. Support and information. (312) 226-0416).

National Foundation – March of Dimes Birth Defects Foundation. 303 Broadway, Tarrytown, NY 10591. (914) 428-7100. Good information and referral resource.

Tourette Syndrome Association, 41-02 Bell Blvd., Bayside, NY 11361. (718) 224-2999.

ILLNESS – CHILDREN IN HOSPITALS

Many hospitals have preadmission programs for scheduled admissions, complete with coloring books and balloons as well as good information. Some of these materials are helpful even in non-scheduled admissions. There are also many children's stories about hospital stays and doctor's visits that help demystify these experiences.

Kushner H. S. *When Bad Things Happen To Good People.* New York: Schocken Books, 1981. Written by a rabbi when his son was born with an incurable illness, this book has found an enormous following by helping people accept the unacceptable.

Lovejoy Fred, and Estridge, David, (eds.) *The New Child Health Encyclopedia.* New York: Delacorte Press, 1987. A very complete (encyclopedic) text on child health issues. Not for the faint of heart; probably contains more than the average family would ever need to know, but certainly would be helpful in a situation involving major health concerns.

The following agencies may be helpful to families with particular health problems:

Hearing impaired. American Society for Deaf Children. 814 Thayer Ave., Silver Spring, MD 20910. (301) 585-5400.

Vision impaired. American Council of the Blind. 1010 Vermont Ave., N.W., Suite 1100, Washington, DC 20005. (202) 393-3666 or (800) 424-8666.

American Diabetes Association, National Service Center. 1660 Duke St., Alexandria, VA 22314. (703) 549-1500 or (800) ADA-DISC. Call for information about local chapters.

Juvenile Diabetes Foundation International, 432 Park Avenue South, New York, NY 10016. (212) 889-7575.

Cystic Fibrosis Foundation. 6000 Executive Blvd., Rockville, MD 20852. (301) 881-9130 (or 6931 Arlington Rd., Bethesda, MD 20814 (301) 951-4422). An organization for support and information for families.

Epilepsy Foundation of America. 4351 Garden City Drive, Landover, MD 20785. (301) 459-3200 (or 3700), (800) 332-1000.

Muscular Dystrophy Association of America. 810 Seventh Ave., New York, NY 10019.

National Association for Sickle Cell Anemia. 4221 Wilshire Blvd., Suite 360, Los Angeles, CA 90010-3503. (213) 936-7205 or (800) 421-8453.

National Hemophilia Foundation, 140 W. 2nd St., 6th Floor, New York, NY 10011. (212) 242-1968.

National Multiple Sclerosis Society, 205 E. 42nd St., New York, NY 10017. (212) 986-3240.

MULTIPLE BIRTHS

National Organization of Mothers of Twins Clubs, Inc., 12404 Princess Jeanne, NE, Albuquerque, NM 87112-4640. (505) 275-0955. An organization with many local chapters aimed at helping and supporting parents of twins (and other multiple births).

Leigh, Gillian *All About Twins: A Handbook For Parents.* New York: Methuen, Inc., 1984.

Twins Magazine. Very useful information and support.

NUTRITION

Breastfeeding: The Art of Mothering. A video approved by the American Academy of Pediatrics, available from Alive Productions, Ltd., P.O. Box 72, Port Washington, NY 11050.

Connor, Sonja and Connor, William *New American Diet: the Lifetime Family Eating Plan for Good Health,* New York: Simon and Schuster, 1986. A very sound book; includes meal plans. Recommended by many cardiologists.

Eisenberg, Arlene, Murkoff, Heidi, and Hathaway, Sandee. *What to Eat When You're Expecting.* New York: Workman Publishing, 1986.

Epstein, Leonard and Squires, Sally *The Stop-light Diet for Children.* Boston. Little, Brown and Co., 1987. A simple and effective approach to controlling intake of unwanted foods or calories. A practical approach to helping a child learn to eat sensibly, whether or not that child needs to lose weight. The behavior modification techniques outlined could be useful in other situations as well. Very detailed instructions.

Gross, Joy and Friefield, Karen *The Vegetarian Child.* New York: Lyle Stuart, 1983. A sound guide to raising children in vegetarian families.

Robertson, Laurel, Flinders, Carol, and Godfrey, Bronwen *The New Laurel's Kitchen.* Berkeley, CA: Ten Speed Press, 1986. A vegetarian cookbook with very sound nutritional information, including sections on infants and children. The original was used as a text in nutrition courses at Berkeley.

Yntema, Sharon *The Vegetarian Baby: A Sensible Guide for Parents.* Ithaca, NY: McBooks Press, 1980. A good guide to balancing nutritional needs with vegetarian beliefs.

Yntema, Sharon *Vegetarian Children.* Ithaca, NY: McBooks Press, 1987. Takes up where the above leaves off.

LaLeche League International, 9616 Minneapolis Ave., Franklin Park, IL 60131. (312) 455-7730. A well-known organization for support and information for breast-feeding mothers; some of their views are somewhat controversial. Check your local phone directory for a local chapter.

PREGNANCY AND INFERTILITY

Eisenberg, Arlene, Murkoff, Heidi, and Hathaway, Sandee *What to Expect When You're Expecting.* New York: Workman Publishing, 1984. A detailed review of pregnancy, month by month.

Eisenberg, Arlene, Murkoff, Heidi, and Hathaway, Sandee *What to Eat When You're Expecting.* New York: Workman Publishing, 1986. As it says.

Expectant Mother's Guide to (Philadelphia, Boston, Washington, etc.). Pittsburgh, PA, Spindle Publishing Company, 1988. These guides are available in many cities, and include short articles and information about products and services.

Friedman, Rochelle, and Gradstein, Bonnie *Surviving Pregnancy Loss.* Boston: Little, Brown & Co., 1982. A pioneering review of the intense grief surrounding pregnancy loss. Miscarriage, abortion, stillbirth, death of a child are all included. Intense and very important.

Menning, Barbara Eck *Infertility: A Guide For The Childless Couple.* Englewood Cliffs NJ: Prentice Hall, 1977. The founder of resolve provides sound advice.

Salzer, Linda *Infertility: How Couples Can Cope.* Boston: G. K. Hall, 1986. A more recent and complete version of the above.

SCHOOL FUNCTION AND DYSFUNCTION

Bloom, Allan *Closing of the American Mind: How Higher Education Has Failed Democracy and Impoverished the Souls of Today's Students.* New York: Simon and Schuster, 1987. A controversial and widely read discussion of moral and ethical impoverishment of education in America and its effect on the individuals and socioeconomic fabric of the country.

Elkind, David *Miseducation: Preschoolers at Risk.* New York: Alfred A. Knopf, 1988. A thoughtful discussion by a well-recognized psychologist arguing against the present trend toward "over-education" of young children by success-driven parents.

Turiecki, Stanley and Tonner, Leslie *The Difficult Child: A Guide For Parents.* New York: Bantam, 1985. A valuable book for any "hyperactive" child.

Association for Children and Adults with Learning Disabilities, Inc. (ACLD). 4156 Library Road, Pittsburgh, PA 15234. (412) 341-1515. Information on diagnosis and therapy.

SEXUAL ABUSE

Gordon, Sol and Judith *A Better Safe Than Sorry Book: A Family Guide for Sexual Assault Prevention.* Fayetteville, NY: Ed-U Press, 1985. A book for parents and children to read together to teach children about avoiding problem situations.

Herman, Judith *Fathers and Daughters.* Cambridge, MA: Harvard University Press, 1981. A major study of the most common form of incest and its effect on all family members.

Newman, Susan *Never Say Yes to a Stranger: What Your Child Must Know to Stay Safe.* New York: Perigee Books, 1985. Gives examples of situations children should learn to recognize, with practical exercises.

Terkel, Susan, and Rench, Janice *Feeling Safe, Feeling Strong. How to Avoid Sexual Abuse and What to Do If It Happens to You.* Minneapolis: Lerner Publications, Inc., 1984. A book for older children with discussion of different forms of sexual abuse and how to avoid them.

SEXUALITY

Bell, Ruth *et al. Changing Bodies, Changing Lives.* New York: Vintage Books, 1987. An excellent, fairly explicit guide to all aspects of sexuality, including homosexuality. Includes references to other books and agencies for further information.

Mayle, Peter *Where Did I Come From?* New York: Lyle Stuart, 1973. Written for children in grade three and up, this is a *very* explicit but non-threatening explanation of human sexuality. Illustrated with equally non-threatening drawings.

Sex Education for Adolescents. A bibliography available from the American Academy of Pediatrics, Publications Department, P.O. Box 927, Elk Grove Village, IL 60009.

SLEEP

Cuthbertson, Joanne and Schevill, Susanna *Helping Your Child Sleep Through the Night.* Garden City, New York: Doubleday, 1985. One of several very useful books about troublesome problems.

Ferber, Richard *Solve Your Child's Sleep Problems.* New York: Simon and Schuster, 1985. An invaluable guide to many of the most common (and some of the less common) problems encountered by parents, including practical advice.

STEPFAMILIES

Berman, Claire *What Am I Doing in a Stepfamily?* Secaucus, NJ: Lyle Stuart, 1982. Useful Reading for younger children.

Berman, Claire *Making It as a Step-parent: New Roles, New Rules.* New York: Perennial Library/Harper & Row, 1986.

Gardner, Richard *The Boys' and Girls Book About Stepfamilies.* Cresskill, NJ: Creative Therapeutics, 1985.

Getzoff, Ann and MacClenahan, Carolyn *Stepkids: A Survival Guide for Teenagers in Stepfamilies . . . & for Step-parents Doubtful of Their Own Survival.* New York: Walker & Co., 1985.

Stepfamily Association of America, 602 East Joppa Rd., Baltimore, MD 21204. (301) 823-7570. Provides information and support to combined families.

TEENAGERS

Bell, Ruth *et al. Changing Bodies, Changing Lives.* New York: Vintage Books, 1987. An excellent, fairly explicit guide to all areas of sexuality, aimed particularly at a teen-aged audience. Much of the information is related in the first person by teenagers.

Esman, Aaron *The Psychology of Adolescence: Essential Readings.* New York: International University Press, 1975.

Spock, Benjamin *A Teenager's Guide to Life and Love.* New York: Simon & Schuster, 1970. Advice by the grand master of child-rearing books; not for every teenager, but very good for some.

The Teenage Survival Book, 4th ed. New York: Times Books, Random House, 1986. A very helpful book which has gone through four editions over a dozen years.

Toughlove. A much-lauded organization with chapters nationwide that helps families deal with very difficult teenagers, including those with substance-abuse problems. Organized somewhat along the principles of AA and Al-Anon.

TELEVISION AND PRODUCT SAFETY

Action for Children's Television. 20 University Road, Cambridge, MA 02138. Tel. (617) 876-6620. A non-profit group started by a mother concerned over the content of children's television; very involved at present in the fight over advertising on scheduled children's programming.

US Consumer Product Safety Commission, 1750 K St., NW, Washington, DC 20207. (800) 638-2772. Agency monitors complaints about faulty or dangerous items and provides information about others.

National Safety Council, 444 N. Michigan Ave., Chicago, IL 60611. (312) 527-4800. Publishes information about toys, furniture, etc.

Information from the American Academy of Pediatrics concerning consumer products, accident prevention, and safety education is available either through your pediatrician or from the Academy directly. Brochures, buttons, and bumper stickers are also available. Contact the American Academy of Pediatrics, Publications Department, P.O. Box 927, Elk Grove Village, IL 60009, or call (800) 433-9016. In Illinois, call (800) 421-0589.

INDEX